Only in Naples

Lessons in Food and Famiglia from my Italian Mother-in-Law

KATHERINE WILSON

FLEET

2016

FLEET

First published in the United States in 2016 by Random House
First published in Great Britain in 2016 by Fleet

1 3 5 7 9 10 8 6 4 2

Grateful acknowledgment is made to Hal Leonard Corporation and
Alfred Music Publishing for permission to reprint an excerpt from "Summertime"
from Porgy and Bess, music and lyrics by George Gershwin, DuBose and
Dorothy Heyward, and Ira Gershwin, copyright © 1935 (Renewed) by Nokawi Music,
Frankie G. Songs, DuBose and Dorothy Heyward Memorial Fund Publishing,
Ira Gershwin Music, and George Gershwin Music. All rights for Nokawi Music
administered by Imagem Sounds. All rights for Frankie G. Songs and DuBose and
Dorothy Heyward Memorial Fund Publishing administered by Songs Music Publishing.
All rights for Ira Gershwin Music administered by WB Music Corp. All rights reserved.
Used by permission of Hal Leonard Corporation and Alfred Music Publishing.

A CIP catalogue record for this book
is available from the British Library.

Hardback ISBN 978-0-349-00629-1
Trade paperback ISBN 978-0-349-00630-7

Printed and bound in Great Britain by
Clays Ltd, St Ives plc

Papers used by Fleet are from well-managed forests
and other responsible sources.

MIX
Paper from
responsible sources
FSC
www.fsc.org   FSC® C104740

For my parents, Edward and Bonnie Wilson,
and for my sister, Anna

INTRODUCTION

In Greek mythology, Sirens hang out on the rocky cliffs near Naples with their gorgeous curly hair, singing songs that entice sailors to the coast. They draw ships in with their voices, luring them to danger—to shipwreck, to death. No one hears their song and comes out alive.

Odysseus was desperate to hear it. The song was meant to be sweeter than anything in the world, and he wanted to be the only human being to experience it and live to tell the tale. So, with a mix of pride, curiosity, and smarts, he made a plan. He got earplugs for his crew and had them tie him to the mast. When his ship passed the Sirens, he screamed to his men to untie him, to change course and head toward land. They didn't, and he survived.

Afterward, I'm sure Odysseus was glad that his crew didn't listen, that his earplugged employees kept him safe. But I'm also sure that he wanted to go back. Not just to see and hear the Sirens, but to set foot on the magical land under the volcano that was called Neapolis, the New City.

And this was before pizza was even invented.

I did not arrive in Naples tied to a mast. I arrived on a packed Delta flight from Washington, D.C., in the fall of 1996. There were no Sirens, but I was sucked in and transformed all the same. My head was full of collegiate curiosity; my body was full of appetites that I didn't quite know what to do with.

Goethe said, "See Naples and die." I saw Naples and started to live.

Only in Naples

'A Pizza

When Salvatore sputtered up in his tiny red Fiat for our first meeting, he was over twenty minutes late. The car looked like a tin can and sounded like it was on its last legs. It spat a steady stream of exhaust, and I started to cough. Salvatore responded with two short honks of his horn and a big smile.

It was the first time I was meeting this guy, and he was twenty minutes late. What was *that*?

I was fresh out of college, and had arrived in Naples a few days earlier to start a three-month internship at the U.S. Consulate there. I was standing outside the entrance of the boarding school where I rented a room, wearing a boxy blue jacket with black trousers.

My internship wasn't as much a career move as it was a rite of passage—members of my family did an "experience abroad" during or after college. Big leather photo albums in my parents' attic in Washington show my father Waspy and smiling in Bordeaux in 1961; my mother all sueded out in Bologna in 1966. They had learned foreign languages, and they'd had the time of their lives. Now that it was my turn, where was I going to go?

Naples was not a logical destination. When I'd visited Italy on vacations as a kid, we avoided the city or passed through it as quickly as we could to get to Pompeii or Vesuvius. Naples was dirty and dangerous, we heard. My grandfather, whose parents were from Calabria, said that Neapolitans could steal your socks without taking your shoes off.

"You really should go to Tuscany," family friends had told me. "Have you seen Siena? Florence?"

The serene splendor of Tuscany would have been appropriate for an upper-class girl like me. It felt like what I was supposed to do, and I'd always been very good at doing what I was supposed to do. I spent my childhood overachieving at private schools, and in college I could have majored in Surpassing Expectations or Making Mommy and Daddy Proud. It was time for a change.

The American consul of Naples was a fellow alum of my parents' graduate school of international relations. I'd been seated next to him the previous spring at a fundraising dinner in Washington, and he asked me if I'd considered Naples for my experience abroad. He could arrange an unpaid internship in the political office of the Consulate if I was interested.

Naples?

I thought, Stolen socks and wallets, the Mafia, and corruption. I also thought, Pizza. I was intrigued.

I bounced the idea off people who asked what I was going to do after graduation. "I was thinking of going to Naples," I told them. That was when I got the Look. The Look was a wide-eyed, *beware* facial expression, accompanied by warnings of "It's filthy!" "It's dangerous!" and even "The good guys and the bad guys all look alike! There's no way to tell the difference!"

Aha, I thought. Sounds fascinating.

I now know that Naples is like New York City: you either

lots of Italians believe that if Americans have money, it's thanks to Texas oil. But in the car that first evening, I didn't know where this expression came from—only that Salvatore greatly enjoyed saying it. Over and over.

And then there was that laugh again.

"My" apartment, for a twenty-three-year-old Neapolitan, did not mean a dorm room or a flat with a roommate. It meant his *parents'* apartment. I had assumed that we would go to a pizzeria or that he would show me around the city. Instead he was bringing me home to Mamma and Papà.

The Avallones lived a short drive from my boardinghouse in Posillipo, the nicest residential area of Naples. Named Pausilypon by the Greeks—meaning "rest from toils"—the hill is the high end point of the promontory that juts out into the Bay of Naples. For thousands of years, before the area became part of the city, the Neapolitan upper classes would summer here in the villas that dot the coastline. Winding up the panoramic Via Posillipo, you can see the stone markers for Villa Elena, Villa Emma, Villa Margherita. Steps lead from these villas down to Marechiaro, the clear sea.

Although the city of Naples is one of the densest in Europe, Posillipo is airy and peaceful. The Avallones' building is opposite the entrance to the Virgiliano, a terraced park with views of the electric blue water and the islands of Capri, Ischia, and Procida, as well as the Amalfi coast. During the day, you can hear the squawks of seagulls; in the evening, the occasional buzz of a motorbike or distant fireworks over the ocean.

You think you're from Posillipo is a Neapolitan expression meaning you're a snooty ass, get off your high horse.

The Avallones' palazzo, which Salvatore's father had built in the 1960s, was set inland. It had twelve apartments, nine of which were owned by the family. The building had survived the massive 1980 earthquake unscathed (although Salvatore later told me he remembered leaving the soccer match he was watching on TV and running down steps that swayed and swelled like the ocean). The palazzo was theirs and it was built well, in a place of beauty and rest.

We pulled into an underground garage maze. It was unbelievable how many vehicles at how many different angles were parked in such a small space. They were nose to nose, side window to side window, bumper to bumper. I was confused: there was so much space outside! ("What," Salvatore would respond when I asked him about it later, "people don't steal cars where you come from?")

He parked the little Fiat between two other cars in one swinging, expert maneuver and led me to the elevator. I hadn't smelled the sea air. I smelled mildew and humidity and exhaust fumes.

We were silent in the tiny elevator that brought us to the third, and highest, floor. Salvatore opened the door to the Avallones' apartment with a bulky silver key and showed me in. "*Vieni, vieni,*" he said as he dumped the keys on an eighteenth-century chaise longue at the entrance to the living room. From the foyer, I peeked into the dark, elegant *salone*, where I could make out statues of gold cherubim and folds of heavy silk. Terracotta vases stood on pedestals.

I waited to see what would come next.

"*Mammmmma!*" he called. That resonant tenor voice that I had found so charming in the car was grating and nasal when he called his mamma. I was beginning to dread meeting his parents. It was hard enough to understand Italian and speak with someone my own age: the last thing I felt up for now was conversing with an imposing, formal, wealthy Neapolitan woman who was surely protective of her son. On her own turf! Also, I was ravenously hungry.

"*Mammmmmmma! È pronto?*" (Is dinner ready? Wasn't he going to say that the American girl was here?) I heard the shuffling of bedroom slippers and in came a man whom I took to be Salvatore's father. About seventy, he was not a scary patriarch, but a gentle, distinguished man wearing a dark sweater and lots of cologne. We shook hands and he introduced himself as Nino. He spoke some English, thanks to the thirty years he had spent managing his family's luxury hotel.

"*Salvató, è pronto 'a magnà?*" Nino reverted to Neapolitan dialect to ask his son if dinner was ready, grabbing Salva's arm. He was as hungry as the rest of us.

I was led into the kitchen, where Raffaella was getting off the phone as she took the homemade pizza out of the oven and closed the refrigerator with her heel. It was all movement, all action, all graceful. She wasn't fat and stationary and stirring pasta sauce. She was gorgeous.

About five foot four and fit, Raffaella wore high-heeled boots and a pink oxford shirt. Her white jeans were tight and cinched at the waist with a rhinestone-studded leather belt. She was fully made up: lip liner melded into gloss, eyeliner smudged naturally into charcoal eye shadow. Her hair was short and blond, highlighted expertly. Despite the sparkles and heavy-handed makeup, her look was in no way trashy, only glamorous. I felt large and gawky in my blue blazer and baggy pants. My mother had called the outfit "slenderizing" in a spacious Washington dressing room, but next to this fifty-six-year-old in white jeans, I didn't feel slenderized. I felt like a silent American slug.

"*Ciao tesoro!* Honey, have a seat. I hope you like Neapolitan pizza! Nino, scoot your chair over."

When Raffaella moved, whiffs of Chanel perfume cut through the aroma of baked dough and basil. The *salone* of the apartment may have been opulent but the kitchen was minuscule. On the right side, a rectangular Formica table was built into the checkered tile wall and sat four people at most. The stove, oven, sink, and some (very limited) counter space were on the left. If more than two people were eating at the table, nobody could pass to get to the refrigerator at the back of the kitchen. Why would any family who clearly had money not build a bigger kitchen? I wondered.

As it turned out, extra space was reserved for the living room with its dining niche, where the Avallones ate when they had guests. The kitchen was for cooking and eating *in famiglia*. You can scooch around and bump into family, after all. Lean over them, step on them, feed and be fed by them. A lot of space isn't really necessary when you're with people you love.

There was no place at the table for Raffaella, but fortunately she wasn't planning on sitting. She was planning on doing at least eight other things, including making the American girl feel at home. At some point Salvatore's older sister, Benedetta, arrived, squeezed in, and introduced herself. She was twenty-six, three years older than Salvatore, and had intimidating turquoise eyes framed by thin Armani glasses. Her light brown hair was long and silky straight, and swished like that of the coolest girls in high school. Strangely (it was only 8:00 in the evening), she was wearing pajamas, decorated with pink and white teddy bears holding balloons, with a ruffle at the neck. *Mi piace star comoda*, she would tell me later. When I'm at home I like to be comfy. Her brother was wearing his comfy T-shirt and jeans and she was in her comfy PJs. Only their mother had spent time getting done up.

"Benedetta lavora, capito? Ha iniziato a lavorare in banca,"

Nino was telling me. His eyebrows were raised and he was grinning. He was clearly very proud of his daughter, and repeated several times that she was already working at the age of twenty-six. She works in a bank, already! This was very early for Naples, I inferred. She had finished university with top grades and in record time, and had been hired by the Banca di Roma in Naples to consult with clients about their investments. She had a *contratto a tempo indeterminato*—a no-end-in-sight contract, meaning that she could not be laid off *ever* and could retire at fifty-five. Life was good: she had hit the jackpot with her job and was planning on getting married the next summer.

"*Matrimonio! Matrimonio!* Wedding, do you know?" Nino was positively jolly. I interjected "*Veramente?*" (Really?) every once in a while and "*Mamma mia!*" to demonstrate my awe. So this slick, superconfident Salvatore was the brown-eyed little brother of the whiz kid with the turquoise eyes. That had to suck.

Raffaella, meanwhile, was saying something about a *multa* as she drizzled olive oil over the steaming pizza. Who had gotten this 50,000-lira parking ticket and who was going to schlep to the post office tomorrow to pay it? If I had known then that *multa* meant a parking ticket and that Salvatore was saying that he was nowhere *near* Via Toledo on that Tuesday at the end of June, and Benedetta was saying that her brother was the only one in the family who regularly *quadruple*-parked, I probably would have stopped saying *veramente* and *mamma mia* at regular intervals.

"Me? Absolutely impossible." Raffaella was now being accused by Benedetta, and she froze to make her case, the scalding pizza in an oven mitt suspended above Nino's head. Everyone seemed to have forgotten about me. Salva was going at it with his sister, Nino was looking around wondering when his pizza was going to appear, Raffaella was still talking about her whereabouts on that Tuesday at the end of June. I realized that this was just family business as usual.

Finally Raffaella placed the first slice of pizza on a plate and passed it over her husband's head to me. Salvatore's eyes, for the first time since we had arrived at his apartment, had settled on me.

What kind of a girl is she? How will she eat this pizza?

I understood immediately that it was important to everyone at the table that evening what I thought of the pizza. The pizza was hot, gooey, and thick—impossible to eat with my hands. So I picked up my knife and fork and tasted it. Objectively speaking, it was the best pizza I'd ever had. But my language skills were not yet sufficient to communicate that. So I said something like, "Pizza great yes thank you very much Salvatore family tomato pizza."

And then there was that laugh again.

I laughed too; it was a laughingly delicious pizza.

This was the first of many times that year that my eating would be a performance. The cacophony of voices would stop, silence would reign, and all eyes would focus on me as I dug in. I would feel enormous pressure as I twisted the spaghetti or cut into a pizza. (Will I flick a piece? Will I miss my mouth? Do I need to finish chewing before I begin the praise?) The question on everyone's mind would be, "What does the chick from the world's superpower think of *this*?" And I would satisfy them. *Mamma mia!* Phenomenal! *Buonissimo!* Never tasted anything like it!

And then I made a big faux pas, a *brutta figura*, as they say in Italian. I started eating the crust before the rest of my pizza was finished. Salvatore got up, came around to where I was wedged between Nino and Benedetta, leaned over me, and cut the rest for me in little pieces. He held my fork and knife in his beautiful manicured hands and I could smell his aftershave, his eyes keeping contact with me the whole time. He was so close!

"These pieces you must eat first," he told me, "not the crust! Always the crust last!" More words were coming at me so fast that it was difficult to understand. What I did get was just how invested he was in how my pizza was going to be consumed. I had potential. He just had to show me the ropes.

I managed to finish the pizza without dropping anything or further embarrassing myself. But some crumbs had fallen on my lap (my paper napkin was crumpled up in my tense, sweaty hand). Raffaella had spun around from the sink and was standing over me. She was silent, and still . . . and eyeing my lap. Before I knew it, she had plunged her hands—emerald ring, manicured nails—into my crotch. What the fuck is happening? I thought.

"*Briciole, briciole,*" she explained. I will never as long as I live forget the Italian word for crumbs, *bree-cho-lay.* There was no annoyance, just a job to be done before the crumbs got all over the apartment. Why would it constitute a problem that they were located in my private parts?

Raffaella started singing a song about a pizza with tomato. It had a "Funiculì, Funiculà" rhythm about it, and she twitched her hips as she sang it. *Conosci questa?* Do you know this one? she asked. Her voice was deep, rich, belting. Everyone else kept talking, mostly about practical matters. So many logistics tied the daily life of this family together, parents and kids in their midtwenties connected by the traffic ticket and when's the plumber coming to fix the leaking toilet? It seemed so strange to me that in the next room there were priceless artworks and vases. It felt like we were in an Italian American kitchen in Jersey City.

I didn't even know if I liked this guy Salvatore, I couldn't understand most of what was being said around me, but I felt that, without any ceremony, rites of passage, or coherent verbal communication, I fit in with this family. Without my fully understanding why, this felt like home.

Department of State

The U.S. Consulate in Naples is a big white square building on the waterfront of Mergellina, the port where motorboats leave for Capri and Ischia. It is surrounded by palm trees, and guarded by several open tanks where smiling Italian soldiers with Uzis keep an eye out for terrorists. In 1996, an enormous American flag and a photo of a very pink President Clinton welcomed visitors to U.S. territory.

My job at the Consulate was low stress, to say the least. I was working in the political office, and fortunately there wasn't much political tension between the United States and southern Italy in the late 1990s. Plus, I was unpaid, and the only intern at the Consulate. My co-workers were a mix of Italian locals with those sweet no-end-in-sight contracts, and U.S. foreign service employees, who were thrilled to be posted in a place like Naples, where they could relax and breathe easy before they got sent to Darfur. I usually came in around 9:30; the first cappuccino break started at about 10:15.

"Are you planning on taking the foreign service exam?" the Americans in the Consulate asked me. In truth, I didn't have any idea what I wanted to do career-wise. Both my parents had degrees in international studies, so I thought I might be interested in becoming a diplomat (or, in my less ambitious moments, becoming the ambassador to some small tropical country where I could throw really fun dinner parties with staff). But neither economics nor politics was my thing. What I loved to do was perform. Growing up, I studied acting at Washington's most important theaters and took private voice lessons with esteemed classical musicians. I participated in every monologue, poetry, and singing competition in the D.C. area. In college, I performed the leading role in nearly thirty plays. I combed bulletin boards for play tryouts, packed snacks for rehearsal breaks, and did homework during tech runs.

Onstage was where I was most myself.

But, according to my family, acting wasn't really a job. It was a great hobby, but I had to have a backup. I'd majored in cultural anthropology at college, which got me no closer to figuring out what profession to pursue—it just reassured me that I was open-minded, and wasn't it fascinating how Inuit women's rituals surrounding childbirth reflected their complex role in society?

My internship in Naples wouldn't give me answers, but it would give me a break before I returned to the States to figure out what I was going to do with myself.

My boss at the Consulate, an imposing, full-figured African American woman from Chicago, took me under her wing. She was smart, funny, spoke excellent Italian, and, I soon realized, had the best life I'd ever seen. In addition to the cappuccino breaks, our days were made up of two-hour lunches with Italian businessmen at yummy fish restaurants near the Consulate. Cynthia would talk most of the time, stopping only to dig into a plate of *calamari fritti*, and the handsome southern Italian magnates who hoped to win American support for some industrial enterprise would sit silently, not really knowing what to make of this Tina Turner with her loud laugh and the chubby little white girl who accompanied her.

My working day ended at 5:30 P.M., at which point I would walk the winding coastal road back to Posillipo. I didn't hear the whistles and catcalls of men on motorbikes—inevitable when a young woman is walking alone in Naples—because I was listening to early nineties rock on a cassette Walkman with fuzzy earphones.

I would get back to my dormitory just in time for dinner.

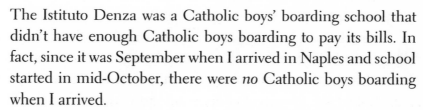

The Istituto Denza was a Catholic boys' boarding school that didn't have enough Catholic boys boarding to pay its bills. In fact, since it was September when I arrived in Naples and school started in mid-October, there were *no* Catholic boys boarding when I arrived.

The campus was lush, with pine and olive trees, magenta bougainvillea, and illuminated statues of the Madonna sitting at the intersections of the walkways. To keep it all up—the greenery, the soccer fields, the buildings—the Barnabite priests who ran the place decided to take in male university students from other parts of Italy who would pay the Denza for room and board. That wasn't enough. They were forced to take in (*ahimè!* horror of horrors!) female "guests."

Nobody explained this to me. A small, shuffling nun in white showed me to my room the first day with only a *"Buon-giorno"* and a *"Prego"*—this way. The room had a single bed, desk, and two windows overlooking the tropical gardens. I could tell from the silence that there was nobody else in the building. Where were the other students in the dorm? I wondered. Was there a Meet the New American Girl social hour planned? Oh, and did they have any extra hangers for the closet?

"Per cena," the nun remembered to tell me before she left, *about dinner* . . . and then she said a whole lot of words I didn't understand. I followed her arthritic hand as she motioned to the left, then to the right. Did she just say past the third Madonna and right at the second soccer field?

"Grazie." I smiled. *"Grazie tante."*

When it was dinnertime, I would follow my nose.

The *mensa,* or eating hall, of the campus was a good ten-minute walk from my building. Other than lizards skitting across the path and mosquitoes digging into my calves, there was no sign of life. A church bell gonged close by, and I hoped it meant *soup's on.*

I finally found the *mensa* (can you call a space with that divine a smell *cafeteria*?), a huge room with marble walls and floors, crystal chandeliers, and many empty tables for six. There was no line, so I got a tray and watched as a nun with an apron ladled out pasta with fried eggplant and tomato. She then handed me a miniature carafe of red wine. *Buon appetito, signorina.*

There were only two tables occupied that first night at the Denza—at one sat four visiting nuns; at the other, three young male college students. I stood with my tray deciding where to sit as they all watched. It was clear that there was a right answer for where I belonged, I just didn't know what it was.

I went with the guys. (Enough with gender division! *Basta,* already!) But as soon as I sat down I knew that it was the wrong choice. No one spoke.

Only a minute had passed when I heard female voices echoing throughout the dining hall. I turned to see that three smiling young women had just walked in the entrance. They were sisters, all with long black hair and almond eyes. They didn't rent a room at the Denza, I would learn, but came to have their meals there. Their parents lived in a small town in Calabria, on the toe of the Italian boot, and the girls had come to the big city to study. When they passed my table and said "*Ciao*," I knew there was a God.

Maria Rosa and Francesca (and their little sister Isabella, who nodded and smiled and was the silent one of the Three Graces) had never met a foreigner. They had never traveled north of Naples, or tasted ketchup. They were full of questions: What did I do at the Consulate? Were all houses in America like the ones in *Dynasty*? Did American women switch their husbands as often as the characters on *The Young and the Restless*?

I held forth in my broken Italian about my homeland. It was a good thing I had a degree in cultural anthropology, because I was able to say things like *America, divorce, very easy!*; *Hospitals, very expensive!*; and *Too much guns*. My friends were enlightened, and I was no longer lonely.

Oreos

I am five feet three inches tall, and in September of 1996 I weighed 155 pounds. The Calabrese girls at the boarding school thought, That's what American food does to you. Salvatore thought, She likes to eat. What no one in Naples would have guessed is that I had binge-eating disorder. I loved food too much to become anorectic, felt disgusting puking it up, so what was left for me? BED: I would binge and then starve myself, avoiding food altogether for a few days or munching on celery sticks for nourishment. Be rational, rein in your appetites, my upper-class, East Coast upbringing had taught me. I tried. And then every once in a while I ate three boxes of Oreos in one sitting.

During my first six weeks in Naples, I stopped bingeing and lost twenty pounds. I did not go on a diet; in fact, I've never enjoyed food as much as I did then. What happened was in part a practical consequence of living in Italy, and at the same time something deeper.

Naples is an anti-binge city. In Neapolitan culture, mealtimes are sacred—food is freshly prepared and consumed *in compagnia.* There is no rushing, and you will hear the Neapolitan *Statte cuieto*—Keep your pants on—if you look anxious or pressed for time at the table. You eat when you are seated without distraction and preferably with a glass of wine. You eat when it is breakfast time, lunchtime, and dinnertime, period. *Punto e basta.*

Stopping in a little café after I finished work at the Consulate, I'd get an espresso, but I couldn't have gotten something substantial to eat even if I'd begged for it. Why would you want to eat at 5:30 P.M.? Pastries are put out fresh in the morning, and desserts are displayed after dinner. When food isn't processed and doesn't have preservatives, eating at random hours means that you eat food that is stale. And only crazy tourists do that.

Because everything I ate in Naples was fresh and full of flavor, at the end of meals I felt satisfied. There were no additives to make me crave more. For the first time in my life I could, along with the rest of the city, get up from the table and not think of my stomach until the next meal.

One evening at the Denza dining hall when I was waxing eloquent about American eating habits, Maria Rosa got a sad look on her face. The problem with your country, she said, is that you eat in a way that is *scombinato.* This means "disorganized" or "messy." I had told her about American college students ordering pizza at 3:00 A.M., and the look on her face—the empathy in those Sophia Loren eyes!—made me feel like I was confessing to heroin use.

The Italian expression for "eating disorder" is *disordine alimentare,* literally "disorganized, messy eating sickness." She had put her finger on it—I was a girl from the land of messy eaters who had an extreme messy eating sickness.

"Non è vero?" Don't you think? she continued, as I took in my messy eating diagnosis. *"Per esempio,* in America, people eat

while walking. They dirty their hands with gooey sandwiches and then suck their fingers. And men in the United States get noodles in little cardboard boxes for dinner. They eat at their desk while they're working, right? *Che tristezza!* [What sadness, what a pity, what sorry lives they lead!] They're really not very good at organizing their meals, are they?"

Wait a second, was an Italian going on about American organizational skills? The flag-waver in me reared her head.

"It's not that they're not capable," I said, trying to keep my cool. "It's just that sometimes Americans eat well, like at a restaurant, and sometimes they grab a bite because they have more important things to do."

My Italian translation of "grab a bite" probably came across as "capture a mouthful." The second, more fundamental idea of "more important things to do" was met by stunned silence. Francesca mercifully changed the subject.

But it wasn't just about organizing my meals. The Italian girls my age all seemed to *live* in their bodies in a way that I didn't. I'd see them draped over a motorbike on the waterfront outside the Consulate. They'd hook their thumbs in each other's pockets, caress each other's hair, enjoy their own and each other's physicality. When it was time to get moving, they'd casually throw a leg over a *motorino*—three or four of them on one tiny little scooter—and unapologetically snake through a traffic jam. The word for what they are is *carnale*. The English word *carnal* is derogatory and has sexual connotations, but in Italian *carnale* is precious and sacred.

When my baby girl was born, ten years after my arrival in Naples, my father-in-law didn't call her *bellissima,* or splendid or adorable. He used the adjective that is beyond all compliments in Italy: he called her *carnale*. Of the flesh—wonderfully, squeezably of the flesh. After all, we are in a Catholic country, and the ultimate gift was the word made flesh. *La parola* became *carne*. In my Protestant background, I seem to have focused on the word part. Lots and lots of words. My relationship with the flesh took second place, my mind was given priority. And every once in a while my flesh demanded three boxes of Oreos in revolt.

———— ☼ ————

After my first dinner at Salvatore's family apartment, there was a lot of kissing of cheeks as I said goodbye. I invariably dove for the wrong cheek (go toward the right first! Right first! I would chant to myself for weeks before it became instinct), and ended up bumping noses awkwardly with Benedetta. (For years, Benedetta's "cooler older sister" aura would cause me to drop things, ram into furniture, doubt my word choice. Whenever I got around the silky hair and turquoise eyes, my best bet was to find a couch and sit in silence.) Salva returned me to my dormitory and said, *"Ci sentiamo."* The literal translation would be "We'll hear each other," but the expression really means "Talk to you soon."

However, at that time, I thought it meant "Call me." So I said, "When?" and Salvatore said, *"Presto."* Soon. I took that to mean tomorrow. So while he was saying his goodbyes with a very noncommittal "Talk to you soon," I was receiving the command "Call me tomorrow." I didn't mind: I liked the idea of hearing his laugh again. I'd never met anyone so *happy*. I'd also never met anyone who smelled that good as he leaned over to cut my food.

So the next day I phoned him. We talked (listened? giggled?) for about five minutes. He called me Pagnottella, after a doughy muffin-like Neapolitan bread (which I didn't understand) and teased, "You like to eat, don't you?" (which I *did* understand). *Te piace mangiare.* He was referring to my chubbiness, and I'd met the guy only once. I should be offended, I thought. But strangely, I wasn't. It seemed that my appetite was endearing to him, possibly even attractive. There was nothing wrong with loving to eat and showing it.

And then he laughed again, followed by *"Ci sentiamo."* I thought, now I need to buy another phone card so I can call him tomorrow.

When I called him the next day (I was a good girl, I always followed orders), he had his sister answer the phone and say he wasn't there. Years later, he told me that what he was thinking was that he'd never seen a girl so desperate for action.

Can a relationship, a life, be determined by a miscommunication? My moving to another continent, my becoming an Italian wife and mother: would it have happened if I had understood the meaning of *Ci sentiamo, Pagnottella?*

'O Sartù

Sartù di riso is a Neapolitan specialty that was invented by the chefs of the Bourbon king Ferdinand I of Naples at the beginning of the 1800s.

After the Greeks and Romans, Naples had been ruled by the Normans, French, Austrian Hapsburgs . . . you name the empire or dynasty, and it ruled Naples at some point. In 1735, Italy was still made up of city-states, and the Bourbon king Charles the Something of Spain (he was simultaneously Charles the First, Third, Fifth, and Seventh depending on which of his kingdoms you were talking about) conquered the Kingdom of Sicily and the Kingdom of Naples and joined them under his crown.

Naples under Bourbon rule was the place to be. In Paris, Jean-Jacques Rousseau wrote, "Do you want to know if there is a spark within you? Run, no, fly to Naples" to hear the master-pieces of Neapolitan composers at the San Carlo opera house. Mozart's dad brought him there on his Wolfgang Wows the World! tour of 1770 (on the trip, they also got some very swank silk outfits from Neapolitan tailors).

Insomma, if you could make it there, you could make it anywhere.

King Ferdinand I was the son of Charles. He was technically named Ferdinando Antonio Pasquale Giovanni Nepomuceno Serafino Gennaro Benedetto. Ferdy loved art, he loved music, and he also loved to eat.

Chefs were brought to his palace in the center of Naples directly from France, the seat of the Bourbon dynasty. They were supposedly the best chefs in the world. Pasta, fish, baked vegetables, elaborate cakes: they made sure that Ferdinand the First went to bed with a satisfied tummy. One day, the king asked his head chef, whom he called *'o monsù* (derived from the French *monsieur*), what was for lunch. He was told that rice was the first course.

"Rice?" King Ferdinand was furious. Rice was for the sick! Even today in Naples, there is an expression, *'O rriso d'o mese int'a 'o lietto stesa:* Eat rice and stay in bed for a month. Rice is considered insipid, insignificant, hospital food. It is even called a *sciaquapanza*, or tummy rinse.

"Please," the *monsù* insisted. "Enough pasta. We'll make the rice hearty! We'll add butter and cheese and . . ."

"Very well. I challenge you to prepare rice that I *like!*"

And so the Neapolitan *sartù di riso* was born. It is made with dense tomato *ragù*, pieces of egg, cheese, sausage, peas, and tiny fried meatballs or salami. Then it is baked in a buttered casserole dish.

The king was thrilled. Who knew? Rice could actually taste good and make for a decent meal.

It was a Saturday afternoon and I was in the Avallones' kitchen while Raffaella was cooking *sartù di riso*, one of Nino's favorite dishes. Salvatore had picked me up at the boarding school—always late, always smiling—and had deposited me in the kitchen with his mother while he finished studying in his room. He was in his third year at the University of Naples, studying law. In Italy, a university law degree is a combination of undergraduate and graduate studies, so after five or six years (or longer for some) "repeating" his books, he could take the bar and begin practicing as a lawyer.

He studied in his room all day, every day, and went every few months to take an exam. No listening to lectures, no comparing notes with fellow students, no interaction with professors. Just memorizing law texts in his boyhood room, which was adorned with teddy bears and third-grade soccer trophies. (I remember describing to Salva later that at Princeton we had precepts, small groups of students who were encouraged to express their opinions on the subject matter to the professor. Salva's reaction: Why would a professor care what a twenty-year-old *thought*?)

I had assumed that when Salvatore picked me up we would do something together. There had been chemistry, I thought, when he cut my pizza into little squares. On the phone the previous evening he had said not just *Ci sentiamo*, We'll hear each other, but *Ci vediamo*—We'll see each other!

And here I was in the tiny kitchen with Raffaella. Who was I for them? I certainly wasn't Salvatore's girlfriend, but I wasn't the Avallones' guest either. There was neither "have a seat in the *salone*, do you take milk or sugar?" nor "Salvatore, honey, why don't you come and show this girl a good time?" Maybe this was how it felt for brides in arranged marriages. Your future husband is busy somewhere, so in the meantime let's teach you how he likes his rice. Would an arranged marriage really be so bad, though, if my fiancé was someone who made me feel as happy and alive as Salva did? I wouldn't *have* to cook for him, after all. Or would I?

What I didn't realize was that I wasn't being judged, and I wasn't being primed. Raffaella's focus was on the *sartù*, and she was making it to satisfy my hunger as much as anyone else's.

Her dance was perfectly choreographed: she simultaneously stirred the *ragù*, fried the meatballs, sautéed the peas. I ducked and dodged. I was at times behind her, at times beside her. She had been to the gym, and wore New Balance sneakers and light green, fitted sweats. How was her makeup perfect after a workout? *"Non sudo,"* I don't sweat, she explained. Ah, that's convenient. The kitchen window was open and sea air was coming in. Look at the volcano! Raffaella pointed. When it's windy like this, you can see the towns surrounding the base of Vesuvius. Even the outlines of the houses. The wind sweeps away the mist and fog.

"Vieni, assaggia." Katherine, taste. Her wooden spoon was suddenly coming at me, full to overflowing with *ragù*, her hand cupped underneath to catch any spills. She stuck the whole huge spoon into my mouth, and I almost gagged on the wood. *"Com' è?"* How is it? I answered that it was *buonissimo*, and she dipped the same spoon back into the pot and tasted it herself.

"Hm."

I was told to cut the hard-boiled eggs into quarters. Raffaella laid the fried meatballs, spitting and sizzling, on freshly ironed dishrags. My Italian had improved enough to be able to ask, "How much egg? How many cheese? How many much peas?" Okay, my quantifying adjectives weren't perfect, but I got my point across. In response, she put her arm around my waist and whispered conspiratorially, *"Più ci metti più ci trovi!"*—the more you put in the more you get out. In other words: That analytical, precise, quantifying brain has no place in my kitchen, girl.

(Many years later, in my mother's kitchen in Bethesda, Maryland, I would find Raffaella staring at a ring of measuring spoons as if they were an archaeological find. "They're for measuring quantities," I explained. "In cooking?" she asked, bewildered. She then shook her head and laughed. "*Americani! Americani!*" Yes, we're a wild and crazy people.)

"*Lella!*" Nino was standing in the door of the kitchen calling his wife's nickname. He was pissed off. What had she done? I wondered. "*C'è una puzza terrificante!*" It stinks in here! Nino, I later learned, has an extremely sensitive sense of smell. He insists that his wife turn on the ventilation when she is cooking so that the smell of food doesn't waft into the rest of the apartment. "*Scusa, scusa!*" Sorry! she cheerfully replied, and turned on the hair dryer–sounding machine. Nino disappeared, still indignant.

Nino was fourteen years Raffaella's senior, and had spent most of their marriage managing the hotel that he and his brothers owned. He left early in the morning and came back late at night, Raffaella told me; it was the least she could do to care for him with a smile when he was at home. He was forced into early retirement because of an ugly family battle that nobody talked about, and now he was at home all the time. She made sure the ventilation was on when she was cooking, served him at the table, and accepted his negative comments about how the pasta was cooked with a smile or a wink and "I think you're right, Nino."

It bugged the hell out of me—she was cooking his favorite dish, for God's sake! But soon I realized that my irritation at Nino's outburst had no place in Raffaella's kitchen, either. "Ketrin!" she was yelling over the fan (the flat *a* and *th* of Katherine were too much of a challenge for most Italians), "make sure you add a little *ragù* first so the rice doesn't stick. . . ." I was forced to move on, to concentrate on the preparation of that rice.

The preparation became aerobic. Raffaella's biceps bulged as she stirred the dense *ragù* in with the rice. I was asked to lay out fresh dishrags (impossibly white) on the table, ousting the baby meatballs (they'd had themselves enough of a nap). I held the tiny balls in my fists until Raffaella offered me the pot with the rice and *ragù*. I plopped them in and she smeared the casserole dish with butter.

Salvatore emerged from his room smiling just as I was helping his mother pour the heavy mass into the pan. He came over and pinched my cheek. "Pagnottella! Did you learn how to make the *sartù*? There's going to be a test later. *Esame, esame!* Princeton!" He found himself delightful. I wasn't laughing. I was hot and hungry. And I really wanted to taste that *sartù*.

<hr />

My mother first put me on a diet when I was in kindergarten. I was never called fat: the words that were thrown around our household in reference to my weight were *chunky, heavy,* and *plump.* As a child, I was probably never more than eight pounds overweight. But for my mother, that was enough to call for drastic measures.

Bonnie Salango Wilson was born in Princeton, West Virginia, during the Second World War. Her father was a Presbyterian minister who was the son of Italian immigrants; they had come from Calabria at the beginning of the century. Although my great-grandparents were devout Catholics, they allowed a Presbyterian Sunday school to use their basement when my grandfather was a little boy. He thought the Sunday school was fun: Protestants were so child friendly! After college my grandfather enrolled in a Presbyterian seminary. His parents never worried about his conversion from Catholicism. It was enough that one of their eight children was a man of the cloth.

So my mother was born to an Italian American preacher in the South. Things weren't easy for a preacher's daughter in the 1950s—Bonnie was expected to be well behaved, accomplished, and, most of all, beautiful. And the definition of beautiful for my mother, a naturally curvy Italian-looking woman, did not leave any room at the seams. Beautiful meant skinny.

Bonnie Salango stopped eating breakfast and lunch in the early 1960s, and hasn't partaken in those daytime meals since. She has never weighed more than 120 pounds, and looks, still, like Elizabeth Taylor in her prime. My mother showed my sister and me the photo of her in a West Virginia local paper when she graduated as valedictorian from Georgetown's foreign service school. When I saw the picture, I didn't feel proud of her achievement. I felt proud of her thinness underneath that robe.

A "chunky" daughter was simply not going to cut it.

So it doesn't surprise me to hear that when I was reprimanded by my mother at the age of three for picking my nose and eating the boogers, my response was, "Why, Mommy, do they have too many calories?" In elementary school, my lunchtime "treat" was a Flintstones chewable vitamin. The teachers at Saint Patrick's were told that when cartons of milk were distributed to the class, Katherine should be given skim rather than whole. "Sweetheaaaaart," my mother would tell me in her Appalachian twang, "remember to always git the *blue*!"

"Mommy, why am I the only one that gets blue and everybody else gets red?"

She explained rationally and I understood rationally. So many extra calories, and for what? I trusted. I felt fine when the box appeared and I saw my blue carton buried in a sea of reds.

And then one day in first grade my best friend, Robin, skinny and blond and a whole-milk drinker until high school, insisted that I take a swig from her red carton. At once my world was shattered and new horizons appeared.

    That first crunchy, steaming bite of *sartù* did the same thing to my twenty-one-year-old body that a swig of cold whole milk had done at Saint Patrick's Episcopal Day School in the fall of 1981. My carnal transformation was under way, and there was no going back.

Laundry

$\mathfrak{I}$t was a morning at the end of September when I arrived at the Consulate with a great big Santa Claus sack of laundry slung over my back. I waved to the soldiers with Uzis, nodded to Clinton, and looked frantically for Cynthia.

My laundry had become an all-consuming preoccupation. I had no washing machine, there were no Laundromats in Naples, and when I took my sullied things to the *lavanderie* (dry cleaners), the women would take the bag and look inside. Shocked, scandalized, they would stare at me and say, *"Ma c'è roba intima!"* There are intimate robes!

What intimate robes? Where?

"You took your bras and underwear to the dry cleaners?" Cynthia asked me, horrified. "Oh, honey, no." She explained that in Naples *roba intima*—bras and underwear and even undershirts—are to be touched by no one but the owner. They are extremely, extremely private. Here I was traipsing around the city with my bag of dirty panties, shoving them in people's faces! How humiliating!

"But what am I supposed to do, Cynthia? I certainly can't

bring my intimate robes to Salva's apartment and ask Raffaella to put them in her washing machine!"

It hadn't occurred to me to do what any Neapolitan woman would have done: buy detergent and hand-wash my panties in the sink. I was raised by a woman who would never *handle* her intimates. She'd do what any respectable preacher's daughter from the South would do: she'd throw her stuff into the washing machine, and turn that temperature up as hot as it would go.

And so the political consul of the United States agreed to let me come over later that day with my unwieldy sack of soiled undergarments to use her enormous GE washing machine (the sack was enormous because my first solution to the no-washing-machine problem was of course just to buy *lots* of underwear). I counted the hours for the working day to end so that I could go to Cynthia's penthouse apartment overlooking the bay. I needed her words of wisdom as well as her washing machine.

"Let me explain," she began, after getting my panties spinning (anonymous in all that American space! How I love the Department of State!). She opened a monstrous bag of Doritos from the military base and set it on the coffee table between us. "There are some things you do *not* mention in Naples when it comes to hygiene and private parts. First of all, they *have* to think you bidet. At your own home, you give guests who ask to use the bathroom one hand towel and one separate bidet towel. When you are invited to someone else's home and you are given a separate bidet towel, *do not say,* 'No thanks, I don't need this.' That is an admission that you, as an American, do not bidet."

"But I don't bidet!"

"*They cannot know that.* They must think that you use the specific *detergente intimo*—intimate detergent, or pussy suds as I like to think of them. And that you dry yourself with the bidet towel afterward."

Her preemptive strike was too late. I remembered with horror that just days before, when Raffaella had handed me two towels when I went to the bathroom, I had actually said, cheerfully, "One's plenty! I'll use the same one for both hands!"

"But don't they understand that toilet paper, used correctly, can do the trick?" Or if not, I hoped, couldn't I be the one to enlighten them on the possibilities of what the Brits call the mighty loo roll?

"No." Cynthia had patience. Oh, did she have patience. "They find it revolting. Not cleaning yourself with a specific kind of soap after doing *cacca* puts you in the category of animals and Gypsies."

We munched on Doritos, and I told her more about Salva and the Avallones. I described how after dinner at the Denza, I would walk down the marble steps to the communal pay phone with a plastic phone card in my sweaty hand. My nerves would settle as soon as I heard his cheerful *"Eh, Pagnottella!"* In Salva's tone of voice, and in the honks of his horn as he picked me up in his little red Fiat to take me to eat his mother's food, I heard: *You are a woman, and you are beautiful, and you are full of healthy, human appetites.* I'd learned a lot of things growing up in America, but I'd missed that part. My whole body was starting to crave the way this guy made me feel.

As I began to fall for Salvatore, though, I worried about the negative preconceptions I had about Italian men. Weren't they all macho and didn't they all cheat on their girlfriends? Cynthia was single, but I'd seen her with several different handsome Neapolitans at events at the Consulate.

"Well, is he a nerd?" she asked.

I didn't know. He was Italian—how could I tell if he was a nerd or not? There weren't many cultural indicators I could read. How did he dress? Like an Italian. How did he express himself? Like an Italian. I couldn't use any linguistic or cultural markers to evaluate him.

"Because if you want to start something with an Italian, he must be a nerd. The others are slick and sleazy womanizers, and the nerds are handsome and charming anyway. Trust me."

"He lives with his parents and studies a lot." I off...

"Good sign."

S...

M' 'a faja dicere na parola? . . .
Chesta è carne c' 'a pummarola.

Here goes with my translation (De Filippo is turning in his
We shall talk o...

Whatever! You decide about the ragù.
I don't want a fight.
But tell me, you really think this is ragù?
I'll eat it just to fill my tummy . . .
but will you let me say just one last thing?
This is simply meat with tomatoes.

The key to cooking real Neapolitan *ragù* is to let it *pippiare.* This onomatopoeic verb in dialect refers to the *pi pi* sound of bubbles popping when the sauce is on a low flame for hours and hours. (Shouldn't I be doing something to it? *"Lascia stare!"* Raffaella told me. Leave it! Leave it! Why do you have to be doing?) Raffaella's mother, Nonna Clara, who had raised eight children in postwar Naples, used to cook her *ragù* for at least twelve hours. Any less and the sauce would be bright red. "You never want your *ragù* to be red, in Naples it must be closer to black and so dense that it's hard to stir," Raffaella told me. Stirring *ragù* for ten people in an earthenware pot for twelve hours: Nonna Clara must have had biceps to rival Rocky's.

I had been to the Avallones' numerous times for dinner. Thanks to the *ci sentiamo* mixup, Salvatore and I talked on the phone almost every day. There were no cellphones, and he lived at home, so I would inevitably talk to his mother first when I called—Beautiful weather, isn't it? How was the Consulate today, and what did you have for lunch? (Young Neapolitans dating could never *not* know each other's parents. An American mother might pass the phone like a baton, but in Naples that would be considered beyond rude. When Salva called my house in Washington months later and my mother said, "Hi! Just a second I'll get 'er," he asked me, *What have I done to your parents that they hate me so?*)

On the evening of my first *ragù*, rigatoni with *ragù*, to be precise, Salvatore had finished studying late. He walked into the kitchen wearing a Mickey Mouse sweatshirt. Even before he sat down at the table, his mother brought a wooden spoon overflowing with her dense *ragù* over to him, and he opened up. She cupped his chin with one hand and inserted the spoon with the other. *Imboccare* is the Italian verb, to spoon-feed.

I was floored by Salva's total lack of self-sufficiency and independence. And pride, for Christ's sake! He was twenty-three! When Raffaella saw me watching, disturbed, she did what she had to do. She used the same spoon to *imboccare* me.

Salvatore and I had swapped saliva but had yet to kiss.

Our plates of pasta that evening were so full of *ragù* that you couldn't see any white of the rigatoni. Raffaella mixed all of the pasta with all of the sauce, spooned it out in the dishes, and then put a whole ladle of *ragù* on top of each serving. "There needs to be enough sauce for the *scarpetta*," she explained. The *scarpetta* (literally, "little shoe") refers to the piece of bread that you use to sop up the sauce after finishing your pasta.

By the time Salva dropped me off at the gate of my boarding

etary? It felt awkward to hear these chic ladies talking about *me*—survivor of an eating disorder and wearer of a slightly frayed sweater that I had gotten at Filene's Basement in 1989.

Mary presided over it all, happy in her electric blue.

There was no hope of seeing a man in the congregation, in part because the Naples soccer team was playing the undefeated northern team, the Milan-based Inter. The men were not missed. In fact, I noticed that churchgoers in Naples were predominantly women. This was their realm, just as the stadium of San Paolo, where the Napoli soccer team was playing, was the realm of men. Boundaries were very clearly drawn, and few women tried to persuade their men to engage in activities together. Why on earth would women want men in church? Why on earth would men want women at the stadium?

"*Nel nome del Padre, del Figlio e dello Spirito Santo,*" an amplified baritone voice cut through the racket, and I turned from a friend of Raffaella's who was caressing and examining my hair to see the priest, Father Giampietro. The flashy colors behind the altar made a perfect backdrop for Giampietro. He was a gorgeous thirty-five-year-old who wore cowboy boots (complete with spurs) under his robe, and had wavy hair, styled to perfection. One day while driving in central Naples, Salva and I saw him weaving through traffic on his motorbike.

"Giampietro!" Salva yelled out the window, teasing. "You're supposed to have a helmet! You're a priest!"

"But my hair!" the priest joked back. "It ruins my hair!" and he sped off around a curve to visit someone's dying grandmother.

That day, Giampietro's microphone whistled and popped. I wish, no, I pray, to DJ Mary that some talented sound technician might pay a visit to all the small churches in southern Italy. How much auditory distress could be resolved with a good sound check! Electronic amplification came on the scene several years ago, and if the truth were told, in most churches it is totally unnecessary, because they have cavernous spaces and domes that would make the acoustics ideal for even the least hellfire-and-brimstone of preachers. Giampietro was in no way hellfire-and-brimstone, mind you. But he was Italian, and his voice projected.

When amplification is used, nobody checks the volume level of the mikes and the piped-in music. And so, as Giampietro began his *Nel nome del Padre*, followed by the sign of the cross, his mike began popping and we heard a painful, high-pitched screech. Many of the women in the church were still talking. "I tried that risotto recipe you gave me but I wasn't sure if the *provola* cheese . . ."

Soon it was time for the responsive prayer. A young woman in jeans took Giampietro's place at the pulpet and instructed us in a monotone voice to repeat together *Vieni, Salvatore*, or Come, Savior, after she prayed for specific intentions. For the Church . . . *Vieni, Salvatore*; for the Christian family . . . *Vieni, Salvatore*; for the sick . . . I kept intoning with Raffaella and the rest of the congregation *Vieni, Salvatore*. Come, Salvatore.

I confess: my mind was on her son, not Mary's. It was blasphemy, I know! But, despite his physical forwardness, despite the miscommunications, despite the fact that I was seeing a lot more of his mother than of him, I realized that I was falling in love with him. I was falling for his long, tanned, graceful body. For the simple sincerity of his attraction to me, and for the smile that defied me to take myself or my problems too seriously.

Who knew? Maybe sitting next to his mother, saying "Come, Salvatore" together, was a sort of incantation and would do good things for our relationship.

As the Communion approached, recorded music began

playing, with a synthesizer beat that sounded like bad karaoke. Wasn't there supposed to be an atmosphere of mystery and serenity for Catholic Communion? This was supposed to be the *actual* body and blood of Christ, after all. I should have realized by then that in Italy, and particularly in Naples, anything is possible. Magic happens. The chaos and noise and colors give way suddenly, unexpectedly, to solemnity. How? The answer is always in the food.

Giampietro fed his girls.

Il corpo di Cristo, the Body of Christ, he was saying, and the ladies were lining up waiting for Giampietro to feed them their wafers. Most of them didn't put their palms out to receive the body of Christ, but opened up their mouths like little girls being fed their *mamma's ragù*. There was silence; the moment was sacred. This is the whole point of Communion, after all, being fed or *imboccati* in silence. Shut up and eat. The sleek sounds of a perfectly rehearsed Broadway show are not necessary.

When the Communion was finished and Giampietro once again made the sign of the cross, *Nel nome del Padre, del Figlio e dello Spirito Santo*, I could tell he had something else to add. Before he dismissed the women, before the cacophony of voices started up and recipes were rehashed, he paid homage to the absent men. He was, after all, a man and a diehard fan of the Napoli soccer team. *"Ricordatevi"*—Remember, he instructed— *"Forza Napoli!"* Let's go, Naples!

If my grandfather Mimi had been in charge, he'd have called me to the pulpit to knock 'em dead with an *"'O Sole Mio"* finale.

Insalata di Polipo

When Salvatore and I were together—in the Fiat, in front of the boarding school, in his room under a big Humpty Dumpty clock—his hands were all over me. *Basta!* I'd insist, swatting. (*They don't get offended*, Maria Rosa had told me. *Slap them if you need to.*) I was a good girl: I tried to be forceful and pretend I didn't like it. I never knew that romance could feel so much like play.

I started to call him *polipetto*—my little eight-tentacled octopus.

Octopuses (or octopi), I learned soon after, are solitary creatures. That's what makes them so hard to catch. They do not live in groups or schools, but can be found alone in a cave or holding on to the underside of a rock, camouflaged against the gray stone. Zio Toto, Raffaella's older brother, explained this to me on the feast day of Sant'Antonio, as Raffaella and her sister Pia prepared a massive meal. The highlight of the lunch was to be a six-pound octopus that Toto had caught the day before.

While no one in the family could be described as a shrinking violet, Zio Toto gets the Oscar for being the biggest *casinaro*.

In Naples, this word refers to someone who is constantly making *casino*: noise, mess, confusion. The word *casino* (cas-*ee*-no) is a different one from *casinò* (cas-ee-*no*), the site of slot machines and poker. Nonetheless, it helps to think of the noise of slot machines in Vegas to capture the feeling of being around a *casinaro*. Zio Toto, *casinaro* extraordinaire, makes a hell of a lot of racket.

He is also totally shameless. *Faccia tosta*, they would say, which is literally a tough face, meaning that he doesn't give a damn what anyone thinks of him. When he came to Washington for our wedding, he spent twenty minutes trying to persuade the ticket seller in the Washington metro to give him a discount. I should mention that he speaks absolutely no English, so it was all in pantomime. I did not offer to translate.

Zio Toto is missing a hand. He lost it in 1972, when he was setting up fireworks for New Year's Eve. In Naples, New Year's Eve is celebrated with explosives. On balconies, terraces, and in the streets, people set off their prized whistlers and bottle rockets until all hours. And every year on January 2, the newspaper of Naples publishes a list of the injured and sometimes the dead. Often they are children. The parents are people who would *never* feed their children mayonnaise or ketchup or let them out of the house without a hat and gloves in October because of the danger to their health. On New Year's Eve, however, they give little Guglielmo a leaping lizard to set off and tell him to have fun.

One would think that losing a hand might have interfered with Toto's octopus catching, particularly because he doesn't use nets, or rods, or underwater guns. (He did use dart guns for a brief while, before giving them up in favor of the visceral thrill of hand-to-tentacle combat.) But the loss of his hand didn't slow him down in the least. *"Che problema c'è?"* he says. What's the problem? He doesn't scuba-dive, so when he gets a glimpse of a *polipo*, he has to take a deep breath and plunge. His long gray hair trails behind him like a merman's as he dives for his prey.

Sometimes Toto hides behind a rock and throws a spearlike instrument into a cave where he suspects an octopus might be lurking. When the little bugger rolls out, Toto attacks. He keeps his left arm and stub close to his body and pumps his flippers to slice through the water to the *polipo*. With only his right hand, he grabs the octopus, squeezes and twists its head, sticks two fingers into its brain, and then pulls it up to shore. The octopus tries to position its tentacles on Toto's stump and pull him down to the depths. When Toto manages to bring an octopus up to the surface, he holds its tentacles and beats its head against a rock (with one hand, somehow managing not to let it slide out of his grip and go flying back into the sea).

Eight arms against one, and Toto is always the victor.

I am in the living room of the Avallones' apartment listening to Toto describe yesterday's slippery battle with the *polipo*. We are sitting on the silk couch, and he hasn't stopped grinning, or talking, for the last twenty minutes. I should be helping to prepare the meal: I am a woman, after all. The sea smell of the octopus overpowers the doughy scent of the spinach pie in the oven. I can hear the shuffling efficiency of Raffaella and her sister Pia in the kitchen, and know that any attempt at "help" would basically mean my getting in the way of their all-important preparation of the *polipo*. Giving my undivided attention to Zio Toto, I've decided, is my most useful contribution to the cause.

"Isn't it dangerous? I mean, the octopus could grab you and pull you down," I ask him.

"*Eeeeh*," he exhales, making a Neapolitan sound which is used to mean, What are you gonna do? That's life. I hear this often in places like the post office or bank, when I protest that they shouldn't be closing at 1:15 in the afternoon—it says on the door they're open until 1:30 and I have a bill to pay! *"Eeeeh,"* on the exhale. That's life.

Toto proudly rolls up the sleeve of his dress shirt. He unscrews his prosthetic hand so that I can get a better look at his war wounds. All the way down to his stub, there are reddish-brown hickeys. *"Quelli s'aggrappano, t'abbracciano."* The little suckers grab on to you and hug you tight. Once, he tells me, he got badly bitten by a particularly aggressive *polipo* (one has to be careful not only of the suction cups but of the octopus's little hidden beak, too!).

The ritual for octopus preparation is this: after the battle, after the triumphant beating against the rock, Zio Toto, with long gray hair and Speedo dripping, delivers the octopus to his sisters, who stick it into a plastic bag. Back home in the kitchen, Raffaella pounds the creature again, this time on a cutting board with a meat tenderizer. Then, after she's cleaned him and removed his hard "beak," she holds his head above a pot of boiling water and dunks his tentacles three times. The tentacles curl up on contact with the water, creating an instant 1960s bob hairdo. There is a cork floating in the water—it makes the tentacles more tender. (Beating against a rock, dunked three times in boiling water with cork: Is this some kind of witchcraft?)

Lunch is ready, and I move to the dining table with the men. (Benedetta is at her fiancé's home, helping her future mother-in-law prepare and serve the Sant'Antonio lunch—there probably isn't one household in Naples that doesn't have an Antonio to celebrate.) Raffaella and her sister are buzzing, tasting, sprinkling things with last-minute salt or parsley or Parmesan. They begin serving. Young, able-bodied, and female, I guiltily wait to be served.

Raffaella has seven brothers and sisters. Their mother, Nonna Clara, cooked three-course lunches and dinners every day, washed sheets and blankets by hand, canned vegetables, and scrubbed floors. Her children, she used to say, "*non hanno voglia di far niente. Sono nati stanchi e vivono per riposare.*" They don't do anything, they were born tired and live to rest. She called theirs a "rotten generation." Seeing Pia and Raffaella baking and serving, and hearing of Toto and his one-handed battle with the octopus, I wonder what Nonna Clara would have thought of my generation. Rotten? Not just moldy but positively in decay.

Toto is still describing yesterday's strategic strikes when Pia's thick fingers (how can fingers be so muscular?) set down in front of me a plate of *insalata di polipo,* octopus salad. I look at the little pieces of Toto's nemesis, mixed with garlic and olive oil and parsley, and feel that I know him. Poor little guy was just minding his own business in that cave when Toto's spear shot through! I put my sentiments aside and prepare to take a bite and exclaim to the table that it is the best *polipo* I've ever tasted.

When everyone has been served, Pia and Raffaella stop moving. They don't sit, they stand at attention behind the high backs of two gilded eighteenth-century dining room chairs. (There is an expression in Neapolitan dialect, 'A *mamma stà assettata, 'o pate stà allerta e 'o figlio fuie.* If the mother sits down, the father gets worried and the kids run away. In other words, a mother sitting is an unnatural sight.) There is silence: Toto has stopped talking, plates have stopped clinking.

We all taste the octopus.

"*È duro 'sto polipo.*"

It is Nino who has broken the silence. He speaks with his mouth full, exaggerating the movement of trying to cut through the chewy octopus with his overworked molars. Have I understood correctly? Has he just said that the octopus is tough, no good?

"*È buonissimo! È buonissimo!*" I start my performance immediately. It's fabulous! It's fabulous! Let's pretend Nino didn't say that!

I am completely ignored.

Salvatore seconds his father's statement. "*Ha ragione Papà.*" Daddy's right.

Boing boing boing go our molars, and I continue my praise. "*Mai assaggiato così buono.*" I've never tasted octopus salad that's so good, I say with the strongest, most authoritative voice I can muster. I swallow a huge chunk whole. My canines have not even punctured the flesh of the animal. I haven't lied—the truth is that I've never tasted octopus salad at all.

No one counters Nino and Salva: apparently, they're right. It isn't tender, it isn't tasty. The only question that remains is, whose fault is it?

After an excruciating silence, Pia declares, "Toto, this octopus you caught is really tough." Not the octopus that we cooked. The octopus that *you caught.* Fightin' words.

"Lella, did you perhaps forget to beat it?" Toto asks Raffaella nonchalantly. Since he is certain that his octopus was not by nature tough, the only question he has for his sister is where she went wrong. Raffaella was supposed to mash the octopus with a hammer before performing the dunking torture, Toto explains with authority, even though I suspect that he has never cooked an octopus. He knows each step in the process, and wants to make sure everyone remembers that.

"Forget?! Of course I didn't forget!" she yells over him. "It's the octopus, it wasn't tender at all." Clearly, the women did the absolute best they could with what they had to work with.

I was glad to stay at the table so I didn't have to watch the sisters wiping the octopus into the trash with oily paper towels. In the kitchen, they talked of the toughness of the octopus; at the table, the men lamented that when women get to a certain age, they don't care for cooking anymore. They forget to hammer the octopus, or they get lazy and figure no one will notice.

"You should have tasted Nonna Clara's octopus salad," Toto tells me. He closes his eyes and imagines it. Succulent, tender.

"Was it much better than this one?" I ask to humor him, knowing the answer.

"*Eeeeeh*" on the exhale is his only reply. What can you do? Life sucks when the preparation of something as important as a *polipo* must be left in the hands of women from a "rotten" generation.

Presenza

"What is that lady's role? What is she *doing*?" I asked Salva. We were watching a soccer program as we snuggled on the sofa, digesting a baked *gâteau di patate* that Raffaella had prepared with potatoes, breadcrumbs, mortadella, prosciutto, and mozzarella. I was happy to be resting my head on Salva's chest.

"*Presenza*. She is *presenza*," he explained.

Presenza can mean physical presence, or can refer to cutting a beautiful or handsome figure when used with *bella*. *Una bella presenza*. This lady was certainly beautiful, and most definitely present.

Surrounding the lady was a group of middle-aged men talking (all at the same time) about the formation of the Napoli soccer team. While the men were all seated in very comfortable armchairs, the *presenza* lady was perched on a stool. A high stool. Which was convenient, given that the camera did not zoom in on her face, as it had with the men, but panned up slowly from her spike heels to her long, strategically crossed legs. The camera hesitated hopefully at her short skirt, even changed angles to see if any more nude flesh could be witnessed. It then continued up, slowly (what's the rush?), to her generous cleavage and stopped, finally, on her face. The men, still arguing in the background, were oblivious to the fact that they were not being filmed. The cameraman, apparently, had eyes only for Roberta.

It was a shame, though, that no one had told her that she was being filmed in close-up. She was clearly bored to tears, following none of the conversation. Instead, Roberta was examining her split ends.

The cameraman, instead of moving on when he found her entirely unengaged, lingered on her. The audience could hear the men in the background arguing about the attributes of this or that goalkeeper, but could see only Roberta and her self-grooming. A few seconds of this had passed when I distinctly heard a whistle. It was someone from the crew trying to get Roberta's attention! On air! She looked up, searching for the camera, and started grinning. A vacant, plastic grin. Believe it or not, she was more interesting to watch when she was examining her split ends.

There is someone sexy, bored, and present like Roberta on nearly every sports program that airs on Italian television. Game and variety shows feature the more energetic *veline*, scantily clad young models who dance and prance. They are more than *presente*; in one game show, a sexy *velina* appears at regular intervals and performs a lap dance with one of the contestants. Everyone else on the show looks on as if it's a natural occurrence—no raised eyebrows or laughing there.

A high point of a *Who Wants to Be a Millionaire*–inspired show is the moment of the *scossa*, or the electric shock dance. A *velina* wearing a bikini a few sizes too small stands on a dance floor under a spotlight and jiggles her stuff. The challenge, the

actress's fundamental conflict and the driving force of her artistic journey, as it were, is to keep the top of her bikini on as she
jiggles without holding it up with her hands. Interestingly, when
she fails at this and her boobs pop out, the camera does not
move to something else. If she can't keep her stuff covered, the
director apparently feels, that's her problem.

There is often a man in an animal suit (and remember, this
is not a kids' program) who does a silly Smurf-like voice and
spends a good bit of time trying to get his paws on the *velina*. He
is very large and red and runs around the studio shouting something unintelligible (as always, everyone except the *velina* is
talking at the same time). The host of the game show seems to
find this hilarious. It's a marriage of Disney and porn: I mean,
what else could you want from TV?

Former prime minister Silvio Berlusconi, as the world
knows, takes great pride in his country's *veline*. News of his
bunga bunga parties shocked the world. But they didn't shock
many people in Naples. The fact that the prime minister invited
veline (some not quite eighteen) to his villa in Sardegna, the fact
that before extending his invitation he perused their photo
shoots—these were simply measures that powerful men take to
ensure that they have . . . stimulating dinner partners.

No, what shocked many Neapolitans was the jiggling. A
boundary was crossed when they learned that Berlusconi sat,
pants down, on an armchair as the *veline* jiggled their bare
breasts in his face. It was choreographed by his chiefs of staff to
ensure that one *velina* from every racial group *bunga bunga*–ed
by and jiggled. In his face.

This wasn't a TV show, it was national news. And he was
the head of the nation's government. Even for the forgiving Neapolitans, that was a bit much.

In 1998, Italians were fascinated by the Monica Lewinsky

scandal. They would ask me what I thought of my country's *brutta figura*. Specifically, they asked me, *"Per chi sei?"* Who are you for? I interpreted this to mean, are you behind the Democrats supporting Clinton or are you Republican and in favor of impeachment? I would answer as best I could that although the president had humiliated himself and his country, I felt that impeachment was too extreme a measure. . . . But no, they would interrupt, we meant are you for Monica or for Bill?

Wait a second. Him against her? That made no sense to me. Monica was not the protagonist but a supporting character. At the center was the president of the United States, who had abused his power and humiliated . . .

"Yes," Italians agreed. "Humiliation. He really could have chosen someone who was more beautiful."

The scandal here was not what he had done, but the fact that he had done it with someone whom they considered overweight and unattractive. So the one who got the respect was Monica. If she, without good looks, could seduce the president of the United States, it was she who deserved to be the star of the lurid *sceneggiata*, or show. The president of the world's superpower, with only one chick, and not even a pretty one at that? That girl must have something. If she were in Italy, they probably would have elected her president.

I know that a big concern of the Italian government at the moment is the continuing brain drain, or *fuga dei cervelli*, of intellectuals from Italy to northern Europe and the United States, particularly in the sciences. Parliament is working on grants and other incentives to keep young, talented researchers from leaving the country. I can't help but think, however, of what would happen if there were a *fuga dei culetti*, or a tits-and-ass drain, in which *veline* found work elsewhere and left the peninsula. Now, *that* would be a national crisis.

Given the context, I think the *belle presenze* on sports programs are one of the least offensive things on Italian TV. For one thing, there's no camera positioned *under* the lady's skirt. But, more important, the *veline* who appear on the soccer programs are, perhaps without even realizing it, so honest and transparent. Roberta is objectified and degraded, yes. But there is something very human underneath: an Italian woman, like so many others, who is just plain bored by men talking about soccer.

A Single Plate of Pasta

I was asked to leave the Denza to find alternative housing in the middle of October. The boarding boys had arrived, and apparently I was a menace. I had unknowingly broken all sorts of rules of the Catholic institution (bidets had nothing to do with it, but I can't help but wonder *if they had known . . .*). I had been seen walking with a student there, a young man. On another occasion I had been seen walking with a different young man. I had not always been wearing a jacket and scarf when I walked with these members of the opposite sex. I tried to explain to the priest who served as the dean of students that I had to walk across the campus to get from my room to the dining hall, and it was eighty degrees! Most of the students were men, how could I help it if we walked side by side for a few meters?

"Da noi non si fa così" was his reply. That's not the way we do things here.

I started looking for a room to rent close by. Since this "experience abroad" was footed by my parents' dollars (and in 1997, dollars went far—thousands of lire far), I had no trouble finding a nice room in an apartment in Posillipo. I saw a big fluorescent yellow AFFITA STANZA (room for rent) sign on a building near the Calabrese girls' flat when I visited them for coffee one day. It was perfect—I would be near them and the Avallones.

"Will you have to cook for yourself?" Maria Rosa asked, concerned, when I said I was leaving the Denza. She and her sisters knew that things could get messy for me when it came to eating. "I'll be fine," I told them.

Salva and his parents worried too. My new flatmates were two girls from Puglia who went home for weeks at a time and kept to themselves when they were in the apartment. No more dinner tray at the Denza, with its scrumptious *scaloppine*, little carafe of wine, and *Buon appetito, signorina:* I'd be left to my own devices at mealtimes.

Most of the time, I ended up at the Avallones'. "What have you planned for your dinner?" Raffaella or Salva would ask me on the weekends, when lunch was over and I suggested that it was time for me to go back to my apartment. If I didn't answer, with conviction, *"Pasta e fagioli!"* or *"Zuppa di ceci!"*—if I hesitated in any way, they would look at each other knowingly. Six hours later I would be sitting next to Benedetta with her teddy bear pajamas devouring Raffaella's lasagna.

It would have been unheard of for a Neapolitan girl to sleep in her boyfriend's room at his parents' house at the age of twenty-two. But the rules seemed to be different for an *americana.* The American women that Italians saw on TV may not have jiggled their stuff on prime-time game shows, but they certainly were promiscuous. In addition, I was from a culture where parents would send their daughter to live and work alone, on another continent, right after college! The Avallones would never have had the presumption to tell me what I was allowed and not allowed to do.

On holidays and weekends, I would find a cot prepared by Raffaella in Salva's room. I accepted the plan: If the Avallones weren't hung up on propriety, why should I be? ("*Non si fa così*," I heard the housekeeper, a middle-aged woman from central Naples, mumble as she remade my cot one morning. Nunzia Gatti echoed the priest at the boarding school: that's not the way it's done. Apparently, my sleeping in Salva's room didn't bother the Avallones, but it certainly bothered their maid.)

"I'm renting a new place," I told Cynthia and my other co-workers at the Consulate. I was grown-up and independent, I wanted them to know. There were two months left of my internship and I didn't want to publicize the fact that I'd basically moved in with my new boyfriend's parents. Or that, when left alone, I didn't know how to eat.

I can do this, I would tell myself on the rare occasions that I cooked in my new apartment. The kitchen was tiny and attracted fruit flies. Hungry, I would open the refrigerator to find nothing. So I'd boil water for some spaghetti, open a can of tomatoes, and then open the refrigerator again, to find that there was still nothing. I learned that it wasn't a great idea to start cooking when I was starved, because that's when my mind embraced dubious mathematical calculations like: If Raffaella's *ragù* simmers over a very low flame for eight hours, it stands to reason that I can let my tomato sauce boil over an extremely *hot* flame for twenty minutes.

As a recovering binger, I had another problem: After years of all-or-nothing eating, it was really hard to know what a "normal" amount of food was when I cooked for myself. I would stare at the pack of spaghetti and wonder if I should boil two noodles or the whole thing. Any amount seemed too much or too little. I needed an Italian woman to sit me down, slow me down, keep me company, and show me what and how much to eat.

I felt that it was important for me to say *no, grazie* every once in a while to the baked gnocchi or *pizza fritta* that Raffaella was making at the Avallones'. I needed to affirm my independence, after all. But as I tasted the spaghetti that I prepared for myself, soupy and insipid, I had to wonder, who was I kidding?

Soft *Stracchino* Cheese Right Out of the Fridge

I was in a flannel robe on the Avallones' living room sofa one evening watching a horrendously dubbed version of *Diff'rent Strokes* when I heard, *"Egoista! Sei un egoista!"*

Benedetta was screaming. Nino was booming. Salvatore and his mother were trying to make peace. All four of them were in Nino and Raffaella's bedroom with the door closed. *Egoista,* Benedetta was calling her father, and though I didn't know exactly what that word meant, I knew that it had to be something pretty bad.

The suffix *-ista* in Italian signals a vocation. So *autista* is a driver, *dentista* a dentist. My all-time favorite word in Italian is the term for the person at the beauty parlor who shampoos: *shampista.* I figured that *egoista* must be someone who was so into their ego that it became a profession (I now know it just means selfish).

Benedetta and Nino were fighting about her fiancé, Mauro. Benedetta had met Mauro only eight months before, and he had proposed almost immediately. Benedetta had had several

previous relationships, all of which had lasted for years. Raffaella told me that three of these boys had become part of the
family, and that when Benedetta had broken up with them (it
was always she who ended it, always the turquoise eyes), Raffaella had been heartbroken. "They were like sons! And I didn't
even get a chance to say goodbye!" When Benedetta dumped
Andrea, the last one, Raffaella made her promise that the next
man she brought home would be the one that she would marry.
It just wasn't fair to put Raffaella through that again.

Mauro was a short cardiologist who, unlike almost all of
Benedetta's previous boyfriends, did not hit it off with any member of the family. So for once the tables were turned: In the
bedroom it was Nino who was attacking, and Benedetta who
was defending her fiancé. The first time Mauro came over, I
later learned, he had opened the refrigerator, taken out a little
plastic container of soft *stracchino* cheese, found himself a fork,
and started eating. The refrigerator of his future in-laws! Without even asking! Where had this guy grown up?

He used the informal *tu* form for *you* with both Nino and
Raffaella. (In English there is only one form for *you*, but in Italian, there are two: the formal *lei* is used when you don't know
someone or you want to show respect, while the informal *tu*
shows chumminess. Or friendship. Or *dis*respect. I don't know!
I still don't know. I *do* know that you have to conjugate all your
second-person verbs based on where you think you stand with
someone. And often, the move from using *lei* to *tu* in a relationship is scarier than asking someone to the senior prom.)

The Avallones were not a formal family. They did not stand
on ceremony, and were far from judgmental. But really, this guy
pushed the limits. Salvatore explained part of the problem when
he told me that Mauro was a communist. Wow, I thought. Italian communists open the refrigerator without asking. They

have the balls to use the *tu* form with everyone. It was kind of refreshing to see someone who totally disregarded Neapolitan bourgeois social norms (which I was just starting to understand myself). *Insomma*, I liked the guy. He made me look good.

That is, I liked him until he embarked on an anti-American tirade one evening at dinner that ended with the phrases "capitalist imperialism" and "worse than fascism" and lots of spit on the table. Now I agreed with Nino. You do *not* open the refrigerator in someone else's apartment without asking.

While Raffaella kept her reservations about Mauro to herself, Nino did not. That evening everyone in the apartment building heard about Mauro taking his shoes off and filling the Avallones' apartment with the stench of his smelly feet (with Nino, it always came back to the *puzza*, the peeyew). Benedetta kept countering with *Egoista! Egoista!* I had never been party to such a row in someone else's home. Part of me was embarrassed and wanted to slip out without making a noise, and another part of me rejoiced in a stunning revelation: families other than mine—even happy, functional families—fought. They didn't just disagree, with respect and calm voices. Other families had it *out*.

I felt perfectly at home.

"Aaayyyed! The ambassador's here!" My mother's West Virginia twang turned my father's two-letter name into one with three syllables, all diphthonged vowels. It was an early summer evening in the 1980s and my father was doing his laps in our pool. He swam with no bathing suit. "It slows me down," he would tell us.

Ed Wilson didn't like to be slowed down by anybody or anything.

My father grew up rich in Chicago. His grandfather, Thomas Wilson, was a captain of industry who had immigrated to the United States from London, Ontario, at the turn of the century. He worked his way up from cleaning manure in the Chicago stockyards to becoming president of the third largest meatpacking company in America. As president, he changed its name to Wilson and Co.

A lot of the canned meat that was unloaded by American GIs in the Bay of Naples and given to starving Neapolitans during World War II was Wilson. The hams baked by my maternal grandmother in a small West Virginia town in the fifties were Wilson.

My great-grandfather, instead of throwing away the cowhides and intestines of the animals, started producing footballs, baseballs, and tennis rackets: *We use every part of the pig but the squeal!* was the slogan. Wilson Sporting Goods was born. Thomas Wilson made the footballs that American kids played with and the hot dogs their parents grilled.

Little Ed was the first grandson, and he had everything he could ever want: his own horse, a chauffeur, tickets on luxury liners to Europe at the age of nine. After Princeton and Oxford, he got his PhD at Johns Hopkins University's School of Advanced International Studies in Washington, where he met my mother, at a reception for new students in 1967.

"He looked like a Kennedy, but fat," she told my sister and me.

When she became Mrs. Wilson, Bonnie Salango gave up her job at a Washington think tank to become a full-time wife and mother. My father was at the Department of Commerce, where he worked with the Bureau of East-West Trade to investigate market opportunities in Eastern Europe. My mother accompanied him to places like Bucharest and Sofia, and at home cooked Italian American meals for pudgy communists.

A *think tank*? I now wonder. A *government job*? The two of them could have taken their Bonnie and Ed show on the road; they could have fought it out in an Edward Albee play, or started a puppet theater for underprivileged toddlers. We would have been better off. But they both had advanced degrees, and they both shouldered lots of parental expectations. It was 1970, and they made "respectable" life choices.

I was embarrassed by my father, always. He couldn't get in a taxi without speaking some exotic foreign language with the driver; he couldn't be served at a restaurant without making sure the Czech waiter saw his imitation of Václav Havel. While the dads of our friends at the country club wore bermudas with little frogs or ducks on them, my father wore a tie that Romanian dictator Ceauşescu gave him ("I'm telling you, Bonnie, the guy likes me," he told my mom, who ignored him) with sheer white bell-bottoms. Ed Wilson needed to be at center stage—he had to be *noticed*. With his clothes and accessories (an obscure Central Asian medal of honor from the last century, an antique walking cane that he didn't need), my father begged to be asked, Where did that come from, Ed? Tell us the story.

My mother hated the way he dressed. She called his see-through pantwear *diaphanous*.

That particular evening, she had told my father that there was no time for him to swim, much less to swim bare-assed. My father paid her little mind, shouting as he dove in, "There is absolutely time, and I can't hear your screaming underwater! Ha!"

Splash.

Despite her anger and embarrassment, I think my mother

English Lessons

My internship at the Consulate became part-time at the end of October. We weren't exactly busy, so I asked Cynthia if I could start teaching English in the afternoons to earn some extra money. It didn't take much to convince the establishment, since I wasn't being paid.

The English-language schools I applied to in Naples had names like the London Institute, Wall Street Academy, and Cambridge Centre, and were located on the second or third floor of crowded apartment buildings downtown. They were made up of two classrooms at most, with cartoonish American and British flags on the walls. I was hired immediately because I was mother-tongue. The school I chose to start at paid 10,000 lire an hour (about five dollars), handed to me in cash by the director at the end of each lesson. He spoke no English whatsoever.

Unbeknownst to the director of the language school, my classes centered on two topics of conversation: What does everyone think of the United States? And, What does everyone think of my relationship with Salvatore and our future?

Like many Americans, I was fascinated by what my students, most of whom had never been to the States, thought
about my country. Could it be that I was homesick? In part, but
it was more that slightly adolescent and narcissistic curiosity
common to a lot of Americans: our great big national desire to
know what they *really* think of us. I had my students write short
essays. Here are some highlights:

"The Americans are a beautiful people because they are
simple. They are always saying what they think. Not like Italian
people."

"I think that United States is a big country full of people
who lives in many different ways, trust in different gods, but
they lives in a same place because they are like brothers and
respect each other. Like blacks, chineses, European people."

"In America, all the streets are crowded by people of different races and colors (whites, blacks, yellows, reds) and this is
beautiful."

"I'd like to go to the U.S. To learn how to be myself and, in
spite of that, to be happy too. Not to make blood in my veins get
water, to get alive."

"U.S. is the place where all things leave before spreading all
over."

"If I will have time in America I'd like to ski in Colorado, in
Aspen of course, running like hell on my skis with big black
sunglasses and a crazy long hat. After this will I get a little tired?
Yes, maybe. And then? Iowa!!!!!! I would go there for two
months, getting fuel for myself, relaxing on the green, kidding
with the dolls. I'd like to rent a big factory [I think he meant
farm, *fattoria* in Italian] and sleep alone a very long time."

After we'd pulled apart their perceptions, and misconcep-
tions, of my homeland, we would move on to grammar.

The question of the day might be: *Do you-all* (plural of *you*, each student can give his or her opinion) *really think Salva loves me?* Or, let's try the third person present interrogative of *love: Does he love me enough to move away from Naples and his parents?* As their English got better, I challenged them to dissect my emotional state. *Am I in love with Salvatore, or with Naples in general?* Or even, *Am I simply in love with his mother and what she cooks?*

Because I enjoyed teaching and sharing the beauty of my mother tongue, it was extremely frustrating for me that Salvatore seemed to have no desire whatsoever to improve his English. We were spending a lot of time together, and I was an English teacher, so wouldn't it have been natural for him to use the opportunity to better his language skills? Did I really have to be subjected to his singing, to the tune of John Denver's "Take Me Home, Country Roads," "Hoven road, in the sun. To the place I rerun! *West Virginia!* [with gusto, he knew that part!] Sunshine Momma, run to road, in the song . . ."?

I understand that when you grow up listening to songs with lyrics in a language that you don't understand, you focus on the melody and the rhythm. A nonsense approximation of the words is just fine. But shouldn't it make him just a tad self-conscious that there was a native English speaker listening? Not in the least.

When I would correct his grammar, for instance by noting, "Salva, the first person of the verb *to come* is 'come.' No *s, capisci?* I come," he would respond with his version of Boy George: *"Cumma cumma cumma cumma comeleon, you giva go, you giva go . . ."* There was no hope. Years later, I would have to leave this teaching job to my bilingual and easily embarrassed children.

At the same time Salva refused to learn English, I was getting more fluent in both spoken Italian and in the parallel language of hand gestures, which is necessary for survival in Naples. Americans use hand gestures too, but they employ them in a completely different way. Except for a few precise ones ("Tsk, tsk" with the carrot-peeling movement of two index fingers; curling up one index finger to mean *Come here*), American hand gestures are large, sweeping, and general. And they vary from person to person. In Naples, they are so specific that there is even a dictionary of *gesti*, complete with pictures of someone's hand and the description of the movement. As a foreigner, you must learn this language just as you learn the verbs or adjectives of the spoken language.

When I first arrived in Naples, I would ask the doorman at the boarding school if there was any mail for me, and he would respond without a sound, looking me straight in the eye. He held, however, his thumb and index finger in the form of a pistol and shook his thumb almost imperceptibly from side to side. My response would be to look him in the eye and ask again, is there any mail for me? Once again, he would do the jiggling-thumb-gun thing, and jut out his lower lip just to make things clear. *Oh, grazie,* thank you! I would say, and wink, thinking I had just engaged in some profound covert communication but still having absolutely no idea whether I had any mail or not. I later learned that that hand gesture means *niente*, nothing, and can also be expressed with a click of the tongue and a hand flicking under the chin.

Watch out, that guy is trying to cheat you is expressed by pulling down the lower eyelid of one eye with the index finger. *Let's eat* is all the fingertips of one hand together doing a pecking motion toward the mouth, while *pasta* is the index and middle finger doing a twisting motion simulating a fork gathering up spaghetti. These are just a few of many, but my all-time favorite is the gesture that means someone has died. It is (get

this!) the index and middle fingers of the right hand straightened upward together, representing the soul of the deceased,
doing a circular, Slinky-like motion up to the sky. The other
fingers are closed in a fist. Along with the hand gesture, a quick
(rather cheerful, strangely enough) whistle is emitted. This is
apparently the sound of the soul of the deceased going to
heaven. Just a hop, skip, and a jump! You will hear people in
Naples (where to say someone is *morto*, or dead, is considered
rather bad taste) describing how Aunt Maria (as soon as the
name is uttered, there goes the soul up to heaven with a whistle
so we remember she's dead!) made the best frittata. . . .

As for my spoken Italian, the language I was learning was
Neapolitan dialect. Not *dialetto stretto*, or pure dialect, but Italian with a marked Neapolitan accent and with many expressions that are unique (I now know) to Naples. The idea of having
a down-home southern accent in Italian did not bother me, because I think in some visceral way it took me back to my mother's Appalachian twang. It's a different language, I know, but I
swear that the feel of it, the pull-up-a-chair-honey-soup's-on of
it, is the same. Ham hocks and beans in southern West Virginia
or fried pizza dough smothered in tomato and mozzarella in the
countryside surrounding Napoli. Tight Italian soccer shirts and
gel in the hair or oversize basketball jerseys and Walmart. The
cultures in many ways are polar opposites. But when you're
called to the table by Mama, or Mamma, in that way, in a way
that goes straight to your innards . . . you could just as well be in
Bluefield, West Virginia, or Secondigliano, Provincia di Napoli.

An analogous situation might be an Italian girl, a bit shy,
pretty in an old-fashioned way, who has come to the United
States to learn English. "Oh, you're from Italy! Whereabouts?"
She responds with a smile, "I's from Rome but learned myself
English in Memphis." That was the sort of impression I gave,

linguistically. In Naples, I learned that any and every verb could be reflexive. I ate myself a plate of pasta, I watched myself a film. My vowels were long and lazy, especially the *a* (in Naples, it lasts so long that you don't know if the speaker is going to get around to finishing the word). My *s* sounded like *sh*. "To have" was for me the Neapolitan *tenere* (which is more like "got myself") instead of the Italian *avere*. "*Tengo na famma 'e pazze,*" I would say, meaning that I was very, very hungry. Or, literally, "I got myself a crazy hunger."

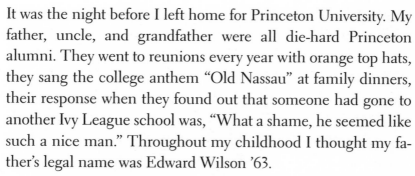

It was the night before I left home for Princeton University. My father, uncle, and grandfather were all die-hard Princeton alumni. They went to reunions every year with orange top hats, they sang the college anthem "Old Nassau" at family dinners, their response when they found out that someone had gone to another Ivy League school was, "What a shame, he seemed like such a nice man." Throughout my childhood I thought my father's legal name was Edward Wilson '63.

So everyone was ecstatic when I was admitted to Old Nassau and decided to go. I was supposed to be ecstatic, too. I was supposed to be "*so* psyched." My mother was supposed to be relieved and proud and ready to enjoy her husband's company in a peaceful empty nest. We both pretended that we couldn't wait. I was going to be Katherine Wilson '96! There were auditions for *Kiss Me, Kate* with the Princeton University Players that very fall! In the checkout line of Bed Bath & Beyond, pulling the biggest suitcases down from the attic, attaching that luggage thing on top of the station wagon, we talked about how "cool" it was going to be.

And then the night before leaving I went upstairs to brush my teeth and set my alarm for the next day. My mother came to my room with an excuse, did you pack your toothbrush or something, and I gave her the opening of a very quiet, very contained, "Mommy, I don't want to go."

"Sweetheaaaart," she bawled, "it's just the worrrst thang thit ever happened to me! My baaayybyyy girl!"

In Naples they say, 'E figlie so' ppiezze 'e core. Your children are little pieces of your heart. But to feel what that expression means, you need to imagine Dolly Parton saying it. No, actually, you need to imagine Dolly singing it. Because this dialect, like that of the American South, lays bare so much suffering and so much love that it does to the body what good country music does—it goes straight from the ears to the gut.

Melanzane a Funghetto

The Avallones' apartment smelled like a geriatric ward. Ben-Gay stung my nostrils as I walked into Salvatore's room to find Nunzia Gatti massaging his bare shoulders and neck. Salva was sitting at his desk; Nunzia was behind him. I was appalled.

The desk where Salva "repeated" his studies faced two French doors through which he could see the Bay of Naples and Vesuvius. "*Dunque*," he was repeating, "*la legge canonica del Settecento prevedeva . . .*" Eighteenth-century canonical law foresaw the enforcement . . . I could not believe my eyes, or my ears, or my nostrils. Had Salva really asked the Avallones' house-keeper of twenty years to massage him with Ben-Gay? Was he really studying his law texts while she did it?

I said nothing. No one noticed me standing there.

"*Grazie, Nunzia*," Salva thanked her when the massage was finished, and she went to wash the Ben-Gay off her hands and to return to chopping eggplants in little cubes to fry. She was making *melanzane a funghetto*, following strict instructions from Raffaella. (Nunzia, born and raised in central Naples, surely knew how to prepare *melanzane a funghetto* when she came to work for the Avallones. But Raffaella had to make sure that the recipe was exactly the same as hers, and so one morning twenty years ago Nunzia followed Raffaella around like a little duckling as she prepared the *melanzane,* learning from scratch.)

"Oh, ciao, Ketrin!" she said cheerfully as she passed me on her way out.

Nunzia came in the mornings to do simple cooking and heavy cleaning in the apartment. What are *le pulizie grosse?* I asked Salva when he described Nunzia's responsibilities, translating the expression in my mind as the Big Cleanings. I saw that Raffaella did a lot of cleaning herself: she swept, dusted, even got up on a ladder to wipe the windows down with old *Mattino* newspapers. So why did they need a housekeeper? "The big cleaning," it turns out, meant keeping things clean in the Neapolitan sense of the word. For this she needed Nunzia Gatti.

In Italy, one's apartment must be spotless. Outside, many Italians think nothing of throwing their cigarettes on the ground or otherwise littering in full view of other people. It is shocking to witness the contrast between the filthy streets of Naples and the shiny, disinfected, pine-smelling cleanliness of Neapolitan apartments. A home should not be superficially clean, or *pulita per la suocera.* (This expression, meaning *mother-in-law clean,* is used in a highly pejorative way and refers to something that is clean for show. An apartment that would pass the test of a five-minute visit from a mother-in-law. Dusted, clothes hung up, no dishes in the sink.) No, one's apartment must be *Italian* clean. Toothpicks getting the crud out of the molding. No dust in the rungs and rivets of the radiator. Outside, *Chi se ne frega!* Who cares! is the mentality, it's not my house.

Many Americans, on the other hand, would not be caught dead throwing a dirty Kleenex on the ground at the park but think nothing of leaving their houses in a state that would have an Italian mother dialing up social services. An Italian grandmother told me of an American mother she knew in Rome in the 1960s who was so much fun! So positive! So kind! *But that apartment.* No one could understand how the woman could live, let alone raise a family, in such a pigsty. *Mio Dio.* Beds unmade and clothes on chairs. Those poor children!

Nunzia Gatti was around sixty and square-shaped. She spoke almost exclusively dialect, and used a *third* form of *you*—the most respectful, feudal form, *voi*, which exists only in Neapolitan—with every member of the family except me. When we first met, I was uncomfortable with the idea of using the familiar form with her while she "Madam'd" me, so I did what I often do: I used the formal *lei* with her, sprinkling it with a few *tus* so I didn't seem too uptight. Pretty soon we were *tu*-ing without saying anything about it. Nobody, including me, would dare say, Let's use *tu* with each other from here on in, whatta you say?

Nunzia, coming from a different social stratum, was a sort of foreigner in this household just as I was. She took it upon herself to warn me in hushed tones about the dangers of getting too involved with a Neapolitan upper-class boy, a *signorino.* "*Vieni qua*"—she would beckon me with her index finger to follow her to the balcony where she was beating the rugs with a long wooden rug-beater—"*Sai come si dice a Napoli?*" You know what we say in Naples? "*Mogli e buoi dai paesi tuoi!*" Wives and cows from your hometown. She didn't mean, as I first thought, that I should be careful of buying a cow or a wife that wasn't from Washington. The idea was that Salva and I would never work as a couple: relationships only work if the husband and wife come from the same place and the same socioeconomic background. "Oh yes," I would reply with a polite smile, "I understand."

I was uncomfortable with Nunzia and with the culture of servitude that made it okay for Salva to ask her to rub Ben-Gay on his neck. It was so servile, so lewd! When I exploded at Salva, wanting an explanation for it, he was confused. "It's no big deal! She works here and my neck was hurting. Your family has a housekeeper too!"

———— ⋇ ————

Doris Belen Hernandez moved to Washington from Honduras in 1984. She was hired by my parents to clean our house several times a week and was responsible for vacuuming, ironing, and making the beds. She called my parents, Bonnie and Ed, "Mrs. Bony and Mr. Head." My mother cleaned up frantically before Doris arrived, worried that she would "just have too much to do, poor Doris!" My mother, the *signora* of the house, would "give orders" that started with "Doris, do you think if it's not too much trouble that you could try to maybe . . ." and ended with "That is, if you have time!" When she needed to be sure Doris was coming on a certain day, she would say, "You're not thinking of coming by on Tuesday, are you?"

Raised poor, my mother was uncomfortable with the idea of hiring "help." She liked to pretend that Doris came because she felt like it, or because she happened to be in the neighborhood.

Doris was not a workaholic. She watched soap operas in our family room. She chatted with her friends on the phone. Our house was large enough that when she cleaned, nobody saw or heard her. We would see the beds made, notice that we were out of potato chips and leftovers, and think, "Oh, Doris must have come."

When we did cross paths, Doris was entertaining. Her English left much to be desired, but this didn't stop her from doing some fantastic imitations of all of us. My father huffing and puffing as he tried to tie his shoelaces for a tennis match, belching and saying "Goddammit!" (with a Spanish accent). "Kaaaaatherine, you're not gonna wayar that are ya?" with tragically scrunched up eyebrows was my mother: Bluefield, West Virginia, by way of Tegucigalpa.

Doris was irreverent and entertaining, and in the Wilson family, that was enough.

"A housekeeper, yes, but I certainly would never ask her to massage—"

"But it's okay to ask her to clean the toilets?" Salva was honestly clueless about the difference.

"Where I come from, you pay a masseuse to massage and a cleaner to clean!"

With a high-and-mighty slam of the door, I went to find Nunzia to hear more reasons why I shouldn't fall into the trap of marrying a *signorino* like Salva.

An Italian friend of mine told me about a recent trip she had taken to the States. "You Americans," she sighed, "some of you have estates as big as Italian villages but no one to pour your coffee in the morning."

"That's not true," I countered. "If you're famous you do."

Raffaella's relationship with Nunzia took me a while to get a handle on. Raffaella gave orders using the familiar *you*, and I got a grammar lesson in the imperative familiar. *"Metti le lenzuola sopra ad asciugare!"* Hang the sheets upstairs to dry! *"Non usare quella scopa in casa!"* Don't use that broom indoors! Raffaella's assertive tone missed that of Cinderella's stepsisters by only a smidgeon, and was quite frankly petrifying to me. When Nunzia made a mistake in her simple cooking tasks, Raffaella didn't call to her from the other room but looked her in the eyes and asked, *"Ma perchè?"*—But why?

Raffaella referred to Nunzia as a *brava donna*, a good woman, faint praise that in Naples basically means "not a thief." It's too bad, though, she told me once, that Nunzia doesn't know how to cook or clean.

To test Nunzia, Raffaella would play tricks on her. One day she took a big piece of *pizza di scarola*, a focaccia-like bread stuffed with escarole, olives, and pine nuts, and put it in the refrigerator, knowing that it was Nunzia's favorite. When Nunzia left, she checked the size of the slice. "Watch this!" she told me mischievously the next day when all three of us were in the kitchen.

"Nunzia, where is the *pizza di scarola* that was in the fridge yesterday?" Raffaella feigned nonchalance, but was seriously enjoying this.

"It's still there, ma'am, in the fridge."

"No, I mean the other half. Somebody ate it."

Silence.

"Who was it?"

"Actually, it was me, ma'am."

"Aaah, ho capito, ho capito." I see. Raffaella looked at me and winked, joyous in her victory.

Nunzia, I assumed, resented her high-maintenance boss. When Raffaella left the room, she rolled her eyes and even flicked the back of her hand in the Neapolitan gesture signifying someone who is *pesante*, or heavy, hard to take.

After episodes like this, it surprised me when I found out that Nunzia came to Raffaella sometimes to get her shots. She had some kind of thyroid problem and had to get shots every month. Since Raffaella was known for her skill in administering shots, Nunzia stood in her employer's marble bathroom and rolled down her thick pantyhose. Raffaella returned from whatever fancy reception she was attending to plunge the needle in her maid's pudgy backside. Dressed in a Chanel suit and balanced on three-inch heels, Raffaella would hold an ice pack for at least five minutes to Nunzia's butt—"*Non ti muovere!*" Don't move! There was that familiar imperative again!—before packing her in the Lancia to give her a ride home.

Pasta e Fagioli

Many of the students in the English school where I taught were college guys in their twenties. *"Teeeacher, we go out later, you come?"* they would suggest in class. Nobody was asking me for a date—it was a group. Sometimes I went. I enjoyed them, especially a smart, unattractive guy named Gianmarco who really liked talking about me, and America.

One afternoon after class, Gianmarco told me that he and some of his high school friends (both young men and young women, *ragazzi* and *ragazze*) were going to Abruzzo to ski over the weekend—did I want to come?

I'd never been to Abruzzo! Skiing was fun!

I asked Salva midweek what his plans were for the weekend. "Plans" can be translated as *progetti* in Italian. Projects. "Do you have plans?" translates roughly as "Any projects up your sleeve?" Often, in Naples, projects are not scheduled more than one day in advance, which can make an American go bonkers (*How do we know we'll be alive?* Salva asks me when I want to book plane tickets a few months in advance).

"Nope. No projects this weekend," he told me.

"I'm thinking of going to Abruzzo," I ventured. "Do you mind?"

His voice was clipped when he answered. "Do whatever you want. *Sei adulta e vaccinata.*" You're a grown-up who's had her vaccinations, an expression meaning you're free to choose for yourself.

He had an exam coming up, so chances were he'd be spending most of the weekend with his *Code of Canon Law* book. I wasn't interested in any of the men I'd be traveling with, so I had a clear conscience. I bought some heavy sweaters with little snowflakes on them and packed a suitcase for the trip.

Much of the Abruzzo region is made up of little towns named after rocks: Roccaraso, Rocca di Mezzo, Rocca Pia. They are nestled in the Apennine Mountains, which cut through the center of the Italian boot. We were headed for Roccaraso, where Gianmarco's parents, like the Avallones and many other Neapolitan families, had a little apartment. Zio Toto, I would later learn, goes skiing there every winter. (But the plastic hand? I asked Salva. "Oh, he duct-tapes it to his ski pole. You've gotta avoid him on ski lifts, because if the tape gets wet and starts to come off, he asks the person next to him on the *seggiovia* to re-attach it.")

Roccaraso is an hour-and-a-half drive from Naples. In the car with Gianmarco and his friends, I noticed castles and fortresses from the Middle Ages zooming by. Gianmarco was definitely nerdy, and not very cute, and still he drove like a maniac. I was riding shotgun. In the backseat two guys and two girls were packed in, and it became apparent as we flew over the mountain roads that they were paired off. The "group of friends" wasn't an amorphous gang hanging out: there were exactly three couples, and the two couples in the backseat were sucking face by the time we reached L'Aquila. This would be a long weekend.

Roccaraso was bombed beyond recognition during World War II ("by the Americans!" one of Gianmarco's friends in the backseat exclaimed, and I decided to keep quiet), so there is nothing medieval about it. The buildings are from the 1960s and are brown and rectangular, with Swiss-like wooden balconies. We parked on the main street and piled out.

I remarked on the silence, the peace, the mountain splendor. "Just wait," Gianmarco said. "Wait till the rest of Naples gets here."

The first cold weekends of the year, the period surrounding New Year's Eve, and the week of Carnevale in February are the periods of the Neapolitan Descent, he explained to me. At these times, the town becomes the site of Neapolitans *in trasferta* (a sports term referring to a team that is playing an away game but that is also used to describe a group that goes somewhere en masse). No serene, tranquil Abruzzese atmosphere then—it's more like an eighth-grade field trip. Naples *in trasferta* is chaos, noise, laughter. Pushing and shoving. Women in full-length furs (which they wear exclusively in Roccaraso; Naples is too warm) doing what they call "laps" down the main street to be seen.

I didn't know Neapolitans were big skiers. Given the way they drove, I was starting to get skeptical about going down the mountain with them. My fears were justified.

After a breakfast of croissants and cappuccinos in his little gingerbread-house apartment the next morning, Gianmarco and his dark-skinned, black-haired guy friends got done up in high-tech Spyder ski attire. The women had hairbands that matched the buckles on their ski boots. They all looked like expert downhill racers who'd just come off the pages of a ski magazine.

I wasn't an expert skier. I took after my mother.

❋

Before they were married, Bonnie Salango made Ed Wilson believe that she loved the outdoors. Sports were very important for my father, and he told my mother he could never marry a woman who didn't enjoy tennis, skiing, and swimming as much as he did. "Oh, I ski," she told him, batting her eyelashes. "We can go *after* we're married."

Their first and last "after-we're-married" ski trip was to Aspen, Colorado. My father didn't think it necessary to verify that his wife could make it down the mountain on her skis. He took her to the top of the highest slope, and after spraying to a parallel stop, noticed that she hadn't managed to get off the chairlift. As he slalomed down (in an enormous Siberian wolf hat that would be a source of embarrassment throughout my skiing career), he looked up to see Bonnie riding the lift back down the other side.

"Bonnie! What in God's name are you doing?" he screamed.

"Ayyyed, ya never told me to get off!"

She went up again, and this time managed to dismount. My father led her to a black-diamond slope. When she saw how steep it was, she calmly took off her skis and pushed them down the mountain. Then she sat on her waterproofed butt and slid down to the base.

"Shouldn't someone help that woman?" a gentleman asked my father.

"Oh, I think she'll be just fine."

My mother never skied again, but my sister and I went to Aspen every year with our father. Anna looked like Suzy Chapstick coming down the mountain, while my lavender ski pants were always too tight around the thighs and my glasses fogged up under my goggles. I never saw any reason to give up the snowplow, which was why my father and sister gave me the nickname Plow.

------------- ☀ -------------

Despite their professional appearance, Gianmarco and his friends had never given up the snowplow either. They pizza-pied straight down the mountain at perilous speeds, snapping photos of each other with their cameras as they went.

It was terrifying. People were coming at me from all directions. It seemed that no one slalomed—they were all on straight daredevil trajectories, from young kids to elegant white-suited *signore*. And their speed didn't stop them from having loud conversations from opposite sides of the slope. They argued about which *rifugio*, or restaurant on the mountain, had the best grilled meats, or the best *scamorza* cheese. Let's meet at the Aremogna at two! No, the Pizzalto restaurant has better *bruschette*!

As if this weren't stressful enough for a nonexpert skier, the "lines" for the chairlifts were great masses of pushing people who had trouble keeping their balance on skis.

"Can you please get your skis off mine?"

"But he's pushing me!"

"She butted. I was after that lady in the white hat."

"I did not! I was here first!"

Katherine, you're going to have to use your poles to push ahead, Gianmarco told me gently when he saw that I'd been standing in the same spot for ten minutes. I could *not* push my skis onto someone else's, butting in line and risking a colossal

fall at the same time. "Don't worry, I'll meet you at the *rifugio*,"
I told him.

The cuisine in this part of Abruzzo is meat- and cheese-
based. You won't find quite as much butter and cream as in the
Alps, and virtually nothing is fried. It is, however, fatty: sausages
and lamb chops, grilled *scamorza* cheese, and salami that is to
die for. The pasta specialties are *cazzarielli e fagioli*, a gnocchi-
like pasta with beans (and sausage, in case you haven't gotten
your caloric intake for the day), pasta with truffles, and in the
summer, pastas with every kind of mushroom you can imagine.
You don't see brightly colored vegetables in this mountain village, and fruit is expensive and hard to come by.

We sat at a long wooden table in the sun. I soon realized
that this was not about refueling: we wouldn't be grabbing a
burger or bowl of chili before we hit the slopes again. This was
a *destination*. The skiing had been a fun mode of transportation
to get us here, and now we could unbuckle our boots and dig
into a heavenly *antipasto*, *primo*, and *secondo*, accompanied by
deep red Montepulciano d'Abruzzo wine. We started with a
platter of fresh ham, *salame*, and cheeses, followed by steaming
cazzarielli e fagioli on plastic plates. When the grilled lamb
chops and sausages came out, I worried that I'd have to roll
down the mountain (or at least slide like my mother had in
Aspen).

"It's normal to feel large in Roccaraso," one of the girls in
our group reassured me. "*Qui, si lievita.*" You get bigger here.
The word comes from *lievito*, or yeast. You expand like pizza
dough. Maybe that's because of all the sausage and cheese and
infrequent trips to the bathroom, I offered. No, the young
woman told me with authority. "It's all the oxygen. You will find
that in Roccaraso you are hungry and sleepy." (I declined to

note that most places in the world have this effect on me.) I would later hear people in Naples talking about going to Roccaraso to *pigliarme nu poco 'e ossiggeno* or "get myself some oxygen."

The *ragazza* finished off the last bone of the little Abruzzese lamb and pulled a foldable aluminum tanning mirror out of her backpack. She held it up to her face to augment the sun's rays as she digested. "This place is so good for your health," she told me. "The best Italian wet nurses were from Abruzzo. Rich *signore* from Rome or Naples or Milan would handpick women from these mountains to nurse their babies. Their milk was rich, fatty, and yellow: the best. Abruzzese food is good for you, Ketrin."

After that lunch on the ski slope in Roccaraso, I felt confident that I could land a job as an Abruzzese wet nurse, no questions asked.

I got back to Naples oxygenated. Gianmarco hadn't tried anything with me, which had been an increasing concern with all the couples smooching around us. I couldn't wait to see Salva and tell him about the skiing and the fabulous meals in Roccaraso.

But he didn't want to see me. He gave monosyllabic answers on the phone, and didn't invite me over. Alone in my little apartment, I wondered what I'd done that was so awful.

"You *what?*" Maria Rosa asked me when I went to get her advice. "You spent a weekend in Roccaraso with another guy?"

"It wasn't a guy! It was a group!"

"Even worse! So American women *are* loose like the ones on *The Young and the Restless*."

"But I did nothing wrong! I touched no one, I kissed no one. . . ."

She thought for a moment, and then said, "Go immediately and apologize to Salvatore if you want to continue the relationship. Tell him that you did not *touch* any other man. That you had a major lapse of judgment, but you've come to your senses."

I did. I repeated the script that she had written for me (with the same intonation of the Catholic prayer of confession *mea culpa, mea culpa, mea maxima culpa*: through my fault, through my fault, through my most grievous fault). After hearing my apology, Salva said, "I just have one question. *Stiamo insieme?*" Are we together? He held eye contact with me. This was something he cared a lot about.

"*Certo,*" I said. Of course.

"Because maybe in your country you can have lots of guys at the same time and it's okay with all of them. But Ketrin? It's not okay with me. *Siamo una sola cosa, adesso.*" We are one thing now, you and I.

That sounded good to me.

Rococò Cookies and Eggnog

As I walked the Via San Gregorio Armeno with Raffaella on December 10, 1996, my mind worked up a list of things that were surely not sold on the street in first-century Bethlehem:

1. sausages
2. swordfish
3. watermelons
4. pizza
5. spaghetti
6. mussels

"There was no pizza in Palestine!" I exclaimed to Raffaella when my mental list was complete. "There was no spaghetti. People didn't sell fish near the manger on a cold December night!"

Raffaella had brought me to this famous street in the center of Naples because it's been the home of the Neapolitan Christmas tradition of the *presepe*, or Nativity scene, since the seventeenth century. Artisans display their handiwork on both sides of the tiny alley from the beginning of November until January 6, but traditionally Neapolitans go between the Immacolata, December 8, and Christmas Eve. On December 10, San Gregorio was one great pushing pack of humanity.

"Ketrin, look at that one! It has a moving water mill." She pulled me through the crowd to look at the crèche close up. It had not only running water, but twinkling lights and a pizza oven that lit up from the inside. A three-centimeter-tall baker with realistic stubble used a long wooden baking paddle to slide a pizza in and out of the oven. It was extraordinary.

But I was not to be stopped. History was history. Jesus's birth was Jesus's birth. "How could washerwomen be washing petticoats in a river? Petticoats near the manger? Raffaella?" My future mother-in-law was fingering tiny terra-cotta shepherds. She had put her glasses on to examine the quality of the workmanship. "There was no river near the manger. There were no petticoats. There were no washerwomen!"

"Which of these shepherds do you like better?"

We were here today because one of the Avallones' shepherds had emerged this year from its tissue paper packaging with one leg missing. The two shepherds that she now held up for me to see were different only in that one had blue seventeenth-century breeches, the other green.

"*Blu! Quello blu.*" I wanted to get back to the Truth.

I was intent on convincing Raffaella that even though I wasn't Neapolitan, I knew about Jesus's birth and the manger and the no-crib-for-His-bed. It was important to me because I had heard a lot of negative press about the way my culture exports its commercial, capitalist Christmas traditions. Christmas trees and Santa Claus (along with Halloween) are recent imports in Naples. In Italy, the *presepe* is the symbol of Christmas, the *Befana* witch is the one who brings gifts, Carnevale is when kids dress up. Why, many Italians feel, must we be subjected to other cultures' *usanze,* or traditions? A tree gets needles all over the floor, and ghosts and goblins scare little kids. Not to mention a big fat man who drives a sleigh and eats your food.

When I was in elementary school, I had an arts-and-crafts project every year at Christmas. With red and green felt, white school glue, and beads that never stuck where you wanted them to (how I hated arts and crafts!), I would make a frame for that year's school picture. With much sticky difficulty, I would slide in the passport-size photo of myself as, for example, a toothless second-grader and present it to my parents as a Christmas tree ornament.

Thanks to these ornaments, the Wilson family Christmas tree documents every stage of my youth, and that of my sister, Anna. Believe it or not, these artifacts have defied every law of Christmas ornament degeneration and are in a perfect felty state, right up to senior year of high school. (At a certain point, we must have stopped doing the crafts, so I'm sure Santa Claus took over.)

Because we need dark recesses to hide our awkward phases and long, exposed branches for the photos where we look pretty, the Wilsons always look for a tree that is scraggly and asymmetrical. No fluffy, well-proportioned firs for us. One shadowy crevice in the back of our tree is the assigned slot for Katherine with Permanent Teeth Before Braces. Another low, hidden area in the rear is home to Anna's I'll Only Wear Fluorescent Pink phase. In the front, one can find the Anna with Ringlets zone, next to the Katherine After Her No-Brownie-or-Anything-Else-Brown Diet section. On protruding, well-lit branches in the foreground, Anna and Katherine are quite serious and beautiful (mouths closed); in the backstage holes, we are giggling kids letting our teeth and pounds show.

One summer on the boardwalk of Nice, I won a stuffed monkey in one of those twenty-five-cent carnival games. He had red shorts and big boxing gloves, and a wide-eyed expression that said, "Bring it *on!*" When we got home, we all agreed that the angel that crowned our Christmas tree had had her day in the sun: it was time for a new cast. The monkey now sits in the place of honor, daring anyone to mess with us or our ugly-ass tree.

That December, instead of decorating our family fir, I helped Salvatore, Raffaella, and Nino set up the Avallones' *presepe.* (Benedetta was with her future husband's family now almost all the time.) Raffaella told me that Neapolitan tradition dictates that the father, the paterfamilias, is responsible for the crèche. *La mamma* is responsible for baking cinnamon *rococò* cookies and making sure everyone is warm and well-fed as they position the figures. There was a look of disgust on Raffaella's face when I asked about eggnog (Milk? Eggs? Alcohol? Together? *La prego no!*), about tea (who ever heard of tea in Naples?), or about cider (big mugs of hot liquid? Why don't you just make chicken broth if you're cold and hungry?). Fine! I gave up. There would be no warm liquids consumed.

"Nino!" she belted to her husband, even though he was sitting right next to her. When there was tradition to uphold, her voice got deeper and louder. Proclamatory. "It's time for you to set up the *presepe!*" He didn't move, just nodded. Raffaella proceeded to unwrap the base, a great slab of wood supporting mountains and caves made of cork. As the three of us watched, munching *rococò* cookies, she used a little eyedropper to make sure the water flowed down the mountain properly. "Nino!" she bellowed when she had finished fixing the *presepe* plumbing. "Now it's time for the *personaggi!*"

Salvatore and Nino and I started unwrapping the figures. We gently peeled open the tissue paper and held up each character for Raffaella to see. "*Il macellaio!*" The butcher! Raffaella called his name like he was an old friend who had unexpectedly turned up after a long absence. She told Nino that the butcher goes on the left side of the highest mountain. "*Il pizzaiolo!*" Salva was cradling the pizza man, awakened after a year of hibernation. To the right, on the second tier, said Raffaella.

Each had his own specific place on the stage. All of them, that is, except the solitary little men in breeches that I kept unwrapping. "Who's this?" I asked, and Raffaella explained that it was a shepherd. The shepherds were to be scattered randomly alongside their tiny sheep across the mountains. "So I can put it anywhere?" I asked. "Yes! Anywhere except in the Nativity cave." I positioned my shepherd next to a little hill of dried branches, at which point Raffaella picked him up and placed him somewhere else.

Then, when Nino unwrapped the shepherd missing a leg, something beautiful happened. "*Poverino!*" Poor little guy! "He lost his leg!" They were all really, honestly upset. Could Salva truly have that much empathy for a tiny terra-cotta figure? We were in Naples: of course he could.

The shepherd was passed around. This is the funeral, I thought, this is the ritual, and then they're going to throw him away. My family said goodbye to our angel, too, before she and her wings got recycled. But no! Raffaella had the solution. "We'll just have to pretend he's sleeping." She positioned the one-legged man behind a tree, laying him down on the moss so that his missing leg wasn't visible. When Raffaella and I went to San Gregorio Armeno two days later, it was not to replace the shepherd but to add one more standing witness to the crowd.

That gimpy shepherd partially hidden by the tree now lives in what my family would call the Land of Katherine's Disastrous Haircuts. He's not perfect, but like the pizza man or a dweeby fourth-grader, he's part of the Christmas scene.

Capitone

One figure was not positioned in the manger scene the day the *presepe* was set up: baby Jesus. Traditionally, the father puts baby Jesus in the crib after midnight on Christmas Eve. Nino's moment with the minuscule porcelain baby was to be after dinner, after mass, but before that big Nordic guy swooped in (the kids all up, the kids waiting, the kids liking this import as much as that fabulous trick-or-treat idea!). The *Befana* witch would have her moment on January 6, the day of Epiphany—no reason you couldn't have both her and Santa bring gifts, the Avallones felt. The more the merrier.

Raffaella hosted sixteen people for Christmas Eve dinner. She included all of her future son-in-law Mauro's family, and Benedetta wanted to be sure that everything was perfect— a *bella figura*—the fancy set of plates and crystal, place cards in silver holders, even little favor bags for the kids. She wore something shimmery and red, and made up her turquoise eyes so that they shot out at you even more than usual.

She left the preparation of the fish to her mother.

The fishmongers in Naples are open all night long the three

days before Christmas. *Le mamme,* wanting to make sure that the fish they get for Christmas Eve dinner is the freshest, set their alarms for 3:00 and 4:00 A.M. They want to get to the fish as the fishermen bring it in, before anyone else has a chance to claim it. The clams must be squirting. The eels must be fat and splashing. The sea bass must have eyes that "sparkle."

"*Nessuno mi fa scema.*" Nobody can make a fool out of me, Raffaella said as she stuffed a wad of cash in her sexy lace push-up bra. It was 5:00 A.M. on December 24, and Raffaella was going down to the Piazza Mercato fish market. "They put eye-drops in the fish's eyes to make them look bright. They put food coloring on the gills to make them look rosy. But I don't fall for that." Nonna Clara was the expert at looking a fish in the eye to see whether it'd been "made up," and she taught her daughter well. The message for Neapolitan women is clear: Go ahead, make yourselves up. Make your eyes look glamorous. But be damn sure that your bass is as natural as the girl next door.

When Raffaella returned from the market hours later, she looked and smelled as if she'd been on a fishing vessel on the open sea for days. She held three plastic bags, one of which was moving in a very disturbing sci-fi way. In it was the *capitone.*

If you look up "eel" in an English-Italian dictionary, you will find *anguilla.* But an *anguilla* is smaller and skinnier than a *capitone,* and is eaten on Christmas only if a family is too poor to buy the thick, powerful, splashing *capitone.* "At my place, we eat *capitone* at Christmas" is a Neapolitan expression meaning, Don't be thinking we're low-class.

When the fishmonger cuts off the head of the eel, it continues to writhe, and the man with his tough rubber gloves has to use serious muscles to keep the bugger on the chopping block. It is really entertaining when the *capitone* escapes and a chase ensues. (When I was having trouble years later keeping my tod-

dlers in check, Raffaella invoked this image, telling me it's normal. Toddlers are like eels, you grab 'em from one end and they
slip away from the other.) Raffaella's eel was chopped into four
chunks, and still continued to thrash in the plastic bag.

The second bag held the clams. The first course of Christmas Eve dinner is *spaghetti a vongole*. Usually, the name of a
pasta with fish includes the preposition *con* meaning "with."
Linguine with shrimp. *Paccheri* with swordfish. But there is no
spaghetti *with* clams because the two become one. A translation
might be "clammed spaghetti." Neapolitans would say "*si
sposono*," they get married. The spaghetti bride and her clammy
husband are an organic, inevitable match.

The third plastic bag held our fresh, bright-eyed beauty, the
sea bass. She was to be baked whole, flanked by potatoes, for the
main course. In addition, there would be the *insalata di rinforzo*, the strength salad. It is made to pump up anyone who
might be gaunt and feeble, and features boiled cauliflower, olives, and carrots. There would also be fried codfish, sautéed escarole, and desserts, desserts, and more desserts.

At eight o'clock on Christmas Eve, I found my place card
(*Ketrin* printed with a gold marker) and settled in for what
would be a three-hour meal. The eel kept reappearing in various incarnations (the thing was five feet long, after all) including pickled *capitone*, fried *capitone*, and *capitone* in tomato
sauce. It nauseated me. It was oily and black. It nauseated other
people too, but that didn't stop them from eating it.

"I don't like eel. I've never liked it. But I'll have a piece for
tradition's sake," Nino told us, and a few cousins followed suit.
Same thing with the cauliflower salad. "I'm stuffed! Plus it
grosses me out. Could you pass me some? *Giusto pe' tradizione*."
The conversation centered on recipes: how someone's grand-

mother prepared her *insalata di rinforzo*; who liked fried codfish and who preferred it baked.

Benedetta's future in-laws spoke knowledgeably about traditional recipes, which surprised me. "His mother left grilled chicken breasts in the refrigerator for him. She never cooked," Raffaella had confided to me about Mauro. Horror of horrors. "Benedetta and I are educating his palate."

When it was time for mass, we had difficulty standing we were so stuffed. The children were bouncing off the walls with excitement—just two more hours until Santa comes!—when we packed into cars smelling of perfume and rarely worn wool coats. Men dozed through the service. The hymn *"Tu Scendi dalle Stelle,"* "You Come Down from the Stars," was sung entirely by the soprano section of the congregation.

We returned home at 1:00 A.M. for the ritual of Nino putting baby Jesus in his crib. "Nino!" Raffaella called her husband to attention, his coat and hat still on. *"Il presepe!"* She handed him the tiny baby in tissue paper and pointed to the *presepe,* just in case he'd forgotten what his job was. This was the responsibility of the paterfamilias. And the real head of the family could relax in the knowledge that there was no chance of a blunder: there was only one place that baby could go.

Pizzetta, Cappuccino, and Orange Juice

My internship at the Consulate ended at Christmas. On my last day there, we had to evacuate the building because a mysterious package that looked like a bomb was found on Cynthia's desk. Nobody knew who had brought it or what was inside. So we all hung out at a café across the street and I was able to say my goodbyes *con calma.* After a few hours, we were notified that it was safe to enter the Consulate. The kind soldiers with Uzis informed us that the package was an elaborate *presepe,* complete with running water, that had been given as a surprise gift to the political consul.

"You gotta love this place," Cynthia said when we hugged goodbye.

My internship was over, but no part of me wanted to go home. There would be time later to figure out my future—for now, I was still interested in figuring out Naples, and seeing where this relationship with Salvatore was headed. Life was organized in semesters, I thought, so I told my parents that I wanted to make this "experience abroad" two semesters rather than one. I planned on going back to America at the beginning of June.

To earn extra money, I took on teaching jobs at other English schools. When I wasn't in class I rode buses and walked the streets. I missed theater, and what I found on the streets of Naples satisfied my craving.

The first dramatic performances of my life were the "lullabies" that my mother sang to my sister and me. They were lullabies that weren't soft or tender. She had no intention of putting us to sleep: we were her audience.

Vocally, Bonnie Wilson was not a soprano but a tenor. With her diaphragm working overtime, she sang Gershwin's "Summertime," sounding something like Luciano Pavarotti singing "Nessun Dorma." Her version invoked the insomnia and anxiety in *Turandot* rather than the sweaty, lazy days of summer on a southern plantation.

Lyrics	Bonnie Wilson's Subtext
Summertime, *An' the livin' is easy*	The livin' will never be easy! There will be shows to put on! Exams to pass! Swim races to win!
Fish are jumpin'	Who the hell cares what's jumpin'?
An' the cotton is high	I've never gotten high, and neither will you.
Oh yo' daddy's rich	Your father and his family were rich but

	not rich enough. He spends too much money, and soon what he had will be all gone. You should worry about that when you're older, if you have the time.
An' yo' mamma's good lookin'	Well, yes.
So hush little baby	If you keep quiet I can finish these last notes
Don' yo' cry	with a flourish.

Vocal energy reminiscent of my mother's singing can be heard at any fruit and vegetable market in central Naples. Men wail, almost tragically, *"Pomodori due euro al chilo!"* Tomatoes, two euros a kilo!

"What are those guys going on about?" my sister asked me, years later, when she came to visit. "Are they mourning? Are they imploring? Are they passing kidney stones?"

"No," I answered, "they are simply stating the price of their tomatoes. With the intention of being heard."

My childhood had taught me that the best thing is to perform; the next best is to be in the audience. I didn't have to look far to witness theatrics in Naples. It became a kind of sport for me to go into a coffee shop, or bar, in the afternoon and order three things that are not, that should never be, consumed together. For example, a small pizza, a cappuccino, and an orange juice. A huge no-no for a multitude of reasons. First, cappuccinos are generally not ordered after eleven in the morning. Second, orange juice can never be consumed alongside anything with milk in it because of acidity. Third, pizzas should be ordered with a soda, beer, or water. Absolutely not coffee or anything warm, or for heaven's sake anything with milk.

So the response of the barista will be, first, incredulity and shock, followed by something akin to missionary zeal. *"Insieme?"* Together? *"La prego no!"* Please, I beg you, no! His eyes pleading, his voice plaintive, with his performance he will try to persuade me to change my mind.

The best performances to be found in Naples are on the sidewalks, in buses, and in coffee bars. I have witnessed arguments, love scenes, even tragic dialogues that rival anything seen on the stages of the Teatro San Carlo or the Bellini. There was a standoff on the 140 bus that runs from Posillipo to Piazza Garibaldi in the spring of 1997, for example. The initial disagreement was over a fart that a middle-aged man presumably expelled in the packed bus. The gentleman didn't have a seat, and stood nonchalantly holding the rubber loops hanging from the roof. An elderly lady sitting near him, holding her nose with a handkerchief, started in. She told the Bangladeshi housekeeper sitting next to her, "It's just rude. We all have to breathe this air." She glared at the man.

"Signora, I agree." The lady behind her declared her allegiance, and now it was just a matter of time before the whole bus, or at least the native Italian speakers, chose sides and put their two cents in. Interestingly, the accused continued to feign nonchalance until the argument got heated. Then he shut everyone up with his bellowing voice and *"Ma come fate a sapere? A sapere tutto?"* But how do you know? How is it that you think you know everything?

This kind of scene makes you want to miss your bus stop and keep riding until the curtain comes down.

I found another very simple way to witness the performance

art that is Neapolitan speech: to ask directions. The rhetoric, the art of saying so little in such a spellbinding way, reminds me of that great rhetorician Jesse Jackson reciting *Green Eggs and Ham* on *Saturday Night Live* twenty years ago. Such a sense of rhythm, such skill at creating dramatic tension. He will not let your mind wander; he will not let you miss one syllable. Nor will he let you *not* care about his green eggs and ham. It makes no difference whatsoever that the words he is reciting are Seussian nonsense.

And so it was with a gentleman, a well-dressed-in-his-Sunday-best Neapolitan gentleman, whom I asked for directions. He was out for a stroll, walking slowly (toes splayed out in that typical way of Neapolitan men) and obviously with no destination in mind. I was a young woman who was also on her own and obviously foreign. These two factors, combined with an innate southern Italian sense of hospitality and the desire to perform, made this man want more than anything else to be of help. But unfortunately, he did not know where Via Noce was. Instead of saying, I'm sorry I don't know, he began a monologue which could have had a score, it was so musical.

"Via Noce, Via Noce." He paused. At this point, I knew that he had no clue where the street was, otherwise his hands would already be in motion. They would be outlining my trajectory, *a destra a sinistra*, right and left with his hand curling up and then a big smile and his arms straight ahead when he came to *diritto! Sempre diritto!* Straight on down!

But he did not know.

"I have grown up in this area, *signorina*. Not too far from here, and I can assure you that this Via Noce, this Via Noce of which you speak, it is not, and I repeat, not, a cross street of Via Toledo. That it is not."

This was the introduction, and it was performed solemnly,

with no hand movements and a somber facial expression. His voice was level. After a pause, it was time to move on to the central piece of the monologue. He became more animated, and took his hands out of his pockets.

"It could be farther up this direction"—his eyebrows were raised in the hypothetical, one arm straightened to the right. "Or indeed it could be in this direction"—his arm straightened to the left, maintaining eye contact with me always. He paused. Oh, there were so many possibilities of where this street could be, given the fact that he did not know! "Because I, to my dismay, do not possess this particular piece of knowledge, I must be truthful. Truthful to you, and truthful to myself." Again, he paused for dramatic effect. He was a man of integrity, he wanted me to understand. The pauses were timed so that the drama was heightened, the tension not dissipated.

"The truth is this," he said, and I understood we'd come to the conclusion. "If I knew, it would be my great pleasure to impart this knowledge to you, a person who does not know, and would like to know, the location of Via Noce. And with this, I wish you a good day, *signorina*." He spun around and walked away. With a flourish.

Fresh Eggs

"*Sai chi era esigente? Nonna Clara.*" The one who was really *esigente*, or hard to please, was Nonna Clara. To hear Raffaella talk of someone *else* being particular in her tastes was ironic. I had told her that I didn't envy her *salumiere*, the owner of the food shop where she buys her cold cuts, bread, and cheese, after she had spent fifteen minutes complaining about the thick and tough prosciutto ham he had sold her the day before. "Like this!" One eye became a slit as she held her thumb and forefinger to show just how thick he had cut it. "You think that's thin? You call that thin?"

A line of customers waited patiently as Raffaella and Signor Buono, the *salumiere*, hashed it out. It was a matter of trust. "To trust is good, not to trust is better," is an oft-repeated Neapolitan expression. Remember, a mother tells her child, it is always better *not* to trust.

Neapolitan parents want to prepare their children for the real world, where cheating and lying are the norm. The worst thing is to raise a child who is *baccalà* (as dumb as a piece of cod), or *addurmùto* (like a zombie). There is no end to the pejorative terms for a person who is naïve and trusting. My favorite is probably *dorme cu 'a zizza mmocca*—he's still sleeping with his mommy's tit in his mouth. The opposite is the highest compliment that you can receive in Naples: to be considered *scetàto*, awake. It's better than being smart. It means that no one can cheat you, you know what's up.

In Mr. Buono's shop, it was fundamental for him to regain Raffaella's trust after the prosciutto episode. The other *signore* could wait.

"I'm easy," she repeated later. Easy? But what about the prosciutto? I asked. "Well, the truth must be spoken. It's in the interest of the *salumiere*. It would be terrible for him if he continued to sell prosciutto like that and no one told him about it!" So she was actually helping him, while at the same time showing him and the other ladies in line that she is *scetàta*, she knows what's up. She's no baby sleeping with a tit in her mouth, or a German tourist who will eat whatever you sell her. "I'm not a difficult customer. Nonna Clara was a difficult customer. It was a nightmare to shop with her. Thank goodness the *ovaiolo* would come to the house."

When Raffaella was growing up, the egg man would come to her home once a week with a basket of eggs and fresh cheeses from the countryside. Nonna Clara would not merely greet the *ovaiolo*, give him money, and take her eggs and cheeses. Oh no. She would invite him in, take his jacket, and they would *buongiorno, buongiorno* each other. She would offer him a glass of water, he would refuse. (Not coffee? Why not coffee? I asked Raffaella. Coffee is for people who are in *confidenza*, she explained. People with whom you share your shit.) They would then sit in two armchairs facing each other in the living room.

It was the moment of reckoning.

Nonna Clara would position herself next to a lamp and remove the lampshade. Then she would take each egg from the basket, one by one, and hold it up to the lightbulb. This way, she

Impepata di Cozze

Winter in Naples is short and wet. By April, it seemed that summer had arrived. Air-conditioning and roll-on antiperspirant became inextricably linked to my nostalgia for and love of my homeland.

I arrived at the hospital of Fatebenefratelli, or the Hospital of the Do-Good Brothers, on a stiflingly hot morning in early spring. I had come to assist Raffaella, currently a patient in the women's ward on the fourth floor. Dressed in a Duke T-shirt and running shorts, sweating as I pressed the call button for the elevator, I noticed a statue of San Giovanni di Dio, arms outstretched, greeting patients and visitors and welcoming them to Fatebenefratelli. San Giovanni's expression was serene, and the statue was exquisite. But why wasn't the elevator coming?

When I was informed that the elevator was out of service, I tried not to think about the what-ifs, about stretchers or emergencies and the inherent logistical problems of a hospital with six floors and no elevator. I told myself to let go of those images of sterile, high-tech institutions where a Visa gold card can get you places. Here at Fatebenefratelli nobody is interested in your credit cards or whether you have insurance or what kind. Your health is in the hands of fate. And San Giovanni. And of the modern-day do-good brothers and their do-good sisters.

Raffaella and Nino had both contracted salmonella at an elegant wedding several days earlier. When many of the guests started getting sick the day after the wedding, everyone thought of the mussels and clams and other seafood that had been served. In Naples, pasta with shellfish is a staple: there would be no Christmas Eve without *spaghetti a vongole*. Children of four are served *impepata di cozze*, or sautéed mussels, parents disappointed only that they can't give their poor little Ciro a glass of white Vesuviano wine to help wash it down. Because shellfish is eaten so often and because hygiene is not always optimal, hepatitis happens.

A Neapolitan friend of ours was violently ill and hospitalized after eating *spaghetti a vongole*. When he recovered, I asked him if he would give up shellfish for the rest of his life. He looked at me as if I had lost my marbles. "The rest of my life?" he asked, incredulous. "My doctor told me I should avoid mussels and clams for a week or so, but I don't know if I can hold out! My mother has found a new *pescivendolo* [fishmonger] who swears by his mussels."

Surprisingly, the results of the investigation about who ate what at the wedding reception (which wasn't easy, given that the dinner lasted four hours and included about forty dishes) indicated that the culprit was a mayonnaise that was served with shrimp. On a hot day, the caterer had left the mayonnaise (made with raw eggs) outside for too long, and many of the wedding guests contracted salmonella.

When I heard this, my heart immediately went out to the bride's parents. In Naples, where a wedding is what you eat and the good impression (or *bella figura*) that you make with your friends is directly related to the quality of the pasta and the succulence of the mozzarella, this was social annihilation. That family has always liked to skimp on what they serve, people started to whisper. The caterer must have been cheap.

Thank sweet Jesus that the newlyweds were vomiting on the other side of the world, at some resort in Thailand.

So this is how we ended up at the hospital of the do-gooders. I climbed the steps to the *reparto femminile* on the fourth floor with trepidation. When I entered the women's ward, however, I was struck by its unexpected beauty. Because the hospital is located on the promontory of Posillipo, there are breathtaking views of the sea out the huge open windows. It is stunning, particularly at dusk, when the fuchsias and violets of the sunset over Vesuvius are as intense as a screensaver. Fatebenefratelli hospital has nothing of the whites and greens of rational science and sterile medicine. It's all fluorescent pinks and blues and bright red blood on white scrubs.

The sounds that you hear are not the beep-beep-beeps of monitors but the constant howl of wind and the screams of patients. Here, you can feel the wind on your face inside, and smell the evidence of doctors and nurses smoking under the RESPECT YOUR PATIENTS, DON'T SMOKE sign. Here you are in close contact with human frailty, with human suffering, right in the midst of nature's beauty and terror. Smells, sounds, and colors are all larger than life.

At Fatebenefratelli, you can see in every direction how Mother Nature really pulled out all the stops in this city. The drama of a volcano would have been enough. But Madre Natura added the sea, the cliffs, the islands of Capri and Ischia. The little island of Nisida, which houses an Alcatraz-like prison. I could only imagine the intensity of watching a loved one perish in such a setting.

Fortunately, Raffaella's condition was not so critical. None-theless, I was in no way relaxed. As the saying goes in Naples, when you're sick, one of the most dangerous places you can be is at a hospital. And here we come to one of the biggest contra-dictions in Neapolitan culture. If you ask an Italian about the United States, he or she will often point to health care as the greatest contradiction in our democracy. All are equal in Amer-ica, right? But a hospital will treat you only if you have insur-ance, or a credit card, or both. This is a hugely simplified way of seeing things, and only partly true, but that's the perception. If you are hurt, or sick, and poor, you are alone.

Here in Naples, there is another kind of contradiction when it comes to health. It is a city where if you fall, or faint, or feel sick as you're walking down the street, you will not have merely one Good Samaritan to help you out. You will have a crowd vying over who has the honor of taking care of you, even of tak-ing you to their home if need be. They will argue over who is most qualified, who lives the closest, who best understands your predicament. I once fainted on a bus in Naples, and apparently after some heated discussion among the other passengers, it was decided that the bus would abandon its normal route and take me and a kind middle-aged lady who had been elected my pro-tector directly to the hospital of the Incurabili, which was the closest. (Yes, there is a hospital of the Incurables.)

The contradiction is this: After such a touching show of love and generosity toward a fellow human in need, you arrive at a hospital where the doctors are smoking in the halls. Where the generator has been broken for a year and nobody has both-ered to fix it (so, if there's a power outage, none of the machines will work). If you have had a heart attack, you risk dying in the waiting room because the diagnosis was performed so perfunc-torily. Or maybe a nurse got a call on her cellphone and forgot about you. *Insomma*, a hospital where unless you have some loving, smart, pushy relatives to take up your cause, you might be better off never setting foot.

Raffaella shared a room with three other women, all of whom had pretty stable conditions. As I entered, I was surprised to see that she had managed to brush her hair and put on makeup. Another surprise was the unmistakable aroma of Neapolitan coffee. I knew that Raffaella hadn't eaten for three days, and coffee was off-limits. "Who had coffee?" I asked, and the four women's eyes darted guiltily to one another. I felt like a kindergarten teacher. One of the patients had pulled her IV drip with her down four flights of stairs to the hospital bar to sneak a little glass juice bottle full of sweet black *caffè* back up to her roommates while the nurses were chatting and smoking cigarettes. I didn't know who the guilty party was, but I saw that the mood of these ladies was sky-high. They were giggling. "Who had coffee?" I repeated.

There was an eighty-year-old patient called Nonna, or Grandma, by her roommates. Her dry, brittle lips were rimmed with black, the black of the syrupy nectar that is Neapolitan coffee. Her lack of teeth and her heavy dialect made it hard for me to understand what she was saying, but whatever it was ended with the gesture of lifting the handle of a little cup of espresso, and with the words *tazzulella 'e caffè* (l'il ol' cuppa coffee). It was so tender the way she said it, and the coffee had obviously done such wonders in improving the ladies' mood, that I decided not to tell the nurses.

It was rare to find a chair to sit in in Raffaella's room. During visiting hours, Neapolitan hospitals are swamped by relatives. It's a lovely thing to see. If you arrive ten minutes before visiting time begins, you find the reception area crowded with families, elbowing each other so that they can be the first out of the gate when the receptionist comes to announce that visiting hours have begun. They are chomping at the bit. It seems that they are not here because they are prey to guilt, or because some sibling forced them to do their "duty." They are here because it is clearly the only place for them to be now, a few days after Aunt Patrizia has broken her hip. They are here to hold her hand, to massage her back, and, most important, to make damn sure that the doctors and nurses don't fuck up.

In the States, if you have a relative in the hospital, you might stop by to see how they are doing, perhaps bring a book or flowers. Here, you come with your job cut out for you. You are responsible for the complicated, time-consuming, and ultimately exhausting job of checking on the doctors and nurses. This means making sure they know that your mother is taking blood pressure medicine. That she is allergic to certain antibiotics. Has this information been communicated, often and to the right people? If you're not sure, you must follow the relevant doctor around (you certainly can't worry if you're bothering him, this is your mother's health we're talking about) and remind the nurses, emphatically and at regular intervals.

I was sitting by Raffaella's bed when a nurse dropped a little white pill on her tray. "Take this," she commanded. If I had been Raffaella, I probably would've taken it. The nurse was very firm, after all. But fortunately, Raffaella grew up in this city and learned early on not to blindly follow orders issued by someone in a position of authority.

"This isn't mine. I think it's Flora's heart medication. She usually takes it at around this time. Hey"—she motioned to Flora's niece, who was reading a magazine next to her aunt's bed—"can you go and find out who this is really for?" The girl set out to find the nurse. This sixteen-year-old surely knew the results of her aunt's last blood tests, which medicines she was to take and when, and which doctor to get furious at when her *zia* was not being tended to correctly. If she was here at visiting hours, it meant that her family had prepped her well.

When it was time for lunch, four completely different menus were prepared and brought in for the four patients. A soft potato dish for Nonna, who didn't have many teeth, a simple pasta for Raffaella, with her stomach problems. Relatives closely examined what had been prepared, and of course complained. They were angry. The food was not fresh enough, the pasta overcooked. To me, it looked and smelled divine. There were cloth napkins and real silverware, a little glass dish of freshly grated Parmesan cheese to put on the steaming pasta. Nothing was prepackaged. It did not even vaguely resemble hospital fare from my homeland. But complaining was the thing to do, and if I said it actually looked good, I would have been laughed at. People would pity Raffaella, who had that clueless American girl to look after her: she might as well not be in the hospital, she'd be better off at home.

I had to show my stuff. I had to be forceful. I had to reassure Raffaella that I was doing my job of *stare dietro,* checking up on the hospital staff.

I put on my best angry face and took the plate of pasta into the hall, searching for the least-scary-looking nurse. When I found her, I tried my hand at the role of protective Neapolitan relative. "This pasta is overcooked! And reheated! It's inedible!" (Meanwhile, I hadn't eaten in hours and was seriously considering taking it into a private corner and scarfing it down.) The nurse issued a rebuttal, which I paid no attention to, so proud was I of my irate outburst. I took the pasta back to Raffaella, who was in turn reading the riot act to another nurse because Nonna's potato dish was also inedible—"*sanno di niente*"—they taste like nothing. "My fish tastes like a bedroom slipper!" a middle-

aged roommate added to the discussion. Oh, man, what energy
it all took. I was exhausted just watching them. This team of
women, patients and relatives together, could have taken over a
small country.

A continuous struggle, conflict and argument and distrust.
Passivity was not allowed. Although the medical care left much
to be desired at Fatebenefratelli, on a psychological level the
combat did these patients good. From the outside, I saw that it
had the same effect as that hit of clandestine coffee. To live in
Naples is to be on your toes, to have a thousand eyes, to stand up
and fight for yourself and your loved ones. When you cannot or
do not do this, it is a bad sign. It might even mean that you're too
sick to risk going to the hospital.

Casatiello

The day after Easter is called Pasquetta, or Little Easter, in Italy. In Naples it is also called Fatta Pasqua, or Easter's-Done Day. If there is one day in the liturgical calendar that is a challenge for Christians, it is Easter Monday, Easter's-Done Day.

I had spent Holy Week catching a mass with Raffaella almost every day. I didn't miss the wooden crosses and perfect harmonies of the Protestant church services I grew up with— I loved the smell of incense and the sound of Giampietro's boots clicking on the marble floors; the dripping wax and Chanel perfume, the cleavage and ringing microphones. Holy Week in Neapolitan churches was that and more. It was also a crescendo of anticipation, of pregnant waiting. There was the palpable sense that something huge was about to happen.

For Catholics and Protestants alike, Easter Sunday is the culmination of that waiting. Out come the fancy clothes and bonnets, the chocolate for the kids and the explosion of orchids. The choir singing Hallelujah, the trumpets announcing the joy of Easter. Pump up the karaoke, He is risen! The tomb is empty!

RRRRrring! goes the alarm clock on Monday morning. Wait, didn't we sing "He is risen!" yesterday? Hallelujah and all that stuff? What do you mean there are lunches to be packed, traffic to battle, life in all its banality to attend to? What a buzz kill.

When I was in high school, my Monday-after-Easter depression was due primarily to a Cadbury Creme Egg hangover. I would wake up on Monday morning in that lethargic, flatulent, morning-after-the-binge state. I would have to zip jeans that were too tight and make it through AP English, trying to get my mind on Elizabethan poetry and out of the rut of "Did I eat four or five chocolate eggs before lunch and six or seven after?" and then "How can I manage to eat only celery until next weekend?"

This is all to say that the day after Easter should be a holiday everywhere for Christians, like it is in Naples. A day to let it sink in: the chocolate, the music, the impossible fact that He died for me and rose again. *Insomma,* give us a moment to digest it all and figure out how we're going to live our lives.

On Pasquetta in Naples, families traditionally do a *gita fuori porta*, a trip outside the city. Usually people take a picnic lunch to the countryside, or a frittata to the beach. When Raffaella was a little girl, she and her family would go to the mountains near Avellino, where her maternal grandparents were from. On the morning of Little Easter, she and her brothers and sisters would come downstairs (wishing each other Happy Easter's-Done Day!) to find eight round *casatiello* rolls on the kitchen table. The *casatiello* is a dense bread made with black pepper, *salame,* lard, bacon, and cheese (provolone, Parmesan, pecorino, *più ci metti più ci trovi!*) and crowned by a hard-boiled egg.

Nonna Clara would make one *casatiello*, of varying size, for each of her eight children. Rosaria, the oldest, would have a roll as big as a tire, while little Nunzio's would be no bigger than a bagel. The kids would start shouting immediately, *"Chist' è mio! Non toccare!"* This one's mine! Don't touch it!

They would wrap their *casatielli* in cloth and hide them under their shirts for the picnic. You knew which one was yours, could recognize it a mile away. You had to protect it. That was your day-after-Easter lunch.

"How did Nonna Clara bake eight rolls, plus two enormous ones for Mamma and Papà, in a nineteen-fifties Neapolitan oven? Was she up all night?" I asked Raffaella.

"What oven? We didn't have an oven!"

Che problema c'è? With the help of her older daughters, Nonna Clara would take the ten *casatielli* to the communal oven, which was located down two sets of stone steps from their apartment on the Vomero hill. The *forno* served the whole neighborhood, and there was always a line. When it was her turn, she'd give a couple of lire to the baker and wait for her babies to brown. She wouldn't leave the spot, staying watchful for the hour and a half it took to cook them. You never knew when other people might come and claim your *casatielli* as their own.

"How could she recognize which were hers?" I asked Raffaella.

Raffaella laughed and shook her head. What questions! "Ketrin, how does a mother know which child is hers?"

~~~~~ ☀ ~~~~~

Raffaella made me a *casatiello* that first Easter Monday I was in Naples. We had decided to go to Caserta, a town near Naples and home to a palace that rivals Versailles (which few people visit, most go to Caserta for the mozzarella), and were planning on having a picnic at the palace gardens. I had eaten, and eaten, and eaten on Easter Sunday. Try the goat with roasted potatoes, Ketrin. The *ricotta salata* and *salame* is the traditional Easter appetizer—how can you not eat it? Taste these two *pastiera* cheesecakes and tell us which one is better, Zia Pia's or Zia Maria's. We need your vote.

So there I was, once again, on Easter's-Done morning, feeling flatulent and sluggish. I should skip lunch, my brain said, or at most find some celery in Caserta. But there was my very own *casatiello* on the counter. It was waiting to be wrapped lovingly. No brothers and sisters were vying for it, Salva and Benedetta had their own and were satisfied. I had no choice.

In 1751, when the Bourbon king Charles commissioned his architect to design the royal palace in Caserta, Luigi Vanvitelli presented him with a model of the building and gardens. It was so beautiful that it filled the king with an emotion "fit to tear his heart from his breast." And this was a guy who grew up in the Royal Palace of Madrid—he knew magnificence when he saw it. The Reggia di Caserta is truly breathtaking. The palace has twelve hundred rooms and the park and gardens extend for nearly two miles. It is considered an architectural masterpiece.

It was hot that year on Pasquetta, and we followed Raffaella to a spot near one of the baroque fountains. She rolled out a blanket and set up the drinks and plates. We took out our *casatielli*. Mine was a little smaller than Salva's, a little bigger than Benedetta's. We compared, and then we dug in.

Sitting on a soft 1970s blanket with the Avallones, I ate it all. I ate the bacon, the lard, the hard-boiled egg. When I'd finished, satisfied (aah, this *casatiello* is not too big, not too small, but juuuuust right!), I rested my head on Salva's lap. Raffaella was carving a juicy melon and talking about where she could find electricity to plug in the hotplate for the little espresso maker she'd brought. Benedetta was spreading coconut sun lotion on her arms. Nino was reading the paper.

I was realizing that I was no longer B.E.D.-ridden.

In all my years of bingeing, it wasn't the actual binge that was the problem. It was the punishment afterward. I had a healthy appetite, and sometimes I ate too much, but I was human. I got hungry again. On depressing, mundane, life-back-to-normal Pasquetta my body needed to be fed just as it did on the sunny, sacred morning of Easter. Even the day *after* the celebration, after the chocolate and the lamb, or the *pastiera* and the ricotta. I realized in Caserta that if I punished and denied myself on Easter's-Done Day, as I had for the last decade, then maybe I was continuing to miss the whole point of Easter itself: The sacrifice was *Jesus's* body, not mine. To us, He said, "Take and eat. This is my body." He didn't say, Take and eat my body . . . and then feel guilty about it and don't eat anything for a while. He said, *Buon appetito, signorina.* Enjoy.

Gelato alla Nocciola

$\mathcal{B}$enedetta's wedding was planned for the end of June in Positano (Nino's objections to Mauro notwithstanding) and the spring was a flurry of wedding preparations. I was part of it all. I went with Raffaella and Benedetta to choose the wedding dress, put in my two cents as to which *bomboniera* was the prettiest. (The *bomboniera* is a little souvenir given at Italian weddings. It is usually silver and small and collects dust in people's apartments for years afterward.) We all went to a huge clothing store near Pompeii to choose the suits for Nino and Salva. Or rather, for Raffaella to choose the suits for Nino and Salva. She pinched and straightened and stuck her fingers all over their bodies. They stood stock-still while she manhandled them, although Salva sent me air kisses across the room. I was asked whether I liked the wider or narrower pinstripe, the Armani or the Ferré, and I did eenie meenie miny moe silently in my mind.

I could not believe that they were about to spend 1,500,000 lire (nearly $1,000 at the time) on a suit. But I realized later, for a well-to-do Neapolitan family, this was borderline thrifty.

Raffaella was a highly talented costumer, and Salva and his father both looked dashing. "You really like the Ferré?" Salva asked me in the car on the way home. We kissed in the backseat, and then he asked, "Now I want to see what you're going to wear, Pagnottella!"

My stomach lurched. We'd never explicitly talked about when I was leaving, but I assumed that he knew I wasn't going to be here at the end of June. Who ever heard of a semester that finished at the *end* of June? "*Vediamo*," I said. We'll see.

From that moment on, everything that happened would trigger tears. I was leaving soon and Salva hadn't even realized that this was the end. The next Saturday I called him, bawling. I loved him and I loved this crazy place and I loved his family, but I certainly couldn't leave my country and move to Naples at the age of twenty-two! Salva sped over to pick me up, asking, What's wrong?

When I couldn't answer in any intelligible way, he said how about *gelato alla nocciola*? His suggestion made me cry even harder. How could I stay here for a man who thought that all of my pain could be alleviated by buying me an ice cream? When my answer was even more tears, Salva took off for Ciro, the best *gelateria* in Naples, and triple-parked. He bought an enormous cone of *nocciola* and got extra Kleenex. With one hand he dried my tears and with the other fed me the ice cream.

It was just what I needed. Once again, I needed to shut my brain off and be fed.

We drove around the city all afternoon, the elephant in the Fiat being my departure and our future together. Finally, I told Salva that we had to talk. He parked in a piazza in central Naples. "About what?" he asked. "About us. About next year," I explained.

"Okay, then, talk," he said. "*Parla.*" (Salva still does this when I say we need to talk. He says, Okay. Talk. It is the one word which makes me, normally a chatterbox, totally tongue-tied.)

"Well, I was thinking . . . I like you . . . I would probably miss you. . . ." As I stammered on, Salva's eyes were not looking at me but out the window at another car that had parked nearby. I had no idea at the time, but Salva realized that they were planning a *scippo*, a robbery. He knew that we had to get out of that spot as quickly as possible if we wanted to keep our wallets, our watches, and our car.

I was telling Salva that maybe I could see about doing a master's in Italy—my parents had both studied at Johns Hopkins University's School of Advanced International Studies, and there was a program in Bologna, a five-hour train ride from Naples. I didn't love political science or economics, but I liked the idea of staying in Italy the following year to see where this relationship was headed. International relations might be an interesting field after all. . . .

But Salva wasn't listening to a word I said. He wasn't even looking at me. He was focused on those guys in the car next to ours.

"*Va bene, va bene.*" Okay, he said, and started the car. He drove off so fast that I thought maybe he was angry that I wasn't staying in Naples the next year. But after a minute or so, he looked at me and smiled. We still had our wallets, we still had our car, and, although I didn't know it at the time, we had a future without an ocean between us. There was much to smile about.

Pasta al Forno

Of Neapolitans are the world's experts at dramatizing the mundane, they are also experts at what they call *sdrammatizzare*: to dedramatize, to undramatize. The *s* at the beginning of a verb makes it the opposite, so *sdrammatizzare* is to suck the tragedy from something and spit it out with a great big smile.

Naples is a city whose history has been marked by occupations, invasions, poverty, and tragedy. Unemployment hovers around 13 percent. The *camorra*, the Neapolitan Mafia, holds business and industry hostage and causes endless violence. Soiled maxi pads and stinking diapers crown the mountains of trash that line the streets. (Naples has the highest garbage collection tax of any city in Italy. Garbage isn't collected, and the money ends up in the hands of the *camorra*.)

How to explain the cheerfulness of Neapolitans? It goes much deeper than great food, great weather, let's enjoy the *dolce vita*! The *dolce vita* is not so *dolce* when people live in poverty, the air reeks of refuse, and corruption and injustice are commonplace. The smiles and songs on the lips of Neapolitans can in large part be explained by the art of *sdrammatizzazione*. They manage to take the drama out of situations that are truly dramatic—when there is tragedy, or suffering, or, quite simply, when the stakes are high.

I had been accepted into the master's program in International Relations at SAIS Bologna, which meant that I would return to Washington for a summer of intensive economics courses. Although I would be coming back to Italy in the fall, I knew that it would be a different Italy. I would be a graduate student in the North. My "year abroad" was over, and this crazy, chaotic, colorful chapter of my life was coming to an end.

Gelato or no *gelato*, I was miserable.

Raffaella organized a going-away party for me the night before my departure. She set out Coke and Orange Fanta and plastic cups. (It was a party for twenty-two-year-olds—if anyone felt like wine or beer they could ask for it, right?) She baked a *pasta al forno*, which she knew was my favorite: a pasta casserole chock-full of bacon, béchamel, and no fewer than four different kinds of cheese. Covered with breadcrumbs, it came out of the oven golden brown and crispy on top. Of course, she also prepared about six other dishes for the party, but it was the *pasta al forno* that I smelled when she opened the door for me that evening.

I told myself that I would hold it together. Enough with the tears! I had been crying most of the day. But when I looked in her eyes, I couldn't.

I started sobbing. *Drammatico*, no? Raffaella's reaction was anything but. It was the amazing, unexpected art of *sdrammatizzare*. Did she cry? Did she Oh-I-understand-honey? Did she even hug me? No, she slapped me across the face. Not so it hurt, just so I would come off it. I was so shocked that I did come off it. Her own eyes were glistening, but her voice was forceful and, yes, cheerful. *"Ué ué!"* (which is like "Hey you!"). "The *pasta al forno* is almost ready, come and see how crispy you want it on the outside. . . ."

I was forced out of my sadness, slapped out of my own personal drama. I followed Raffaella into the kitchen to help (read: watch, dodge, and whimper).

Salvatore came in and said, *"Ciao, vita mia!"* He had given up calling me Pagnottella, Little Muffin, and was now using the Neapolitan expression "my life." I mean, please! Couldn't he have chosen a term of endearment like *sweetie pie* or even *darling?* "My life" sent me back into my drama once again, and the tears started flowing. My tears started Salva crying too: no macho stiff-upper-lipping for him. We were hugging, he was repeating *"Vita mia!"* and we were pathetic. We were also physically in the way of the *pasta al forno.* Something had to be done.

Another slap would have been difficult for Raffaella, as she still had her oven mitts on. So she slapped us with her words.

"Ué ué! Vogliamo fini?" Y'all want to come off it now? She was smiling. She was cheerful. She was a master in the art of *sdrammatizzazione.*

As a parent, Salvatore has drawn on his mother's lessons. There are no sobbing *"vita mia"* moments when one of our children cries. Before I manage to Oh-honey them, before I arrive with my furrowed eyebrows and I-understand-your-pain-let-me-feel-it-with-you, he's there. He's there with his finger outstretched and a smile on his face. He's touching their tears. "Mamma Ketrin! Let's taste these tears to see if you put enough salt in the water when you were making this little one." He always tastes them. Not for pretend—he really tastes them. And guess what? The amount of salt always happens to be just right.

Caffè Macchiato

When I arrived back in the States in June of 1997, I missed Salvatore, I missed the Avallone family, and I missed Naples. On top of it all, I desperately missed Neapolitan coffee.

I should mention that in both suburban Maryland and downtown Naples, coffee is essential to my being, and staying, human. And the sounds that are linked to the experience of coffee consumption trigger in me a drug addict's vein-jumping response. In the United States, there is the squeaky Styrofoam sound of "to go." There is Billie Holiday singing in a Starbucks, a background to the barista's (or Starbucksista's) efficient assembly-line voice calling out, "Venti chai" or "Skim soy latte" (isn't life complicated enough as it is? I wonder). There are people standing in line who are not talking.

In Italy, the sound of coffee in a bar is clinking porcelain. It is cacophony, racket, loud voices arguing and laughing over the *sssssshhhh* of the espresso machine. These sounds, a prelude to the hit of that syrupy black nectar that is called *caffè*, remind me that everything is possible. I can fight the good fight.

I think the fundamental difference between the experiences of coffee in the United States and coffee in Italy comes down to the concept of "to go." In America, coffee is taken to go because there's a lot of liquid to be consumed. It accompanies you as you go about your morning. There is comfort in the feel of large quantities of lava-hot liquid under your fingers, of knowing that this coffee will be with you for hours. Your big hot cup of American coffee or latte or macchiato or whatever else Starbucks has decided to name it, will be held close, cuddled and nursed. Your very own grown-up sippy cup, thanks to that marvelous plastic mouthpiece (a *beccuccio*, or little beak, they would call it in Italian), which enables you to sip without spilling or scalding your mouth. Sipped and dripped. American coffee is sippy and drippy. It is like the saline bags that are linked to an intravenous drip: the level of fluid in your bloodstream never drops below a certain level.

Italian espresso, on the other hand, is a hit. A fast, intense bang to your veins. It is a one-gulp switch of the wrist that wakes and revs you up in an instant. For this reason, Italian coffee to go makes no sense. Or rather, it makes sense only when you can't make it to the bar and the uniformed barman brings it to your office on a tray, in a porcelain cup (you'll bring it back, you're trusted, they've got plenty of them). You can get your one-gulp hit somewhere other than the bar as long as it's close by and the whole endeavor is performed quickly.

Many Italians, particularly in Naples, ask me with a big smile whether I prefer American or Italian coffee. Their faces tell me they know the answer, they know the only possible answer. They are fishing for a great big national compliment. No one can say that Italians are not patriotic—I mean, really, who cares whether you're a superpower if your coffee is bad? Most Italians (and particularly Neapolitans) find coffee in America terrible. I have heard it called *brodaglia*, or bad broth, and *acqua sporca*, dirty water. Many find even the idea of it, particularly coffee poured from a pot (reheated! *Ahimè!*) disgusting.

With a revolted but curious look on her face, Benedetta picked my brain about American "dirty water": "I've seen in movies and on TV those big cups that sit all day on American desks. What do you call them? *Moogs?* They can't really be filled with coffee, can they?"

"Mugs, and usually, yes, they are."

"All that liquid is coffee?"

"Yes."

"Doesn't it get cold?"

"Eventually, yes."

"And Americans drink it anyway? When it's getting cold?"

"Yes."

And then the crux of the matter. "You don't actually like that dirty water that they call coffee in America, do you?"

"I do."

Truthfully, I don't mind the taste of a Venti, I enjoy the relaxing experience of Billie Holiday singing in a Starbucks. People waiting in a line. A straight line, in which you know your position. It's not that no order exists in Naples when it comes to ordering a coffee, it's just that the "line" is a very amorphous formation. To an American, it may seem that people are crowded around the cash register trying to elbow each other to be first. Some people are, and do, but often people do know their place in Italian "lines"—they are simply not physically standing one in front of another. They remember who has entered before and after them: the order is an unspoken reality. They feel no need to re-create this order physically, because, after all, we all know that the lady with the white hair is after the young guy with the leather jacket and before the man with the beard, right?

So the person behind the cash register, seeing three or more people standing shoulder to shoulder, asks, *"Chi c'era?"*—Who's next? I, not remembering who came in when, sure only that I've been in that spot an awfully long time and am in dire need of caffeine, do not say, as I should, *"Io!"* (Me!) and order. I look at the people on either side of me, and trust. If no one is in too much of a rush, one of them will point graciously at me and say, *"La signorina."* Ahhh, it's nice when that happens. Authorized, I order my hit. What stress.

So when I went to Starbucks that first summer home, it was so relaxing that I sometimes felt like maybe I didn't even *need* a hit. But I would often go with a friend, to talk over coffee. To talk while drinking. Yes, we Americans multitask! And talking while drinking means that you need liquid, large quantities of it. So I would order a Venti, a drip drip drip sip sip sip into veins that were used to the sudden rush of the godly nectar that was my espresso. The Venti tasted good, though. As long as I didn't think of it as *caffè*.

Burgers and Fries

"*Fidarsi è bene, non fidarsi è meglio,*" Raffaella reminded me on the phone when I called from Washington. Again the trust thing: to trust is good, not to trust is better.

Raffaella was using the expression not in reference to a person, however, but in reference to hamburgers. I had said that I was missing Italy but enjoying American hamburgers. "Better not to trust hamburgers?" I asked.

"When you eat at restaurants, you don't know what they put in the food." She worried about me like I was her daughter, and she doubted my judgment. Now that I was far away, she realized that I was naïve, a babe in the woods. I needed her protection. For all she knew, I was living on the edge, performing daredevil maneuvers like ordering meat in restaurants where I didn't know the owner. American restaurants where I didn't know *anyone* in the establishment! How could I be sure that the meat was decent?

"*Mi raccomando,*" she said, using a term that means, Watch out! Heed my advice! And keep me in your mind! all at once. "When Salva arrives in Washington, you two can cook at home."

Salvatore had started planning his trip to the United States as soon as I left Naples. We missed each other and he wanted to see America. "Yes!" I said, "Come visit! We can see Washington and New York! I'll introduce you to American food courts!" I was thrilled.

He bought his tickets. "*Allora*, I arrive on July fifteenth and leave on August thirtieth," he told me over the phone. Wait, I thought. Did he just say a month and a half? I couldn't wait to see him, of course, but I was taken aback. A month and a half under my parents' roof?

Words like *visit* and *vacation* are tricky. You think they can be easily translated from one language to another, from one culture to another. *Una vacanza* is a vacation, right? *Visitare* is to visit someone. But for a Naples university student, *vacanza* meant, apparently, between one and two months. The translation in American English would more accurately be a "summer internship" or an "experience abroad." It could even be translated as "taking up an alternative residence."

———— ✸ ————

In my family, anything that lasted over two weeks was the stuff of résumés and college admissions. Vacations, on the other hand, were no longer than two weeks and usually meant a cruise. Our Wilson grandfather traditionally took our family on vacation every other year, alternating with my father's brother's family. My mother and aunt planned these vacations, which meant that while our friends from Washington went to Hilton Head or Cape Cod, we went on a cruise in Southeast Asia or the Galápagos.

My mother couldn't admit that we cruised because it was a fun thing to do, and because our grandfather was paying for it. She would come up with creative reasons for why it was "impor-

TanT" (with the pronunciation of the two *ts* very marked when it came to talking about spending money on oneself) that the children *understand the differences* between Asia and America. Or that they *experience firsthand* the ecosystem of the Galápagos.

Anna and I pretended that we were Captain Stubing's daughters from *The Love Boat*. We relished the fact that there was no argument between our parents over where to have dinner, no battles over the price of entrées. A cruise director could direct the show that was our family, and we could be kids in between the ports of call.

Salvatore arrived in America with gel in his hair, wearing a checked dress shirt tucked into beige pants. He was carrying a man-purse and pulling a suitcase packed with gifts for every member of my family. Raffaella had bought an Armani scarf for my mother, a Marinella tie for my father (a brand that is worn by Berlusconi and sold only in Naples), a necklace for my sister, and a number of other gifts that she instructed Salva to give to "aunts, uncles, godmothers . . . whomever you think appropriate."

For me, she had packed Neapolitan *taralli* crackers, made with lard, pepper, and nuts.

My parents were standing in front of the ornate columns of their big suburban house when I pulled up with Salvatore after getting him at the airport. They seemed to be on unusually good behavior. My father welcomed him with *"Benvenuto!"* and my mother smiled. Who were these people?

We showed Salva into our modern, gray kitchen. I thought he would be taken aback by the size of the room and the fact that it looked out over our pool and extensive lawn. But he seemed unimpressed. He started fumbling around in his suitcase to find the

wrapped gifts, and handed them to my parents, saying, "For you."
I'd never heard his accent so thick, or so adorable. He was sweating, even with the freezing American air-con.

"This will go great with my Bali pants, *grazie mille*," my father said.

My mother spun around the Formica island trying on her
scarf in different ways, and cooed, *"Gentilissimo grazie grazie
Salvatore!"* She'd gotten a *Parlo Italiano* audiotape and was listening to it every day in her car so that she could outdo my father linguistically when Salva arrived.

He blushed and laughed. I'd never seen him blush. I'd
never seen him at a loss for words.

"I didn't know what form of *you* to use with your parents,"
he told me later, "I wanted to show them respect!"

I reassured him that there was only one form of *you* in English, and that they would happily answer to Bonnie and Ed (or
Bony and Head). He relaxed and started to enjoy the antics of
what he considered a "typical American family." (*Typical American fathers do not swim nude,* I had to remind Salva when we
got back to Italy. *They do not make loud animal noises in elegant
French restaurants; they also do not buy live lobsters at Whole
Foods so they can swim with them and then boil them for dinner.*)

My mother planned three weeks of travel for the four of us.
While a Neapolitan *mammà* would have spent time organizing
and preparing typical dishes for my boyfriend to taste, Bonnie
Wilson was compiling a folder with maps, brochures, and tickets for the Show Salva the U.S.A. tour. We hit New York and
Los Angeles, Boston and San Diego. My mother organized the
strategic strikes with great efficiency: Who knew if Salva was
ever going to come back to America? We had to get as much in
as possible.

At the end of the trip, she booked us tiny, internal cabins

(we certainly couldn't afford a porthole!) on a Carnival cruise
going to the Caribbean. If Salva was ever going to really fit in
with the Wilsons, he had to know how to cruise.

Salvatore's English was improving, but he had begun to develop his linguistic trademark of adding one incorrect letter to
English words. (Years later, at our son's Catholic school, the
teachers were *nunts*; my best friend Leo from college was *Lero*.)
What we took to the Caribbean was a *cruiser*. My parents and I
regularly corrected him with a loud *crooooozz* in unison over
the racket of steel drums or announcements about muster stations. Salva snapped his fingers to the beat of the reggae, ignoring us.

My father's clothing choice and loud voice fit in, and Salva
ditched the Armani suits his mother had packed after the first
day and pulled out his T-shirts with bubble letters. We rocked
the cocktail bar and the karaoke lounge. When he got back to
Italy, Salva told his friends how much fun the cruiser had been.
It was a shame, though, that we hadn't really stopped at any
ports of call.

"What do you mean?" I asked him. "We went to the Cayman Islands, Cozumel—"

"But the ship only stopped for a few hours. We didn't *visit*
those places." There was that verb again, *visitare*. For Americans
like us, cruising was a way to *get in* lots of places in a short time.
We *did* Grand Cayman, Cozumel, Belize . . . in just one week.
What more could you want? But for the Neapolitan in Salva, we
might as well not have gone. When you dock at 9:00 and leave
at 4:00, you don't even have time to taste the island's typical
dish.

Our cruise ended in Miami, where a Princeton classmate of
my father's had a house that he wasn't using. It was a sprawling
estate in South Beach, and on our arrival, a handsome young

maggiordomo showed my parents and me to our bedrooms in the main house. Salvatore, he told us, would be staying in the guesthouse, a separate structure across the lawn. It was a young man's dream come true, complete with a Jacuzzi and beers in the refrigerator. A bachelor pad! I thought Salva would be thrilled.

During the afternoon he seemed to be. He asked me to take pictures of him to show his friends in Naples: in front of the house, relaxing in the hot tub, reclining on a lounge chair. But after dinner, when we kissed good night before going our separate ways, I sensed that something was wrong. "Is this the only key?" he kept asking. "*Solo questo?* You just turn it once like that?"

Hollywood has conditioned the world to think that an isolated house in America is inevitably going to be a site of violent crime. Plus, Gianni Versace had been killed just a few weeks before in Miami, and newspapers were still covering the story. My father thought it very funny to tell Salva that Versace's murderer was a serial killer ready for more Italian blood.

I was preparing for bed when I heard a tentative knock at the door.

I opened it to find Salva in pajamas printed with flying soccer balls. "*Mi sono cagato sotto,*" he whispered. I got scared, shit-in-my-pants scared. He crawled into the single bed with me. "It was so quiet. And those wooden doors wouldn't keep out a fly."

Back in Washington, Salvatore and I went against his mother's advice and trusted—we ate out. We consumed burgers at restaurants. We drank bottles of ketchup. We got free refills. Salva was awed by straight lines of customers, by waiters who told you their name, by eighteen-wheel trucks. We hopped from enormous thing to enormous thing, from shopping malls to supermarkets to sports complexes. Having grown up in Naples, he had never seen spaces like these.

At one point, I feigned interest in joining a Gold's Gym in Rockville, Maryland, so that we could get a full tour. The trainer shook our hands, and smiled with a lot of very white, very American teeth, telling us that his name was Gary.

"Why is he telling us his name?" Salva whispered to me in Italian. "What does he want from us?"

"*Tranquillo, tranquillo,*" I reassured him. "He's just going to show us around."

Salvatore marveled at the high-tech equipment and the spacious changing rooms. When we finished the tour, Gary invited us into his office to discuss prices for membership and various personal training programs. What are you most interested in? he asked us. Cardio? Weight lifting? I was about to answer (Salva's English was still shaky, and I wanted to get out of there as quickly as possible to introduce him to the great American phenomenon of fudge at another food court) when my boyfriend spoke up.

"She needs . . . how to say . . . the leg part . . . here?" He turned to me and pointed to his thigh. "*Ketrin, come si dice* coscia?" How do you say *thigh*?

Silence. I did not translate. I would not translate.

I had a vague sense of where this was going.

But Salva would not be stopped. Nor would he let the language barrier get in his way. Oh no, this was too important. "Do you have some machine for *thees*?" Now he pointed at my thigh. "To make more slimmer?"

Now, I should mention that I have a character flaw the Italians call *permalosità. Permalosa* is the word that is used to describe someone who is thin-skinned, who takes everything personally. Like, for example, me. Watch what you say around Katherine, she's *permalosa*. Oversensitive, easily offended. I readily admit that I have never, and will never, like sentences that start with "Don't take this personally, but . . ." I don't like them and I don't like the creature who utters them. If you know that I may take it personally, that I probably *will* take it personally, just keep your mouth shut, no? I am highly *permalosa*. And, like many young Anglo-Saxon women, nowhere is this more the case than when it comes to body image.

So, if I weren't *permalosa*, I might have seen this episode as an example of my boyfriend's encouragement, of his desire to lovingly nudge me and my thighs toward self-improvement. But since my ego and hence insecurity were about as enormous as that Gold's Gym, I asked the personal trainer if there were any machines that would make my boyfriend's biceps look like they'd lifted something heavier than a fork. There was confusion and fear in the eyes of that trainer as he quickly dispatched us, handing over a brochure and telling us to call if we needed any more information.

Bologna

The typical dish of Bologna is *tortellini in brodo*. Traditional Bolognese sauce (which is not anything like Neapolitan *ragù*—it has almost no tomato in it, in fact) is eaten with tagliatelle or fettuccine, while the meat-filled tortellini must be swimming in broth. At hardcore restaurants in Bologna, they will refuse to serve you *tortellini al Bolognese*. Only *in brodo*.

At restaurants in Naples, pasta doesn't swim. Get a soup.

When I arrived in Bologna to begin my year at SAIS, Salvatore and I decided that we would see each other every other weekend. He came north bearing Styrofoam care packages from his mother, which he would toss on my desk before undressing me. The *parmigiana di melanzane*, mozzarella, and *pasta al forno* could wait.

"She told me it's all for you," he would say, after we had gotten our fill of each other and were hungry for food. "Mamma made me promise not to eat it. I get it all the time and you don't. She said you're *sciupata*." *Sciupata* is the Neapolitan word for scrawny, but it also means pale and generally unhealthy. It's what one becomes when one doesn't have a *mamma* in the kitchen. When, for example, one pursues a master's degree in a city where the pasta is swimming in broth.

My fellow students, my fellow *sciupati*, were from all over the world. They were smart, sophisticated, global. They were twentysomethings who could write cover letters in three languages to attach to their impressive résumés. They hopped continents frequently, had work experience in places like Burma, and most already emailed in 1997.

Meanwhile, Salvatore stayed in Naples, memorizing by heart three-hundred-page law texts in his room of teddy bears and elementary school soccer trophies. We both purchased cellphones as big as small toaster ovens and talked in the evenings. My head was full of kinked supply curves and what was happening in Bosnia, while he would tell me what wonderful things he had had for dinner. "And what did you eat, my *pagnottella*?"

I refused to answer him. Word would get out.

In the United States that summer, Salvatore had been enthralled by what was, in 1997, a consumer culture that was much more advanced than that of Italy. Although he was challenged by verbs like *to be* and *to go,* he immediately learned expressions like *reward points, preferred customer,* and *supersaver.* What intellectual energy he had left after eight hours of rote memorization of his law texts he used to redeem coupons to get a 20 percent discount on bath soap (yes, on another continent), or to write letters to places like Walmart (with my linguistic consultation) that went something like this:

Dear Sir/Madam,

I would like the new Bonus Club Membership. Please. Thank you.

Salvatore Avallone
Via G. Pascoli, 4B
Napoli, Italia

In economics class, I learned that southern Italy was the Appalachia of the EU. Unable to withstand regional shocks and bounce back with labor mobility, it was a place where market capitalism was turned upside down. How did young Neapolitans do that and manage to get away with it? By living at home until they're thirty, by working in the black market, by ignoring the rules and being so very *grounded*. Neapolitans turned the global system on its head in one *gesto*, like a flick of the spatula when frying a frittata.

The young people I knew in Naples didn't seem the least bit interested in being mobile, flexible, independent, global. *No, grazie*, they seemed to say. We're just fine here, with our extended family, smelling things simmering in a pot for hours. But we do like that supersaver discount idea; do we qualify?

Every other Friday afternoon, I would get the Eurostar to Naples, to soft sheets and deep red *ragù* and the world of sensory satisfaction and emotional connection. Five hours passed quickly. Medieval Bologna, Renaissance Florence, the aqueducts outside Rome. (They always made me remember the signs on the Beltway pointing to Washington, the unquestioned seat of the Empire in 1997.) When I saw the sea at Gaeta, I knew that Naples was near and I was coming home.

Pulling into the Napoli Centrale train station, I could see the laundry (intimate robes, pajamas, and all) on the lines that connected the buildings to each other. *"Pronto, Mamma?"* Cellphones would start ringing as we neared the station, loudly, all at the same time. From middle-aged businessmen to young girls in university up north, everyone got a call from their *mamma.* Their conversations were the same, no matter the age or gender: Yes, the train is on time, that sounds good for lunch, but did you get the mozzarella? *Sì, sì, see you soon, love you, Mamma.*

My to-do list in Bologna:

Write a paper on the Warsaw pact
Exercise
Read econ chapters
Figure out a job in which I can earn money and have fun
Destroy the judging mother in my head
Become famous
Take calcium pills

My to-do list in Napoli:

Make sure when cooking crustaceans only to use sprigs,
    not the flowers, of parsley
When going back to bed for afternoon nap, put full
    pajamas on (no half-assed siesta)
Tell Nino to get extra ricotta for me
Bring full array of eye shadow
Kiss Salva on the soft spot behind his earlobe
DON'T EAT CRUST OF PIZZA FIRST

Tonino Reale

The SAIS master's program includes a year in Bologna and a year in Washington. It was understood that after my year in Bologna, I would go back to the hum of central air-conditioning, to "Have a nice day!" and a linear career path. As my fellow students organized their summer internships and their upcoming semesters in D.C., I started buying bags of chocolate amaretto cookies. I discovered Bolognese binge food.

It wasn't just that I missed Naples and the Avallones (although it would have greatly helped to have been spoon-fed some of Raffaella's lasagna on a regular basis at that point). Once again, I was hungry for the stage. Although I'd performed my way through high school and college, I had never acted professionally. It was time for me to work in theater as a grown-up: I wanted to take a risk and see if I could make a living doing something I loved.

When I told my mother that I'd decided not to finish the program in Washington, she reminded me that I wouldn't have an advanced degree: all I'd have to show for my year in Bologna was "a *di-plOH-ma,* sweetheart"—that long "O" making it sound like a certificate for winning points at a boardwalk arcade. She told her friends that her younger daughter had decided to take a temporary (at least I *hope* it's temporary!) "leave of absence." When I explained my decision to Raffaella, she said, "Okay," and then asked what I was planning for dinner. Salva said, "Oh! We have a showgirl!" He pronounced it *show-gEErl*.

I spent the summer working on audition pieces, and came back to Italy in the fall ready to find out where the Italian productions were and to try to get cast. Little did I know that though I was in the land of Dante's *Divina Commedia*, the comedy of Italian theater wasn't always so divine.

~~~~~※~~~~~

My first audition in Italy was for the Neapolitan director Tonino Reale's musical version of *The Picture of Dorian Gray* at the spectacular baroque Teatro Bellini in central Naples. I brought my "I Could Have Danced All Night" sheet music and the text of a Blanche Dubois monologue from *A Streetcar Named Desire* in Italian. I was nervous, and looked anxiously for the waiting room, expecting to commiserate with other water bottle–nursing actors dressed in black. What I found instead was a hot eighteenth-century salon that stank of BO and powder. The communal stage fright of the scantily clad *velina* types was palpable.

There was a lot of exposed flesh and thick Pan-Cake makeup. I should keep my eyes down, I thought, so they don't land inadvertently on cleavage or thongs. I sat down and opened my *Un tram che si chiama Desiderio* text to keep busy.

"*Che cos'è? Che fai?*" An absurdly beautiful adolescent girl was leaning over my script. Her boobs were touching my forearm! She wanted to know what I had brought. What play is that? Why are you doing it? Can I hear you do it? You need a little more eyeliner. I have some, you want to borrow it?

Minding one's own business was not part of the deal. I told her about myself, that this was my first audition in Italy. When I mentioned that I was American, a great big *oooooohhhh* rose up in a wave from the girls. They were wide-eyed and even silent for a moment, until a blonde in spike heels said, "*Vabbò, io me ne vaco a casa!*" They all laughed. An American's here? Maybe I should just go home.

Fortunately, the director had made the same assumptions about American talent that the girl had. As I was singing the very first "I could have daaaanced . . ." he interrupted me to say that I was cast. God bless Italy! I was emotionally prepared for "Don't call us, we'll call you," even "*No, grazie.*" And here I was cast without even a callback, and without bringing out Italian Blanche. Kindness of strangers, indeed.

I stayed in Benedetta's old room while the play was in rehearsal. After Benedetta and Mauro's Positano wedding, the newlyweds had moved into an apartment on the first floor of the building where Salva and his parents lived. Some friends warned that living in the same building as parents and in-laws was a recipe for disaster, but others congratulated Benedetta and Mauro on their luck at having a *mamma* just two floors down. Lasagna could be sent up in the elevator. Shirts could be ironed free of charge. When children came, the *nonni*, or grandparents, would be babysitters in residence. An intercom was built in to save on phone bills, for the daily Mamma, do you have an onion? Or, Can I substitute *provola* for *scamorza* cheese in my stuffed peppers?

Raffaella was busy. She now fed not two children but four

twentysomethings. When Benedetta asked her mother for lasagna, Raffaella would bake it (remembering to leave out the sausage—Mauro didn't like pork) and then buzz her daughter to say, "It's in the elevator." So as not to intrude on Benedetta and her new husband, she would not bring the lasagna herself, but would put the hot pan on the floor of the elevator (oh, how that smell would linger! A *ragù* cooked for hours, tiny fried meatballs hidden in the layers of pasta . . .) and push the button of the floor where her daughter lived. Benedetta would walk out of her apartment to find the elevator doors opening, opening to the smell and the sight of that aluminum-foiled labor of love inside the little lift.

One morning, about a month into rehearsals, I was running out the door of the Avallones' to grab a taxi for the theater, when Raffaella told me that she had made a *pizza di scarola* for my snack. I had to go, I was already late, I told her, to no avail. Raffaella had to make sure that the focaccia-like pizza was properly packaged. The director could wait.

By the time I made it out the door, I was majorly, unjustifiably tardy. In addition, all of downtown was in gridlock. As I sat in the taxi, watching the meter ticking away, I asked the driver if there was a strike or a demonstration. Yes, he told me, it was the demonstration of illegal aliens, and it would block traffic the entire morning. Policemen were escorting the African, Bangladeshi, and Southeast Asian demonstrators in an attempt to keep some kind of order. I wondered: but if they are illegal . . . and these are cops . . .

The demonstration would not be a viable excuse—I was now disastrously tardy. I had been late for rehearsal once before, a matter of about fifteen minutes, and had expected to discreetly join the rest of the cast, score in hand and causing not a ripple (maybe just mouthing *Scusa!*). Instead, the director screamed, *"Chi sei!"* Who are you? as soon as I entered the room.

It confused me. Did he really not know who I was? Granted, I was not the lead. Nor was I an important supporting character. But we had been rehearsing the musical for almost a month, six days a week, and there were only about eighteen members of the cast. So I would have liked to think that the director, Tonino Reale, knew who I was. He had cast me, after all.

Many international theater professionals have not heard of the Neapolitan director Tonino Reale. He is an actor/director/ narcissistic tyrant who bears a striking resemblance, physically and temperamentally, to Rumpelstiltskin. He has been known to jump onstage during performances, whisper "You suck" to the lead, and play the role for what remains of the show. He is usually wearing a black T-shirt printed with nonsense English phrases like GOING STRONG UNIVERSITY. When he sings, a sort of hoarse, screaming sound that disregards notes and rhythm, he totally blows out his voice (which is already suffering from the pack of cigarettes he smokes each day). For curtain call, he likes to keep coming back onstage for applause until all of the audience has left. Sometimes as many as seven times. Needless to say, he has not been nominated for any Italian Tonys.

That's why I was more than a little tense in the taxi on the way to the Teatro Bellini. I had some idea how the ogre would react to my being thirty minutes late. When I arrived, I braced myself for the worst. I entered the theater and found the actors doing some blocking on the stage while Tonino surfed the Internet on his laptop in one of the ornate boxes that had been reserved for royalty two centuries ago.

Maybe he wouldn't see me! Hope! I ran onstage and tried to blend in with the other members of the cast.

"Americana!" he screeched. The sound of his voice was not tempered by all the red velvet. But, looking on the bright side, at least this time he remembered who I was.

"Multa!"

A fine? For being late? But just a few days before, the director had failed to show up! Twenty people waited for him all day long! And he never even explained his absence when he came to rehearsal the next day.

So it went that I had to pay a twenty-euro fine for my tardiness. But at least I was saved the humiliation of being the object of a ten-minute tirade. On another occasion, the director, instead of suggesting that I move a few feet stage left, screamed, "Girl with the nineteenth-century ass! Move over! You're blocking the people I *really* want to see!"

––––––––– ☀ –––––––––

I learned the hard way that stage actors in Italy have a tough lot. Very little money. Exhausting tours. School matinees where high schoolers throw food onstage and shout "Take it off!" and teachers stand up every few minutes to shout *"Basta!"* This, compounded with Tonino Reale's howling onstage and off (and his regular groping of the actresses) persuaded me to take my wobbly soprano voice, bizarre accent, and nineteenth-century ass to a dubbing studio.

If an actor in Italy is not interested in being on a reality show, perhaps his or her most promising (read: most lucrative and stable) future is in the world of dubbing. All foreign films in Italy are dubbed into Italian. "Subtitles cause headaches," Italians often say. And so each big American star is dubbed by one Italian voice. The voice of Tom Cruise is a friend of mine and a phenomenal actor. Sylvester Stallone is dubbed by a fat character actor famous throughout the country. The Italian public is

very attached to these voices, particularly the voices of stars like
Cruise, Tom Hanks, and Sharon Stone. There was an uproar
when Tom Cruise's dubber was replaced in one of his films be-
cause of a contract disagreement. My friend Roberto, the Italian
Cruise, was *tranquillo*, however. "They will rehire me. I am
Tom."

Italians are so attached to the stars' Italian voices that they
can be greatly disturbed when they hear the Americans' real
voices. "The voice of *our* Robert De Niro is so much better than
yours," someone told me recently, apparently not concerned
about the fact that the English-language version is the man's
real voice. But I agree that some performances are greatly enhanced by dubbing. Not the Fonz, and most definitely not
Meryl Streep, but Jean-Claude Van Damme, for example, and
Keanu Reeves.

Good dubbing is an art form. Not only do you need to understand the character and "find" the voice, like any good actor,
but you need to pay close attention to "synch"—the ability to
start speaking the second the actor opens his mouth, take
breaths when he or she does, and keep the rhythm so that you
finish the line exactly when the actor does. Dubbing successfully depends of course on having a translation, or rather an
adaptation, that works. But it also takes talent and skill.

I started to get calls from studios in Rome to dub in English.
Since Italian dubbing studios are some of the best in the world
(and cheapest to use—you could pay dubbers and technicians
under the table), we would get all kinds of work: Chinese mar-
tial arts films, Philippine horror movies, Brazilian cartoons. Basically anything that was headed for distribution in English-
speaking countries, or that needed an English version on DVD.
I immediately fell in love with cartoon dubbing. I could go crazy
with my voice without having to worry about following the

mouth of the actor onscreen. Although a dubbing director might suggest that I could let my British woodchuck get in touch with her anger, or that my melancholy marshmallow could incorporate a touch of bitterness, I generally was not told "you suck." That was important for someone as *permalosa* as me.

So I was happy when I got a call for a turn (three hours in a dubbing studio) for the English version of *Snow White and Her Seven Dwarves*. I hopped on a train for Rome excitedly. Snow White! My voice would be perfect. I should have paid more attention to the possessive pronoun in the title, though.

I soon realized that this Snow White was not a cartoon. The film was intended, in fact, for a very adult audience. The director came into the studio, fitted me with my headphones, and put a chair behind me. "In case you start hyperventilating," he told me.

Hyperventilating, in fact, is the greatest risk in porn dubbing. Fortunately for the dubber, the director can usually use the heavy breathing in the film's original language. But every once in a while, along comes an *"O Dio!"* or some such cry. The dubber has to record an "Oh God!" and all the cries and breaths surrounding it. I'm telling you, it's exhausting.

Snow White's director listened behind the glass division, looking bored and sleepy. He'd watched these scenes thousands of times, having already dubbed the dwarves into English, Spanish, Portuguese, and Chinese. He stopped me mid-wail, and with a tone of voice that I'm used to now with Italian directors, told me that I sounded like I was tired and in pain. Bianca Neve (Snow White) isn't in pain, why should I be? Relax and enjoy it, *Americana*.

A Manicure Before Mass

"Before we go, Ketrin, could you cut my fingernails? It will only take a minute." We were walking out the door, late for the service. The baptism of Benedetta's newborn son, Emilio, was to begin at ten o'clock, and it was now 9:55. The organization was difficult because there were so many of us: Benedetta and her husband, Nino and Raffaella, Salvatore and myself, Zio Toto (owner of the aforementioned fingernails), and Benedetta's Sri Lankan nanny and housekeeper, who was the only one sitting in the car downstairs ready to go. *"Mi raccomando!"* Raffaella had announced that morning, meaning I trust you all will listen to me. "Don't be late. We must leave the house no later than nine-thirty!"

I was in Naples on break from tour. I had been cast in the Italian production of Andrew Lloyd Webber's *Jesus Christ Superstar,* and had been traveling for months with a group of thirty dancers and singers throughout Italy. We hopped from city to city, baroque opera house to baroque opera house, seedy hotel to seedy hotel. When there were breaks, I would come to Naples and stay with the Avallones. Salva had a few more exams left, hospital. The room was filled with about ten people when mother and son were rolled in immediately after the C-section. The baby was still crusty and blood-streaked; Benedetta looked pale and nauseous. Raffaella was opening a bottle of champagne and fumbling with fifteen plastic cups. She left the job to one of her sisters when she saw her daughter and grandson. She strode over to grab the baby out of Benedetta's arms and lift him for all to see. *"Ma quanto è bello!"* How gorgeous he is!

I thought, There's no easing into this, Emilio. You've had your nine months of peace and quiet and personal space. Now, as they say in Neapolitan, *"T'è scetà!"* Gotta wake yourself up.

I was about to slip out to visit a bathroom (if nobody else washed their hands or used disinfectant, at least *I* would) when the baby was literally passed to me like a football. These women of Salva's family had handled newborns and knew something about it. I had never held a baby in my arms, let alone one that still had his plastic ID bracelet on and umbilical cord attached. But there was no time to protest, the fuzzy black head was resting against my chest and everyone was talking about something else. I was a kinswoman, and my body was forced to grasp that concept immediately even as my brain needed a little more time.

And so it was, packed in the car going to mass, that I transformed from a punctual priss to a gushing, emotional mess of a *zia*. Toto, apparently satisfied with his manicure, came out to find that there was no space for him in the car. *"Che problema c'è?"* He grinned. He had his motorbike. Raising his plastic hand, he called out, "See you in church!"

A Home for Good

The tour of *Jesus Christ Superstar* led to a tour of *Evita*, which led to small roles in Italian sitcoms. At dubbing studios, I was called to lend my voice to heroines in low-budget Filipino horror movies, or to neurotic badgers in Brazilian cartoons. There was work, but none of it was in Naples.

As I got ready to go onstage in Mantova, or Cremona, trying desperately to find a pocket of oxygen in a dressing room that was a haze of cigarette smoke, I would call Salva in Naples. The whole family was gathered for risotto and *arrosto* to celebrate Santa Benedetta, or San Salvatore. Or it was Nino and Raffaella's wedding anniversary, and they had gotten fresh *gamberi* for the linguine. It was Emilio's first birthday, and I should have tried that *caprese* cake! The family gathered, and I was missed.

How much longer, I wondered, until I can come home for good?

"How many years do couples usually date in Naples before getting married?" I asked Salva on the phone one evening, trying to sound like I was performing a sociological survey. He had only one exam left to complete his university degree, and I wondered where we stood.

Well, Salva told me, his cousin Giorgio had been with his girlfriend for fourteen years. Another friend was going on sixteen years, with no engagement on the horizon. Hard to tell.

"*Comunque, più di dieci*," he decided. More than ten years for sure.

"That is a decade. Of dating."

"The reason is economic," Salva explained. Italian *ragazzi* don't earn enough to rent their own place. (He didn't mention mothers, or lasagna.) You can't get married if you're still economically dependent on your parents, after all.

It was time to tell him about my family's history, and the money that my grandparents had set aside for their grandchildren, in the form of a trust. This was difficult, since there is no Italian translation for the term. Italian children who inherit wealth usually get it in the form of apartments or land or jobs. When their parents die, they get whatever they get directly. Taxes? *Eeeeeeh*, on the exhale—you don't pay them during life, you don't pay them after death.

"I have a trust fund." (To trust is good, not to trust is better: *Fidarsi è bene, non fidarsi è meglio!*) I tried to explain. "It's this American thing where we skip generations." My translation made it sound like all Americans like to hop over their kids on principle. "It isn't my parents' money, it was set up by my grandparents."

"Why? They didn't trust your parents?"

It was a conversation going nowhere. The truth was, I had no vocabulary to translate terms like *estate tax* or *loopholes*. In reality, I didn't even know what they meant.

~~~ ☀ ~~~

I was very confused about money as a child. I knew that we had an extravagant house, and that we took a lot of nice vacations. But my parents reminded me often that we weren't as rich as other people thought we were. Our family had never actually *owned* Wilson. My grandfather was just a shareholder when it was sold and it wasn't sold for much and I should just laugh when my classmates in elementary school asked me for a free tennis racket. When my family socialized with the Marriotts and Firestones, my mother always commented that "these people are just in a different *league*, precious." And she was right, they were in a different league if you were going to compare the rich with the superrich. But my mother pushed the point so much that my sister and I believed that we were one step away from food stamps.

So I realized only embarrassingly late that the trusts in the hands of family bankers, the studying of tax loopholes, the bizarre generation skipping—all meant that we had money in our names. My father's grandfather, the industrial magnate, left him trusts. My grandfather, in turn, left me trusts. But these trusts, my mother believed, were not meant to be spent. "They exist to avoid estate tax," she would tell me when I asked what a trust was. Interest could be skimmed off for emergencies, but the phrase *tapping into capital* was akin to *shooting up heroin*.

For Bonnie Wilson, money that you don't earn shouldn't really be yours. Rags to riches is a heroic story to be told. It is the American dream, Calvinism exemplified! Riches to doing just fine—not so much. Better to pretend you're poor.

The trusts that I inherited were enough to allow me to buy an apartment in Italy, and Salva and I could establish ourselves as an independent couple. I explained this to him, but he seemed strangely uninterested in the matter.

"Ho capito, ho capito." Oh, I get it, is what he said. After a pause he added, "Why don't you buy new sneakers? The ones you have are all worn down," and that was the end of it.

Inheriting money from your grandparents was a quirky American way of passing money down, he seemed to think, but there was nothing momentous about it. Salva came from a family that had had money, and had lost money, and were doing fine. He would graduate from law school, and find work. He would never be dependent on me or anyone else. As his parents had taught him, *Fidarsi è bene, non fidarsi è meglio.*

'O Purpo

"*Facciamo la strada o le scale?*" Raffaella asked. Do you want to use the road or the steps? We were in Positano, carrying beach bags stuffed with towels, thick sandwiches, peaches, bottles of water, sunscreen, a change of clothes—a load of stuff—down to the beach. The Avallones have a house high on the cliff overlooking the water, and to get to the small pebbly beach there are exactly . . . I don't know how many steps. A lot. Salva, when he was little, would count the steps every day of his two-month summer vacation in Positano, and every day he would come out with a different number.

Salva would run down these steps barefoot, with no parental chaperone, at the age of seven. He would stop on the way down to the beach only to buy a chocolate *cannolo*; on the way up, a lemon granita made with those Amalfi coast lemons as big as a human head. The little granita cart that is strategically positioned at the Piazza dei Mulini made enough lire in the summer months to support three Positano families all year long.

The road, meanwhile, is winding, narrow, and petrifying, whether you are on foot or in a vehicle. In Italy, hairpin turns present no reason for cars, buses, or motorbikes to slow down. The use of brakes is limited to the moments when two wide vehicles meet head-on (the tiny roads on the Amalfi coast are mostly two-way). It is not uncommon to see the Interno Positano bus reversing and then scraping up against the cliff to leave space for the Montepertuso bus to pass. The clown-nose honking of horns echoes frequently through Positano. When you are walking down to the beach and vehicles whiz by, or two buses have a honking tête-à-tête, you have to hop to safety either by jumping onto and clinging to the cliff or by ducking into one of the chic jewelry shops carved into the rock.

Road or steps? *"Le scale,"* I tell Raffaella. Definitely the steps.

As Salvatore's callused little soccer feet ran down these steps thirty years ago, his mother's pedicured feet never stopped moving around the kitchen of their villa. She would bake all sorts of delicacies to bring down to the beach for lunch: *polpette al sugo, frittate, peperoni saltati.* "It was simple," she told me when I suggested that food shopping, cooking, cleaning, and generally managing small children in hot, vertical Positano must have been exhausting for her as a young mother. She was on her own most of the time, as Nino, like most of the other fathers, stayed in Naples and joined his family for weekends and August. "We just ate sandwiches for lunch." Well, yes, but the sandwiches weren't peanut butter and jelly—they were sandwiches filled with something she had *baked* that morning.

At the beach, the family rented umbrellas and lounge chairs close to their friends from Posillipo. There is a hierarchy to the positioning of the chairs: those closest to the water are the families who have been coming to Positano the longest and who spend all summer. Farther back are the families who don't have vacation homes, who come to Positano for only a few weeks.

The Avallones' umbrellas and chairs have always been in the first row, despite the fact that they would spend at least a month every summer away from Positano, at their apartment in Roccaraso. They were, and are, prominent in the preening Posillipino-Positanese posse.

My one-piece bathing suit and last-minute depilatory efforts did not, I realized as we neared their *ombrellone*, cut it. Raffaella was wearing a Pucci caftan, and somehow, even in early June, was already deeply, uniformly tanned. She moved from umbrella to umbrella (only in the first row; her friends were as linear as a chorus line), praising wraps and pinching grandchildren, while somehow negotiating the sharp pebbles along the beach in her high-heeled flip-flops. *"Conosci Ketrin?"* she asked. Do you know Katherine? The *americana* girlfriend of Salvatore was introduced as I struggled to stay upright. (How did one stand on rocks that felt to my bare feet like fiery shards of glass? My New Balance sneakers were up in the changing room.)

We had come to Positano to celebrate Salva's graduation from university. Raffaella and Nino were so proud: their son had graduated with top honors and was now Dr. Avallone. Hallelujah! He had done it. Six years of pulling teeth, of sweating bricks, of memorizing tomes, and now he was a free man. Free, I assumed, to marry me and move out of his parents' apartment. Everything else was immaterial.

But every time I uttered the word *marriage*, Salva would change the subject.

A Neapolitan expression that Nino taught me helped me to avoid a diplomatic coup d'état and dramatic breakup: *'O purpo s'ha dda cocere dinto a ll'acqua soia*. Literally translated: An octopus must be left to cook in its own juice. After boiling an octopus, apparently, you turn off the flame and leave it in its pot, where it continues to emit its own juices. You can write emails or pick up the kids from soccer practice while the big, slimy, puckering animal stews, because the longer the *polipo* steeps in its own dark pink liquid the better.

Nino taught me this expression that fateful weekend in Positano. When, on Sunday night, Salva hadn't popped any questions except of the "Do you like the stuffed calamari or the steamed *cozze* better?" sort, I confided in Nino and Raffaella. Salva was showering after our day at the beach, and I was sitting with my future parents-in-law on the terrace of their villa. The twinkling lights of Positano were reflected in the blackness of the sea below; the light breeze and smell of orange trees added to the aura of potential romance.

On the other side of the mountain we could see a religious procession, complete with a band playing music that resounded against the rocks. From the terrace they looked like the tiny figures of a Christmas *presepe*. With raised banners and statues of the Madonna, the Positano faithful slowly snaked their way around the winding roads. What a perfect setting to dispatch the parents, get on one knee, and present a ring! Any goddamned ring!

I came out with it: Why does Salva change the subject every time I bring up the idea of getting married? Is it because I'm American? Is it because he wants to stay single, living at home and eating magnificent dishes? "He's like an octopus," Nino replied. "He has to be left to cook in his own juice." Raffaella nodded in agreement. I was not to pressure him or add any external stimuli, but let him come to the decision on his own. Salvatore is a handsome guy, and I was attached to the image of him on one knee asking for my hand in marriage. Instead, I was presented with the image of a bubbling sea creature who, perfectly content for the time being to stew in the pot *by himself,* needed to cook for another five years or more.

Apparently the whole "Will you marry me?" scene with ring and candlelight is an American tradition. It took me a surprisingly long time to realize this, but at a certain point it came to me in a flash. People don't do that here! They just start planning for the wedding. I was waiting for the Easter Bunny! When I tell Italians that in the States, a proposal is often romantic like in the movies, they can't believe it. It cracks them up. We thought that was just another *americanata*, they say, a cheesy and dramatic exaggeration invented by Hollywood.

Having grown up in fast-paced, do-it-yourself North America, I realize that letting people and situations cook in their own juices is decidedly not my forte. (This is probably why my *ragù*, even after eighteen years in Italy, tastes nothing like that of my mother-in-law.) So, to leave Salva alone and trust him to come to a decision without my prodding was a challenge. I succeeded, I am proud to say, for exactly twenty-one hours after that conversation. I probably would have managed longer, except that I found myself, returning from Positano, in a position in which I thought that I was surely going to die.

My puckering *polipo* and I were returning to Naples in his tiny Fiat, on the narrow two-way coastal road. The view of the crystal-blue ocean five hundred feet below; the sea air coming in the open windows: it could have been an enjoyable and picturesque drive. Except that Salva was speeding like a madman around the curves and actually passing other cars. He would honk his horn. (The English verb Salva uses is *to horn*. As in, "I was just horning! The man is going too slow.") I thought this was the moment for our conversation, as it was probably my last.

"So are you going to ask me?" I yelled. We had trouble hearing each other for the wind.

"What?"

"To marry you!"

"*Who? What?*"

"Wedding! *Matrimonio!* Us!"

"*Okay!*"

"*Fine!*"

"*Fine!*"

The octopus was cooked.

Till Dessert Do Us Part

ecently, I overheard two Neapolitan ladies I had never
seen before talking about "that wedding in America."
Sitting by the swimming pool and gossiping, one said to the
other, "Did you hear? All the friends of the bride wore *the same
dress*! There was a *rehearsal*. And everyone got up from the table
to dance, during dinner!"

I felt proud. Proud that in some way I helped a group of
Neapolitans understand that one can party without pasta and
live to tell the tale.

———— ✵ ————

There is a word that you will not find in your Italian-English
dictionary: *sfamarsi*. Like *sdrammatizzare*, *sfamarsi* uses that
little *s* to turn a verb into its opposite. *Sfamarsi* is to dehunger
oneself. I learned at my wedding to Salvatore that it is very difficult for Neapolitans to dehunger themselves without pasta.

No one will come if we get married in the United States,
Salva had said. It's too far. It's too expensive. (He didn't say, how
will we dehunger ourselves? That came later.) So we planned

the wedding for mid-August, when all of Italy is on vacation anyway. My mother organized a four-day affair in Washington. Months before the event, Salva's Neapolitan friends and family got an invitation that looked like a book. It contained individual invitation cards for the rehearsal dinner, the ceremony, and the Sunday barbecue, as well as maps, pickup times, contact numbers, and dress codes. In Naples, they'd never seen anything so organized. They got their butts to the travel agency, bought tranquilizers for their fear of flying, and signed on. Forty of them.

The Neapolitans who arrived for the Wilson-Avallone wedding averaged three suitcases a head. After they finished their American tour (and learned a new word in English: *outlet*, pronounced *aauutlet*), that number rose to four. The women's sporty casual look was white and pastel oxford shirts with tight, tapered pants and ankle boots. Big rhinestone-studded sunglasses held back their perfectly styled hair. The men wore linen jackets and moccasins that were red or lilac. Most had a terra-cotta tan.

In the evening, necklines plunged and heels soared. The ladies' chiffon wraps seemed to match their husbands' silky-soft made-to-order suits. My aunt and uncle hosted a buffet dinner for out-of-town guests two nights before the wedding. "Katherine," my aunt whispered to me soon after the Neapolitans had stepped down from the bus in their stilettos and Maglis and partaken of the buffet, *"there's nothing left to eat."* The caterers had brought huge platters of baby lamb chops, sautéed vegetables, cheese wheels. *"They've already eaten everything."*

What had happened? These were not bingers, and no one was obese. Benedetta later explained to me that the Avallones and their friends had dehungered themselves in the only way possible. "We were just trying to *sfamarci*. We don't know how to do it without pasta, *voi americani come fate?*" How do you Americans do it? How do you satisfy yourselves in this Land Without Pasta?

When it came to determining the menu for our wedding reception, Salva and I decided that rather than serving pasta that would surely not taste like the *primi* Italians were used to, it would be better to stick to typical American dishes. Actually, "Salva and I decided" is perhaps a simplification. Our conversations about the day of the wedding went something like this:

> ME: Shrimp, crab cakes, prime rib. It'll be fine. So, after the first dance, my father will . . .
> HIM: And the shrimp cocktail will be followed by . . . ?
> ME: Give the toast.
> HIM: Toast?
> ME: We need to decide the music for the first dance.
> HIM: We're having toast?
> ME: *Steak!* Crab cakes and steak!
> HIM: And the pasta course?
> ME: I think the seating at our table should be . . .
> HIM: And the pasta course?

He could not get over the fact that at our wedding there would be no pasta. On the most important day of his life, he would not eat pasta: this was extremely difficult to *mandare giù*, to send down or swallow. He and his compatriots would have to eat an entire cow and a school of fish to dehunger themselves. On top of that, they would have to focus their attention (at least part of the time) on something other than the food.

Italian weddings are about what you wear and what you eat. And what other people wear and what they eat. I have been to weddings in Naples where I have sat, masticating, for five straight hours. No dancing, no mingling. Conversation is limited to what is being served and what color sandals the mother of the bride is wearing (with some inevitable soccer discussion among the men).

"Hi, nice to meet you! Where are you from? What do you do?" I do not recommend this line of conversation at a wedding in Italy. I have tried it. Feeling like a bored overstuffed pig, I have ventured out into the taboo territory of putting questions to people I don't know. The response is usually "Here," and the job description is one or two words with the subtext, "I do it because I have to but count the minutes until my next vacation." That shuts me up and sends me back to examining the twelfth plate of food that has been set before me. Praise the food, dissect the consistency of the risotto, and you will find people interested in conversation at Italian weddings, I have discovered. At least that way you'll find something to do with your mouth other than chew.

It is tradition in Naples for the mother of the groom to hand the bride her bouquet, ceremoniously. The photographer is there, ready to record the ritual. The bride and her future mother-in-law look in each other's eyes, faces glowing with respect and love. Other emotions are hidden for later: *Now you're the one who's going to have to make his* pasta con piselli, *grinding up the little pieces of onion! Ha!* Or, on the other side: *You'd better not even think of coming over to our place uninvited!* This is a moment of calm before the storm of daily life and grandchildren, and the photo of it is usually displayed in a silver picture frame in Neapolitan newlyweds' living rooms.

No one told me about this tradition. I had to figure it out for myself. Unfortunately, I figured it out after the photo op.

At the entrance of Washington's National Presbyterian Church, Salvatore and his Neapolitan groomsmen stood tall in white tie and tails, greeting the American guests in their best English. They looked gorgeous. I had explained to my future husband that in the States, tuxedos can be rented, and after his initial terror of powder blue and ruffles, he agreed to let my mother and me herd him and his six buddies to Bob's Tuxedo Junction a few days before the ceremony. The fact that we Americans had successfully costumed the Neapolitan men, and that their women kept saying that they were *elegantissimi! Elegantissimi!* was a great source of pride.

In the women's dressing room, my bridesmaids were adjusting their matching sleeveless sky-blue dresses and putting the finishing touches to their makeup. Benedetta's two sons (Claudio had been born after Emilio, and I was getting the hang of being a *zia*, falling deeply, hopelessly in love with both boys) were playing tag in their ivory silk ringbearer outfits. My sister was trying to fasten my grandmother's necklace around my neck. It had a minuscule silver clasp from around 1910 that was impossible to hook. My mother was in such a state of tension that at a certain point she just started doing laps around the perimeter of the room, managing to look stunning in her eggplant strapless gown despite her anxiety-induced dementia.

The photographer arrived, and told us he wanted to get some candid shots of the wedding preparations. That's when Raffaella came up to me with my bouquet. She was silent, and she was still, two things that seemed odd for my future mother-in-law. I said, "Oh, thanks!" and then laid it down on a coffee table so I could have my hands free to touch up my lipstick again. After a few minutes, she came up to me again with the bouquet. Again I said, "Oh, thanks!" and then gave it to my cousin to hold while I adjusted the netting under my gown.

Apparently, the third time she alerted the photographer. He snapped what is possibly my favorite picture of our whole wedding (followed closely by the one of Zio Toto doing the twist with a Waspy Massachusetts schoolteacher aunt). In it, Raffaella's two hands are holding mine and the bouquet. She is looking at me with acceptance, gratitude, and love. I am looking over my shoulder, mouth open, shouting something about a safety pin to a bridesmaid who was having an issue with her bra strap.

Maybe it was a good thing that I didn't know about the bouquet ritual. Oblivious to the significance of the moment, I unwittingly was the one to *sdrammatizzare*, and nobody's mascara ran before the ceremony.

Rome

If you asked somebody in one of the lands that Rome conquered two thousand years ago what the Romans were
like, you would probably hear that they were arrogant, aggressive know-it-alls who thought they were the shit. I asked Salva
why he didn't like Rome, and he said that Romans were arrogant, aggressive know-it-alls who thought they were the shit.
Center of the world, and all that (well, they were for an awfully
long time, I wanted to point out . . .). Plus, they don't know how
to cook.

Salva and I had moved to Rome in 2001 and rented a loft in
Trastevere. We didn't sit down with a bottle of wine and decide
our future; we didn't map out, as some couples do, the pros and
cons of staying in Naples or moving north. There was very little
free will in the matter, because we were literally shoved out by
my mother-in-law.

The Avallones owned two apartments on the first floor of
their building in Naples. One was Benedetta's, and the other
was destined for Salvatore and his wife. It was rented out when
Salva was finishing his studies, and I assumed that when we

were married we would move in. We were next in line for the
lasagna in the elevator, after all. I'd even gotten the hang of the
recipe advice via intercom! But Raffaella had other plans. My
mother-in-law almost never speaks in dialect and is careful to
use correct Italian when speaking with family members, but
when she heard us talking about moving into the apartment in
Naples, she used pure Neapolitan. *"Te nè 'a í,"* pronounced *tuh
neh ayeee*. You gotta get outta here. Her middle three fingers
pointed down and sliced the air, showing me that we needed to
leave, and we needed to leave soon.

Wait, wasn't a Neapolitan *mammà* supposed to wring her
hands and beg us to stay close by? Wasn't she worried that her
grandchildren would be raised on processed food, without cud-
dles and the sea and the music of Napoli? No, she wasn't.

"Ketrin, there is no future here. Go to the U.S.! To Rome,
Milan, northern Europe! Anywhere. Naples would be a waste
for you. For me, *figurati che gioia!* It would be such a joy! But for
your family it would be the end. *Niente, non c'è niente a Napoli."* There is nothing in Naples. "I will bring you the food in
my suitcase, wherever you go."

I was shocked. Salva's roots and the Avallones' love ran so
deep that I'd assumed that if we ever suggested leaving, there
would be resistance, a battle even. The opposite happened: the
lady basically kicked us out. She was loving, but she was forceful.

When Salvatore and I talked about it, it was clear that the
idea of leaving Naples didn't make him happy. But he would
follow the plan. In true Neapolitan fashion, the man might be
pampered, but in the end it was a woman who would decide.

Naïvely, I believed that the Eurostar line connecting Italy's
most important cities (Milan, Bologna, Florence, Rome, Naples) was a longitudinal measuring stick in which culture got

more southern in degrees. If people in Florence are more laid-back than in Milan, I figured, then they are very relaxed in Rome, and in Naples, life's a beach. If everyone plays by the rules in Milan, most do in Florence, a few do in Rome, and no one does in Naples.

What I didn't realize was that Italy is a young country. Unification didn't come until 1861, and for a thousand years before that what is now Italy was composed of city-states, each with its own language, culture, and identity. *Insomma*, Naples is not just a more southern version of Rome. It's an entirely different country altogether.

Salva got an internship at the Rome soccer team. He was in the marketing office, working with their sponsorship group. Salva's passion had always been sports. When he graduated from law school, I encouraged him to look for something in sports marketing. After all, the law stuff would come in handy sooner or later. But he left our apartment in the morning with the face of someone going to work in a sweatshop. *It's not my team, Katherine,* he explained to me when I wondered at his lack of enthusiasm. I would find him sitting in a chair near the window looking at the "view" of the building across from ours in Trastevere. He might as well have been uprooted and dumped in Detroit.

Raffaella advised me about what to cook. *Maybe we shouldn't have moved to Rome after all* was met with, "If you can't find *friarielli* greens at the market, Ketrin, try *broccoletti*." She knew that if her son ate what he loved, things would work themselves out. *He mutters under his breath how he can't stand Rome,* I would tell her. So? she answered. Let him mutter.

During the week, I spent my time reproducing Raffaella's recipes and keeping Salva away from the Romans. But every weekend and holiday, we were on the train for Naples.

San Gennaro

O ne such holiday was the feast of San Gennaro, the patron saint of Naples. "He ain't no second-class saint," a wizened man told me in the Duomo on the nineteenth of September when I went to witness the miracle of San Gennaro. Only a few weeks before, the government had issued a decree eliminating the holidays of patron saints. There are about twenty important saints' days throughout the year, and the government decided that they could be attached to celebrations on the Sunday before or after. The decree would mean that those delicious long weekends, or *ponti* (bridges), when Saints Peter and Paul fell on a Friday in Rome or Saint Ambrose fell on a Monday in Milan—or even when it fell on a Tuesday, the vacation bridge spreading over four days!—would disappear. Most Romans thought, Shucks, that would be a shame. Most Milanese thought, Too bad for us but it had to happen sooner or later.

Neapolitans went positively ballistic. Not because they would miss another day off work (although that would be bad enough—"Work makes you throw away your blood" is an oft-heard Neapolitan expression) but because whatever scandalous thing you do in Naples, whatever combinations of food you order, however you eat your pizza, *you do not under any circumstances mess with San Gennaro.*

The old man in the Duomo was a San Gennaro groupie. He came to the Duomo to witness the miracle every year, he told me, he wouldn't miss it for the world. The idea of taking San Gennaro's day away? "You can't just ask San Gennaro to liquefy his blood on Sunday the sixteenth because on Wednesday the nineteenth you have better things to do! *Ma stiamo scherzando!*" You've gotta be kidding.

The decree was a sacrilege, an offensive blow to Neapolitans and to their history and identity. Not to mention, my gentleman friend reminded me, that it would piss off San Gennaro himself, and then the trouble would really start. "San Gennaro loves us. He protects us. *Ci ama. Ci ama . . .*" He kept repeating "he loves us, he loves us," almost inaudibly.

Gennaro was the archbishop of Benevento (a city not far from Naples) in the fourth century, and was beheaded for his Christianity by the Roman emperor Diocletian. Legend has it that a woman collected an ampoule of his blood and conserved it as a relic to be worshipped. The blood solidified, or rather goo-ified. It is kept in an elaborate golden safe at the Duomo, an exquisite church hidden in the dense, old center of Naples. The blood did not, however, remain solid: two times almost every year for centuries (in May and in September) a miracle occurs— the blood in the vial liquefies.

On those rare occasions when the blood has stayed solid, disaster has struck the city of Naples—or so it seems to Neapolitans. They will point out that after San Gennaro's blood failed to liquefy in 1980, an earthquake struck Naples and killed nearly three thousand people. Another solid-blood year was 1528, when plague devastated the city. If the blood stays solid, Naples could be prey to any catastrophe from the eruption of Vesuvius to international terrorism.

So it is no wonder that women stay in the church the day and night before praying to San Gennaro to liquefy his blood and thus protect the city. These faithful *signore* don't take their eyes off the statue of the saint, which is displayed next to the altar. He has a pointy red hat, a red cape, and a pose that is serene and Buddha-like. He's kind of grimacing, though, and honestly looks a little pissed off.

The women flatter him. *"San Gennà, comme si bbello,"* how handsome you are! And *"Tu si 'o primmo santo nuosto,"* you are our first, our most important saint! (As the competition between the saints is ferocious, the women have to reassure him that he's their guy.)

We were packed like sardines in the side chapel of the Duomo, where the safe was located. In just a few minutes the mayor of Naples, with the archbishop, would open it with a special golden key to take out the vial of blood. When the vial was removed, there would be a procession into the narthex and we would all follow the blood, the priests, and the politicians to the main altar, where the blood would be placed next to the statue of the saint. Only then would we learn whether the blood had liquefied.

I had come to the ceremony alone. "I want to go with you to San Gennaro," I told Raffaella when she described the blood and screaming and magic that went on at the Duomo. "Oh, we don't go to San Gennaro," she told me. Then she continued to tell me how women weep and wail all night long to the saint.

They fall on the floor! They start screaming curse words at him if the blood doesn't liquefy—even the eighty-year-olds! They . . .

"Wait—you don't go?" I was surprised. Raffaella is devout, and she is Neapolitan. Yet she had never been to the Duomo on September 19 to witness the miracle? I couldn't figure out why. "Can I ask Zia Pia?" Raffaella's sister Pia is even more devout than she is. She regularly makes pilgrimages to Lourdes and Medjugorje with twenty of her friends. Recently I got a call from her as her tour bus was en route to the Medjugorje shrine. Earlier, I had asked her about her frittata and she wanted to make sure I had the recipe right. In mid-conversation I heard a booming voice amplified by the microphone on the bus. "Our Father, who art in Heaven . . ."

"Gotta go! It's the *Padrenostro*! Remember, one egg for every one hundred grams of spaghetti! And then throw an extra egg in at the end for good measure!" (One Lord's Prayer for every ten Hail Marys is the rosary ratio. Zia Pia probably throws in an extra *Padrenostro*, too—she's that kind of lady.)

Surely Zia Pia would be at the Duomo praying to the saint all night long, I figured. But when I asked her about the miracle, her sentences (like Raffaella's) started with, "*Si dice che*"—I've heard that . . . She'd never been, either.

I soon realized that it was a matter of class. San Gennaro is a saint of the *popolino*, the "little people," the working class. The Duomo is located in the poor inner city of Naples, and the ceremony itself is viewed by many middle- and upper-class Neapolitans as a hocus-pocus ritual that gets the ignorant *popolino* worked up.

That is how I, a Protestant, a rational anthropologist, ended up alone at the Duomo. I expected folklore. I expected voodoo. I didn't expect to be profoundly moved.

The tension in the side chapel grew. The ornate, frescoed chamber smelled of incense mixed with BO. I rested my arm on what I thought was a pedestal but soon realized was a lady's shelflike hip. We were that close. As we all waited for the muckety-mucks to arrive with their Alice in Wonderland golden key, there was silence. There was no wailing. There was no screaming. Even the man next to me had stopped murmuring, "*Ci ama*." There was only prayer.

Only prayer . . . until a cellphone started ringing. Its standard default ring signaled that the owner was of the older generation. It was in a purse wedged in the middle of the crowd, forgotten by the owner (whose mind was certainly on San Gennaro's blood). There were a few whispered, "It's yours!" "No! It's yours!" until one of the priests waiting next to the safe shot his finger to his lips and performed a hearty, loud *Sssssshhhhhh!* that involved his entire cassocked body.

When the mayor and archbishop arrived with the key, people started pushing and standing on their tippy-toes in a futile attempt to see whether the blood was liquid. "*Si vede?*" Can you see? they started asking each other. "*È liquido?*" Is it liquid? And then, "He's closing the safe! He has the blood!"

The man next to me had begun to cry quietly. He was wiping his nose. He saw me looking at him. "*Signurí, lloro 'o ssanno! Lloro sì e noi no!*" They already know! They know and we don't. It was almost unbearable that the priests knew whether the blood had liquefied and we would have to wait.

Thankfully we didn't have to wait for long. We followed the procession, led by the vial of blood (held in a golden reliquary high above the head of the bishop) to the altar where the statue of San Gennaro watched over the proceedings. The bishop po-

sitioned the reliquary near the altar—ceremoniously, calmly,
God! he was taking forever!—and we tried to distinguish
whether the black that we saw in the ampoule was liquid or
solid. It was impossible to tell.

Then the bishop raised a white handkerchief, the symbol
that the blood had liquefied.

At that precise moment, San Gennaro, with his red cape
and pointy hat and pissed-off expression, became a rock star. He
was the Beatles, he was Elvis, he was Madonna at Madison
Square Garden. The crowd gave it up, cheering and clapping
and crying. Outside, fireworks started popping. The bishop announced, bellowing over the crowd, that when he opened the
safe, the blood was *already liquid*. "People of Naples!" he
paused, waiting for the commotion to quiet down. "San Gennaro loves us! San Gennaro will protect us!" The crowd answered with shouts of *Evviva San Gennaro!* Long live San
Gennaro! Then he repeated, *"Cari Napoletani,* dear people of
Naples, the blood was *already liquid."*

My gentleman friend shook his head in amazement and
gratitude. *"Era già sciolto,"* it was already liquid. His subtext was:
Despite my hard life, despite the fact that I'm unemployed and
my son has gotten in with the *camorra,* despite this, *I am loved.*
I am so loved that it was already liquid. And there I was worried
and lacking in faith!

The blood, in its magnificent orbed scepter, was carried by
the bishop down the aisle, lined today by a red carpet. The
pushing became ridiculous. I touched (I think) boobs, thighs,
elbows, wispy old-man hair, sweaty underarms. And I was
touched in ways that probably would be considered molestation
in some countries. But what everybody wanted to touch was the
blood.

Again, we would have to wait. After mass, the bishop announced that the relic would be available for kissing between four and six that afternoon. Only those hours. (So it's pointless to get your hopes and puckers up before that!) He also announced that someone had lost a set of keys—he would keep them at the altar after the service.

There was one last, explosive *Evviva San Gennaro!*, followed by applause, before everyone left the Duomo, exhausted but renewed. Confident of the protection and love of that little Buddha with his pointy hat.

Wall-to-Wall Carpeting

Raffaella visited us often in Rome. We decided to look for a bigger apartment—Salva's internship had become a job in sports marketing, and he had made some Neapolitan friends in Rome and wasn't grumbling so much about the Romans. We were planning (read: I was chomping at the bit) to start a family. Raffaella helped us find and remodel a new place near the Colosseum.

From the time I was a little girl, I imagined that my home as a grown-up would have wall-to-wall carpeting. I didn't have a specific mental image of where my home would be, whether it would be a house or an apartment, in the city or in the country, in the United States or abroad. But I knew that when it was my turn to decide for myself, there would be no talk of area rugs or parquet. My family's and my bare feet would sink into soft, thick, creamy carpets in our home.

My parents' house in Bethesda, Maryland, is not cozy. The living areas (called "the sitting room" and "the craft room" by a team of designers in the eighties, no TV room or actual *living* room for us) look a little like Louis XIV met up with Liberace and went to a Sotheby's auction. The walls are painted to look like marble. Statues of whirling dervishes stand on gilt pedestals. There are small, valuable Persian rugs on the wood floors.

My childhood longing for wall-to-wall carpeting bespoke a desire for us to be a "normal" suburban family, and a need for comfort, quiet, and peace. I could hang out barefoot and in PJs on a carpet. Loud voices would be absorbed, not echoed. One day, when I was big, I would cuddle with a golden retriever or a child of my own on my carpet (in some soft pastel color) without being eyed by a nineteenth-century nude lady in a painting.

"*Amore*, there is bug inside," Salva told me gently, when he understood that the wall-to-wall carpeting issue was close to my heart. He was trying to talk me out of it with sensitivity, using English instead of Italian, since he knew it was a touchy subject. What he meant was that wall-to-wall carpeting was not hygienic, particularly in Italy, where there is so much dust in the stone buildings.

"Do you mean dust mites? What, dust mites can't live in area rugs? Or you just want to get freezing marble so if we have children they'll be forced to wear ski socks in the apartment and probably crack their heads on the travertine?"

"*Shh, shhh*. There now."

I had known the battle was coming. I had never seen wall-to-wall carpeting in Italy. I didn't know whether it was a matter of aesthetics, or the fact that marble is inexpensive, or the reality of the "bug inside." Whatever the reason, people looked at me like I was nuts when I said the word *moquette* (there's not even an Italian word for it! They had to use the French word! Where had I ended up?).

There were so many decisions to be made. How big to make the *salotto*, or living room? Will the dining room be a room of *rappresentanza,* for formal entertaining? Should the kitchen be small and compact, or American with Formica and room to play? These questions brought to a head the central one: What kind of people are we, American or Neapolitan?

Since Salva was working, it was Raffaella who jumped on the train and accompanied me to the architects, the carpenter, the upholstery guy, the marble cutter. These artisans, after they understood that the apartment was mine, would explain to me the advantages of this or that molding, this or that kind of wood for the paneling. Then Raffaella would take over. Of course they need a separate room and bathroom for their live-in nanny (but the apartment is small! And we didn't even have children yet!). Of course they prefer a small kitchen, because it's easier to cook well in a small kitchen (but I'm uncoordinated and will burn myself!). Of course the curtains must have brass rods with curlicues and the door handles must have silk tassels tied on them (but if we have kids?). The countertops near the stove should be travertine, though it's a shame that you can't put lemon or anything hot on them. Can't spill on them, in fact. *Ma sono bellissimi!*

What did I want for my home? What kind of wife and mother would I be? I hadn't figured it out yet. I listened to Raffaella's advice and nodded and said, "I'll talk it over with Salva" until Raffaella offhandedly said these words: "Oh, and I meant to tell you, when Nino worked at the hotel he had a client who sold beautiful Persian area rugs. We have a bunch of them in the basement. The colors are gorgeous—deep red, midnight-blue . . ."

When I get riled up, you can tell from my upper lip. It starts to quiver. It's where I hold my tension. Not in my stomach, or my shoulders. My lip started to tremble, but Raffaella didn't notice. She was talking about the carpenter and the kitchen cupboards. Finally, when she said, "off-white trim," I burst into tears.

"*No! Non ce la faccio più!*" I can't take it anymore. And I stormed off.

I canceled all my appointments with Raffaella for the next week. Oh, I have to meet a friend on Tuesday. Wednesday I have a dubbing turn . . . that lasts all day. No need to come to Rome, thank you very much. I snapped at Salva and didn't answer Raffaella's calls. I wanted this home to be mine, bug inside or not.

By the time we got to the bug-in-the-rug conversation, Salva was handling me with kid gloves, because he could see how upset I was. He folded me in his arms when I started to cry, blubbering and letting it all out. "But I want a playroom, *amore*, I want to spill on my counters! I don't want to *rappresentare* with our dining room! I don't want a lady from the Philippines living in a closet! I don't want tassels on the doors. I want air-conditioning everywhere! *I want the bug inside!*"

"Have you told my mother these things, Ketrin?"

"Not exactly."

"She wants to help us. She won't be offended if you say what you want. She's not *permalosa*."

"But when we talk about choices for the apartment she says things like *si fa*—this is what's done. Like it's the only way to do things here. She's the expert."

"*She* decides for her home and *you* decide for ours. That is what's done here."

I loved him a lot.

I answered Raffaella's call on my cellphone the next day. My end of the conversation was tense and fake. Hers was relaxed. She'd heard of an acupuncturist that she wanted to get

Nino to; the stuffed zucchini she had made for a lunch the day before had turned out exquisite. Surprisingly, she didn't mention the architect or the carpenter or any of the arrangements. "Ketrin, my friend Paola wants to meet you. She said Saturday afternoon we can stop by for a coffee, what do you say?"

Salva and I were going to Naples for the weekend, but I didn't feel like accompanying her to the *salotto* of one of her chic friends. I didn't want to listen to her tell her friends about "our" decisions regarding shower stalls and shelves. But I felt guilty saying no after I'd been avoiding her for a week. And I had been working up a monologue in which I described how although I found the doorknob rosettes she had chosen lovely, I wanted first to make sure that there was air-conditioning, everywhere.

Paola Martone lived on the top floor of an apartment building overlooking the Bay of Naples. Raffaella and I squeezed into the tiny elevator, the sweet smell of her perfume enveloping us. She pushed a stray hair from my forehead. "You'll *love* her apartment," she told me. Oh, would I? I was irritated. I wanted to get this over with and go home.

A blond, curvy lady with enormous collagen-filled lips opened the door. *"Raffffffa!"* she cooed, as my mother-in-law hugged her with a *"Paoliiiiina!"*

That's when I looked down to see the lady's elegant beige Magli heels resting on thick, royal-blue wall-to-wall carpeting. I understood why we were here.

"*Paoliii*, thanks so much for having us, honey. I wanted to show Ketrin what's possible with wall-to-wall carpeting. Yours is the most beautiful in Naples."

Autospurgo

S oon after we moved into our new apartment, I learned that there was no surer way to provoke a fight with my husband than to throw the wrong thing down the sink, the bidet, the shower drain, or the toilet. We, along with most young couples who redo their homes in Italy (with even more likelihood if there is a foreigner in the mix), have major plumbing problems.

The ancient Romans figured out how to flush toilets, and imported water from miles away for their sinks and elaborate fountains. This was over two thousand years ago, when the rest of the world was using buckets and digging holes in the dirt. But that expertise didn't trickle down to contemporary Italian plumbers. It seems that the basic rule for Roman toilets is: the longer ago the system was put in, the better it works.

While Raffaella and I picked out curtain rods and searched high and low for synthetic countertops that would stand the test of my acidic American salad dressing, our plumber was screwing up big-time. He decided to put one tiny drain, which would service the whole apartment, in the corner opposite the kitchen and bathrooms, far away from the fixtures.

Along with the wall-to-wall carpeting and air-conditioning, a disposal in the kitchen was one of my longings. The Avallones had never seen one. I explained how convenient it would be, especially given this country's garbage collection difficulties. Our plumber installed one, but did not communicate three important facts: 1) that disposals are illegal in many parts of Italy, 2) that ours could never be used because the tubes for the plumbing in our apartment were too small, and 3) that he had rigged our pipes and our drains in a such a way that nothing could ever go down the kitchen sink but water.

Salva had a sense that the disposal (*tritarifiuti* in Italian—chop up the trash) was a recipe for disaster. "Let's not use it, Ketrin, okay?" Oh, I thought, he's just a traditional Neapolitan man who is wary of technology. Especially newfangled appliances in the kitchen. His mother still has clay pots, for Christ's sake! I will introduce them all to the wonders of the microwave! I will usher them into the twenty-first century in our high-tech American kitchen! These were my thoughts as I stuffed the contents of a two-pound bag of *erbette*, spinach-like greens, down our new disposal.

The *erbette* had gone bad. I had bought them and forgotten about them, which is something that you just don't do in Italy. Nobody was home, and I wanted to eliminate all traces of them. I wanted to mince them to oblivion. They never existed, I told myself as I turned on the disposal. The green mass went down okay, it was only a minute or so after the procedure began that I saw green goo start to slime up from the bubbling drain.

Salva and I were Lucy and Ricky Ricardo that evening when he got home. "*Amore?* There are plumbing problems."

"*Perchè hai quella roba verde dappertutto?*" Why are you covered with green slime, dear?

Physically speaking, the locus of anger in many American men is their chest. It is a puffed-up chest, a *who-do-you-think-you're-messing-with* chest. The arms are still, the head up, and the torso rotates from side to side. It is a torso that is looking around to see who else might be trying to fuck with it. *Bring it on.* American men often become larger in their anger, more horizontal and more intimidating. Salvatore, meanwhile, like many Neopolitans, gets angry with his legs close together and his feet in first position. His heels touching and toes splayed outward, he moves vertically. There was a Neapolitan toy sold after the war, when people would invent anything to make a few lire, called *scicchegnacco int'a butteglia*. It was a marble suspended in a bottle that would go up and down when children shook it. It is this image that best conveys Salva's up-and-down anger, his long, lean body expressing its *furia*.

I know that it's not healthy or psychologically enlightened to engage in name-calling. I know that would be the first thing that we would learn in an anger management seminar. But have the leaders of those seminars ever had to call the *autospurgo* at 3:00 A.M., after six hours of wiping and plunging and dumping? (Collins translates it as a "gully sucker." My not-so-technical translation would be "a man who comes, sucks, and pumps.") On that night of the green slime, we were not managing our anger in any sort of enlightened way.

"*Ma quanto sei scema!*" (How stupid you are! His hand hits his forehead at a forty-five-degree angle in the Neapolitan gesture meaning there's nothing inside your head, your brains are gone.)

"*Sei uno stronzo.*" (You're an asshole. No hand gestures, but boy, is my upper lip quivering.)

"*Pigliati una camomilla.*" (Have a chamomile tea, but no, it's not the kind suggestion that I might benefit from the calming effects of an herbal tea. The translation might be something along the lines of get a grip on yourself. His hand is doing the motion of lifting a cup of tea.)

"*Vaffanculo.*" (Fuck you.)

"*Stai dando i numeri!*" (Literally, you're giving the numbers. His hand hits his forehead perpendicularly, which means that I've gone from being just stupid to being out of my mind.)

"The numbers" in Naples refers to the centuries-old *tombola*, a game similar to bingo. Each number from one to ninety is associated with a person, an object, a concept, or an event. So, for example, the number 61 is hunting and 51 is a garden or yard. If I dream of hunting for a mouse outside, I might be advised to play the number 61, 51, and 11 for mouse at the lottery the next day. I must consult an expert (usually an old wizened Neapolitan grandmother who has "the gift") who can interpret the numbers.

When must I play the numbers? Either when I have a strange dream or when something completely out of the ordinary occurs. For example, several years ago I had my wallet stolen in Rome the day after my sister had her wallet stolen in New York and the day before my mother had her wallet stolen in Washington. Now, either word had gotten around the globe about the Wilson ladies' absentmindedness, or something supernatural was up. My father-in-law called me immediately when we realized the "coincidence."

"I've found someone who is *bravissima*, an expert at interpreting your numbers," he told me. "You're going to play them, aren't you?"

I didn't, in fact, play them, but learned that my number would have been 79, 70, and 52 (79 for thief, 70 for a tall building, New York, 52 for *la mamma*).

Benedetta, at one point during her teenage years, was dating a guy named Luca who was unstable and had abandonment issues (his nickname was 'o *pazzo* or Luke the Crazyman). When my sister-in-law decided to break up with him, he threatened suicide, calling out from the top of the rocky promontory of Posillipo where he lived that he loved her and would throw himself into the Bay of Naples below if she didn't take him back. In the crowd that soon gathered around him, there were of course people trying to dissuade him from jumping. But there were others who, in hushed tones among themselves, whispered, *"Sta dando i numeri"*—he's giving the numbers. It was an event that was out of the ordinary, and smart Neapolitans knew they had to find a soothsayer in the crowd to interpret the numbers so they could play the lottery. There was even, Salva tells me, one man calling to passersby on the road, "Ladies and gentlemen, there's a crazy man about to jump. Come and find out the numbers!"

So, back to our fight. According to my husband, I am so out of my mind that I'm "giving the numbers," and according to me, he is quite simply being an asshole. I remember with nostalgia the days when we were first dating and I didn't understand Italian and he didn't understand English. What wonderful discussions we had! How we saw eye-to-eye on everything! It was idyllic. As I learned more Italian and he learned more English, though, our communication became more complicated.

I realize now that the real difficulties began when we mastered the subjunctive and the conditional. When you are limited to the present indicative of verbs, you are inevitably drawn to the present: to needs, to wants, to likes and dislikes. *I need to pee. I like ice cream, do you?* What you say is necessary and true, and that makes for great relationships. Just look at the simple beauty of second-grade friendships as evidence.

Unfortunately, though, if you know how to use the subjunctive and the conditional, the relationship changes. You start thinking, and then saying, *If you hadn't insisted on the disposal, we wouldn't have stayed up cleaning pipes* and *I wish you weren't such an asshole.* Life is no longer in the here and now but is being compared to some ideal in your brain. Gone are the days of *I'm hungry* and *Do you want to cook* erbette? It is now *I wish we had hired a different plumber* and *There wouldn't be any green slime if you hadn't said we needed to eat more vegetables.* Your life and the person you love are measuring up (or *not* measuring up) to the ideals that you've created with your fancy old verb forms.

I suppose I must be grateful that, despite the complicated nuances of our language of litigation, in the language of making up, nothing is lost in translation. I threw a balled-up Kleenex at him as a peace offering. He grabbed me in his arms and said, "*Ma quanto mi fai arrabbiare!*" You get me so darned mad! We admitted to each other that neither of us liked *erbette*—they were nothing compared to the *scarole* sautéed with olives that you find in Naples.

"Promise me that you won't use the *tritarifiuti*? Ever again?"

I promised him. It has stayed under our sink, unused, ever since.

Pasta alla Genovese

After our frequent plumbing rows, there were frequent occasions of making up. In the summer of 2004 I found out that we were pregnant with our first child.

I learned that what a Neapolitan mother eats during her pregnancy is very, very important. I'm not talking extra protein, or cutting out caffeine and sushi. I'm talking cravings. If the lady doesn't satisfy her cravings, the baby will pay. Things can get ugly.

"I really have a *voglia* (craving) for *rigatoni alla Genovese*," I told Raffaella sometime during my fourth month. I didn't realize at the time how important this comment would be, that it would set a great ball rolling. In Naples, if a pregnant woman has a craving that is not satisfied, her baby will be born with a *voglia*, or a mark. Usually this mark is a skin discoloration in the form of the object of her craving: a strawberry, for example, or a little cup of coffee. In the case of *pasta alla Genovese*, the birthmark might come in the form of a great big onion tattoo.

Despite its name, *la Genovese*, the sauce has nothing to do with the Ligurian city. Various theories have been offered to explain why this typically Neapolitan dish is called the dish from Genoa (one is that the Neapolitan cook who invented it was nicknamed 'o *Genovese*), but nobody knows for sure. The fact is that you cannot find this recipe anywhere in Italy except Naples.

It is a kind of *ragù*, in the sense that the sauce is cooked with meat, but it is characterized by the kilos of Montoro onions that are sautéed to give it flavor.

Raffaella immediately dispatched Nino to the market to buy the onions, and bought her train ticket to Rome. Her grandson would not risk being born an onion face.

I was shamelessly spoiled, but honestly didn't feel guilty about it. I deserved to have my cravings satisfied; I deserved to see the schedules of my husband's entire family governed by my every whim. I deserved to be spoon-fed onion *ragù*, and lie on the couch watching bikini-clad starlets dance. I deserved all of this not simply because I was pregnant, but because the rest of my time was spent at the painful, exhausting, humiliating *centro di analisi*.

The folder that contained the results of the lab tests was so thick you could almost call it a binder. The receptionist at the diagnostic center handed it to me, closed with a sticker for privacy, and I had the same feeling as when I was little and it was time to see my report card. Let's see how I've done, or rather how my blood and urine have done. Do I eat right? Is my lifestyle healthy? I can't wait to see!

My excitement turned to disappointment and confusion when I opened the folder to find that my lymphocytes were at 1,800 per microliter of blood and my cytokines were at 1.4. What did that mean? I leafed through the folder to find very ambiguous graphs that had disturbingly sharp peaks and cavernous lows . . . my C-reactive proteins were doing some pretty funky stuff. Did I have something serious? To find out, I had to make an appointment at another office on another day in another area of the city. This center did not diagnose, it only took your blood, urine, and stool samples, then ran the necessary tests.

When I went the first time to have my blood taken, I was unprepared. I had had breakfast, and blood is taken only on an empty stomach. So I was told to go home and come back the next day. When I showed up hungry and cranky the next morning, the receptionist asked where my pee was.

I really did not know how to answer, the matter being complicated by the fact that I did not know the word for bladder. So I repeated the question: *Dov'è l'urina?* The ball had been deftly bounced back into her court. *"Non l'ha portata?"* You didn't bring it? Now, whether it's linguistic, or because of my *permalosità* (oversensitivity), I tend to interpret questions formed in the negative about what I've *not* done as accusations. They're really not, particularly in Italian. They are simply factual. "Did this lady before me with the accent not bring her own pee?" the receptionist was asking.

It proved to be a problem. Once again I was sent home, this time with instructions to buy a little plastic pee cup at the pharmacy and to come the next day with my pee. But not any old pee, only the *first pee* of the morning. The purest pee. This kind of pee is best for the tests, apparently. Don't be coming in with any of that watered-down stuff, the *centro di analisi* clarified, we want the yellowest, smelliest pee you got.

This was all logistically problematic given the fact that I had to drive in Roman traffic the next morning with my plastic pee cup, without having had any sort of coffee or breakfast. Where was I to put the pee? The cup had a lid, yes, but it was flimsy. Aha! A lightbulb turned on in my brain. I didn't have to hold it in my hand or balance it on the seat next to me. I could put it in the little coffee cup holder! It fit snugly, and I was off.

Tutto a posto, or everything in its place, everything going well, until a kamikaze *motorino* swerved in front of me and I had to slam on the brakes. I need not delve into the details of where my pure pee ended up, but my next stop was the car wash, not the *centro di analisi*. When I returned to the center, I did so on foot, carrying my deep yellow pee cup very carefully by hand.

I really wanted to find out from those little old ladies how they did it: I now noticed that everyone who entered the *centro di analisi* was discreetly carrying their pee. A veritable bring-your-own-pee party! At my doctor's office in Maryland, there is a sterile bathroom where you put your pee in a cubbyhole. From there, it mysteriously disappears—you don't have to hand it off, or even write your name on it. It's a totally anonymous procedure.

I struck up a conversation with a grandmother next to me, pointing to the plastic cup in her hand and saying, *"Difficile, no?"* "No!" she answered. "It's more difficult with the feces." What were they going to make me do next?

Mercifully, the feces examination was reserved for Salvatore. To be present at our son's birth, he had to be tested for salmonella. He was given a little transparent gelato cup and a plastic spoon and told to bring his sample to the *centro di analisi*. Now it was bring your own poo.

"Ketrin? Mi porti un giornale?" His request for a newspaper was the first coherent communication that emerged from behind our locked bathroom door the next morning. Salva had been in there muttering and cursing for the better part of an hour (the Virgin Mary had been called all sorts of unkind things

in Neapolitan dialect). The atmosphere was tense. I was confronted with the choice of giving my husband the *Gazzetta dello Sport* or the *International Herald Tribune*. Was the newspaper to help him relax enough to relieve himself or to be implemented in another way?

I was taking too long.

"*Ketrin!*"

"*Ma per . . . leggere?*" If it was to be read, then I should definitely go with the pink *Gazzetta* with the picture of the star soccer player Buffon jumping for a miraculous save against Milan.

"*No! Macché leggere?*" Not to read! What are you thinking?

And so I handed him the *Tribune*.

Our bathroom was plastered with the advertising supplement of the newspaper—really, there are so many reasons to visit Vietnam!—when Salva emerged. He'd been stabbing at turds for an awfully long time, poor guy. In his triumphant hand was the little plastic cup, on which he wrote his name with Magic Marker: SALVATORE AVALLONE. He was ready for show-and-tell at the *centro di analisi*.

"*Ecco.*" Here it is, he told the receptionist later, and placed his poo proudly on the counter.

Recently my father told me that he had to send a stool sample to a lab in suburban Maryland. I was interested to find out how that worked in America. As in Italy, a little plastic ice cream spoon was provided, but it blew my mind when he told me that he *sent it away in the mail*. You mean you took your little transparent cup to the post office? No, he told me, he put the little anonymous prestamped package in the door slot!

"Now, that's what I call a great country, where you can send your shit out anonymously into the world without carrying it anywhere!" I was about to break into "The Star-Spangled Banner" when my father told me the addendum: the sticker with the lab's address had come off and his poo was returned to sender.

Vestiti

After Salvatore and I had survived the *centro di analisi*, there was nothing that could rock our confidence as new parents. That is, until we tried to figure out how to clothe our newborn.

The following are comments Raffaella has made to family members who are not properly dressed:

"*Nino, mi sembri un sacco di patate.*" Nino, you look like a sack of potatoes.

"*Amore mio, mi sembri figlio di nessuno.*" Sweetheart, you look like the child of no one.

"*Che sei? Uno scaricatore di porto?*" What are you, a dockworker?

Family members are subject to these comments if their shirts are untucked, if there is lint on their sweaters, or if one of their pant legs is hitched in a sock. If they have a stain, or a collar that has not been ironed to perfection, they might get a simple "Don't worry, there's time to change before we go."

I am off-limits—I do not receive these comments. This may be because I am a daughter-in-law. It may be because everyone knows I'm *permalosa*. I think, though, that it has more to do with the fact that Raffaella first met me in fleece: there was nothing but room for improvement. There was nowhere to go but up from my bingeing, intellectual feminist look of 1996.

I get a proud smile if I wear something that matches. I get a *come sei carina!* You look great! if I so much as put a belt around my jeans. That beautiful freedom, however, that license that I hope lasts until I enter an Italian nursing home, does not carry over to my children.

When I was eight months pregnant with my son, the private clinic where I was to give birth gave me a list of clothes to bring with me for the newborn. There were articles of clothing that I'd never heard of before: *bodino, ghettina, tutina*. They all ended in *-ino* or *-ina*, which meant they were little and cute, but what were they?

If this wasn't enough to send my hormone-assaulted brain into a spin, the clinic specified the required type of fabric. So my fetus and I set out to find a *ghettina di lana leggera* (light wool leggings) and other outfits that would compose his first foray into the world of Italian fashion.

My plan was to hand the list to the lady in the store with my credit card and be done with it.

The shopkeeper was around sixty, a beautiful, gravelly-voiced grandmother. I was done for. Approximately two hours and hundreds of euros later, my fetus and I emerged, sweaty and agitated. The *signora* had regaled me with questions. Which kind of cotton do you prefer? Lace at the collar or on the sleeves? Oh, she was full of questions. But somehow I couldn't get up the nerve to ask mine. I had only two, and they were fundamental at that point in time.

Which is cheaper? And, where is the bathroom?

Later, I handed my completed assignment over to Raffaella.

She put her glasses on to examine the list and to feel the tiny garments. She was Giorgio Armani before a *Vogue* photo shoot. She was a Hollywood image consultant. She described the workmanship of each minuscule article, saying things like "cross-stitch embroidery" and "cream and sky-blue appliqué." I tried to figure out if these descriptions meant the clothes passed the test. I did not want to visit the exacting, gravelly-voiced grandmother at the baby store again.

My son was not yet at term and his look was already being scrutinized. He would have to be stylish and elegant as soon as he saw the light of day. Weren't they going to give him a couple of months to get into the swing of things? Couldn't he be given a few weeks of leeway on account of his American, sweatpant-wearing mother?

"*Hmmmm . . .*" Raffaella would have to think about it, work on it, match some of these things with items she had bought. But it looked like my job was over. Hallelujah.

"You know, in the U.S., we usually buy baby clothes that can go in the washing machine," I ventured, finding renewed confidence in my ninth month.

"Are you serious? They get ruined that way! What about the satin lock-down stitch?"

I didn't mention that we also tend not to spend two hundred bucks on a wardrobe that would last less than a month, and that was destined to be covered with milk and vomit. It was pointless. I didn't want my son to get the *figlio di nessuno*, the "no one's kid" label, as soon as he was born, so I let Nonna Raffaella handle my newborn's wardrobe. After all, I figured, who cares what they dress him in? I had enough on my mind.

So it's ironic that what I remember most vividly about the birth of my first child is a tiny cardigan of merino wool. When the nurse brought Anthony in, an hour after our C-section (I do not believe that the disproportionately high percentage of cesareans in Italy has nothing to do with aesthetics. The mommy looks better, the baby looks better. The mommy can get her hair done and hands manicured the morning of the birth; the baby's head is a perfect orb. I mean, natural delivery? *Per favore!*), he was wearing a pinstripe lambswool sweater. It was cerulean and cream, and must have been chosen by Nonna Raffaella and approved by a panel of nurses. His hair had been combed to the side, a dab of cologne had been applied behind his ear.

My first thoughts were: What if he doesn't like me? What if I have bad breath? What does my hair look like? Can somebody please get me a *mirror* in here?

I was ready for fatigue, depression, joy. I wasn't ready for an eighth-grade crush. No one prepared me for the butterflies in my stomach, the dry mouth, the sweaty hands. Oh Lord, help me. For the second time in my life I was falling for an Italian man.

"*Mamma!*" Raffaella came into the room and used a term that nearly paralyzed me with its weight of responsibility. All those *m*'s spoke of lasagna made by hand, ironing shirts for a thirty-year-old, and a love that was *totale*. She saw my face, she saw Anthony in my arms looking for my breast, and she knew that it was time to *sdrammatizzare*. "Did you see the pullover? It's so elegant!" Yes, he was elegant, and the sweater was a jewel. Let's focus on the lamb's wool.

But where was Salvatore?

"He's splashing some water on his face. [Read: bawling for joy in the men's room.] Tomorrow I'm thinking that Anthony would look dashing in the white silk romper suit. What do you say?"

"I totally agree."

Extracomunitari

The women of Salva's family assumed that I would hand over my baby—the piece of my heart, as they say in Naples—to someone from the Philippines, Ukraine, Sri Lanka, or Brazil. It was assumed that this lady would be not too attractive, not too expensive, and would live in a corner of our apartment and have Sundays off.

Things that were not taken into consideration were: carpet time, take-out dinners, sweatsuits with vomit stains on them. The concept, *insomma*, that mothering would be my job.

Immigrants from Sri Lanka are dirty, and *The great thing about Filipina domestic workers is that they stay out of your way,* or *Brazilians are too pretty to be live-in babysitters* are all comments I heard from Italian mothers. Mothers who otherwise seemed to be kind, sensitive people dismissed whole continents because *fanno schifo,* they're gross. I, too, was an *extracomunitaria,* I reminded them. No, Ketrin, Americans don't count! *Extracomunitari* are people from North Africa, from Asia, from poor areas of Ukraine . . . people who don't look like us and who work for us.

Oh, and by the way, Ketrin, why don't you have one?

When Emilio was born, Benedetta had hired a lady named Marieli from Sri Lanka. At the same time, Raffaella and Nino hired her cousin, a young man with a Yankees baseball cap named Mitzi. (Nunzia the working-class Neapolitan had retired—Mitzi helped with the cooking as well as the "heavy cleanings." He was young, strong, and knew how to fix appliances.) Both Raffaella and Benedetta would complain, however, that "they"—referring to Marieli and Mitzi—have no idea what hygiene is (they don't even bidet!); that "they" are clueless when it comes to packaging leftovers. "Look," Benedetta told me one day, holding out a plate of sausages and *ragù*. It was covered with cellophane, but the edges were coming loose. "Marieli did this. This apparently is how they package things in Sri Lanka. *Limitate, sono limitate.*" They are mentally deficient. (Note to self: When in Benedetta's or Raffaella's home, get rid of leftovers and pretend you ate them. Do not try to wrap.) She obviously considered me an Italian *signora*, a lady of the house, who had nothing in common with these *extracomunitari* domestic workers.

But she was wrong. I have the same work permit issues as these women. I am far away from my home like these women. I don't know how to get Italian plastic wrap to stick around the edges of a bowl, just like these women. And I don't bidet. Sure, there are huge differences. I have a lot more resources and a lot less courage than these women. But on a human level, when I hear Neapolitan *signore* complaining about their domestic workers, how they *just don't get it*, I feel like they are talking about me.

How could people feel this way about "the help" and then hand their babies over to them? I wondered.

So I resisted. I became a stay-at-home mom, American-style. I was sleep-deprived and overweight (no bingeing, just eating what I wanted when I wanted it). I wore no makeup, didn't fix my hair. For me, these were the consequences of being a full-time mother with a baby. In a way, I was proud to look so bad: my scrunchies and sneakers were badges of honor, showing the sacrifices that I made for my "work" as parent. I don't sit around pampering myself, my crusty velour pantsuits said, I take this mothering thing *seriously*. I suffer for it.

For the Italian women in my life, my appearance was the start of a slippery slope that would end with unwaxed legs and microwaved dinners. "*Sta diventando una scema appriess'ai bambini*," I heard a friend describe another mother whose nanny had left and who was reduced to wearing sweats at the park like me. She's becoming demented being around the kid so much.

They were not just worried about what I looked like, they were worried about my mental health.

When Anthony was about one and a half, I got a call from Zia Pia. "Ketrin, have you thought about the babysitter idea? You need it. You're with that boy way too much. *È troppo legato a te*." He was too attached to me? But he wasn't even two! Pia's children lived at home until they were thirty! I got riled up. I interpreted her comments as an attack, a judgment on my mothering style. What I didn't understand was that she was not saying I was a bad mother, or that Anthony would suffer. She was saying that I needed to take care of myself. She was thinking of me.

Inexpensive child care is a mixed blessing. In southern Italy, you can hire a live-in nanny for a month at the same rate you would probably pay a New York babysitter for a day at Central Park. It made it *very* hard for me to say no thanks, I like my vomit stains. I like eating from a can, and asking Salva to pick up pizza five times a week. It's *so* good for my child. After all, he gets to be with me, on a carpet!

So I agreed to have someone come in during the day. No serving lunch at the table, or massaging necks, just some cooking and cleaning and taking care of Anthony while I went to get a cappuccino. Of course, he would *never* want to be with her. He would put up with it and count the minutes until I got home. I would help him understand that Mommy needed a little time for herself, too.

One of Anthony's first English expressions was "When de Jackie come?" He would waddle over to the door and sit there, waiting. Another early expression was "Mamma leave now, okay?" Jackie would race him to the park, tell him about climbing to the top of the volcano near Lake Taal in the Philippines when she was a little girl, pretend she was a goalkeeper of the Series A soccer league.

I, meanwhile, learned how the vacuum cleaner worked. I found a fantastic lemony anticalcium spray for cleaning the toilets. I had a blast. I didn't need to get a cappuccino or go to the beauty parlor. I simply needed to do *anything* that did not involve interacting with a two-year-old brain. I had judged my friend who said that you can become demented being around a kid so much, but I started to realize that she could be right. Admittedly, my excitement about getting the crud out of the bathroom tiles was a little disturbing.

For the first time since my English classes in Naples, I decided to go back to teaching.

Act the Food

I strongly believe that acting is the best way to learn another language, to really learn to speak it. Everyone has to create a new persona when they learn a language that is not their own. So, I told Italian friends who wanted to learn English, instead of spending all your time studying grammar, try some dialogues and improvisation exercises. Create a character. The language will get inside you, emotionally and viscerally. You will free yourself of the little judge in your mind who says things like, "Wow, you really sound stupid! Are you *sure* that's the third person singular of that verb?"

An acting school located in a tiny black-box theater near the Colosseum hired me to teach a course for Italians called Acting in English. About ten actors in their twenties and thirties came for the first class. They didn't feel confident speaking English— they'd studied it in school but couldn't seem to *sbloccarsi*, or unblock, themselves with the language. Be an animal in English! I told them. Get pissed off at this other actor who has just stolen your girlfriend! Invent a joke and make us all laugh! Do whatever's necessary to free yourself and go for it.

At the end of the course, I told my students, we would work on dialogues from *Pulp Fiction* and *Death of a Salesman*.

To help my Italian actors find their characters' truth (and focus on something other than their linguistic limits), I introduced some improvisations to tap into their emotional memory. To try to get them to remember the feeling of their first kiss, their rage in an argument with a family member. A moment of joy with a friend. Surprisingly, I got almost nothing from them. Or rather, what I got was fake, demonstrated, showy. I tried to get them to talk (in English, I know it's not easy) about their relationships with their mothers. Rather than tears and depth of feeling, I got "My mother is a little rigid" or "We are different in character, my mother and I." Voices were level, faces were inexpressive. Were these really *Italians*? Talking about their *mamme*? These were people who, when describing the traffic they had encountered coming to class, were as dramatic as Jim Carrey in *Batman*.

Part of the difficulty was cultural. While an American actor will dissect and analyze his parents, an Italian will protect them. There is, still, a certain respect for family. Young Americans often bond by dumping on their parents: Italian *ragazzi* most definitely don't. There are no who-has-the-most-dysfunctional-family competitions.

But the problem was more complicated. I didn't want the actors simply to air their dirty laundry in class, I wanted them to feel and then express with emotional intensity in English. I mulled this over as I walked home from school. Then the light-bulb suddenly appeared above my head. Duh! What was I, a dunce? How long had I been living in Italy? How was it that I kept forgetting that the answer was always in the food?

I put away the Stanislavski and Uta Hagen acting texts for the next class. I told the students that we were going to skip the sense memory exercises, I had to ask their advice on something. I wanted to try out some new recipes for my husband—we'd had a tough period with the baby not sleeping and had been fighting a lot. I wanted to cook something special for him. Can you each describe your favorite dish? If you remember, tell me about the person who makes it for you and how they do it. I need to learn.

The first actor was from Salerno, just south of Naples. He described his grandmother's ravioli. He showed us how her fingers pinched off the little balls of ricotta and *spinaci* and folded the dough in pockets. "In *this* way," he specified, making a perfect *th* sound, tongue between the teeth and all! His eyes were full of tears; he didn't need to tell us that his *nonna* had passed away.

Barbara from Turin showed us how her mother cut the vegetables for the *bagna cauda* stew, and again we knew without being told that Barbara loved and hated her with a passion. She told us that her *mamma* cut everything in *ssstrips* (good—not ztrips! I had been working with them for ages on *s* plus a consonant! *Sssssnow*, not *zznow*. *Seven snakes slept in the snow!*). They lived the emotions honestly through food; they remembered through recipes. They spoke in English, with almost no accent.

Toward the end of our course, when we began to work on dialogues from movies and plays, those actors had so much to think about. The character's truth, their own truth, those big fat American *a*'s that felt so weird in their mouths! But my job as a teacher/director was easy. When they got lost in their brains, when they stopped being honest and started to fake it, I knew how to direct them. Michele, ravioli. Chiara, *pasta alla Genovese*. Barbara, *bagna cauda*. Tap into that and you will give us a performance that is nothing less than inspired.

Cotoletta alla Milanese

When Anthony was two and a half, Salva and I decided it would be a good idea to enroll our son in nursery school. Actually, Salva thought it was a great idea, and I felt like I was dispatching him to a forced-labor camp. Anthony had become a *mammone*, a southern Italian mama's boy, and it was 100 percent my fault.

Before I gave birth to an Italian boy, I had passed judgment quickly and cheerfully on all the mama's boys in Italy. Actually, I had passed judgment on the mothers. After all, the problem with Italian men is really Italian mothers, isn't it? You will never hear blame being placed on an Italian thirty-year-old who still lives at home and has a special "Me and You" telephone contract so he can call his *mamma* free of charge to tell her to put the pasta on, he's coming home from work. That's the *mamma*'s fault, of course! Why does she let him do it? Why does she put the water on to boil?

Before having an Italian son, I thought it was because these Italian women didn't know better. They cooked for and pampered their boys because they obviously hadn't read any books with titles like: *Helping Your Toddler Thrive* or *The Childhood Handbook* or *The No's That Help Them Grow* or *Boundaries and Love*. I mean, would it really be so hard to order some parenting books and make life a lot better for these young men and their future wives?

I was quite sure that my son would never become a *mammone*. I had read the books. Plus, I was American: food would not be the expression of my love. My love as a mother would be expressed by teaching, by guiding, by enriching. By reading! By practicing letters! Mother to son, brain to brain. The bodies and tummies of my son and me would be separated by some good old healthy Anglo-Saxon distance.

That was my thinking before having Anthony. Before hearing his first "*Mammmmmmà*," already the intimate Neapolitan dialect for Mommy; before seeing his little hand twisting his finger in his cheek (in the Italian gesture meaning *delicious*) after nursing from my breast. Um, can I return that *Independence and Boundaries with Your Toddler* book and get my money back?

So I confess that I am *guilty*. Guilty of aggravating Italy's problems—if things follow the *mammone* template, my son will not be part of a flexible and mobile workforce, but will hang out in his boyhood room with soccer trophies and Garfield stickers into his thirties. There will never be an empty nest. (Ah, the laughs I have gotten from my Neapolitan friends when I translate that expression! What do the mothers and fathers do when the kids go off to university so young? they ask. *Si guardono in faccia?* They stare at each other's faces?)

I was trained in my *mammone*-raising not only by my mother-in-law but by the nuns at Santa Chiara nursery school. When I would go to pick up Anthony, the elderly nun at the door, Suor Alfonsina, would tell us how the day went before letting us into the garden to collect our little ones. The conversations went something like this:

"Hello, I'm Anthony's mother. How was he today?" (Read: Did he hit/kick/spit/injure/offend, reflecting horribly on me as a parent and his environment at home?)

"Anthony, Anthony . . . *ah, sì!* He finished most of his pasta but ate none of the *cotoletta.* Does he not like veal cutlets?" She was worried. What *was* the situation at home?

"No . . . I mean yes! We're working on that. At home. And . . . did he play with the other kids?"

"Play?" Suor Alfonsina must have extra patience with this American mother who asks well-intentioned but totally irrelevant questions. "Well, I'm sure he did. And tomorrow maybe we'll start with the meat." She turned to another mother. "*Mamma di Emanuele?* He was such a good boy! He finished all of the pasta with lentils!"

The *mamma* was proud. She beamed.

The menu of the week at the Santa Chiara nursery school was posted next to Jesus on the cross. The fact that conversation at pickup time was relegated to "Leonardo ate all of his tortellini but left some of his meat" and "Does Enrico have a problem with fruit?" made me wonder how these nuns remembered such details. And why did they care?

Anthony had major separation issues when I first began taking him to nursery school (okay, fine! I had major separation issues too. The *mammone* thing implicated both of us). He was so miserable in the mornings that he would vomit almost every day before we left home. I tried to talk to the other mothers about our problem. I learned the Italian terms for *letting go* and *separation anxiety.* I got a lot of advice. They cared, and they shared. One said lay off milk in the morning. Another said it was a problem of acidity—was I giving him orange juice? They discussed among themselves whether it might have been my tendency to give him too much cereal in the morning. Finally a grandmother came up to me and put her two cents in.

"Dear, I went through exactly the same thing with my son, for years. I know what you're going through." I was starting to feel relieved, looking into her wrinkled face. I was talking to someone who really understood my predicament, and her time-tested advice about mothering with boundaries and love was going to be wise and true. "I'll tell you the secret," she whispered, "*no* breakfast at all! He'll have nothing to puke up!"

I accepted this advice with genuine gratitude, even though, as a woman raised in a culture of psychoanalysis, it offered me no solution to my problem. I knew that for the grandmother this was not something trivial. A *nonna*, after all, telling you *not* to feed your child was a rare event. She too had suffered, and she had found her answer.

<hr>

When kindergarten began, Salvatore and I set up a meeting with Suor Alfonsina to talk to her about Anthony and his behavior. He was misbehaving big-time at home—challenging Salva and me, refusing to take time-outs, jumping on the furniture, you name it. I wanted Suor Alfonsina to help us understand what was going on at school and maybe give us a few pointers. I was working on the veal cutlet issue; she could give me a hand with the discipline thing.

We were flabbergasted to hear that Anthony was an angel at school. She used the words *obedient, social, sensitive,* and—get this!—*caring.* Anthony Avallone? Were we talking about the same kid? Brown hair? Wears a Naples soccer jersey twenty-eight days a month? After verifying that we were in fact talking about Anthony, I expressed my contentment that at least when he was out of the house he knew how to behave. Better that way, I later told Salvatore.

"What, are you crazy?" my husband replied. "It would be much better if he behaved himself at home and misbehaved at school! Then someone *else* would have to deal with his tantrums, not us!"

I, as an American, felt that our son's behavior outside the home was a positive indicator that in the future our son would perform, socially and professionally . . . and then I realized that for a Neapolitan, your behavior *inside* the home is the real indicator of your character. Not in the workplace, not in school. Sure, it's nice to look good when you leave your home, and make a *bella figura*. But in terms of your identity, the most important thing is who you are with your parents, with your children, with your cousins. The important thing is how you behave with the people who *really* matter.

Pants on Fire

As soon as Anthony learned to walk, he joined in the free-for-all to open Nonna's suitcase and dive into the *pizzette* and *mozzarelline* she brought when she came to Rome. Anthony and Raffaella loved each other with a passion. Raffaella spoon-fed him, cuddled him, played with him.

She also lied to him, regularly. I was ready to embrace a whole lot about the Avallones' Neapolitan parenting style, but when it came to telling the truth, my American cultural conditioning ran deep.

One of Anthony's favorite games as a toddler was Memory. Because I have never liked to make life simple for myself, I gave my son a Memory game of horses that included about thirty pairs—all of which looked almost exactly alike.

Raffaella and Nino were visiting, and it was Anthony's bedtime. He wanted to play Memory with his *nonna*. I told Raffaella it would take too long, to which she replied that I should distract Anthony in the kitchen and she would try to memorize the position of the cards so she could win quickly. "I'm good at cheating," she explained. "We'll be fast."

"What's Nonna doing?" Anthony asked me. Raffaella, sitting on the living room floor in a Fendi suit, was memorizing the stallions as quickly as she could.

"She's setting up Memory, sweetheart," I told him. I was complicit in the cheating. The child would take drugs and lie about it as soon as he hit puberty.

"*Siamo pronti!*" Let's start! She was excited about the game. Not surprisingly, she racked up pairs quickly, peeking at the cards whenever my son looked away. It was a challenge, and she was having a blast. Anthony was suspicious. Every once in a while he said, "Nonna! You peeked!"

"What are you talking about? *Quando mai!*" she laughed. But never!

I expressed my reservations later to Raffaella, saying that it might be a good idea to teach Anthony that it's better not to cheat. It's better not to lie.

"But didn't you want a quick game of Memory?" she answered, confused. "Who knew where those damn stallions were? And now he's sleeping soundly!"

"I understand," I tried to be diplomatic, "but in the long run . . . cheating at Memory could mean cheating at school—"

"What does school have to do with it?"

And at that point I remembered Salvatore's reaction when I was in graduate school and complained about a difficult exam. His response would be, "Wasn't there someone who had studied sitting near you?" His law exams were all oral, but little slips of paper and huddled desks were common when there was a written exam in Naples.

"We can't do that. We don't do that."

"You could save yourself a whole lot of trouble. You Americans, why is it that you are always making life so difficult for yourselves?"

———— ※ ————

In Naples, people do not lie. They re-create, artistically and playfully, their own truth. It is normal to tell untruths, creative reconstructions of reality. These untruths are told with great calm and finesse. They are told not only to dupe or deceive but also to protect, out of love for the person being misled.

In a culture where the truth is like a game, relationships often focus on trying to *svelare*, or take the veil off, a friend's version of the truth. This is done with very little drama, and almost no condemnation or judgment. So what if a person just invented and described an imaginary experience? He could be, using the vulgar vernacular, a *cazzaro*, or a person who tells *cazzate*, meaning lies. In Naples the expression would be *spara cazzate*: he shoots off the lies.

"That's fascinating that Alessio went to India for a month!" I say to Salva.

"Oh, Alessio's a *cazzaro*," he'll reply, not all that interested whether his friend lied or not.

But the friendship sails along smoothly, despite Alessio's tendency to shoot off lies. Nobody's pants are on fire or anything drastic like that. As an American, I immediately take this tendency to the next level. I assume that if he lies to you about a vacation, he'll lie to you about important things. Where's the trust in that friendship? Just like Clinton: If he cheated his wife, he'll cheat the country, right? If he lied under oath about sex, he's capable of any sort of deception.

But in Naples, that is not the line of thinking. What does sex have to do with politics? It's totally irrelevant. What does a lie about a vacation have to do with what kind of friend he is?

Disturbed, I continued to try to talk it through with Raffaella. How about Pinocchio? I asked my mother-in-law. Wasn't the moral of Italy's most famous fairy tale that one should never tell a lie?

"Oh, that Pinocchio story," she began, and I understood immediately that Pinocchio was not Neapolitan but northern, and thus foreign. "I guess it can be useful to teach children not to lie to their parents. But Pulcinella . . ."

She went on to describe animatedly how Pulcinella, the Neapolitan clown from the commedia dell'arte, lies regularly and gets caught only because he isn't smart about it. Now *that's* an important lesson for a kid.

I heard a revealing conversation take place between my mother-in-law and my son, the evening of a dinner party and bridge tournament at the Avallones' apartment. About forty people were to arrive in a few hours. The new Sri Lankan housekeeper Mitzi was frying zucchini to make *zucchine alla scapece*, a marinated zucchini, mint, and garlic dish. He had already set up the card tables in the living room, and had collaborated with Raffaella on the other nine dishes that were going to be served when the players took their ten o'clock break.

Raffaella wanted to get Anthony to sleep before the guests arrived. The only way was to tell him that nothing was happening later.

"Nonna, are you having a party tonight? Are people coming over?"

"*Ma no! Che dici?* No, of course not. What on earth are you talking about?"

"I saw the card tables in the living room. . . ."

"Oh, those! I set them up for next week when your grandfather is going to have a meeting with his friends."

"Meeting? Nonna! That's not the truth!" He was smiling,

and adorable. He was thrilled that he'd won the little truth game. She started laughing and enveloped him in a hug.

"Amore mio! Quanto sei scetàto!" My love, you are awake!

Kissing and tickling him, Raffaella was so very proud that Anthony had called her out on her lie. Her grandson wasn't no kid sleeping with his mama's titty in his mouth. He was being raised well.

Anthony accepted the Find the Truth game as just that, a game. He knew that he could play it with his Neapolitan grandmother, aunt, and cousins. But if I was around, his little eyes made contact with mine as if to say, Mommy, I'm going to ask you later what the real answer is. As he grew, Anthony enjoyed the game less and less, and sought out the truth more and more. He knew where to look.

After all, this wasn't a game his American mommy knew how to play.

Eggplant Parmesan

enedetta and Mauro's marriage was on the rocks. Salvatore noticed that Benedetta was buying her groceries at the discount supermarket: that's how he knew.

At the beginning of their marriage, love was expressed through both Benedetta's and Raffaella's cooking. It was a mother-daughter team. Raffaella had prepared her daughter well—Benedetta knew that peas were to be cooked in May, that eggplants were not to be canned when she was menstruating. (One day I tried to help Raffaella pack her boiled eggplants in jars, and she asked me, "Do you have the *ciclo*?" I didn't have the cycle, but wanted to know why it mattered. "They say the eggplants will become acidic," Raffaella explained, "because hormones are transmitted through your hands. Better not to take the risk.")

A weekly menu was established based on what was fresh that moment, which vegetables were particularly good in the countryside around Naples that year. (Neapolitan women have found it genuinely funny that I cook sausage in the summer or asparagus in the fall. She must come from a place where they grow asparagus in September! This is considered akin to wearing ski boots in July.)

As her relationship with Mauro deteriorated, so did Benedetta's cooking. She no longer asked Raffaella to make her specialty casseroles. All she asked her mother to do was to cook for her two boys—don't worry about Mauro! He can eat anything, it doesn't matter. Benedetta's dishes were *arrangiati*, meaning put together with no care. She was cooking without love.

Was this the woman who had made *tagliolini* casseroles for her husband, taking special care to use the cheeses that Mauro preferred? Who went across town to get the ricotta that was the freshest? The woman who based her (and her mother's) cooking on "how Mauro likes it"?

When Salvatore saw the plastic bags from Tuodì supermarket, he confronted his sister and asked her what was going on.

Benedetta had fallen out of love with Mauro. "He doesn't do anything here. He's never even changed a diaper! He's a *peso* [a burden]." That word, *peso*, which literally means a weight, was the same word that I'd heard other Neapolitan women use for their husbands. "Things are so much easier without him" was another sentence that I had heard before.

I told Benedetta that I was surprised. In the early years of their marriage, she would often say what a caring and helpful partner Mauro was. Her response now was an *"Eeeeh"* on the exhale—what are you gonna do? That was before children. "You know? He's never even given the boys a bath! He doesn't know how to screw in a lightbulb, or fold a shirt. I mean, come *on*."

My sister-in-law did something that would have been impossible in Naples in the past: she left her husband. (Well, I shouldn't say left, since it was she who kept the apartment and the kids and the lasagna in the elevator.) Salvatore tried to mediate. He understood his sister and the problems she had with Mauro, and at the same time felt for his forty-five-year-old brother-in-law who had to move back in with his mother. (Live on his own? That option wasn't even considered. Mauro didn't know how to fry an egg! How would he survive?)

Is there any chance that he could get custody? I asked Salva. In Italy, no. The mother has to be a drug addict or a prostitute, and even then, she usually gets custody of the children. *"La mamma è sempre la mamma"* is an expression that you hear all the time: Mama will always be Mama, there's no one like Mama. The subtext being that Papa is a nice addendum, but never a substitute.

It seemed to me that Salvatore was an objective mediator. He had the necessary emotional distance. He wasn't blinded by anger and showed respect and consideration for all involved. That is, until the Day of the Eggplant Parmesan.

The whole family had gathered for Sunday lunch. Benedetta's two boys played with their little cousin Anthony; Raffaella cooked and served. Salva, Nino, Benedetta, and I sat at the table and consumed. No one mentioned Mauro. Benedetta seemed to be happy—she had even started dating a man she worked with. She'd been separated from Mauro for a few months, but it would be years before they could officially divorce. (In the best-case scenario, when a husband and wife are consensual, an Italian couple can apply for a divorce after three years of separation. If not, it can take closer to a decade. This was the case for Benedetta and Mauro.)

Tutto a posto, everything in its place. In a new place, granted, but in place. There was peace and children's laughter and magnificent food.

Benedetta's new flame lived a short drive away, by himself. If I had been raised in Naples, I probably would have thought,

It's Sunday, and Benedetta's new boyfriend is alone! What's the poor guy going to have for lunch? but it didn't occur to me. After we had eaten the pasta with beans, the sautéed *friarielli* greens, huge milky balls of mozzarella, and the most divine eggplant Parmesan Raffaella had ever baked, Benedetta got up and asked her mother for a plastic plate.

"What are you doing?" Salva asked her as she cut a hunk of the deep purple *parmigiana* and positioned it on the plate.

"Can you give me some plastic wrap, Mom?" she said.

Salva stood up menacingly. "What are you doing?"

Benedetta was wrapping the cellophane around the plate. Once, twice . . .

"Who is that for?"

Salva knew that his sister was planning to take their mother's *parmigiana* out of their home. She was going to put it on the passenger seat of her little Fiat and take it to the apartment of her new partner. She had fallen in love and this was the way she expressed it.

But Salva saw it as a betrayal. His mother had dried the eggplants in the sun for two days. She had then fried them in strips. Raffaella had even used the tomatoes that she canned herself. All this to satisfy the appetite of his sister's lover? Suddenly that dark purple *parmigiana* was so sexual. Salvatore never spoke of honor, or of family, or used any words that a Neapolitan brother would have used just one generation ago. But he lost his *shit* over that eggplant Parmesan.

My husband's knees bounced and his hands flew. Benedetta cried and screamed and used expressions in Neapolitan dialect that I didn't understand. I swept Emilio, Claudio, and Anthony off to the bedroom, where I taught them rock, paper, scissors in English. When I heard silence at last, I came back to the kitchen to find the plastic plate with the *parmigiana* snapped in two and the floor splattered with blood-red tomato sauce. Everyone else had stormed off and Raffaella was alone with that heartbreaking mess. How could I help?

Raffaella put on her magic yellow kitchen gloves ("When I put these on I'm more efficient," she told me once. "Without gloves I don't even know where to start!"). She picked up the chunks and wiped the oil away with newspapers. Then she started mopping. She was a cleaning machine.

I felt sick with pity for this mother who for forty years had stirred and fried and baked her love for her daughter, and for the last ten had learned to do the same for a son-in-law. Suddenly she had to unlove him at the drop of a hat. She had to not care anymore what he ate and start learning instead how Benedetta's new partner liked his *pasta e fagioli*, whether he preferred his Easter *pastiera* cake with or without candied fruit.

After wringing out the dishrags, my mother-in-law looked me in the eye and I saw her concern. There was no Neapolitan tradition that told her where the *parmigiana* was to end up in a broken and blended family. Her Catholic church didn't give instructions on how to uproot someone from her heart, someone who with great effort she had taught herself to love.

But I had misinterpreted Raffaella's concern. "*Tesoro*," Honey, she said, and grabbed my hand, "did you want another piece of that before it went on the floor?"

Jealousy

"What do you have to do with it?" Raffaella asked me, genuinely baffled.

The problem was Anthony's jealousy. My son had turned into an eighteenth-century southern Italian, sword-brandishing, jilted lover. One of the things I appreciated about my husband was that he didn't have the possessive love that so many Neapolitan men have for their women. The *You're not wearing that, are you?* to short skirts or plunging necklines. The *When you go out, we go out together.* It exists, still. Although Salva is passionate and chivalrous, he has never had any macho possessiveness. I always credited his mother for having raised him to respect women's independence.

But apparently, mothers have nothing to do with it. The character trait jealousy—just like *permalosità*, shyness, aggression, you name it—is something you inherit from your relatives just as you would blue eyes or curly hair.

"*Zio Renato era geloso,*" Raffaella informed me. Apparently Anthony had gotten the trait from an uncle on his grandmother's side who was known for his possessive jealousy.

I was pregnant with a girl, and Anthony was on fire with rage. He spent his time glaring at me as if he had caught me in flagrante with a nemesis. It made no difference how I played with him or doted on him or spoon-fed him his favorite dishes: he was ready to pull out the saber and sing a Puccini aria before putting an end to it all.

Anthony and I had been spending a lot of time together at the park of the Domus Aurea—Nero's golden palace, on the Oppian Hill above the Colosseum. While the Italian mothers chatted about what they were preparing for lunch, I loaded my pudgy love on my back and pretended I was a racehorse at the Kentucky Derby. Faster, faster, *here's* the starting gate, Mommy! Not there. *Here!* I neighed, very loudly. Everyone thought I was insane. I was having more fun than I'd ever had in my whole life.

The doctor told me when I was pregnant that it was probably better not to reenact the Preakness at the park with my son.

"We can play with Legos!" I told Anthony. "And pick-up sticks!" He wasn't interested. "Horsey wasn't fun, Mommy," he told me. "No fun. Never."

I neighed. I thought we'd had something good.

He didn't want to go to the park with me anymore. He didn't want to *see* me. Although he'd been potty-trained for a while, he pooed in the middle of our living room, and said, "Mommy, something in *salotto*. Clean it up."

I asked Raffaella for advice. Where had I gone wrong? It must have been the way I'd handled it. I shouldn't have told him . . . I should have waited . . . I shouldn't have . . .

That's when she asked, "What have you got to do with it?"

As an American mother, I assume that every negative behavioral trait that my children have can be traced back to me. Specifically, to what I did or didn't do. This is absolutely unheard of for a Neapolitan. What a strange Anglo-Saxon cocktail of omnipotence and narcissism! Sure, *la mamma è sempre la mamma* and all that, but what can you do if your kid inherits Aunt Mary's rudeness?

I was off the hook. When we went to Naples for the weekend and Anthony had a tantrum, I was spared the *Katherine really should handle the situation better.* At most, Zia Pia or Raffaella would murmur *Good thing the jealousy gene skipped over Salvatore!* or *Yup, that's Zio Renato's jealousy there. Remember the time he camped out near his girlfriend's apartment?*

The period of my daughter's gestation and birth was a haze of tantrums, rage, and exhaustion. There were enormous amounts of caffeine and a lot of shouting. Anthony fumed; Salva and I fought. There was no Mozart played for the fetus. The books would say that didn't bode well for having a healthy, happy baby.

Luckily, my little girl inherited not only the name but the character of her *nonna.*

One of the most miraculous things about a newborn is her hands. I'm sure that little Lella's hands were tiny pink gems. At some point they probably rested, inert, on an embroidered sheet in her bassinet. But I have no memory of them. Because I have no recollection of Lella's hands ever being still.

It seems that from the time she was born, my daughter's hands were showing me how to do things. They were blending the blush on my cheeks (*dis no look right*), defending herself from her brother (*me hold up fist like dis*), braiding her best friend's hair. *This is the best way to cut potatoes, Mommy!* (Where'd you learn that?)—and the little fingers would fly, showing me the width of the strips.

When I told her, "I know it's hard for you when Anthony . . ." she waited patiently for me to finish, stroking my arm as if to reassure me that what I had to say was important. Then, it was: "Okay, *me* talk now. Remember, Mommy, it's always better to . . ." and there were the hands, showing me how to tie shoelaces, or fold wrapping paper.

At school, she cheerfully organized playdates for the other kids. "Simona wanted to go over to Francesco's house. I made sure they worked it out and told him what she likes for snack." *Li ho sistemati*, I set them up. With a great big smile, the girl got people where they needed to be, doing what they needed to be doing. She made sure her mommy looked decent, put her brother in his place, and learned how to make her grandmother's tomato sauce by the age of six.

Che problema c'è?

Air-Con

On the early years of Anthony's and Raffaella junior's lives, my priorities as a mother were to raise children who were:

caring
principled
intelligent
accomplished
entertaining
disciplined
bilingual

Salvatore's priorities as a father were to raise children who were:

well fed
warm
dry
fans of Napoli and not of Roma soccer team

If Salva was fixated over these priorities for Anthony, the birth of a defenseless baby girl took his fixations to the extreme.

During the first summer of little Raffaella's life, Salva's fathering was dependent on two all-important remote controls, each kept in a separate pocket of his velour dressing gown. The television remote was used every five minutes to check on the ranking of Napoli in the Italian seasonal tournament. The other remote regulated our air-conditioning units, or as Italians call them, our "splits."

We have remote-controlled wall units in all rooms of our apartment, and they are usually (even in the worst heat of the summer) turned off. This is not because air-conditioning per se is hazardous to your health (although it is! Don't you know that?) but because the splits create drafts that cause, among other things, the common cold, neck cricks, and bronchitis. In the worst-case scenario (among the very young and very old), they can provoke pneumonia and paralysis. "Drafts" can be translated as *correnti,* a word Italians pronounce with a menacing rolled *r.*

Hence the importance of my husband's vigilant control of the splits. Who is responsible for regulating the air-conditioning at my house in Washington? I have been asked by my in-laws. Who has the holster for the sacred remote? My mother, who is *freddolosa* (always cold) or my father, who is *caloroso* (would downhill ski in his Speedos)? No one? With central air, we just set the temperature and forget about it. It astonishes them that day and night, morning and afternoon, there's *no regulating.*

When Raffaella junior was tiny, I would strap her into her high chair far away from her roaming, raging brother. No matter the room, Sal Quick-at-the-Draw would find her. He would find his daughter—buckled in, immobile, defenseless—regulate the vents with his remote, and exit. It would happen in a nanosecond. We would not hear the sound of footsteps, nor would we get a glimpse of him in his loungewear. Sal's presence was heralded by the *beep-beep-beep* of the remote control. *Beep-beep-beep*, another child rescued from a *corrente*, and he'd be gone.

Recent sightings of Quick Draw Sal have revealed that, even in summer, he dresses in layers. The Italian expression is *a cipolla*, like an onion. His loungewear begins with a white short-sleeved undershirt. Then come the pajamas—long-sleeved gray pajamas printed with little white curly-tailed cats interspersed with fluffy clouds. The legs of the pajamas are tucked into his very long navy-blue knee socks, so that no chilly air will come up his pajama legs. The undershirt and pajama top are tucked into the pants tightly so that, once again, no air will make its way to his belly. As a general rule, air is not to touch exposed flesh unless one is at the beach in Sardinia and it is 101 degrees. Salvatore's dressing gown, worn over his pajamas, is soft velour and is tied (tightly) around the waist.

Bedroom slippers are often mismatched in our household. In Italy, and in Naples in particular, bare feet are not to touch floors, even in the summer. When I wake up in the Avallones' apartment, I find slippers already on my feet before I put them down on the parquet. Some concerned kinswoman does not want me catching a cold, and everyone knows that I, as an American, have been known to walk around the apartment barefoot and sometimes even with wet hair. Salvatore, careful not to touch the floor, dons the slippers closest to the bed when he wakes up in the morning. There have been times when one of those slippers is pink, has feathers, and is mine.

In Naples, most sicknesses can be directly traced to one of three culprits: the aforementioned drafts or *correnti*; a moment when a person has *preso freddo*, gotten a chill; or, worst of all, *preso umido*, has taken humidity into their bones. For me, much of the difficulty of raising small children in this country comes down to the fact that I, as an American, do not recognize these dangers. I take my children out when it's fifty degrees and not raining. I know enough to keep them bundled in hats, scarves, and gloves, with no inch of bare skin showing. But if it's humid, or if all of a sudden it starts to get windy, I do not grab them and sprint to the nearest shelter.

Once, when Anthony got a cold, I overheard some Neapolitan family members talking about how I had taken him out on Wednesday. Yes, Wednesday! The day of that humidity! They tried their best to understand. "Maybe in Washington, where she grew up, the climate is so dry that they don't know what humidity is!"

Since the possibility of humidity and the risk of getting a chill loom large during winter, you can only imagine the stress of an outing with children when it rains. If it rains, children should stay at home, and adults should go out only if absolutely necessary.

If anyone has any negative preconceptions about Italians and their organizational abilities, they should watch a family with small children getting out of their car when it's raining— a family that has made the decision to venture out in the *tempesta*. In our family, Salva briefs me on how the tag team is to proceed with the umbrellas as we're about to arrive at our destination. "I will drive up to the front door. You should have the small umbrella in your pocket. I will open the big umbrella and accompany you with Lella in your arms into the building. Leave her inside and give me the small umbrella. I'll give you the big umbrella. Go get Anthony from the car and I'll go and park the car with the small umbrella."

The whole relay proceeds without a glitch. It is fast, it is efficient but also highly stressful. The fear that the kids might get wet is so real and so intense that I forget that the drops that are falling from the sky are only water.

I've come to realize that the number of sweaters and ski jackets that my husband puts on members of his family is in direct proportion to the love that he feels for us. If I manage to leave the apartment in winter without his accosting me, pinning me down, and zipping up my ski jacket, it means that he is angry with me. Let her go out with no jacket in March. To hell with her! Let her dig her own grave.

When it comes to the children, the smaller and more vulnerable they are, the more sweaters they get. As babies, Anthony and Raffaella were often hot and sweaty and fussy. It drove me crazy to see Salva pile on the layers, so, as soon as he was out of sight, I would strip them down. This was complicated, though, because they were small and uncooperative and confused by the continual costume changes. In a moment of particular tension on this front, my sister (an accomplished seamstress and costumer) told me that she thought our marriage could be saved and the harmony in our family restored if she just got rid of our zippers and buttons and Velcroed us all.

The reason I tend to get angry and a little bitter is that it's hard enough to have kids who are sick, without being accused of provoking it. My rational brain tells me that colds are viruses, and they get passed from person to person. I don't mention that to people in Naples, though. One way to find yourself friendless and ignored in Italy is to start a sentence with "Studies show" or "Scientists have found."

So I've decided to go with the flow, avoid *umidità* and *correnti*, and bring along my CVS disinfectant so that all the bases are covered.

Total Hunger

In ancient times, rich Romans would go to the seaside near Naples for the summer. It made sense. It still does. Without the ocean, Rome gets hotter than Naples in the summertime, and when you can't turn on the air-conditioning splits, and you're breast-feeding, and you're not allowed to sweat . . . the only option is to pack the kids up like *signore* have been doing for thousands of years and go to the beach. Or, if you happen to be American, to a swimming pool.

Salva finds my preference for swimming pools (no fiery rocks, or sand in crevices, or seaweed—the reasons are endless) immoral. Preferring a swimming pool to the ocean is akin to preferring frozen pizza to a fresh one right out of the oven. But I was hot and sleep-deprived and nursing and my husband knew what was good for him.

He called his friend from high school, Enrico, and told him we were coming with the kids for lunch and a swim.

Enrico had grown up in a *basso* in the dense center of Naples. The *bassi* are the street-level apartments that house extended families in the Spanish Quarter. "What adorable little restaurants!" I gushed to Salvatore the day he stripped me of jewelry, wallet, watch, and cellphone and took me on a tour of the Quartieri. I saw little tables propped up in alleyways, just outside of kitchens with lace curtains. The smell of peppers frying made me drool. "Do you think they're open?"

"What restaurants? Those are people's homes, and if you stand there salivating any longer they'll invite you to lunch."

Motorbikes whizzed by, missing us by millimeters. Salva, despite the fact that this was not his hood, could tell me which young guys on the bikes were thieves and which were undercover plainclothes cops. ("You can tell, that's all," he explained when I wondered how he could distinguish them.) Neither category wore the obligatory helmet.

"*Enrico abitava qui,*" he told me, pointing to an alley strung with laundry. He had a friend who lived here? I was surprised. "Who *used* to live here," he clarified.

Enrico had grown up heading soccer balls against the graffitied stone walls of his *basso*, but now lived in Bacoli, a suburb full of single-family villas. It's where many stars of the Naples soccer team (most are South American or eastern European) have chosen to live. In Bacoli there is space, there are pools. Gone is the stench of garbage and the constant buzz of motorbikes. Even robberies are high-class affairs: they are not *scippi* (pickpocketing and purse snatching) like in the Spanish Quarter, but full-fledged team efforts with drills and other power tools, performed by "expert" thieves. (A psychologist friend in Naples told me that one of her patients proudly noted that her husband was a *mariuolo di case*, a house thief, rather than a simple pickpocket. There is a major difference in terms of job profile.)

Enrico and his family made their money in clothing stores. They are *commercianti*, store owners, a term that is used by the Neapolitan bourgeoisie with not a little prejudice. Store owners who have been economically successful are considered nouveaux riches, but the term's Neapolitan translation, *cafoni arrichiti*, doesn't need to be uttered—it's enough to say *commerciante*. The Cardones have worked hard and moved up in the world. They have sacrificed, skipped afternoon naps, brought lunches from home to their stores (which don't even close! Some of the first stores in Naples not to close even for lunch!).

We arrived at the Cardones' villa in Bacoli just before noon on a scorching Saturday in July. The cameras on their high-tech alarm system ("Best ten thousand euros I ever spent," Enrico told us, and Salva later explained that a telltale sign of *commercianti* is that they speak in numbers, never afraid to tell you exactly how much something cost) blinked blue as the electric gate buzzed open. It was a slow curtain opening for Enrico's mother, who greeted us center stage in a tiny sequined bikini holding a one-year-old grandchild on her hip.

"*Salvató! Viene ccà!*" she called in a voice that was not of the gravelly grandma variety but a high, hysterical trumpet. Her voice told me she didn't smoke; her body told me she had other vices. She held the arm that wasn't supporting the baby out to hug Salva, and he disappeared for a moment into her 250-pound, dark-skinned embrace. She wore Ray Charles sunglasses and sported a platinum-blond bob. The sequins were under severe garment duress.

"This is Ketrin," Salvatore told her. When she didn't move

her head but just reached her hand out to pinch my chin, looking for me with her bloated fingers, I realized that if she was not totally blind she was close to it. *"Che nome è? Kay-tree?"* What kind of name is that? "Salvató, where did you go to pick this chick up?" They both laughed and I joined in. Kay-tree! Go figure!

She led us to the pool where her daughter-in-law Giada sat on a deck chair reading the riot act to her three-year-old child. Giada and Enrico had three daughters under the age of six. The girls, dressed in Ralph Lauren, Tommy Hilfiger, and Lacoste, were all blond and scowling. ("See that little horse, American flag, and crocodile? Five hundred euros a month," Enrico told us later. "That's Giada's clothing allowance for the girls.")

Giada had told her daughters that they could not go in the swimming pool today. There was a little wind; Ludovica had had a cough last Tuesday. This is never going to work, I thought. They're being asked to spend all afternoon moving between their grandmother's hip, deck chairs, and a lunch table? Listening to grown-ups talk and gazing at the crystal-blue water? When it's ninety-six degrees?

Little Raffaella was already splashing her feet in the water and Anthony was doing cannonballs. I was not going to veto that. It was ninety-six degrees.

Enrico's oldest daughter started to whine, and Giada shouted, "No is *no!*"

Before I knew what was happening, Giada had smacked her daughter across the face with speed and efficiency. Were my children and I responsible for child abuse? Giada saw my concern. "What, you never hit your kids?" The exact words that she used in Neapolitan dialect were: *"Nu' ll'abbuffe maie 'e mazzate?"* Whop them upside the head, I think would be the most accurate translation.

In Naples, it's still common in schools for teachers to strike kids with rulers, or spank them. When I taught English to a group of preschoolers, the director of the school told me on the first day that if things got out of hand I shouldn't hesitate to hit them. Not hard, of course. Just to get them to listen to you.

But I had never seen skill like this woman's: bam bam! Front of the hand! Back of the hand! Before I knew it the girl was sitting immobile next to her mother and Giada was talking to her mother-in-law about the state of the stuffed peppers.

Giada doesn't call her mother-in-law Mrs. Cardone or Angelica. She uses the term that Neapolitan daughters-in-law are meant to use: *Mammà*. With the accent on the final *a*, it is down-home dialect for the Italian *mamma* (accent on the first *a*) and thus even more intimate. If *Mamma* is Mom, *Mammà* is Mommy.

Since Enrico and Giada live with his extended family, the two women spend all their time together. While their husbands man the stores, Giada and Mammà plan, buy the ingredients for, and cook the three meals that are nothing short of feasts at the Cardone household. (Cleaning is done by a uniformed, thin Brazilian maid. To see the women of the house all overweight and the help skinny seems a throwback to the last century.) Breakfast consists of homemade cakes and *crostate*, or fruit pies, and lunch and dinner include a *primo*, or pasta course, a *secondo* that is meat or fish, and at least two labor-intensive vegetables. Because the gentlemen do not come all the way back to the villa for lunch, the team of wives package up their husbands' lunches for them to take to work.

In Naples, packaging food is an art form. Newspapers, rubber bands, Styrofoam, freezer bags, soft rags, string, and twine are used. Temperature and distance to be traveled are taken into consideration, and obstacles such as customs regulations in a foreign country or the length of a transatlantic flight are seen as exciting challenges. A friend who is an Alitalia flight attendant told me that Neapolitans can always be recognized by the packages of food that they hold close on board a plane. They often refuse to put them in the overhead compartments—after all, who knows what the exact temperature is up there?

The last time I flew back to Washington, D.C., at Christmas, Zia Pia called me a few days before the flight. "We've figured out a way!" she told me. A way to do what? "To get the octopus to your father!" Aunt Pia knew that my father loves *insalata di polipo* and damned if she wasn't going to get it to him. In my already packed suitcase. Her plan involved nestling the slimy creature in the underwear compartment of my pull-along. Bubble wrap and rags would do the trick. What if it starts to drip? I asked her.

"*Eehhh* [on the exhale] . . . *che vuoi fa'?*" she answered. What can you do? These are just the risks one has to take.

Because the Cardone gentlemen's fried eggplant, roast veal, and baked pasta casseroles only have to travel across town, Giada and her *mammà*'s packaging job is simple. All they need is some old *Mattino* newspapers, Tupperware, and heavy-duty rubber bands.

Mr. Cardone appeared from inside the house wearing a Speedo. He was tall and thin, with lots of white hair and skin the color of dark clay. He introduced himself, sat down, and lit up a cigarette.

"*Giada, vedi nu poco i peperoni a Mammà.*" Angelica too had lowered herself onto one of the deck chairs and wanted Giada to check the stuffed peppers in the oven, which smelled like the Quartieri Spagnoli, where the family had its origins. Her sentences, whether she was commanding, cuddling, or cursing, always ended by underlining the relationship she had with her listener. Her words brought her family members back to her broad brown bosom. To her daughter-in-law, Can you check the peppers for Mammà? To her niece, Oh, how beautiful you are to your aunt! To her granddaughter, Baby girl, wipe your nose for Nonna.

"*Kay-tree, viene ccà.*" She motioned me over. I wasn't part of the family, so her sentence didn't end with Mammà, Nonna, or Zia. American with the weird name, come here.

Angelica had focused on the fact that I was from the United States. Although I know absolutely nothing about medicine, I am often considered a medical expert simply because I am American. People ask me about new procedures that are being performed in the States, and which American doctor is the expert of which disorder. So many Italians have blind faith that in the land of miracles any condition can be cured, as long as you have money to pay. I assumed that Angelica was going to inquire about new laser technology for her eye problem, but no.

"In America, they've gotta have a pill that you can take to make you lose weight. Can you ask around for me, honey? I'm ready to pay."

Angelica's hunger is described by her skinny whip of a husband as *totale*. An all-consuming, black hole of an appetite. Her smile and sequins glittered as Carmine described an incident from the early years of their courtship, when Angelica climbed over a neighbor's spiked fence at 3:00 A.M. to get a *cornetto Algida*, a chocolate ice-cream dessert ("I knew what I was getting into," he told us). Later in life, unable to drive because of her eyesight, Angelica made her son, at the age of fifteen and with no driver's license, drive her two hundred miles to a sandwich joint in the mountains of central Italy ("*Tenevo na famma 'e pazze*"—I had myself a crazy hunger—"and I'd heard it was the best"). After undergoing an operation on her hands, she developed the skill of eating pasta with her elbows (and actually gained weight! she told us proudly).

I listened and laughed, my sweaty thighs sticking to the plastic deck chair. I was hungry, too. Angelica and I both knew just how much it sucks to feel fat and hungry. And hot. But once again in Naples, my hunger, my readiness to dig into the steaming stuffed peppers that Giada brought from the kitchen (barking at the little blond toddlers that got in her way, *"Ué, te vuó spustà?"*—Hey you! Git, why don't ya?) didn't feel pathological. It felt human.

As I sat next to this smiling woman with an overwhelming hunger, I thought about the days when I would put away three boxes of Oreos. I imagined Salva bragging about it someday to friends who came for lunch.

"So," she asked me, "do you Americans have this pill that will let me eat what I want and not be fat?"

In Naples, a hunger like Angelica's is not seen as pathological or as a disorder but, like the love she has for her children and grandchildren, quite simply *totale*. So I didn't tell her about Prozac or appetite suppressants. I simply informed my hostess that even in the land of medical miracles, that is a condition for which we have yet to find the cure.

Peanut Butter

In Neapolitan culture, foods that could potentially damage children's health include crackers, ketchup, hot dogs, cold milk, anything in a can, anything that has ever been frozen, and anything that has ever been in a microwave. Oh, and anything that comes from a supermarket. Fish must be consumed regularly. But not *pesce di allevamento*, farm-raised fish—only fish from the ocean. And which ocean matters: there's a difference between Adriatic and Mediterranean sole, for example. Fish from the Mediterranean is almost always superior.

Nino, who had rarely interfered in our decisions as parents, called once a week to find out whether little Raffaella had had her fish, and which fish. I threw little George Washington out the window and started lying through my teeth.

We lived in Rome, for God's sake. Salva was at work all day. No one would find out that I gave my kids Cheerios and crackers! I refused to spend my time boiling vegetables for hours, when I was sure that those vegetables were the wrong vegetables, and when I was sure that my kids would ball them in their little fists and hand them back to me. Wasn't it better to sing "Ten Little Monkeys Jumping on a Bed" and tap-dance to it?

The problem arose when we visited Naples and Anthony got to the point of expressing himself well in Italian. Much to my dismay, he often told the truth. It must have been my fault. What was I thinking, telling him all that garbage about the cherry tree? I should have read up on that smart Neapolitan Pulcinella clown who lies and gets away with it!

"Mommy opens these cans with . . . how do you say *baked beans* in Italian? I like them but Lella doesn't so she just eats crackers. Can I have some more *ragù*, Nonna?"

"Sweetheart," I would tell him later, "you don't always have to tell Nonna everything, you know."

"Are baked beans a secret?"

"No, sweetheart. The beans are fine. It's the *can* that's a secret! *Cans* are always secret! And bottles! Or jars! Ketchup, mayonnaise . . ."

"And peanut butter?"

"What are you talking about?"

"That you eat on the couch when Papi isn't looking."

"*Sssshhhhhh!*"

How did he know about that?

My best friend is a woman from Connecticut named Katrina who moved to Italy around the time I did. Fresh out of Smith, she started out in 1998 wearing scrunchies in her hair and respectable Banana Republic tops, and soon found herself dating testosterone-driven Italian boys with too many hands in too many places. Now, seventeen years later, we call each other with life-altering dilemmas like this one: in the absence of chocolate chips and double-acting baking powder, is it possible to bake chocolate chip cookies and, if so, will they have the consistency of cobblestones?

Like me, Katrina is an adult woman with a family, a career, and an advanced degree who is forced to eat peanut butter in hiding. We call each other at the precise, delicious moment that we sit down on the couch with crackers, Diet Coke, and a jar of Skippy. We have to do it when our husbands are out of town; ours is a clandestine crunch. We've analyzed Italians' aversion to peanut butter, and have realized that it's not just the consistency (*O mio Dio!* It sticks to the roof of your mouth!); it's not just the fact that it comes from the United States (Do you know what they put in food there?), but is primarily classist.

It's not that Italians consider people who eat peanut butter low-class. It's the peanuts themselves that are low-class. Katrina's husband, Gianluca, who is not only Italian but also works in the food industry, explained to me that certain nuts are *nobile*, others aren't. The most noble, or aristocratic, nuts are apparently pistachios. Walnuts are also pretty hoity-toity, followed by hazelnuts and cashews. The most *cafone*, or low-class, are— you guessed it!—peanuts. To have a wife who not only eats hick nuts but eats them in processed, American form, on the *couch*, is a kind of disgrace.

Anthony had found me out. *Non vi preoccupate*, don't worry, I planned to tell my father-in-law if word got out, I may have a problem, but your grandchildren are safe from the processed hick nuts.

I couldn't say the same about sandwiches.

'A Marenna

"Fishing is not just about catching fish. It's about stillness, becoming one with nature. Breathing the ocean air. Hearing the lapping of the waves. It's about the process, not just the result. And if and when fish are caught, we are going to throw them back." Nobody was interrupting me. I was having an environmentalist, humanitarian field day. After all, this was an invaluable opportunity to teach my son a lesson! I was an American mother who would not see her children plundering, taking from the world! Who would not see her son brag about numbers, swaggering back to his preschool to tell how many fish he caught and how long they were! I would not have a little Mussolini triumphant in Ethiopia!

Nonna Raffaella waited patiently for me to stop.

Anthony totally ignored me, focused as he was on helping his father get the bait, a slippery little shrimp head, stuck on the hook.

It was early spring of 2009, and we were in Naples for the weekend. We had come down the steep steps to Marechiaro, a breathtaking corner of the rocky coastline. A restaurant down the shore had advised us where the fish were biting. Far from the discharge of garbage, the water was crystal-blue and we had each found a flat part of rock for our buttocks. The sun was shining, the kids were excited, and I was brimming with life lessons.

I was also in a particularly good mood because that day, for the first time ever, my children would eat sandwiches for lunch in broad daylight. In front of their grandmother. I had insisted on this, much to the confused dismay of Nonna. I wanted everyone involved to understand that the world would continue turning if we didn't schlep home to make pasta with vegetables or pork roast. It was a gorgeous day: we could get sandwiches and stay out at lunchtime.

Lessons and sandwiches! I was positively euphoric.

We had stopped at a little *salumeria* before starting down the steps to the water. The old man behind the counter with dirt (or maybe oil? basil?) under his fingernails was patient with all of our questions: "Anthony, do you want tuna? What kind of bread?" and "Will Lella eat *prosciutto crudo*?" and "Katherine, do you want to do half and half with peppers and *fior di latte*?" The *salumiere* waited, he advised which cheese would be best with the fried eggplants, and he said no when I asked for ricotta with zucchini. (Those two *non sposano bene*, they do not marry well. In fact, they fight big-time, he told me.) We were in his shop for the better part of an hour.

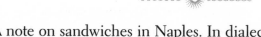

A note on sandwiches in Naples. In dialect, a serious sandwich is called a *marenna*, which sounds like the word for snack, *merenda*. This I think is indicative of how a sandwich is considered: it is not a legitimate meal. *Marenne* are eaten at construction sites and at soccer stadiums. Substituting a *marenna* for a real *pranzo* with first course, second course, vegetables, and fruit is one of the sacrifices that Neapolitan workmen make for their jobs and that Napoli fans make for their team.

When Salva was in middle and high school, the Napoli team had its heyday. Thanks to the "golden feet" of Diego Maradona, Naples crushed every other team in the Series A league, including the historically strongest teams of the North—Juventus, Inter, and Milan. Maradona led the Napoli team to win the national championship twice, after sixty years of northern victories. (Diego Maradona is an unofficial patron saint of the city. Devoted fans still light candles and lay fresh flowers at an altar dedicated to him in downtown Naples. He's fortunately kicked his cocaine habit and coaches in the Middle East.)

On Sundays during Napoli's glory days, Neapolitan *ragazzi* who didn't have tickets for the 2:30 game would get up at dawn and risk life and limb to climb the gates and sneak inside the San Paolo stadium.

Salva and his friends had tickets, and would bring their sandwiches to the stadium. That is, all his friends except Gino. Gino waited to hear the results at home, because he could not bring himself to eat a sandwich.

Recently, my family and I traveled to Munich to watch the Naples soccer team play Bayern Munich. There were thousands of Napoli fans, some of whom we met on our Alitalia flight to Germany. After takeoff, we could smell fried peppers. The expertly packaged *marenne* had been opened—and it was 8:00 A.M.! I decided to ask one of the young men about his sandwich. "*Signó*," he began. (Oh God, I'm old! These guys don't think twice about giving me the formal *signora*.) "*Siamo in trasferta. Chisto è 'a marenna.*" It's an away game, ma'am. This here's our sandwich.

They were well-mannered *ragazzi*. I went back to my seat

with half of one of the most succulent sandwiches I'd ever tasted. I had protested: "No, thank you." "Really, I just had my cappuccino." "Come on, you'll want it for the game." None of my comments registered. I shouldn't have even tried. It was clear that I had no choice but to share the *marenna*.

~~~~~~~ ※ ~~~~~~~

"Papi, when are the fish gonna come?" Anthony had been holding the rod and staying still for a good twenty minutes. He wanted to catch a fish, and he wanted to catch one *now*. There you go, Salva! Now you can talk to him about the process, about patience. . . . But instead, it was: *"Adesso, amore. Lo sento!"* Now, my love. I feel it in the air!

Nonna Lella was sending text messages on her cellphone. Ever the multitasker, she was also playing peekaboo with little Lella and offering words of encouragement to Anthony and Salva. "Of course you're going to catch some! And I'm going to fry them tonight!" she offered cheerfully. I had stopped spurting my philosophical advice, and was starting to realize that I too would be extremely frustrated and pissed off if we didn't catch anything.

"I'm going to the bathroom! Be right back." Nonna Lella took off for the restaurant that was down the rocky beach. When she came back, Anthony and Salva still had not caught anything and we were all hot, hungry, and frustrated. Nonna told Anthony that she had seen a crab behind that rock over there—see if you can catch it, *amore*! At which point she produced from her Louis Vuitton handbag a plastic bag of dead fish and a small pasta strainer.

"The crab was crawling right over there! It can't have gone too far. . . ." She distracted him with her words as her hands flew. The plastic bag disappeared and she dumped three of the fish into the strainer and lowered it into the water. She was ready. *"Anthony! Vieni!"* Come! Look!

There was amazement in my son's face as he pulled up the pasta strainer. Nonna Lella grabbed it from him immediately so he wouldn't see that the fish were dead. "Three of them! You got three of them! And they're at least ten centimeters long! *Amore, sei bravissimo!"* Watch out, Ethiopia.

We looked in to see that they were not only dead but headless.

Nonna had gone to the kitchen of the restaurant and asked the chef if he could give her some fish for her *creatura*, her little grandchild. "He's fishing, and will be so disappointed if he doesn't catch anything. . . . How about those?"

"Ma'am, I've already taken the heads off. Was just about to fry them—"

"They're fine! Oh, and while you're at it, do you have a net or something so it will look like the boy 'caught' them himself?" *Che problema c'è?*

"This is a very rare kind of fish. It's called the headless haddock," Nonna was explaining to Anthony when he asked why the fish he had caught had no heads. "They're so hard to catch. And they are delicious. Tonight, *frittura di pesce*! Now it's time for our *marenne*."

Throw them back? The process not the result? Patience in life? She had even invented the name of the fish! So much for lessons. Now at least we had the sandwiches for consolation.

I opened the bag and thought, Damn, we should have made labels so we knew whose sandwich was whose without having to open them all up. *Vediamo*, let's see. I pulled the first one out and saw something scribbled in ink on the brown paper packaging. *Entoni?* What did that mean? I got out the next one: *Nonna.*

Then *Papi Salva. Piccola Lella.* When I got to the big oily luscious monster at the bottom I saw *Mami Ketrin.*

While we conversed in the shop, the man had focused on and remembered each of our names and, of course, our relationships. The sandwich man didn't just write Salva, or Ketrin, but included the *papi* and *mami.* These *marenne,* the first sandwiches of my children's lives, were made specifically, personally, lovingly, for each of us. The sun was still shining, and we had caught a rare, delicious species of headless haddock with a pasta strainer. Lessons or no lessons, things could have been a lot worse.

Raffaella Junior

Nonna Raffaella had three grandsons, whom she tried to dress in lace well into elementary school. When a granddaughter was born, Raffaella's costuming instinct went ballistic. For as long as Nonna Raffaella could get away with it, little Raffaella wore things that were gorgeous, scratchy, expensive, and couldn't go in the washing machine.

And then my little Neapolitan American girl *s'è scetàta*, as they say in dialect. She woke herself up.

As a child, I knew one thing as a deep, unshakeable truth, and it was that my mother was beautiful and that she knew how to dress. I also knew that only dumb, lazy rich people shopped at places like Neiman Marcus and Lord & Taylor (we certainly couldn't afford to shop there, my mother convinced us, and wouldn't have, even if we could!).

Women who were smart shopped at one store, and one store only: Loehmann's.

We learned math by calculating the Loehmann's Red Dot

Sales prices for Mommy. She would ask us, "What is the 'compare at' price?" (Read: How much did your smart mommy save?) Anna and I learned addition, subtraction, and percentages at Loehmann's. We learned that you *can* get a Ralph Lauren evening gown for the National Symphony Ball for $13.99 and look fabulous in it. If you're smart.

We also learned about death and mortality at Loehmann's, when we saw an elderly lady collapse under a pile of clothes that she was going to try on in the dressing room of the Rockville, Maryland, store in 1984. "Girls," our mother told us, "that's probably how your mama's gonna go."

Unfortunately (and tragically for my mother), Loehmann's did not have children's clothes. So when it came time for Bonnie to bring clothes from the States to her granddaughter, my mother brought cheap, comfortable clothes from other discount stores. She waited with anticipation for her granddaughter's rite of passage: the day when she could take little Raffaella to the Loehmann's dressing room to find the bargains beyond all bargains. In the meantime, there would be no lace collars or subdued pastels. There would be $2.99 T.J.Maxx leopard skin leggings and Marshall's $6.99 (compare at $19.99!) fluorescent off-the-shoulder sweatshirts.

Little Raffaella ate them up. *These* were clothes.

My mother-in-law despaired. When we went to Naples, she would lay out pink cashmere wraps and dresses with frills on little Raffaella's bed as a "surprise." Silently, when no one was looking, little Raffaella would fold them neatly and replace them on her grandmother's bed.

"Raffa, amore, hai visto il regalo di Nonna?" Sweetheart, did you see Nonna's gift on your bed? Raffaella would ask over lunch, her smile concealing how important the outfit was to her.

My daughter would ignore the question and ask for some

more *pasta al forno*. "È *buonissima, Nonna!* It's the best *pasta al forno* that you've ever made."

She would *not* be wearing the frills.

I didn't get in the way. I was proud of her. My girl could negotiate her two worlds, her two identities, with *naturalezza*. She could appreciate the divine dishes that her *nonna* prepared but say no thanks to embroidery and lace.

When Nonna Raffaella finally gave up, little Raffaella was almost seven. My mother-in-law came to Rome with a shoe box in one last-ditch effort to save her grandchild. "*Le scarpe, Ketrin, solo le scarpe,*" she whispered to me, on the verge of tears. The shoes, just the shoes. Give me that, at least.

They were patent leather Mary Janes. There was no chance. Once again, I stayed out of it, leaving the two Raffaellas in my daughter's room to hash it out. I heard a few words through the door, though. "*Amore, hai visto come stai meglio? Come sei elegante? È tutta un'altra cosa!*" Love, can't you see how much better you look? How elegant they are? You look like a different person!"

And then my daughter. Trying to make her grandmother understand, patiently explaining an obvious truth. "Nonna, don't you see? I can run *so* much faster in these sneakers! And if they get dirty it's no big deal. Bonnie got them seventy percent off at Target."

Lasagne

If there were a New Testament play in Neapolitan, I imagine Nonna Raffaella in two possible roles. One is the female lead, the Virgin Mary, and the other is a man who is not named, who is simply called a friend.

First, Maria. Her most important line is one word, and one of my favorite expressions in Italian. *Eccomi.* Here I am. But even simpler than "Here I am," because it is just one word, fluid vowels flowing into consonants. *eh-ko-me:* one word that sums up her approach to life. When the Archangel Gabriel came to give Mary the Son-of-God-in-Your-Tummy announcement, Mary's response was *Eccomi.* It was not "*What the **?!*" or "Actually, I'm not even married" or "When were you thinking, 'cause I was planning on finishing my degree?" It was a very simple *Eccomi.*

This is the expression that Nonna Raffaella uses when someone asks her for help, for time, or for lasagna. "Raffaella? Salva is really down and stressed about work. Can you make him a *sartù di riso?*" *Eccomi!* "Raffaella? I'm worn out by the

kids. Can you take them for a few days so I can rest?" *Eccomi!*
No questions asked or emotional price tag attached. Here I am.

The other role for Raffaella would be the man who figured
out a way to get his paralyzed friend into the crowded house
where Jesus was performing miracles. The tiny house was
packed and there was a multitude outside the door, trying to
make it in. A crowd of the crippled, the sick, the desperate. The
friend cut a hole in the roof, and with some helpers lowered the
paralyzed man down to where Jesus was preaching.

Che problema c'è? I imagine Raffaella saying to her friend
paralyzed on a mat. I'll get you in. Who needs a door?

I imagine her cheerfully studying the logistics of the house
and finding the right instruments. I imagine her calling three
friends (all Neapolitan women, all in Pucci caftans) to help her
cut a hole in the roof. I imagine them lowering their friend
down to Jesus, not even seeing Him themselves. Lowering their
friend through the roof and making it home in time to prepare
lunch for the family.

Last summer Raffaella invited some of her blond, Botoxed
friends to Positano for a girls' beach week. No men allowed.
"And Nino?" I asked her. Her husband is past eighty now, and
depends on her for everything. *"L'ho sistemato,"* she answered—
I set him up. "Mitzi will take care of cooking, and I've organized
a gin rummy playdate for him every afternoon. *Ketrin? Ci
vuole."* Katherine? I need it. I need to take care of myself, too.

Five *signore* packed their sparkly fuchsia bikinis in Louis
Vuitton suitcases and headed to Positano to join Lella for beach
week. During the day, they sunbathed and read magazines. In
the evenings they played cards until 3:00 A.M. And the food?
"Sometimes, Ketrin, you don't feel like cooking."

Raffaella had Mitzi cook platters of risotto, *insalata caprese*, and *babà* cakes in Naples. She had trained him well, and the dishes tasted almost like hers. It sounded like she was coming close to trusting him. How did he get the stuff to Positano, though? Mitzi doesn't drive, and Raffaella certainly couldn't bring it several days in advance!

A hole in the roof big enough for a paralyzed man? The delivery of a feast on the beach of Positano? Why not?

Sri Lankan Mitzi with his New York Yankees baseball cap arrived from Naples on the *aliscafo*, the motorboat that crosses the bay. Raffaella, in her flowing beach cover-up, met the boat at the pier flanked by three of her cohorts, and examined the trays of food to be sure that Mitzi had cooked them to her satisfaction. "Make sure Nino is dressed properly for the gin rummy game at four," she reminded Mitzi after thanking him for his delivery. She bought him a croissant and a glass of cold milk on the pier before sending him back to Naples on the next *aliscafo*.

When beach week was over, and Nino went to pick up his wife at the port of Naples, he found her radiant and rejuvenated. Stepping down off the *aliscafo* with her posse, all talking at once, she rushed up to Nino, kissed him, and caressed his cheek. Her giddiness was like an adolescent's, not that of a sixty-five-year-old *signora*. She was ready to go home and embrace domestic life just as she embraced her beach week with the girls. When Nino sulked a little bit, miffed that she had left him for a week and that she had such fun without him, she asked what she could prepare him for dinner.

"*Lasagne*," he replied. Elaborate, time-consuming, his favorite dish. Mitzi, after all, doesn't make it just the way she does. And Raffaella's response to her husband of forty years was one word: *Eccomi*.

Salad

I make really good salad dressing. It's in my blood. My grandfather, the southern preacher of Italian origins, was known for his salads. When his church, in Hinton, West Virginia, hosted potluck dinners, the congregation would not expect my grandmother to bake a casserole. She didn't melt marshmallows over sweet potatoes or baste a pot roast. She bought the lettuce, picked the tomatoes, got out the great big wooden bowl, and left Reverend Salango to it.

I can't say how much oil, vinegar, salt and pepper, or garlic he used or my mother uses or I use. Impossible to quantify the amount of feta cheese or onion; impossible to describe in words how we do it. Which is a sign, I learned in Naples, that we know how to do it really, really well. Salads are in our DNA.

It was in my Americanized kitchen in Rome that I first made a salad for Raffaella. She had opened her magical suitcase, with eggplant Parmesan, mozzarella, lasagna, and *pizzette* from Naples. The kids and Salva dug into the suitcase, and I asked Raffaella what *she* wanted for lunch. She'd been up since 6:00 A.M. baking, buying the freshest mozzarella, and had just arrived on the Eurostar train. *"Solo insalata,"* she said. Thanks, Ketrin, just a salad.

I got to work. Without thinking, measuring, or judging, I made the salad that I know how to make. I told Raffaella that she had to sit down and eat, the kids could wait. I served her.

"Ketrin, è fantastica!" This is the best salad I've ever tasted, she said. I'm having a lunch for the ladies next Friday—could you teach me how to make it? Is there more? Could you make some more?

I reached for a jar to fill with my salad dressing. As I squeezed the garlic and poured the vinegar, I heard the kids and Salva in the living room, laughing and fighting over the contents of the suitcase. Papi, I get the mozzarella! That's mine! Lella, those *pizzette* are for us, too!

There's enough to go around, I called out to my children. Nobody's going hungry.

I screwed the lid on the jar of salad dressing and wrapped it in cellophane. Then I rolled a sheet of newspaper around it and fitted on some rubber bands to keep the packaging in place. It was ready: Raffaella could take it with her on the train back to Naples.

Please appreciate the numbers that are included in the following recipes. They weren't easy to get. As Raffaella plopped and poured, stirred, and talked, I called Mitzi surreptitiously in from his living room rug cleaning to ask how much oil was in the pot, or how much that piece of mozzarella weighed. I had to use the stopwatch function on my iPhone to know how long the meat had been frying. It was better to do this unbeknownst to Raffaella: running numbers by her resulted in a confused, pained look on her face. It was enough to take the Joy out of Cooking.

Ragù

(Serves 6 to 8)

1 small yellow onion, diced

½ cup extra-virgin olive oil

¾ pound *gallinella di maiale,** divided in three quarter-pound,
2-inch cubes

¾ pound veal shank, divided in three quarter-pound, 2-inch
cubes

2 pork ribs (about ¾ pound together), split lengthwise in
2-inch pieces

1 glass red wine

2¼ tablespoons tomato paste

Six 15-ounce cans of the purest peeled tomatoes you can find
(Check ingredients! See below!)

Salt to taste

A few leaves of basil

1½ pounds rigatoni

A handful of large-grain salt (sea salt, for example)
for boiling pasta

1 cup grated Parmesan

Fresh bread

**Gallinella di maiale* is Neapolitan dialect for the meaty muscle from the lower part
of the pig's thigh. (I come from the *We use every part of the pig but the squeal!* Wilson

My mother-in-law knows you're busy (*"Chiste hanno 'a fa,
non tengono tiempo,"* she says. These people don't have time,
Ketrin, they've got things to do), so here's the three-hour *ragù*
recipe rather than the twelve-hour one. She also knows you'd
prefer olive oil to lard, and that you probably don't have a pot
that's made of hardened clay. So here's what you need and
here's what she'll give you: a recipe for "rushed" *ragù.*

First, put an apron on, and don't think of removing it until
you've turned off the stove. When the *ragù* starts to spit, it takes
no prisoners. Get a pot that is not only wide but tall. (The
height is important when the sauce spatters—Raffaella is worried about your kitchen as well as your clothes.) Dice the onion
and put it in the pot with the olive oil.

Non ti ho detto di accendere ancora. She hasn't told you to
turn on the flame yet, so keep your pants on. Position all the
chunks of meat on top of the oil and onion, and scrunch them
in tight with your fingers. Shanks and hocks, pigs and cows—all
down there together, at the bottom of the cool pot.

Now it's time to turn on a medium-low flame. *Si deve im-
biondire la cipolla,* the onion has to become blond, and the
meat has to *rosolare,* pinken. You can put away dishes, or wash a
pan in the meantime. You'll be tempted, like me, to keep walking over to the pot to make sure something bad doesn't happen.
But you've got to leave it alone. It's like raising kids. They're
always there, in your mind, but you don't have to hover over
them. Don't be a helicopter parent to your *ragù.*

Move the chunks of meat around every once in a while
with your wooden spoon so they don't stick to the bottom of the
pot. After 8 or 9 minutes, turn the pieces over. The meat is re-

---

family but have no idea what this is called in English. Boned pork foreleg, possibly?)
Talk to your butcher. The important thing is that it is fleshy and divided in three
quarter-pound, 2-inch cubes.

leasing water, and will continue to do so for about 20 minutes. As long as there is water in the pot, it's too early to add the wine. You know there is water because of all the brown bubbles. (I thought that was oil boiling, but no, it's water. Oil doesn't boil. *What, do you fry blindfolded, Ketrin?*)

When the meat is a dark crusty brown, the onion looks a little burned, and there are fewer bubbles, turn up the heat to high. Pour a few drops of dark red wine on each chunk of meat, like you are performing a baptism. (*Nel nome del Padre, del Figlio, e dello Spirito Santo.*) Enjoy the sound it makes. After a minute or two, repeat until you have poured the whole glass of wine.

Continue to scrape the sides and bottom of the pot regularly. The chunks of meat should slide around more easily now, and the sides should look like you are never in a million years going to get this pot clean.

In the pools of dark purply-brown liquid in between the pieces of meat, drop half-teaspoon dollops of tomato paste. After plopping in each dollop, *stemperatelo*, mash it with the back of your wooden spoon. The paste should become one with the liquid in the pot. (You've been at this for around 45 minutes now, but don't despair! The *avviamento* of the *ragù*—setting it on its way—is almost completed. The time is coming when you're going to send this *ragù* off to college.)

A word on the tomatoes that you are about to pour in. The six cans of peeled tomatoes sitting on the counter ready to be ground up would ideally have been canned by you, during hot summer days, with your womenfolk. Since they probably haven't, you must trust the brand you have chosen. The ingredients should say: TOMATOES. *Basta.* Okay, salt we can let slide. But if it says anything else . . . Raffaella will teach you how to can your own. Oregano? Garlic? Preservatives? *Scordatelo.* Forget about it.

With an immersion blender, grind up three cans of the tomatoes you've chosen and add them to the pot. Continue to scrape the bottom and sides of the pan. After a few minutes, grind up the other three cans and add them to the now red *ragù*.

Turn the flame down as low as it will go—*piano piano piano piano!*—gently gently softly softly!—and cover the pot. Now you can get back to your busy life. (But remember, don't take off your apron, because in about an hour, your *ragù* is going to start spitting up a storm.) The sound that until now has been a frying *zzzzsssssssshhhhhhh* now should become a very mellow *bloop . . . bloop . . . bloop,* which Raffaella calls *purpullià.* (I thought the verb was *pippiare,* but I've heard *pappulià, pippulià . . .* apparently there are as many Neapolitan terms for the slow boiling of *ragù* as Eskimos' terms for snow.)

Check on your *ragù* every half hour or so. Take the cover off the pot, and wipe away the water on the underside of the lid that has accumulated from the steam. Add salt and the basil leaves. Stir the *ragù*, and make sure it doesn't stick to the sides and bottom of the pot. Admire how it is becoming denser, darker, and more *arraggià*—Neapolitan dialect for angry, but meaning tense and dense. A spitfire.

Cover the pot again. After hour two, you can take out all the pieces of meat except the ribs: leave them in until the end. When the *ragù* has been cooking for three hours total, turn off the flame. Boil rigatoni in salted water (use coarse sea salt for the pasta water, never table salt!) and after straining, dump the pasta into the pot of deep red *ragù*. Sprinkle grated Parmesan and serve with fresh bread to sop up the *ragù*. The pieces of meat can be served *after* all the pasta has been consumed, never together.

Ecco fatto: all done. Now you can take off your apron.

Insalata di Polipo

(Serves 6 to 8)

One 2-pound octopus
¼ cup chopped parsley, extra for garnish
½ cup extra-virgin olive oil
1 clove of garlic, cut in quarters
Salt to taste
¼ cup lemon juice, extra lemon slices for garnish

Raffaella starts her preparation of the octopus with this warning: You must make sure your *polipo* is *verace*. *Verace* means authentic—an octopus that is a real Neapolitan, and not some impostor from the Indian Ocean. You may trust your fishmonger; for all Raffaella knows, he may have been the best man in your wedding. But still, my mother-in-law asks you to double-check that he has sold you an octopus that is *verace*: a real, fresh, just-yesterday-he-was-clinging-to-a-cave-in-Marechiaro octopus.

The way you do this is to look for a "double crown" of suction cups on each tentacle. Two parallel rows of suckers, or you've been had. If he's the real thing, get out your meat hammer and cutting board and go to town. Pound the octopus as hard as you can on the cutting board with a meat tenderizer.

Crush his squishy, slimy brains out. Then, in a calmer mode, put him under running water and caress his body, gently pulling off any little black filaments.

Turn his slippery head sac inside out with your fingers (*Peekaboo!* Raffaella sings with a sly smile), and take out all the gloop. Dig your fingers deep under the head to remove the *polipo*'s hard "beak."

In a large pot, boil water with the cork from a wine bottle. Hold the octopus by the head above the pot and dip its tentacles three times in the boiling water. Check out the octopus's curly new hairdo. Put the whole animal in, turn down the flame, and cover. You must maintain a *bollo dolce*, a gentle boil, meaning that the water continues to boil without spilling over the sides. To do this, Raffaella poises her wooden spoon between the lid and the edge of the pot.

Cook the octopus for 20 minutes. The water will become a dark pink, like rosé wine. (This piping-hot pink octopus water used to be drunk with salt and pepper on January 5, the night before Epiphany, in downtown Naples. It was served with the end of the octopus's tentacle, or *'a ranfetella*, floating in the cup, and it really warms you up, apparently. If someone gives you an espresso that isn't strong enough and you want to tell them it's too watery, you can say, "Hey, this octopus water is missing its tentacle!")

Turn the flame off, and let the octopus stay in the water until it cools. This can take a long time, so if you want to speed things up and the weather's chilly, take the pot outside. When it has cooled, take the octopus out and snip it into ½-inch pieces with scissors. Cut the parsley leaves (again, with scissors is the easiest way) and mix them with the octopus, olive oil, garlic, and salt. Let the *insalata* sit for at least one hour at room temperature. Add the lemon juice before serving, and garnish with slices of lemon and parsley leaves.

PS: Raffaella is worried about the fishy smell of your kitchen, your cookware, and your fingers. She hopes, for your own good and that of everyone in your family, that you've turned on the ventilator. For the bowls and your hands, smush damp, used coffee grounds around the pots with your fingertips before washing them with dish soap.

Parmigiana di Melanzane

(Serves 6 to 8)

> 4 pounds eggplants (see below for physical requirements)
> Two 15-ounce cans of Italian peeled, whole tomatoes
> 10 basil leaves
> 1 clove garlic
> Salt to taste
> 2 cups peanut oil
> 1 cup grated Parmesan cheese
> 1 cup *fior di latte* or other soft mozzarella-like cheese,
>   cut in cubes a little smaller than dice

Your eggplants must be long, skinny, hard, and so dark they're almost black. *Insomma*, like a tall, fit Italian woman after a summer on the beach in Positano. Eggplants with the least pulp and seeds (found in summer and early fall) make the best *parmigiana*, Raffaella says. The ones you find in winter tend to be fleshy and moist inside and need to be dried out for at least a day. Otherwise all their white flesh will absorb the frying oil and you'll get a greasy *parmigiana*. One of the worst insults you can lay on someone's *parmigiana* in Naples is that it's greasy.

Cut the stems off your eggplants, and use a carrot peeler to take two long strips of skin off each of them, from opposite

lengthwise sides. Then cut them (again, lengthwise) in slices
½ centimeter thick (¹⁄₁₀ of an inch). Each slice will be framed
by some skin, but no slice will have an entirely purple side.
Place the slices of eggplant on an unlined cookie sheet and
set them out to dry. (Letting them sunbathe on your roof or
balcony is ideal, but if that's not possible, lay them around the
house. Warn family members not to knock them over, Raffaella
reminds you.)

To get rid of the moisture in the eggplants, let them per-
spire for as long as possible. When you take them off the tray
to fry them, you'll notice wet patches on the tray where they've
been lying. This is good: it means they'll fry quickly and lightly,
without absorbing oil.

Before frying the eggplant slices, begin your tomato sauce.
With an immersion blender, grind up the contents of the cans
of tomatoes (remember, the ingredients should say: TOMATOES,
e basta) and put them in a pot with a few of the basil leaves and
one smushed garlic clove. (*Gli dai un pugno in testa, e si toglie
la camicia*, Raffaella says: Punch it on the head and its shirt will
come off.) Cover the pot and cook on low for about 20 minutes.
(After 10 minutes, take the lid off or wedge your wooden spoon
between the rim of the pot and the lid. We don't want watery
sauce.) Add salt to taste.

As the sauce simmers away, turn back to your bathing beau-
ties. Line a tray with paper towels, to receive the slices of eggplant after they've been fried. Heat up your peanut oil so that
it's hot enough to make the pieces sizzle but not so hot that they
smoke. (Try the sizzle test with the edge of one piece before slid-
ing them all in. If the piece bubbles, the oil is ready.) Now ease
the slices in for their hot bath. Put in enough pieces to cover
the surface of the oil, but not so many that they're crowded on

top of each other. (Think of vacationers on the beaches of the Amalfi coast in mid-August. People are touching each other, but it would be uncool to get on top of anyone.) Flip them after about a minute, and then take them out when you see that they are becoming light brown. (This should happen pretty quickly if they've sweated properly beforehand.) Use a skimmer to take the slices out, and hold them over the pan to let the excess oil drain off before positioning the eggplant on the paper towels. Cover the slices with more paper towels to absorb the oil (Repeat: *My* parmigiana *will not be greasy!*). Make sure the oil is still hot enough for the next batch—if not, pump up the fire. After frying the next round of slices, position them on top of their predecessors, separated by paper towels. Repeat the process until you've fried all the eggplant. Preheat the oven to 375 degrees.

Now assemble the layers of the *parmigiana* in an 8-by-8-inch casserole dish. Start by putting a few spoonfuls of tomato sauce on the bottom of the dish and smoothing it into a red carpet with the back of your wooden spoon. Then arrange the first layer of eggplant slices (slightly shriveled and brown now, as if they've spent too much time at a tanning salon) side by side across the bottom of the dish. Spread another layer of tomato sauce on top of the eggplant, and sprinkle a few spoonfuls of Parmesan cheese evenly across it. Tear some basil leaves with your fingers (never touch basil with a knife, because it alters the taste! *Mi raccomando!*), and drop the torn leaves to the north, south, east, and west. Then distribute about a third of the *fior di latte* cubes.

The next layer of eggplant slices should be placed crosswise to the one before, so that the *parmigiana* is easier to cut. Continue with the same pattern—eggplant slices (each layer running crosswise to the one before), sauce, Parmesan, basil, and *fior di latte*.

Stop the pattern after the Parmesan. The top of the *parmi-giana* should be Parmesan-dotted red, with only a vague hint of the brown treasures inside. Bake at 375 degrees for about 25 minutes, or until you see a crust forming on the top. Serve at room temperature.

If your *parmigiana* turns out greasy or is swimming in oil, please don't mention to anyone where you got the recipe.

Sartù di Riso

(Serves 6 to 8)

RAGÙ
1 small yellow onion, diced
½ cup extra-virgin olive oil
2¼ pounds of meat (boned pork foreleg, veal shank, pork ribs.
    See recipe for *ragù*, page 268) in 2-inch cubes
1 glass red wine
2¼ tablespoons tomato paste
Six 15-ounce cans of peeled, whole tomatoes
Salt to taste
A few leaves of basil

MEATBALLS
2 cups day-old bread (the soft inner part of a loaf works best)
¾ pound ground beef
1 egg
Salt
⅓ cup Parmesan cheese
About 2 cups peanut oil

SARTÙ FILLING
5 eggs

3 tablespoons extra-virgin olive oil

2 small (¼ pound each) fresh pork sausages

½ white onion

One 15-ounce can cooked peas or 1½ cups frozen peas

Salt to taste

1 pound arborio rice

Butter for casserole dish

1½ cups grated Parmesan cheese

2 cups *fior di latte* or other soft mozzarella-like cheese,
    cut in cubes a little smaller than dice

4–6 leaves of basil

The *sartù di riso* isn't hard, Raffaella reassures you, it just takes organization and assembly. (And a big table, I would add. And an efficient, empty dishwasher. And a well-developed capacity for multitasking. And a few other things . . .) The various elements can be cooked ahead of time, frozen, and defrosted if need be. It's particularly helpful if you've already made the *ragù* and the baby meatballs.

(Heads up! Have *ragù* at the ready and make the baby meatballs first! Raffaella says, *che problema c'è* if you haven't prepared these beforehand. But I would argue that there is a *problema*.)

Prepare the *ragù* if you haven't yet (see page 268).

For the meatballs: Take off your rings. In a bowl, soak the day-old bread in 4 cups water. Smush together the ground beef, egg, salt, and Parmesan. Squeeze the bread to release as much water as possible, add it to the meat mixture with your greasy, sticky hands, and work it together like dough. Then roll out little marble-sized balls. Put the peanut oil in a tall pot or deep fryer and heat it over a high flame. As the oil heats up to its sizzling temperature, line a tray with paper towels. Fry the little balls for a few minutes or until they become light brown (they should float around in the oil, bubbling away. Don't skimp on the oil and don't crowd the meatballs). Remove them with a skimmer, and place them on the paper towels. Like anything small and fried, they are at risk of being stolen by hungry, roaming family members. Keep your wooden spoon at the ready: these *polpettine* are destined for your *sartù*.

For the *sartù* and to assemble: Boil 3 of the eggs in a pot of water for 10 minutes, and while they are cooking, put 1 tablespoon of the olive oil in a small skillet with 1 cup water. Cut the ends off the sausages and poke holes in them with a fork. Put them in the oily water, cover the skillet, and cook over a medium flame. The water will boil off and the sausages will brown. This will take 10 to 15 minutes.

When the eggs are done, place them in a bowl of ice water for a few minutes so you can shell them more easily. Take the sausages off the fire, cut them into 1-centimeter (quite thin) rounds, and set them aside in a bowl. Dice the onion, and in another skillet, heat the remaining 2 tablespoons of olive oil. Sauté the onion over a low-medium flame until it starts to brown. If you're using canned peas, drain them first and then put them in the skillet with the onions; frozen peas can be thrown in still frozen. Cover the pan and let the peas and onions cook for 5 minutes (10 to 15 if you're using frozen peas). Put the pea mixture in a bowl, then form an assembly line with the *ragù*, Parmesan, peas, sausage rounds, meatballs, *fior di latte*, and basil. Shell the eggs, cut them in quarters, and put them next to the sausage rounds and cooked peas on the assembly line.

In a tall pot, bring to boil 34 ounces (1 liter) of water mixed with two ladles of *ragù* and some salt. Put your rice into the orangey-red boiling water and stir. Take out a few ladles of the liquid and put them in another small pot on the stove. (The rice should absorb all the water like a risotto, but if it gets too dry, this hot broth will be useful. Ten or twelve more burners on your stovetop and a sous-chef would also be useful at this point.) Cover the pot of rice. Make sure you maintain the *bollo dolce*—the gentle boil that keeps on boiling!—and stir regularly. Turn off the fire 2 minutes before the advised cooking time of your rice, so that it's not crunchy hard but al dente. If the rice is cooked too much, your *sartù* will become a *papocchia*, or pigs' mush. (*Per carità!* Lord help us.) Let it cool.

Preheat the oven to 400 degrees. In a large bowl, beat the remaining 2 eggs with a fork, add a pinch of salt, and set aside. Using a piece of paper towel, spread butter over the bottom and sides of a deep casserole dish (Raffaella's is 3 inches tall, 9 by 13 inches across) to make a *velo di burro*, a veil of butter. Plop a ladle of *ragù* on the bottom of the pan and spread it out with the back of your wooden spoon. Make sure your rice is cool, then stir it into the beaten eggs. (If the rice isn't cool enough, you'll inadvertently scramble the eggs. Please. These eggs are what holds the *sartù* together—Raffaella says *unite* the *sartù*—important eggs, for heaven's sake.) Now stir into the rice pot one ladle of *ragù*, 2 spoonfuls of grated Parmesan cheese, a third of the sausage rounds, a third of the meatballs, a third of the peas, and a third of the *fior di latte*.

Put down a 1-inch-thick layer of *sartù* on the *ragù*-lined bottom of the pan and level it out with the back of your spoon. Spread out another layer of *ragù* on top: your rice needs to be *ben salsato*, or sauced up, Raffaella says, otherwise it will stop in your throat. Not pretty. Distribute a few more spoonfuls of Parmesan, a third of the peas, sausage rounds, meatballs, cubes of *fior di latte*, and a few torn-up leaves of basil. Start again with another layer of rice.

Now it's time to pretend you're the Easter Bunny and hide 6 of the hard-boiled-egg quarters in the middle of the casserole where nobody can find them. Don't tell anyone where you put them. Dig little holes if you need to. (Raffaella puts her glasses on for this hide-and-seek.) Repeat the pattern once more: rice, sauce, Parmesan, the last thirds of the peas, sausage, meatballs, *fior di latte*, and basil, and make the Easter egg hunt with the remaining hard-boiled-egg quarters. End with sauce and Parmesan. Bake at 400 degrees for 20 minutes or until the *sartù* forms a crust on top. Dollop some hot *ragù* on each slice before serving.

ACKNOWLEDGMENTS

It isn't easy when you're a *mamma* to let your baby go. You need people to hold your hand, put up with your craziness, and look at your little one, the piece of your heart, and say, "Hey, she's got a blob of something on her chin" that you hadn't noticed. Or "Don't you think it's time for a training bra?" You need loving, smart people to help her grow. It does take a village.

The village that has raised this book extends to both sides of the Atlantic. Without my agent, Anna Stein, the baby would be a pile of crumpled-up pages spat out by my wonky printer. She believed in it from the get-go and knew exactly what it needed, always. David Vine is a friend with a great big capital Quaker F for leading me to her. To the bicontinental guardian angels at Aitken Alexander, including Sally Riley, Nishta Hurry, Lesley Thorne, Alex Hoyt, and Clare Alexander: thank you for guiding me along the way.

At Random House, Andrea Walker is not only a brilliant editor but manages to be therapist and friend at the same time. She has been a true partner in raising the baby with *calma,* laughter, and peace of mind. Your little Tillie is blessed. Thanks also to Andy Ward for his help in the literary kitchen. And rather than thanking Susan Kamil in words for her passion and faith in this story, I'm going to help my mother-in-law get that *parmigiana di melanzane* to her office in New York (fresh, and at the right temperature!) so, hopefully, when we manage that, she'll be able to taste our gratitude.

Thank you to Ann Patty, who got me on course, and to John Thavis, who helped me stay there.

Early readers and friends Josh Conviser, Josephine Scorer, Dave Digilio, Massimiliano and Mireille Paolucci-Smit, Marco Maltauro, Alejandra Pero, Leo Kittay and Kim Dooley Kittay, Lynn Swanson, Heather Perrault, Silvia dell'Olio, Mercedes Roza, William Pratesi-Urquhart, Mike Rudolph, Laurie Kaye, Azar Burnham-Grubbs, Fee Huebner, and Doris Rametsteiner: *grazie, danke, bedankt.* I am so grateful for the atrium of Ambrit International School in Rome, and for the help and support of Paolo Isotta, Kris Dahl, Jennifer Gilmore, Renato de Falco, and of Ken, Vickie, and Alix Wilson.

Giovanni Vitale's rules of Neapolitan dialect (expertly compiled in his *Dialetto Napoletano: Manuale di scrittura e di dizione*) were an invaluable resource. *Grazie assai.*

The friendship of Kiersten Miller is a jewel at the center of my chaotic Roman life. At her Milk Bar, I've learned that when the going gets tough, the tough need to hang out for a little while with bighearted women from Naples and New York. Preferably over Ponzu.

Theo and Jim Yardley: Thank God you came to Rome. You are *maestri* of the craft and true friends.

Thanks to Monica Barden for her constant encouragement, generosity, and inclusiveness. Pia and Giuseppe Signori, Giorgio and Claudia: you have taught me the deepest meaning of family. And Antonio Mormone, I hope your spirit never wanes. The world needs it.

Katrina Smith and Gianluca Franzoni have come to the rescue often, and our friendship is a *punto di riferimento* that I cherish. The image of the two of you laughing together over the manuscript on your porch in Bologna was what I needed at just the right moment. Katrina, I hope we're smuggling Reese's Peanut Butter Cups into an Italian nursing home together one day.

Gracias infinitas to Irene Hernandez, my mentor from Madrid, who didn't say "I'm here for you," when on the verge of tears I suggested lighting a bonfire, holding hands, and throwing my manuscript in page by page. She said, Please! Will you stop being so *Neapolitan?*

Antonella Dugo is the grandmother of this book, and Andreas Giannakoulas its grandfather. You helped me to find and trust my voice, whether it was wobbly and off-key or full-bodied and right on pitch. Thanks also to my soul sister Jackie, for keeping me laughing no matter what. And for screaming at me, often, *Mommy! Write your book!*

To the Crossley family and especially my friend Tara, I am grateful every day that people of such faith have crossed my path. Thank you, Tara, for being an example of pressing on toward the goal, and running the race. And for reminding me always of what the prize really is.

To the whole Avallone family: My father-in-law asks me never to say thank you. Thank you assumes you're not family. So I won't say thank you, I'll say read the book. But I'll add that there are two people whose place in the story is infinitely smaller than their place in my heart: my nephew Claudio d'Albore and Nino himself. Thank you for loving me like a daughter.

And, finally, Salvatore, Anthony, and Raffaella: *Siete la mia vita.*

About the Author

KATHERINE WILSON was raised in Washington, D.C., and educated at the Sidwell Friends School and Princeton University. For the past nineteen years she has worked in theater, television, and film, as well as freelance translating in Italy. She lives in Rome with her husband and two children.

katherinewilsonwriter.com
Facebook.com/KatherineWilsonWriter

About the Type

THIS BOOK was set in Electra, a typeface designed for Linotype by renowned type designer W. A. Dwiggins (1880–1956). Electra is a fluid typeface, avoiding the contrasts of thick and thin strokes that are prevalent in most modern typefaces.

GLADSTONE AND WOMEN

Gladstone and Women

Anne Isba

hambledon
continuum

Hambledon Continuum
A Continuum imprint

The Tower Building,
11 York Road,
London SE1 7NX,
UK

80 Maiden Lane,
Suite 704,
New York, NY 10038
USA

First Published 2006

ISBN 1 85285 471 5

A description of this book is available from the
British Library and from the Library of Congress.

Typeset by Carnegie Publishing, Lancaster,
and printed in the United Kingdom by MPG Books Ltd, Cornwall.

Contents

Illustrations   vii

Acknowledgements   ix

Introduction   xi

1   Early Years   1

2   Eton and Oxford   13

3   Catherine   31

4   Helen   49

5   Lady Lincoln   71

6   Fallen Women   99

7   Daughters   123

8   Harriet, Laura and Olga   153

9   Victoria   177

10 Final Years   201

Notes   212

Bibliography   241

Index   245

for
Jean Gilliland

Contents

Illustrations   vii

Acknowledgements   ix

Introduction   xi

1   Early Years   1

2   Eton and Oxford   13

3   Catherine   31

4   Helen   49

5   Lady Lincoln   71

6   Fallen Women   99

7   Daughters   123

8   Harriet, Laura and Olga   153

9   Victoria   177

10   Final Years   201

Notes   212

Bibliography   241

Index   245

for
Jean Gilliland

Illustrations

Between Pages 80 and 81

1   Gladstone as a young man

2   Rodney St, Liverpool

3   Seaforth House, Lancashire

4   Helen Gladstone, Gladstone's sister

5   Helen Gladstone's medicine chest

6   Catherine Gladstone, *née* Glynne

7   Agnes Gladstone

8   Catherine Jessy Gladstone

9   Mary Gladstone

10 Helen Gladstone, Gladstone's daughter

11 Hawarden

12 Fasque

13 Group photo at Hawarden in mid-1880s

14 Group photo at Hawarden, August 1874

15 William and Catherine Gladstone

Between Pages 144 and 145

16   Susan, Countess of Lincoln

17   Harriet, Duchess of Sutherland

18   Queen Victoria

19   *Lady with the Coronet of Jasmine*

20   Laura Thistlethwayte

21   Meeting at the Corn Exchange, Manchester

22   Plate of William Gladstone

23   Plate of Catherine Gladstone

24   A London prostitute

25   Olga Novikov

Illustrations Acknowledgements

The author and publishers are grateful to the following for permission to reproduce illustrations: Aberdeen Art Gallery and Museums Collections, no. 19; Athenaeum, Liverpool, no. 1; Flintshire Record Office, nos 11, 13–15, 22, 23; National Trust for Scotland, no. 16; Royal Archives, no. 18; Scottish National Portrait Gallery, no. 17; Robin Thistlethwayte, no. 20.

Acknowledgements

I should like to thank, first of all, Sir William Gladstone and Mr Charles Gladstone for allowing me to quote widely from the Glynne-Gladstone manuscripts, to reproduce family images, and for giving me access to the Temple of Peace at Hawarden and the Gladstone home at Fasque. Also in this context, the staff at St Deiniol's Library, Hawarden, and the Flintshire Record Office have been consistently kind and supportive in facilitating access to the Gladstone family papers and other important material. Oxford University Press have generously given permission for extensive use of the Gladstone *Diaries* and Blackwells have agreed to the reproduction of material of mine first published in *History* magazine, the research for which was funded by the Wellcome Trust. For all this I am very grateful.

The value of support provided by family, friends and colleagues cannot be overstated, and I thank them for it and for their forbearance. For extra information on specific aspects of Gladstone's relationships with women, I should like to acknowledge the help provided by David Bebbington, Ruth Clayton, Colin Cruise, Michael Lynch, Mark Nixon, Kim Reynolds, Richard Shannon, Virginia Surtees, Scott and Pauline Traynor, David Vincent and Chris Wrigley. At Hawarden, Bill Pritchard was an endless source of valuable insights into the private life of the Gladstones in the nineteenth century. Thanks also to Martin Sheppard at Hambledon, a fund of good ideas and a generous and enthusiastic editor.

My greatest debt by far, however, is to Jean Gilliland. Jean was closely involved both in research for the Gladstone diaries (whose editor, Colin Matthew, was her nephew) and, more recently, for the *Oxford Dictionary of National Biography*, to which she contributed many articles. No one understands more than Jean the significance of women in Gladstone's life. Her generosity in sharing with me not only this knowledge

but also her friendship and hospitality has made writing this book –
which could, by rights, be hers – a pleasure and a privilege. Thank you,
Jean.

Introduction

It was the afternoon of 3 February 1927. In the packed courtroom of the King's Bench Division of the High Court in London, the atmosphere was electric. For five days, the jury of nine men and three women in the case of *Wright* v. *Gladstone* had heard recounted every serious rumour about the sex life of William Gladstone. Now they had withdrawn to consider their verdict. At stake, nearly thirty years after his death, was the good name of nineteenth-century Britain's greatest statesman. The question the jury had to decide was: were Gladstone's sons Herbert and Henry justified in calling Captain Peter Wright a coward and a liar for accusing their late father of hypocrisy and immorality?

It was a complicated case. In a book entitled *Portraits and Criticisms*, Wright had inserted almost gratuitously, at the last moment and apparently without the knowledge of his publishers, a passage to the effect that Gladstone had 'set the tradition in public to speak the language of highest and strictest principle, and in private to pursue and possess every sort of woman'.

It is not possible to sue for libel of the dead. The only route open to the Gladstone sons was publicly to insult Wright so outrageously, via an open letter to the press, that he had no choice but to sue them for defamation, after which the issue could be thoroughly aired in the courts. This is what had led to the case.

The trial gripped the imagination of the nation. A quarter of a million words were recorded by the court stenographers and the leading newspapers reported the proceedings in merciless detail. In an attempt to prove his case, Wright aired the whole range of scurrilous rumours, including that Gladstone had fathered an illegitimate child, and had enjoyed a string of liaisons with prostitutes, ex-courtesans and actresses – Lillie Langtry among them – and even with a Russian spy. Although the allegations had never before been aired so publicly, they were not new. They had surfaced periodically in whispering campaigns ever since Benjamin Disraeli had succeeded Gladstone as Prime Minister in 1874. Indeed, the *Times* newspaper questioned 'whether the better course might not to have been to treat [Wright] and his book with silent contempt'.[1] But the elder of the two surviving sons, Herbert, Viscount Gladstone, felt that the family had had no alternative course of action available if they were to preserve his father's reputation for posterity.

> Because Mr Gladstone was dead we could not take legal action ... If we took no legal action, it would have been open to Wright or anyone else to say the charges were true because two of Mr Gladstone's sons were alive when they were made and dared not take any action. Such statements would have the appearance of truth. We held that if we did nothing, we should fail in our duty as sons ... My brother and I, being of advanced years, realised that when we were gone there would be no one to give the evidence that we alone could give.[2]

Herbert Gladstone won much public respect for his stance. The nation and the press were strongly behind him. The *Manchester Guardian*, for example, quoted at length from the memoirs of Salvation Army chief, Bramwell Booth, the ultimate arbiter on rescue work, to explain the innocent nature of Gladstone's prostitute contacts and his utter disregard for public opinion. Booth recalled walking down Regent Street one afternoon when he saw the then Prime Minister on the other side of the street.

> No one who knew him at all could mistake him. The vivacity which belonged to his speaking and action showed itself in his very gait, and he conveyed something of himself in the varying changes of his facial expression. On this occasion he was accompanied by a young woman, and I, probably quickened in my perceptions as the result of Salvation Army experience, instantly saw that she was one of a sorrowful class. Mr Gladstone was evidently speaking to her in the most kindly and fatherly manner. I did not, of course, hear what he said, but there was something about his whole attitude and about the girl's appearance also which lead me to feel that he was appealing to her and bestowing some kind of favour upon her.[3]

Booth added that, in such instances, the 'risk of misinterpretation' was made clear to Gladstone, but he was 'so sensible of the purity of his motives that he was proof against expostulation'.[4]

As the trial progressed, Wright's case was systematically demolished as witness after witness refuted the interpretations he put on what was the flimsiest of hearsay. In his summing-up Mr Justice Avery went so far as to suggest that Wright had inserted the offending passage solely to sell his book and 'to pander to the vicious taste of that section of the reading public who live on scandal, particularly if it is scandal connected with the private life of a public man'.[5] So it came as no great surprise, but no small relief either, when the jury returned to the courtroom after two and a half hours' deliberation and announced that they found Lord Gladstone's opinion of Wright to be true. They found unanimously for Herbert Gladstone against Wright for the calumny of his father, awarding him costs of £6000.

But that was not all. In the growing tide of applause that broke out in the courtroom on hearing the verdict, it was just possible to hear the foreman say that the jury would like to add that it was their unanimous opinion that the evidence placed before them had 'completely vindicated the high moral character of the late Mr W. E. Gladstone'.[6] The *Daily Mail*, which had taken the credit for first drawing public attention to Wright's accusations, reported the scene in court.

> As the foreman sat down, Lord and Lady Gladstone and Mr Gladstone, another son, sank back with obvious relief. The hands of the two brothers met and clasped ... The murmur of applause swelled, and several people in the gallery began to stamp their feet. Mr Justice Avery brought instant silence with a stern threat that the next demonstrator would be committed for contempt of court. Even before the last words of the foreman of the jury had been said, Captain Peter Wright, who had paled at the verdict, rose from his seat – a few yards away from the Gladstone family – and walked out of the court with his head bowed. He went out alone. From all parts of the court people were advancing on Lord and Lady Gladstone. Some of them were people they knew, some spectators they did not know. There were handshakes for all comers, and messages of thanks which were the only comment they would make on the case. 'We are all happy now – all vindicated', said Lady Gladstone, smiling on all around her. Lord Gladstone said it was the only verdict possible, the verdict that all who knew Mr Gladstone had expected.[7]

As the Gladstones left the court, they were greeted outside by yet more crowds of cheering well-wishers. Many of the demonstrators can hardly have been born when Gladstone was a towering figure in British politics; but a belief in the integrity of the 'People's William' clearly continued to live on in the popular consciousness.

Of the women defamed by Wright's assertions – for they, too, were victims of the calumny, as Winston Churchill pointed out in a letter to the Press Association – most were already dead and unable to defend their reputations.[8] Gladstone's friend Laura Thistlethwayte, the courtesan turned evangelist, had died in 1894, four years before him. Katharine O'Shea, whom Gladstone was accused of using as a go-between to the Irish nationalist Charles Parnell while knowing of their adulterous affair, had died in 1921. That year also saw the death of Olga Novikov, whom Disraeli called 'the MP for Russia', allegedly sent to London to seduce Gladstone into siding with Russia against Turkey. The only prominent woman to survive was Lillie Langtry, by then Lady de Bathe and aged seventy-four. She sent an immediate telegram to the court from her home in Monte Carlo, repudiating Wright's 'preposterous statement' that she had had a liaison with Gladstone, and suggesting that Wright should 'reflect upon the necessity for accuracy in a modern volume of memoirs even when dealing with people almost belonging to a past generation'. Speaking to the *Daily Mail*'s Monte Carlo correspondent, she was more forthright, insisting that 'in the old days a thing like this would have been settled by a horse-whipping in the Haymarket'.[9] She had only met Gladstone half a dozen times in her life, she added, the first occasion being when he had visited Millais' studio where she was sitting for a portrait.[10] 'He seemed to appreciate all the difficulties that lay ahead of me in my theatrical career, and always left me feeling that he was an essentially good man.' She valued his 'comprehensive mind and sweet nature', his 'wisdom' and the 'uplifting effects of his visits'.[11]

After the Wright case was over, the *Daily Telegraph* spoke for the entire nation when it said that 'Mr Gladstone's moral character emerges from this trial wholly unscathed'.[12] But there were two other important documents, and potential pieces of evidence, on the Gladstones' side that were not presented in court, on the advice of their counsel. One was Gladstone's diaries. 'Our root difficulty', Henry suggested to Herbert in 1926, was the diary's 'introspections, its spiritual misgivings and half accusations and in the fact that confessions of human weakness are definitely connected with the other sex'.[13] But the second item that their legal team advised the Gladstones against producing in court could have been even more compromising. It was a document about Gladstone's sexuality known within the family simply as 'The Declaration'.

On 7 December 1896, Gladstone, increasingly aware of what he called the 'successive snapping of the threads' that bound him to this earthly existence, had decided to set down on paper a remarkable statement about his private life. It was a dramatic enough revelation for any person to make, let alone one who had four times been Prime Minister. Conscious of the rumours circulating even then about his alleged sexual activities – although he would not have described them as such himself – and knowing that, once he was no longer there to defend himself, these activities would be examined by his enemies in greater detail than ever before, Gladstone took an important stand. He made the point of insisting that he had never – not ever – been guilty of marital infidelity. This statement was placed in a sealed envelope, on the outside of which he wrote: 'only to be opened after my death'. He gave the document into the safekeeping of his son Stephen, rector of the family church at Hawarden. It read:

> With reference to rumours which I believe were one time afloat, though I know not with what degree of currency: and also with reference to the times when I shall not be here to answer for myself; I desire to record my solemn declaration and assurance, as in the sight of God and before His judgement seat, that at no period of my life have I been guilty of the act which is known as that of infidelity to the marriage bed. I limit myself to this negation, and I record it with my dear son Stephen, both as the eldest surviving of our sons, and as my pastor. It will be for him to retain or use it, confidentially unless necessity should require more, which is unlikely: and in any case making it known to his brothers.[14]

Gladstone died eighteen months later. The envelope was not opened until two years after that, in September 1900, and only then for possible use by John Morley, who had been appointed by the Gladstone children to write their father's life. The existence of 'The Declaration' – and the qualified nature of the 'negation' – was not disclosed in Morley's biography. For it was a document that raised more questions than it answered about Gladstone and women.

1

Early Years

William Ewart Gladstone first saw the light of day in December 1809 in a substantial double-fronted house in Rodney Street, Liverpool.[1] He was the fourth son and fifth child of six born to the wealthy and ambitious Scottish merchant John Gladstone and his devoutly evangelical wife, Anne. Gladstone's father John (1764–1851) was a self-made man. His career typified the combination of personal ambition and commercial acumen that made Britain a great trading nation in the late eighteenth and early nineteenth century. Thomas Gladstones, John's father, had been a corn dealer in the Edinburgh area, although the family came from Biggar in the Scottish Borders.[2] John Gladstone, who had originally worked in his father's corn business, amassed a great fortune trading with North America and the Baltic. His business interests encompassed grain – following in his father's footsteps – as well as property and shipping. In the West Indies he invested heavily, and successfully, in sugar, cotton and slaves.

Ambitious and driven though he was, John Gladstone retained old-fashioned Scottish Presbyterian values, including duty, probity and charity. None of these compromised his material success. From the beginning of the nineteenth century until 1828, when William fulfilled his father's dearest hope by going up to Christ Church, Oxford, John Gladstone's assets had grown from around £40,000 to well over £500,000.[3] This was a family for whom money was not a problem.

Some of his money John Gladstone used to buy himself a seat in Parliament in an unreformed Britain where 'pocket' boroughs were readily available for cash. In this capacity, he represented in turn Lancaster, Woodstock and Berwick on Tweed. The world should have been his to command, except for one sorrow. In 1792 he had married Jane Hall, the daughter of a Liverpool merchant. Unlike her husband, she was never physically strong. Shortly after their marriage, she began visiting spa

resorts but they did her no good. As John's fortunes continued to prosper, his wife's health continued to deteriorate until she died, childless,
in 1798, leaving him a widower at the age of thirty-four.

In 1800, after the period of two years required by decency, John married again. Anne Robertson Mackenzie was twenty-eight, beautiful, shy,
an intensely religious Episcopalian and, like her predecessor, frail. She
was also well above her husband in social status, being the descendant
of Highland gentry on both sides of her family, tracing her ancestry as
far back as Robert the Bruce.[4] Her father and grandfather were both
leading lawyers in Dingwall, a centre of social and political Highland
life, and she claimed Seaforth clan connections. Money no longer being
a main consideration, improving his family's social standing became
one of John Gladstone's ambitions.

The increasingly invalid Anne provided him with four sons and two
daughters. The eldest and youngest of the Gladstone siblings were girls:
Anne Mackenzie, born on Christmas Eve 1802, and Helen Jane, born in
June 1814. These two sisters played a crucial role in influencing William's
attitude to women for the rest of his life. William's three elder brothers
were Thomas (1804), Robertson (1805) and John Neilson (1807).

John was entirely devoted to his family. 'He had', wrote William, 'a
large and strong nature, simple though hasty, profoundly affectionate
and capable of the highest devotion in the lines of love and duty.'[5]
He was particularly devoted to his wife; but her nature, though saintly
and noble, was nervous. Like her elder daughter, she exemplified the
'pure but supine' woman that was to condition William's image of
ideal womanhood.[6] There is no doubt that her nervous condition
held the family back from achieving the social standing that John
Gladstone craved. The chronic illnesses of his wife and daughters
prevented entertaining and required frequent peregrinations to fashionable watering-holes.[7] But there is no indication that John Gladstone
valued his wife any the less for that. Indeed, he invested his considerable wealth to bring to Liverpool as many members of his own and her
own family as desired to come. At one time John Gladstone owned as
many as nineteen houses in fashionable Rodney Street, many of them
rented out to members of his wife's family.

In 1811, when Rodney Street was no longer grand enough, John Gladstone began building Seaforth House, some five miles out of Liverpool,

on the banks of the River Mersey. It was an impressive and ambitious project, named after his wife's clan, and one which he kept changing and adding to for years, earning the house the nickname 'Guttling Hall' from young Anne. In addition to the mansion, the estate eventually comprised a home farm, small hamlet, St Thomas's church and an attached school. In the early stages, the Gladstones divided their time between there and Rodney Street. The final move down river was completed in 1815, when William was five years old. It was an idyllic setting for a young boy to grow up in. There was just one other house between Seaforth and Liverpool. There were barns, stables and lofts to hide in; orchards, woods and fields to play in; and a long windswept beach in front of the house along which to race ponies and watch the merchant ships – those symbols of the family's wealth – sail up and down the river.[8]

The physical freedom afforded by life at Seaforth was, however, in no way matched by intellectual freedom. Gladstone and a dozen or more boys from his extended clan were taught by the rector of St Thomas's, William Rawson. Rawson had been brought from Cambridge by John Gladstone, at a salary of one hundred pounds a year, to run both the church and school he had built. Rawson was a weak teacher – particularly in classics, the central subject for a gentleman's education. Like Mrs Gladstone, he was a pious but relatively submissive personality. As a result, the school remained as resolutely evangelical as home, and strictly under the control of John Gladstone.

The physical helplessness of the two Annes made a lasting impression on young William. For the rest of his life, he saw illness bravely borne as a sign of nearness to God, and women – rightly or wrongly – as noble creatures that either occupied, or needed to be returned to, a moral state equivalent to that occupied by his mother and elder sister. Gladstone remembered Anne Gladstone as a 'dear and noble mother', 'a beautiful and admirable woman', 'a woman of warm piety but broken health'.[9] He rarely knew her in good health. One of the first entries in the first volume of his diary of 1825, when he was his fifteen years old and away at Eton, reads: 'Mother ill'. It would become a leitmotiv of his journals. But despite her perpetual invalidism – combined with a self-effacing, nervous disposition which made it difficult for her to manage servants, let alone social contacts – her genuine goodness and sense of duty set the tone of family life. While her frailty held the family back from social advancement, there seems no doubt as to the sincere and deep, if anxious, devotion which all members of the family felt for this traditional angel of the hearth.

If it was Anne Gladstone senior who defined the moral parameters of family life in the God-fearing household, it was young Anne Gladstone – at least in the early years before ill health began to drain her own vitality – who shouldered much of the day to day responsibility for its management. As young as twelve, she was left in charge of the family home while the parents were away; and she reported diligently back to them on domestic affairs. She was specifically responsible for the welfare of her one-year-old sister Helen. 'It is no small comfort to me', her absent mother wrote, 'to know my little pet has one who will pay every kindness and who so well comprehends all her wants.'[10]

Anne was two and a half years older than her first brother, Tom. William, the fourth boy, was two and a half years younger than John Neilson, the brother above him. By contrast, there was less space than this altogether between the three middle boys, Tom, Robertson and John Neilson. As a result, young William stood apart from the core group of brothers; he gravitated towards the care of his elder sister, and later into a position of authority – bossiness even – towards Helen, four and a half years his junior. William was devoted to Anne, who was, he insisted, 'a perfect saint. In later years she lived in close relations with me, and I must have been much the worse but for her'.[11] For, unlike her, he was not, he claimed, a particularly good person: 'I have no recollection of being a loving or winning child: or an earnest or diligent or knowledge-loving child ... I did not lie or habitually practise falsehood, meanness or indecency: but I could be drawn into them by occasion and temptation'.[12] In old age, he wrote of his childhood:

> I wish that in reviewing this period I could regard it as presenting those features of innocence and beauty which I have often seen elsewhere ... The best I can say for it is that I do not think it was actually a vicious childhood. I do not think ... that I had a strong natural propensity then developed to what are termed mortal sins. But truth obliges me to say this against myself ... [I was] not a devotional child ... neither was I a popular boy ... I was a child of slow development: there was perhaps more in me than in the average boy,

but it required greatly more time to set itself in order ... and if I was not a bad boy, I think that I was a boy with a great absence of goodness.[13]

It was his sister Anne, who was his conscientious godmother as well as his surrogate mother, who encouraged him to keep a diary in order to be able, on the Day of Judgement, to give an account to God of the use of his time. (William later tried to pass this advice on to Helen, though with less success.) Anne it was who sent spare socks to Eton (where he went at the age of eleven), who wrote to him about the antics of the family cat, and who discussed every possible subject with him from contemporary political and theological issues to his latest visit to the circus and the new tooth-brace of his school chum, Charles Canning. He called her his 'little witch' and the family's 'Secretary of State for Foreign Affairs, Home and Colonial Departments', keeping him up to date on all that happened back home at Seaforth.[14] His relationship with Anne was the most significant of William's young life.

> Her mental gifts were considerable, her character most devout and fervent; her religious rearing had been in the Evangelical tenets but her mind was too pure for prejudice. She must have infused into me some little warmth, and I think she started me on some not very devious bypaths of opinion.[15]

As his spiritual mentor, it was Anne who explained the practical day to day significance of the high moral tone set by their saintly invalid mother; and established the almost impossibly demanding standards that William would strive to meet for the rest of his life.[16]

In the autumn of 1823, however, Anne became seriously ill. It would be another sixty years before the tubercle bacillus was identified, but it seems that tuberculosis was almost certainly the cause of her six-year decline. Brothers Robertson and Tom were also regularly sick during the first two years of Anne's illness, suffering a series of persistent infections from which they, unlike their unfortunate sister, eventually recovered. The Gladstones invested in every medicine and treatment that money could buy for Anne, but to no avail.[17] At twenty to three in the morning of Thursday 19 February 1829, at the age of twenty-six, she died at Seaforth House, 'without a struggle or a groan'.

It was Saturday morning before Gladstone, now in his second term at Christ Church, Oxford, received the news. He packed up his things immediately and travelled home through the night 'at first much dismayed but afterwards unable to *persuade* myself of the truth of the news'.[18] Yet he cannot have been surprised. There had already been one earlier false alarm when he had been summoned home from Eton. And his diary entries about Anne indicate his growing sense of anxiety, particularly during the last two years of her life. When at home, he recorded her almost obsessively as they talked, as if in an attempt to capture on paper what he expected, sooner or later, to lose. And now he had.

Around midday on Sunday, Gladstone arrived at Seaforth where he

> found all in great grief ... Saw the pale remains of dearest Anne, but felt in weeping over them that my tears were entirely selfish. Blessed and praised be God's Holy Name for thus calling to Himself first from among us one who was so well prepared, so thoroughly refined, so weaned from earth, so ripe for Heaven ... Listened to the accounts given of dearest Anne's death-bed scenes, with an interest which must be felt under such circumstances even by those whose feelings are as little tender and as much abstracted as my own.[19]

The following day, Gladstone rebuked himself for not being able to experience gratitude for Anne's life, instead of the dismay he felt at the sight of her remains,

> considering how many opportunities I had enjoyed of conversation and intercourse with my dearest deceased sister: of knowing her character: of estimating her powers of mind and her tenderness of heart and her numberless Christian graces; how unworthy I had been of the love, and the attention, with which the departed saint had honoured me, as well as other more worthy ... *she* was happy, and ... our first and highest duty, after suffering the tribute of tears to be paid [should be] to seek what she had sought, and to honour her memory in following ... her footsteps.[20]

William Gladstone had no such noble thoughts; he simply missed his sister. Two days later, 'the remains of dearest Anne were inclosed in their last earthly house. The lead was soldered over and all placed in the outer coffin'. She was buried next day beside her grandmother.[21] 'The day was very rainy and seemed ... to suit our occupation.' William spent the next few days drawing up an inventory of Anne's books, with Helen's help, and copying out her papers; throughout his life, creating order provided a source of comfort in times of stress. A week later he was back in Oxford.

Early close bereavements are difficult, if not impossible, to overcome; and to some extent William never got over Anne's death. Her spirit lived on as an additional conscience, a silent observer and arbiter of all he thought and did. Her birthday, on Christmas Eve, had always been a special event for him – one year he wrote an epic poem for her on the subject of death and salvation – and for most of his life he continued to commemorate it as a significant day of pious reflection, almost of religious conversion.

William left behind at Seaforth a grief-stricken household. Most obviously devastated were Mrs Gladstone – who had exhausted her already depleted physical and nervous resources in caring for the daughter who had once been her main domestic support – and Helen, not yet fifteen. Helen was desperately lonely without her sister. A week after her death she wrote to William implying he was the only real source of emotional support left to her:

> Sometimes, I think, I must bother you by making my letters in one sense so barren, but I cannot help it. My earliest recollection of you ... is as loving you almost more than any other, and now, I cannot avoid looking to you as my principal friend.[22]

In the difficult weeks that followed William and Helen were particularly close. 'Let me say how I long for you every day', she wrote to him at Oxford.[23] It was a relationship so close and exclusive that it provoked trouble within the wider family, already edgy with grief. The other brothers discovered that William had been discussing with their young sister, but not with them, his thoughts of making a career in the Church. In an angry postscript to a letter from Helen to William in May, Tom asked why his brother had failed to give him 'some intimation of it'. And again in April, Tom wrote:

> I will merely say explicitly but I hope kindly, that you are the undoubted selector of your friends; that I have ever wished to count myself as one of them, in addition to the title of 'brother'; but that I have never sought and never will seek a confidence that is not spontaneous and reciprocal.[24]

The episode hints at an early indication of one aspect of Helen's character – her capacity to stir trouble within the family through the manipulation of information. Later, she would occasionally be found opening letters marked 'private', particularly at times when she felt (rightly) that her behaviour was being monitored and discussed behind her back.

By the time of Anne's death, Helen was already becoming a handful. Once simply a bright and bouncy child in a house of invalid women, she had begun to receive laudanum for abdominal pains in her early teens and had since often become moody and unmanageable.[25] It had been impossible to retain a governess for her. She had never felt worthy of Anne, or as loved by her family as the 'dear departed' had been. In a letter to her on her fifteenth birthday, doubtless kindly meant, William did nothing but reinforce this.

> She that is gone was to you a treasure more beyond price than to others. Oh! My dear Helen, now while your recollection is yet unimpaired, and her excellences deeply imprinted upon it, cherish every one of them and engrave them deep on your heart, for never never will you again have afforded you so beautiful an example as you were blessed with in her chaste and chastened spirit. I often think that when years shall have gone by, and time weakened our present strong impressions, it will be impossible to picture to ourselves [the extent of] her goodness, or to believe that she *could* have been, what we now know she was. Her only joys were in the good of others; and none was more intense than that which she experienced in promoting what she knew to be your happiness – while you live, let this recollection be with you, and on each succeeding birthday may you find yourself nearer to that model of human excellence.[26]

Now, after Anne's death, Helen was allocated her sister's role as companion to her invalid mother, with all that this implied. She began herself to enjoy ill health, travelling round the country from spa to fashionable spa in pursuit of the latest medical treatment. Nor can Helen's fragile self-confidence have been helped by a pact she and William made after Anne's death. In memory of their sister, they undertook to continue her spiritual mentorship, with each undertaking to provide constructive criticism whenever the other's behaviour seemed in need of correction.[27] Gladstone took an early opportunity to exercise this privilege. Helen expressed her gratitude for his interest, in the absence of her dear late sister's guidance. 'I feel who is wanting, [not knowing where] to look for guidance and comfort. I owe a great deal to your example and counsel, and this debt I am most anxious to increase. Be to me a real *censor*, my friend, my own dear William.'[28]

William continued to suggest corrections to her behaviour, and the lonely girl continued to be grateful for attention of any sort, even negative. A few months later, as he was about to leave Seaforth and return to Oxford for start of the Michaelmas term, he wrote again to Helen (who was in the house at the time), offering nine pages of detailed suggestions for correcting the shortcomings in her dress sense, her use of time and her personal expenditure.

> I take advantage of the present hurried opportunity of addressing you in conformity with a covenant long tacitly held by us and within a short time openly ratified, considering it, hurried as it is, to be preferable to my only other alternative – silence. We have agreed to perform for our mutual benefit one of the most painful, one of the most profitable, and one of the most sacred offices of friendship – we have agreed to tell one another's faults, small and great, without fear or favour. I have taken upon myself to act *first* upon the provisions of this agreement, not I trust from believing myself better qualified to offer advice to you than to receive it from you, but because it may be considered by you, and perhaps is, my duty, as the elder, to make the first assay.[29]

After a three-page preface justifying his actions, explaining his reasons for writing rather than speaking to her directly, and extolling the virtues of 'the blessed principle of submissions', he launched into the substance of his criticism.

> On dress, let me say in the first place that I am far from wishing to bring you to the level of my own ideas. This much however I will state. I think you dress *not more plainly* nor more fashionably than the generality of those who are what is termed 'out'. I think too – you will know whether I am correct or not – that it is usual for those who are not 'out' to dress somewhat *more plainly*. Thirdly it appears to me that those who wish to be guided by the principle of doing all, as much as lieth in them, to the glory of God, should decidedly keep within rather than go beyond the general rule for handsomeness of dress, and refuse compliance with any fashion which they in their conscience after due deliberation believe to be extravagant. More especially, dear Helen, I believe your habit from childhood has rather been to press my Mother towards letting you have such articles, than to hang back and follow her leading: and I do certainly think that you are a good deal beyond those of your own age generally in your manner of dressing.[30]

He stressed that in this and all other matters he left her to follow her conscience, accusing her only of 'ideas of propriety which are I think a little overstrained'. On her use of money, he was more pleased with her except for urging her to save more. On her time management he had more concerns: 'I know you have difficulties to contend with'. Echoing Anne's advice to him to keep a diary as an account to God, he recommended practising

> that abiding and pervading and habitual energy which dictates making the most of this or that particular season but of every time: which girds up its loins not only to attain one end, but to raise up and then seek another to succeed it without intermission, and delights to seize the flying moment and compel even its airy wing to bear aloft as it passes on its course a proportionate offering to the shrine of duty ... Let me recommend again ... division of time and appropriation of specific seasons to specific purposes.[31]

Rather surprisingly, he concluded: 'After all you see I have been able to find but little to scold about'. Quite apart from the insufferable priggishness expressed by a brother towards a young woman who still had the full complement of parents to monitor her behaviour, this letter says far more about nineteen-year-old William than fifteen-year-old Helen. His anxiety about her appearance, which he deems too forward for her age, hints at an uncomfortable awareness of his sister as a sexual being. His comments about her being spoiled by their mother, when he has lost his own surrogate mother in Anne, suggest a certain jealousy. And his attempt to position his brotherly advice within the context of doing all one can to the glory of God is little short of juvenile arrogance. But, as usual, Helen was humbly grateful for any attention rather than none, and wrote back:

> When I first read [your letter], my natural pride and self-love were awakened fully, yet I trust I even then felt thankful that I was not left alone, and suffered to stray further without being warned. For that warning, so much needed for all its, to me, exquisite affection, I can never be sufficiently thankful.[32]

Throughout their lives, Helen was to bring out in William a controlling streak that at times descended into outright bullying, whether kindly meant or not. Perhaps the two sisters represented the two sides of his own personality. Anne represented the goodness and self-restraint to which he aspired; in Helen, he recognised the wilful, headstrong, undisciplined – and sexual – side of his own nature, and the possible consequences were it not kept under control.

Helen's letter to William on his next birthday, his twentieth, contained no such criticism of him; instead, it was a sad young girl's brave attempt at providing some comfort for them both.

> Darkened as the last year has been, I feel satisfied you can rejoice in it, nor do I doubt that a dispensation which has deprived you of our best of earthly counsellors, has been a faithful messenger, leading you to seek, more and more earnestly, the source of spiritual light and salvation. To us both (for neither would exclude the other) may the ensuing year bind us together in love, whether through weal or woe. May we extend the warmth of charity to each other, and may each failure be laid at the throne of Him who is mighty to love, that in our prayers also we may be together led by the spirit of God. I feel ashamed to put myself even nominally on your level ... may you increasingly be the joy of your parents, and be enabled to repay all their tenderness ... I have been, I feel, a cause for anxiety, though unwillingly.

The cause for anxiety seems, at this point, to have been Helen's ill health rather than bad behaviour. 'Your sister thank God is better', their mother wrote, 'but we have had so many drawbacks that I must not be too sanguine ... this morning she looked so like our departed Angel.' As Helen came increasingly to assume the invalid position previously occupied by her late sister, her ill health formed a central theme of their mother's letters to William, as Anne's had done previously. Yet Mrs Gladstone took comfort from the thought that what does not kill makes the victim stronger: 'I fear Helen has suffered a great deal, but I know she is provided with courage to endure it, and they that suffer and support suffering, are far happier than those who do neither.'[33] She was found to be suffering from bad teeth, gumboils, foul tongue and earache. 'You cannot wonder that this dear child is my theme', her mother wrote, 'and [as] if to enhance her value, her voice and manner sometimes recalled that of our Angel.' Comparisons with Anne were something Helen would always have to endure. As late as 1835, the year before her death, Mrs Gladstone was still calling Anne 'our sainted darling', while Helen was 'my remaining darling'.[34] After Anne's death, it was William, rather than the former 'little pet', who became the family's golden child, as he progressed through Eton and Christ Church, and into Parliament, in pursuit of his father's ambition for him.

2

Eton and Christ Church

Gladstone's years at Eton and Christ Church years, 1821–31, did little to extend his acquaintance with women beyond domestic servants and Eton 'Dames'.[1] But, unsurprisingly, the male friends he made during that decade, from the age of eleven to twenty-one, provided the introductions to many of his future female acquaintances. Of his friends, contemporaries and near-contemporaries at school and university, two became brothers-in-law (Stephen Glynne and George Lyttelton), while two others narrowly escaped this fate (Walter Farquhar and Francis Douglas). Scandal surrounding the wife of another (Henry Lincoln) furnished one of the most dramatic escapades in Gladstone's private life. Others who became political colleagues, firm friends or both included Francis Doyle (the best man at his wedding), Sidney Herbert (who with Gladstone and Lincoln would form the core of young Peelites), Henry Manning (until his conversion to Rome), Arthur Kinnaird and Thomas Acland (with whom he founded 'The Engagement', from which his prostitute rescue work originated) and Martin Tupper. Two other close friends – both, interestingly, from a pronounced Whig background – were James Milnes Gaskell and Eton's golden boy, the poet Arthur Hallam, with whom Gladstone had a relationship bordering on the romantic, and who died tragically young in 1833.

When Gladstone went to Eton at relatively late age of eleven, he went unencumbered by much prior learning, either at home or at school, a lack which he felt keenly when comparing himself with some of the other boys. He had hitherto received 'very little benefit of teaching'.

My father was too much occupied. My mother's health was broken. We, the brothers, had no quarrelling among ourselves: but neither can I recollect any influence flowing down at this time upon me, the junior ... Mr Rawson was a good man ... He never showed any violence in school ... everything was unobjectionable ... as to intellectual training, I believe that like the other boys I shirked my works as much as I could. I went to Eton ... after a pretty long spell in a very middling state of preparation, and wholly without any knowledge or other enthusiasm, unless it were a priggish love of argument which I had begun to develop.[2]

Mr Rawson's school was free of violence; but the same could not be said of Eton at the time under the notorious regime of the diminutive, red-faced martinet of a headmaster, 'Flogger' Keate, said once to have beaten eighty boys in a single evening. With only a handful of assistants to control several hundred boys, discipline was extremely bad. School rules were strict, but not applied. During Gladstone's time, the younger son of Lord Shaftesbury died as the result of a drunken brawl. The college's reputation in terms of religious teaching and practice was also appalling. This was clearly outweighed, however, in the minds of Gladstone's parents, by the social advantages that an Eton education would confer. Robertson, their second son, had left after two years to join the family firm, but Tom, the eldest, was still there (with mixed success) after four years when William arrived. Despite his brother's company, William at first found Eton an alien and hostile world, for which his home background had provided no training ground whatsoever. Together with the harsh and arbitrary nature of the discipline, there was the 'beastly' cold, the iniquities of the fagging system and bullying. He also took an instant dislike to his first Dame, Rebecca Sherry, 'the most horrid, stingy brute that ever was known or heard of '.[3]

Gladstone was not particularly concerned to do well academically at this time, nor was he particularly good at sport: 'There was not in me any desire to excel. My first pursuits were football and then cricket: the first I did not long pursue, and in the second I never managed to rise above mediocrity'. A family friend tried without success to interest him in the classics: 'The subject only danced before my eyes as a will of the wisp and without attracting me. I remained stagnant without heart or hope'.[4]

All that was about to change when, around Easter 1822, Edward Craven Hawtrey became Gladstone's temporary form master. Hawtrey, Gladstone recalled, was 'always on the look out for any bud which he could warm with a little sunshine' and 'it was with as much astonishment as delight that I was filled [as I began] to learn'.[5] Hawtrey, who went on to become headmaster, was Gladstone's form teacher for six months.

During that time he [set] me up for good. It was an event in my life: and he and I together for the first time inspired me with a desire to learn and to do, which I never wholly lost, though there was much fluctuation before it hardened into principle and rule at a later period of my life.

I well recollect ... the morning of this (for me) great occurrence. I was ordered to repair to Mr Hawtrey's house. There I saw him and he went through the verses very carefully with me, making such corrections, or improvements perhaps, as he thought necessary. The novelty of the situation to me was extreme, for he all the way through maintained the kindest manner, and appeared to feel an interest in me, which I, a boy of twelve, thought singular and unaccountable, but at the same time enjoyed with much fluttering and a thrill of new hope and satisfaction.[6]

After leaving Eton, Gladstone continued to see a great deal of this 'excellent and most accomplished man, full of taste and knowledge, of liberality, and of modesty', who had kindled a flame in him. Until he was taken under Hawtrey's wing, Gladstone's efforts at Eton were, by his own admission, 'of perhaps the purest plodding ever known'. Hawtrey undoubtedly provided the catalyst that galvanised Gladstone's intellect, turning an average schoolboy into a student capable of both diligence and insight.

One of the boys who lodged with Hawtrey at Eton was Arthur Hallam, the *jeune homme fatal* of the school at the time.[7] Like many others, Gladstone was captivated by Hallam.[8] He became 'my earliest near friend',[9] ousting William Farr, 'my nearest friend of the first period [whose] friendship however was not all good to me'. His relationship with Hallam Gladstone saw as 'the zenith of my boyhood', a 'high privilege though ... to this hour I am unable to conceive how on his side he could have for it any sustaining amount of nourishment'.[10] It was clearly also an emotional attachment, as Gladstone confided to his diary on 24 September 1826.

Breakfasted with Hallam, Walk with Hallam. I esteem as well as admire him. Perhaps I am declaring too explicitly and too positively for the period of our *intimacy* – which has not yet lasted a year – but such is my present feeling.[11]

Gladstone was also in awe of what he perceived to be Hallam's superior intellectual qualities, which had been encouraged from an early age.

We were I think at almost all points contrasted more or less. He had been from the first of early and quick development: I was very slow in growth. Of philosophy he already had a tinge: I was outside it. In poetry he was I think on the right lines ... I think he had in one point a large advantage over me ... He had evidently from the first a large share of cultivated domestic education: with a father absorbed in business, I had little or none. I cannot recall to have had a sense of ever having learned anything until I went to Eton, and had been there some little time.[12]

Hallam enjoyed wide popularity at Eton, and seems to have played the field to some extent. At times, Gladstone was unsure of their relationship, whose progress he later charted in painful detail in his diary.

The history of my connection with [Hallam] is as follows. It began late in 1824, more at his seeking than mine. It slackened soon: more on my account than his. It recommenced in 1825, late, more at my seeking than his. It ripened much from the early part of 1826 to the middle. In the middle, [Farr] *rather* took my place. In the latter end [of 1826], it became closer and stronger than ever. Through 1827, it flourished most happily, to my very great enjoyment. Beginning of 1828, [Hallam] having been absent since he left Eton, it varied but very slightly. Middle of 1828 [Hallam] returned, and thought me cold ... Early in 1829, there was friendly expostulation ... and affectionate reply ... At present, almost an uncertainty, very painful, whether I may call [Hallam] my friend or not.[13]

At the time of writing this, Gladstone was in his second year at Oxford. Hallam went on to Cambridge where he enthralled Alfred Tennyson, whose sister Emily he became engaged to marry, and who immortalised him after his death in the poem *In Memoriam*. Sixty years later Gladstone and Tennyson, by then Prime Minister and Poet Laureate respectively, could still feel jealous over Hallam's affection for the other.

Hallam was a couple of years younger than Gladstone but Morley pointed out that, at Eton,

such was the sympathy of genius, such the affinities of intellectual interest and aspiration spoken and unspoken, such the power and the charm of the younger with the elder, that rapid instinct made them close comrades. They clubbed together their rolls and butter, and breakfasted in one another's rooms. Hallam was not strong enough for boating, so the more sinewy Gladstone used to scull him up to the Shallows, and he regarded this toilsome carrying of an idle passenger up stream as proof positive of no common value set upon his passenger's company.[14]

As for Hallam's appreciation of Gladstone, he wrote to his friend on 23 June 1830, by which time they were at Cambridge and Oxford respectively:

> Never since the time when I first knew you, have I ceased to love and respect your character ... It will be my proudest thought that I may henceforth act worthily of their affection who, like yourself, have influenced my mind for good in the earliest season of its development. Circumstance, my dear Gladstone, has separated our paths, but it can never do away with what has been. The stamp of each of our minds is on the other. Many a habit of thought in each is modified ... which would never have existed ... had it not been for the old familiar days when we lived together.[15]

Another young Etonian friend of Gladstone's who also basked in the glamour of Hallam's affection was James Milnes Gaskell. Together they founded the Eton Society of Literati ('Pop').[16] But when it came to choosing between Oxford and Cambridge after Eton, Gaskell's clear preference was to follow the solid and reliable Gladstone to Christ Church. Writing home to his mother, who seemed to favour Cambridge, Gaskell gave three reasons for his preference: first, because a man could be much more independent at Oxford; secondly, because the debating club at Oxford was respectable and gentlemanly; and, thirdly, because Gladstone was going to Oxford.

> Gladstone is no ordinary individual, and perhaps, were I called on to select the individual I am intimate with to whom I should first turn in an emergency, and whom I thought in every way pre-eminently distinguished for high principle, I should turn to Gladstone.[17]

A few days later, he wrote again to stress: 'Such friends as Gladstone ... I appreciate the more as I begin to lose, and if you decide finally in favour of Cambridge, my separation from Gladstone will be a great sorrow to me'.[18] In his last letter home before leaving Eton, he repeated that 'the idea of being separated from Gladstone is really distressing to me, in fact writing upon this subject is enough to make me melancholy'.[19]

In the event they both went to Oxford. As he left Eton, Gladstone expressed the feeling that 'the happiest period of my life is now past ... if anything mortal is sweet, my Eton years, excepting anxieties at home, have been so! God make me thankful for all I have received here. I am perhaps very foolishly full of melancholy'.[20]

After a shaky start, Gladstone had made the most of his Eton career, in and out of the classroom. He had won no prizes, but he had made a definite mark in the debating societies. He had rowed and ridden, played bowls, billiards, football and cricket. He had taken part in school plays and concerts, drunk alcohol (regularly supplied from home for 'Mr Tipple', as his friends called him) and played cards (sometimes even for money). He was still a serious young man – his friend William Farr accused him of 'taking jokes to pieces',[21] but he was beginning to develop a sense of direction. On 3 December 1827, he left 'my excellent friends, my long known and loved abode' and headed home for Seaforth.

Before Oxford, there was a period of cramming to be endured. Tom had been taken out of Eton a year early to prepare for Oxford with a tutor in Bristol, but William was sent to Wilmslow to study classics and mathematics with the Reverand John Turner, in the company of fellow Etonian Charles Wood, and Horatio Powys, a Cambridge graduate and ordinand. It was not a successful project. Gladstone found the change 'a very great one, not on the whole pleasant'. The work was undemanding 'and time rolls on here in the most monstrous manner imaginable'. Fortunately, the ordeal was cut short when his wife's illness obliged Turner to end the arrangement. Gladstone returned to the family, spending the summer holidays at Seaforth, Scotland and Leamington, before embarking on a second period of intense study at Cuddesdon, near Oxford, under the supervision of the acting vicar, Augustus Page Saunders, who was to be one of his tutors at Christ Church. As well as studying, Gladstone also taught at the local Sunday School, an activity he regularly carried out at various locations in his early years.

Gladstone went up to Oxford in October 1828. He found he liked it 'very much, though not as well as Eton. We are not overworked by any means'.[22] Apologising for his delay in replying to a friend's letter, he commented: 'Did I read as I threatened and wished to do, my reading would excuse my delay; but the quantity and quality of my studies have hitherto not been such as to furnish me with any such justifications!'[23] At university, he continued the interests he had enjoyed at school; he reinforced existing friendships – there was a vast contingent of Eton boys at Christ Church – and forged new ones. Debating remained his first enthusiasm, primarily at the Oxford Union (as it became), where he famously carried a motion against the proposed Reform Bill, and at the Essay Club, Oxford's equivalent of the Cambridge Apostles, known throughout its short life by Gladstone's initials.

James Milnes Gaskell remained a particular friend, mentioning Gladstone in almost every letter home. In May of their first year, he wrote to his mother: 'I see as much of Gladstone as ever and Mr Saunders (our lecturer) said he did not know anyone at Oxford today, whom he would select as his friends before Gladstone and Acland'.[24] Two months later, he wrote: 'You will be glad to hear that I paid off all my bills yesterday, and that I am as regular as Gladstone himself'.[25] But he was annoyed at some of the contacts Gladstone was making outside Christ Church, and in November he complained to his mother:

> I much regret that Gladstone has mixed himself up with the St Mary Hall and Oriel set, who are really, for the most part, only fit ... to live with maiden aunts and keep tame rabbits.[26]

In the nineteenth century, Oriel (of which the medieval St Mary Hall is now part) was a leader in the intellectual revival of Oxford, a place where critical and rational argument was valued. The 'Oriel set' included Newman, Keble, Pusey, Froude and R. I. Wilberforce, all men associated with the Oxford Movement, which had fostered the revival of catholic practice within the Church of England.

Gladstone may not have worked hard in the first two years at Oxford, but his father expected him to aim for the top. So, in the summer of 1830, it was time for him to return to Cuddesdon for the entire long vacation. There, as he wrote to his friend Farr, he launched himself on the 'unintermitted succession of reading to which I have at last been compelled to resort', during which he worked for ten to twelve hours a day.

> I have never tried any real work before this long vacation, anything I mean calculated to interfere materially with the pursuance of my own pleasure. I find it at times intolerably irksome but it gets lighter as I go on, and perhaps my being so extremely indisposed to it only proves the necessity which existed for this or some other discipline for my mind.[27]

It was a tense and exhausting time, but an experience that would stand Gladstone in good stead in public office. Of the period before taking his final exams, he wrote to his father:

> Taking into consideration together the amount of mental labour and physical trial, and the anxiety arising from the uncertainty of results, it is the sort of thing which ought not, I think, to come more than once in one's life, though for once it is very well, and the benefits exceedingly great.[28]

Gladstone had stretched himself to the limit and discovered what he was capable of achieving under pressure. In December 1831, after failing to win many prizes at Eton or Christ Church, the self-confessed 'plodder' took a double first class honours degree in classics and mathematics.

It was common for young men of Gladstone's class to mark the transition between the end of education and the beginning of professional life with a Grand Tour of continental Europe. In January 1832, Gladstone set off on such a tour with his brother John Neilson, who had taken leave from the Navy to accompany him. While they were travelling, Gladstone received a letter from the Duke of Newcastle, the father of his school and college friend, Lord Lincoln. The letter offered him the opportunity to stand as a candidate for the position of Tory MP representing the Duke's 'pocket' borough of Newark. At Geneva, Gladstone wrote in his diary on 15 July that he had agreed to stand but was uncertain of success: 'There cannot be ... anything approaching certainty, in a case where the constituency consists of 1600 voters, but be that as it may, I stand pledged to this bold and terrible experiment: and it constitutes, considering the general unimportance of my being and life, a situation of no ordinary interest'.[29] He returned to England and in mid-December the voting took place at Newark. There were three candidates. It was a close call but, on 14 December at nine in the morning, William Gladstone was proclaimed to be the new Member for Newark by 89 votes, 'and may the Almighty give me the strength to perform the duties of this solemn office'.

Gladstone took his seat when Parliament convened in the New Year, 'in company with a large number of contemporaries and friends, but

> provided unquestionably with a large stock at least of schoolboy bashfulness. The first time that business required me to go to the arm of the Chair to say something on business to the Speaker (who was something of a Keate),

I remember the revival in me bodily of the frame of mind in which a schoolboy stands before his master.[30]

Six months later, he made his maiden speech in Parliament on slavery in the West Indies. In his fifty minute oration, he attacked the terms under which slaves were to be emancipated, while supporting the principle. The speech earned him congratulations from Sir Robert Peel. The following year, Gladstone was offered a place in the Tory government as Junior Lord of the Treasury, followed by a few months as Colonial Under Secretary, before the government's defeat in April 1835. In a few years, his political career had gone from strength to strength.

Not so his romantic career. He was out of office, with time on his hands: what better moment to begin looking for a wife. In July of that year, there was already one family engagement to celebrate. Tom had announced that he was to marry Laura Fellowes. On meeting her for the first time, William wrote to his mother at Fasque, the estate in Kincardineshire in Scotland which in 1833 had become the Gladstones' main residence outside London, that Miss Fellowes displayed 'every social and domestic excellence: she is artless without being shy ... you will be extremely pleased and delighted with her'.[31] The couple were married in London in late August, with William present.

Normally Gladstone would have spent the summer at Fasque. But romance was in the air that season. Within five days of Tom's wedding, he was explaining to his mother that his reason for remaining in London was Caroline Farquhar, the sister of his Eton and Christ Church friend, Walter.

I have become attached to a person of whom I think, should it please God to join us, you would not disapprove – Miss Farquhar. Her brother is a much valued friend of mine ... Her mother Lady Farquhar is a very fashionable person ... her father, Sir Thomas ... a banker. She has been very much in London society, without, as I believe, being in the smallest degree tainted by it, or enslaved to it, On the contrary, I believe that she is governed in all things by ... religion. Without that belief I should have held it my first duty to stifle in its earliest stage every feeling that might grow into mature attachment. She is a person of great beauty and accomplishments ... [Her] many attractions ... persuaded me to break the subject to her parents just before going down to Norfolk last week ... Walter Farquhar entertains strong religious views, at variance with those of his mother: and the family

think that I approximate more to Walter's opinions than would comport
with their peace and comfort ... Lady Farquhar opened this subject to me in
the frankest manner: we had a conversation ... that seemed to give her some
satisfaction. But ... I have this day addressed to [Caroline] a letter of considerable length on the subject ... I leave it in the hands of the Lord with
perfect satisfaction ... that the issue will be for the best.[32]

Gladstone had first made the acquaintance of Caroline Farquhar at a
concert given by Lady Antrobus in London in May that year, and was
clearly impressed by her.[33] He began calling on Lady Farquhar and was
frequently out and about with Walter and other members of the
extended family in the late spring and summer. In July, he spent the
night at their place near Dorking. The following morning he recorded:
'In London, I cannot get up: here I could not but get up on wakening ...
after breakfast went reluctantly to town with my excellent friend:
looking forward however to another visit next week'.[34]

Two days later Gladstone rode with members of the family to the
penitentiary at Millbank, where he was about to become a Visitor. The
following week he went with them to visit Bedlam, rode out again with
them and continued to pay regular calls at their London home. In
August, he was still anticipating a favourable outcome to his acquaintance with Caroline Farquhar. He appears not to have countenanced a
refusal.

I lay and ruminated on that which lies before me, and about which I have
said to myself often enough within these last weeks, shall I grasp at it, shall
I dream of grasping at it? There is a sweet image which comes to me with
delight ... I recognise in her that which one should wish to find in the being
whom God should appoint to be as a guardian angel to the soul.[35]

Gladstone was in regular correspondence with close family members
about his plans and received warm support and encouragement from
them. Before making a formal proposal, he had written to his father
about the important role of religion in securing domestic bliss.

Marriage is a subject which, in a general form, has been enough in my mind,
but I feel myself beset perhaps with some peculiar difficulties: inasmuch as it
would be my first duty if possible (and by seeking strength above it must be
possible) to keep a strict guard over my own feelings, until I could have
ascertained that the object which might attract them was endowed with those
religious convictions which are the only permanent foundation of happiness,

and whose necessity in my own case I should not rest upon special merit, God knows, but upon special need in myself.[36]

It was a wise strategy. Unfortunately Gladstone failed to abide by it. Before, rather than after, he had established the true extent of Caroline Farquhar's religious conviction, Gladstone wrote to Sir Thomas on 25 August 1835, requesting 'access to her affections', with a view to marriage. On receiving news of his matrimonial interests, Lady Farquhar – who continued nevertheless to encourage his association with her family – replied that, although she had discussed his proposal with her daughter, no concrete response could be expected at this stage.

> [Caroline] expressed extreme surprise at the communication, not having the smallest idea that you entertained any preference for her. She told me she considered the acquaintance of so short a duration, it was impossible to own any decision as to the future, or whether on intimate acquaintance a congeniality of opinions might lead to any warmer sentiment than at present exists … she seemed pleased and flattered at the preference you have expressed for her, and seems desirous of cultivating your acquaintance. I trust, my dear Mr Gladstone, I may not, most undesignedly, have wounded your feelings in speaking this openly, but I have been anxious, most anxious, to guard against implying a preference on her part, which must be more a creation springing from any future intercourse, than from any past acquaintanceship.[37]

In short, Gladstone's interest had been noted, but Caroline Farquhar's options remained open. Her brother Walter, who reassured Gladstone that he knew his sister 'to be entirely free', warned his friend that Caroline feared 'your ideas on the subject of religion might be of a stricter kind than she feels it right to embrace'.[38] Strangely, considering the impressive Gladstone wealth, he added that her financial fortune was limited, 'lest you might suppose it larger than it is'.[39]

On 3 September 1835, Gladstone wrote an eight-page letter of excruciating tedium to Lady Farquhar, outlining his moral and religious principles and their importance in married life. Her ladyship replied by return that Caroline 'felt the responsibility too great'.[40] Crestfallen, Gladstone wrote to his mother that he planned to return almost immediately to the family home at Fasque.

> My hopes are now altogether crushed and the cord which bound me here [in London] is snapped. I have a letter this morning from Lady Farquhar kindly

and with regret but I fear decisively apprising me that her daughter, as well as herself, sees in my view on religion so much that is likely to cause disunion and distress, that they can no longer think of a connection which might otherwise have led to much happiness. Being unable so to read this as to persuade myself that I had any right to solicit further explanations, I speedily felt that remaining here alone and within six or seven miles of that which was my delight ... I could have little hope of regaining my self-possession ... Thus quickly have I passed out of a gentle and delightful dream into a painful reality ... I do not say that even yet I have entirely extinguished the last glimmering of my happy anticipations ... because it is not that I have found one worldly whom I hoped spiritual, or one cold whom I hoped affectionate ... and yet if this be all past and the future wholly void, still ... I ought to be thankful: for to have beheld with emotion that which is less tainted than myself, must have an elevating effect on the mind ... and [be] healing to my heart.[41]

John Gladstone had been irritated by Lady Farquhar's indecisiveness as to whether or not his son's attentions to her daughter should be encouraged.

Lady F's conduct has been highly reprehensible in first inviting a renewal of intercourse and then cutting it off without any new cause arising to justify such conduct, but in showing such a disposition, whilst I feel for her daughter who seems sacrificed to such selfish views, I regret the less that you are not to be connected with such a person ... thinking so differently from you on subjects so important. It might have become a source of great future unhappiness.[42]

Now Mrs Gladstone, too, wrote words of sympathy, sensibly reminding her son that, as this was a short acquaintance, he should not be too upset. Admitting the 'unaffected pain' his news had caused, she added that her feelings were 'not unmixed with pleasure derived from the manly and high principled tone with which you treat the subject ... I trust too that your feelings had not become so deeply implicated as to cost you much difficulty in forgetting what has passed'. She concluded in a postscript – implying he had enjoyed some choice in the matter of his refusal: 'Yours has been a sacrifice to duty and to know that must ever afford you a pleasing recollection'.[43] More letters of commiseration and support soon followed from Gladstone's brothers.

In January 1836, Gladstone spent a week at Hawarden Castle outside

Chester as the guest of his Oxford friend Stephen Glynne. At this stage
he still entertained some hope that Caroline might change her mind. In
mid-February, however, after he had a meeting with Caroline's brother,
he wrote to his father: 'I saw Farquhar this morning and the result of
our conversation was ... that I am convinced that the matter is practically at an end'.[44] John Gladstone repeated that he thought his son had
been poorly treated: 'If [Lady Farquhar] had no serious intention of
affording you an opportunity to endeavour to gain her daughter's affection and to receive you as a son-in-law ... she ought not to have
proposed a renewal of intercourse.'[45]

The reality was that by now the Farquhars had other plans for their
daughter. In March, they announced her engagement to Charles Grey,
second son of Earl Grey. On hearing the news, Gladstone agonised that
he was perhaps doomed never to marry; but he reiterated his conviction
that 'my wish for marriage was chiefly on religious grounds. For what is
the wife of a baptised man, but the gift and the instrument of God our
Redeemer?'[46] Caroline Farquhar married Grey on 26 July 1836. Grey
later became Private Secretary to Queen Victoria. After his death, Caroline became a Woman of the Royal Bedchamber.[47] Over fifty years
later, in 1886, Gladstone was kneeling at the communion rail in the
Savoy Chapel in London when Caroline looked up and saw him. 'She
rose without a second's hesitation and left the church without taking the
communion.'[48]

Having one's first proposal of marriage rejected paled into insignificance compared with the next blow Gladstone had to face. He had just
noted in his diary the first anniversary of the death of his 'earliest near
friend' Arthur Hallam, when his mother's health began rapidly to deteriorate. A week later, on 23 September, Anne Robertson Gladstone, too,
was dead. She died at the age of sixty-three, less than three weeks after
her son's rejection by the Farquhars. Gladstone was twenty-five. Mrs
Gladstone had been deeply upset by the recent deaths of her sister and
brother-in-law. Despite the demands of his first courtship, William had
spent much of his time nursing his mother during her final decline.
Helen, too, had shown – as she always would – true strength under
adversity:

> Much impressed with Helen's nerve and fortitude. With perfect self-
> possession as well as the deepest interest she watched the advances of

Death upon the frame of her parent. A sense of emotion in the morning on my Father's reading prayers from my being asleep: as I had been in my Mother's room from eleven to five. We gathered finally in the evening to see her die ... at a quarter past midnight her soul went to blessedness.[49]

Gladstone's mother had been a shadowy, remote figure and Gladstone was much less affected than he had been by the death of Anne. It was also to Anne that Mrs Gladstone's thoughts returned as she lay dying: 'In one very pleasing reverie she evidently dwelt on her daughter in heaven: "Oh my first – dearest – beloved – precious – she was blessed".'[50] He recorded the passing of his mother – 'tender, affectionate, unwearied in love and devotion' – in classic evangelical style.

She departed in seraphic peace, like the gentleness of her own disposition, like the serenity of her everlasting home. She was eminent in the discharge of every duty: she sorrowed for sin: she trusted in the atonement of Christ ... perfected through suffering, she had no new thing to learn, no fresh character to assume, upon translation to the world of spirits; her mind and affections had received already and for ever their mould and their bias, and she has but carried the one vital principle of love which cannot be bound in death, from a thick and clouded atmosphere to one of perfect purity and freedom. Two only have been taken from our family: and both are angels in heaven.[51]

Almost immediately, Gladstone received a kind note from Lady Farquhar, which he recorded in Italian, in which she expressed regret that she had ' "broken things off so abruptly"; and this pleased me, impelling me to thank God's wisdom without too much disturbing my heart, made clearer and more stable by grief '.[52] His mother was buried five days later in the vault in the church at Fettercairn near Fasque.[53]

We laid a body in the grave: but, from whatever cause, I do not feel separated from the spirit which possessed it: and which I rejoice to think is now very near us, and associated again with that of her beloved daughter ... and now they are both blessed. May the fullness of the love of God make them glad for ever.[54]

To the world, Gladstone put on a brave face but any outward sign of pleasure 'in no way matched my inner feelings'.[55] He felt himself 'so poor a creature in every way'. More and more he was confiding to his diary in Italian (perhaps also because he was also reading Dante at the time).

> Thought over my affairs; it is necessary to get out of the tangle: and more and more I feel what a wretched gift I would be as a husband. And there is such a difference between intention and practice; and of the two halves of my nature, which would be the one that married?[56]

It was in the summer of 1837, while he was campaigning on his father's behalf in Scotland, that Gladstone renewed a former slight acquaintance with Lady Frances Douglas, daughter of Lord Morton. Wooing again mainly by letter, he quickly proposed marriage, again stressing the over-riding importance of religion. He received no reply. Towards the end of the year, his Edinburgh friends Isabella and Edward Bannerman Ramsay (later Dean of Edinburgh) undertook to make discreet enquiries on his behalf. The result was a clear and definite rejection. Again, Gladstone's obsessive tendency took over, and he wrote to Edward Ramsay repeatedly – more than once a day at one point – for clarification. On 15 November, Ramsay passed on a warning from Lady Frances's parents that 'respect and regard may not be mistaken for a reciprocation of feelings'.[57] In a second letter the same day, Ramsay stressed again that 'the decision is definitive ... because there is reciprocation of none of those feelings that are required for a different verdict'. He stressed the point that Gladstone's mother had made over Caroline Farquhar: 'I fondly hope that as this has not been a matured or long cherished affection, the seam of its excision will soon heal'.[58] The long-suffering Ramsay also tried to point out kindly to Gladstone that he was in danger of being over hasty in his wooing.

> You have been precipitate – had our young and lovely and pure-minded young friend accepted on so short an acquaintance she would scarcely have been deserving of such a glorious gift as you have offered ... she must have had *time* allowed to receive those impressions which might have made your happiness. Another time, dear Mr Gladstone, be more guarded of yourself – your conduct is noble and generous, but you must give yourself time and opportunity to win – I cannot conceive the possibility of failure when you do yourself this justice.[59]

It was a 'crushing letter'.[60] Yet, a couple of days later, its recipient 'felt as if the bitterness were past ... and that it is good for me'.[61] But

Gladstone, who was staying in Norwich after Christmas, still continued to hope and pester, and on 8 January he rose early to answer
'another extinguishing letter from Mr Ramsay'. That same morning,
he walked into Norwich Cathedral for an early service, and found
unexpected consolation in the anthem being played on the organ.

> Sometimes I could not tell whether the music was made on heaven or on
> earth, and I willingly stayed rooted to the spot. I heard it saying to me, 'Thy
> wife shall be as a vine, upon the walls of thine house. Thy children like the
> olive branches, round about thy table. – And thou shalt see thy children's
> children, and peace upon Israel'. Was not this really a Providence for me?
> And entirely without my playing any part. And a promise as well: not of mar-
> riage, but – as I firmly believe – of that eternal love which hitherto has
> preserved me.[62]

But thoughts of marriage continued to obsess him until finally, on 13
January 1838, even Ramsay seemed to lose patience. 'My conviction now
is to repeat the word "never" to you – this my dear friend is painful to
write, but the truth ... is precious ... and when truth is sought, the
sooner it is found, the better.'[63] Two weeks later, it was Isabella Ramsay
who wrote a frank and affectionate letter to Gladstone, possibly
prompted by Lady Morton's apparent anxiety that the affair might
become public and compromise her daughter's prospects elsewhere. She
also reminded him that he was a 'one-off' and would need a special sort
of wife, more special than Lady Frances.

> All things are rightly and wisely ordered for God's children, dear Mr Glad-
> stone, so think [so] of your disappointment ... Lady Frances Douglas is
> charming – nay lovely and loveable in no common degree, but the mind is
> not suited to yours, never could be ... if the feeling which you have given
> had been reciprocated, there were qualities of character to reconcile the dis-
> parity, but believe me it is best as it is ... the very richness of your mind ...
> requires that your companion for life must be similarly gifted, or you would
> be left alone ... this would inevitably have been your loss. There is a child-
> like buoyancy of heart and spirit that seem to set aside all tendency to deep
> thinking in Lady Frances Douglas – she is younger in character than years.

Gladstone was not consoled. It was one blow too many, leaving him
miserable and depressed. He continued to put on a brave face, and
endeavoured to see the will of God in all things, but life had become

grey and joyless. At the end of March 1838, he gave a speech in the Commons that was warmly received by all parties, but he took no comfort from his success.

> Isolated from love, and my greedy heart unappeased by a thousand consolations, I am half insensible even in the moment of delight to such pleasures as this kind of occasion affords: I feel as if the side of me, which lies towards the world, were ice, and all I see in it a dream: I long for that which is within, above: but this is a dangerous and a carnal state: indifference to the world is not love of God: may I have that love within me, as the central principle governing all others, cleansing me by discipline from my intolerable sinfulness, and filling me with an earnest affection to all my fellowmen.[64]

Gladstone was unable to shake off his melancholy. On 28 April 1838, he confided to his diary, again in Italian:

> The world outside me seems somehow dismantled now, because of the icy coldness of my heart ... I walk among the splendours of the world like a dead man ... with a heart of stone ... It may change. Meanwhile, it is hard.[65]

Two months later, he was still suffering 'the daily sadness that is upon me in the midst of this painted life of inward trouble'.[66] In early June, he attended the funeral of his cousin Eliza Robertson, the favourite playmate and closest friend of his dear dead sister Anne, and found the ceremony

> beautiful and soothing. I am tempted to desire to follow; I ought to be happy here, having the means to be useful; yet I live almost perpetually restless and depressed. Active duty brings peace: what I have then to pray for is to be kept always at it, and to be content, strictly, with my daily bread.[67]

Within weeks, Gladstone had a chance meeting with Lord Morton at a social event hosted by the Duchess of Buccleuch, and discovered that Lady Frances was to marry Lord Milton. 'Lord Morton shook hands cordially', he wrote, adding in Italian: 'The marriage is arranged: may they be happy'.[68] Like her predecessor in Gladstone's affections, the young woman had accepted an aristocratic husband within weeks of rejecting him. Gladstone wrote to the bride's father to congratulate the family and received 'a kind note from Lord Morton. So ends this for me saddening episode'. Morton was clearly relieved that Gladstone had taken the news so well: 'We have received many gratifying letters on the subject but none of [whose] warmth and sincerity ... we feel more convinced. I hope we may meet in Scotland on your way to the North this year'.[69] Gladstone took up the offer and enjoyed the Mortons' hospitality at Dalmahoy en route to Fasque.

For the meantime, Gladstone was still deeply sad. The previous nine years had been the emotionally bleakest period of his life. In 1829, he had lost his beloved sister Anne when he was just nineteen. Gladstone was anxious and overwrought and had twice suffered from hallucinations of a religious nature. There was trouble with Helen as well. On 28 June 1838 his younger sister celebrated – if that is the right word – her twenty-fourth birthday, and it was 'a gloomy one', Gladstone wrote in his diary. Whether the gloom reflected his own unhappiness or hers is unclear; but certainly she must have been at least as distressed as her brother. The death of her sister and mother left Helen the only woman in a family of relatively dour, busy men with interests that excluded her, and left her with no useful role. Now totally bereft of intimate female companionship and isolated at Fasque, Helen was in danger of taking excessive comfort in food and laudanum. For both brother and sister, a change of scenery seemed sensible, and on 11 August they set sail for an extended stay on the Continent. The plan was to settle Helen with acquaintances in the fashionable German spa town of Bad Ems, while William carried on touring Europe. Shortly before departure, Gladstone wrote in his diary: 'Breakfasted with the Misses Glynne'. There was no indication of any further agenda. But, fortuitously, a Glynne family party was also on the point of leaving for the Continent.

3

Catherine

When Gladstone set sail for Rotterdam in August 1838, he was twenty-eight years old. He was in possession of a generous allowance from his father. His career showed considerable promise: he was Conservative MP for Newark and had already held office as Junior Lord of the Treasury and Under-Secretary for War and the Colonies. His first book, *The State in its Relations with the Church*, was about to be published. There was much to make him feel both thankful and proud. But it was a truth still universally acknowledged that a single man in possession of a good fortune must be in want of a wife. Certainly, Gladstone felt that to be the case. He was a young man of strong sexuality and tender curiosity.[1] And, as he embarked on his continental tour, he was almost certainly still a virgin.[2] He longed for marriage. Yet Gladstone had an awkward way with women – eligible, attractive young women in particular. In their presence he was anxious and embarrassed; and he covered up his shyness with what looked like priggish and pompous posturing. He tried to analyse his discomfort, and rationalise the civilising benefits of respectable female company:

> Do I mix in society (wretchedly capacitated for it as I am) for the gratification of self? My opinion of it has been in some measure changed: or rather I have had little opportunity previously of forming one. But it seems to me that female society, whatever the disadvantages may be, has just and manifold uses attendant upon it in turning the mind away from some of its most dangerous and degrading temptations.[3]

His lack of ease was hardly surprising. Until he left Oxford, Gladstone's close female contacts were very limited. His mother and elder sister, now both dead and therefore easier to idealise than living women, he saw as the embodiment of female perfection to which all others must be raised or restored. With servants and school staff he was comfortable

but distant.[4] There was not much in between. There had been little
scope for socialising at home, given Mrs Gladstone's nervous disposition and Anne's pious but somewhat censorious views on having fun, in
her later years at least. While he was often invited to the balls and soirées
of the grand political hostesses of the time, such events made him feel
uncomfortable and had to be endured rather than enjoyed. Despite his
reluctance to be party to frivolous gatherings, and with the shadow of
Anne admonishing him, on Good Friday 1838 he drew up a list of no
less than thirty-nine reasons why it might be acceptable for a religious
young man to attend balls.[5] One item read: 'Some of us might add, and
that not from superior spirituality, that to them these are not pleasures
but upon the whole a burden'. As a burden, balls and the like were
acceptable – but not as a pleasure.

Gladstone's two attempts at courtship had failed miserably in the face
of his rigid and apparently obsessive religiosity. He also made the double mistake of wooing too fast, and wooing by letter, rather than trying
to win over the girl gradually and in person. There is no doubt that,
throughout his life, Gladstone was much warmer, and a more charming
and interesting companion, in person than in his writings. As a result,
the fact that he spent so much time abroad, informally, in the company
of the Glynnes, as he did in the winter of 1838–39, provided the ideal
opportunity for the strengths and virtues of this singular young man (or
'peculiar', as Isabella Ramsay wrote to him, in the kindest way) to reveal
themselves slowly to Catherine Glynne, herself a singular type of woman,
according to her friends. She, who had been told by an acquaintance to
mark young Gladstone as a future Prime Minister, had already suffered
a number of romantic disappointments of her own. Like Gladstone, she
was experienced in that respect, but wary. 'The feeling that all men are
not sincere will make you more eager to return the one true love', a
friend had predicted after a particularly disastrous affair.[6] Catherine was
already twenty-six years old, and astute enough to see the potential in
someone she clearly regarded as a most unusual young man. Gladstone,
for his part, was desperate to find a spouse. In September 1837, he wrote:
'I know not whether any other boon, except the holy treasure of a wife,
could make me love this anxious load of life.'[7] It was a promising start.

Gladstone arrived on 16 August at Bad Ems, near Koblenz, where his
first task was to ensure that all was well with Helen, who, in a state of

physical and mental exhaustion, had left London ten days earlier and was installed in a hotel under the protection of family friends, Sir Samuel and Lady Scott. He stayed in Bad Ems for three weeks, during which time the Glynne party – Henry Glynne (the rector of Hawarden), Catherine and her younger sister Mary, and their widowed mother Lady Glynne, who was still feeling the effects of a stroke suffered some years earlier – stopped overnight at the spa resort on their way to Italy via Switzerland.

The Glynnes were an old aristocratic family. Both Catherine's parents were descended from crusaders. Her father, Sir Stephen Glynne, was twenty-fourth in descent from William de Percy, a Norman chieftain who had come over to England from France in 1066 with William the Conqueror. Through the Percys, Catherine could claim direct descent from Charlemagne. Her mother, Mary Neville, daughter of Lord Braybrooke, was eighteenth in descent from Richard de Grenville, who had died in the Holy Land in 1147. Lady Glynne was related to four Prime Ministers: two Grenvilles (her grandfather and great-uncle), Lord Chatham (great-uncle) and William Pitt the Younger (cousin).[8]

The marriage of Catherine's parents was cut short after only a few years by Sir Stephen's death in 1815 at the age of thirty-three, while the family were staying on the French Riviera in a desperate attempt to improve his chest condition. It was the year of Waterloo. Napoleon had escaped from Elba, and only with difficulty did the young widow and her four small children – Stephen, Henry, Catherine and Mary (all under the age of six) succeed against all odds in returning unscathed to England. Once back, Lady Glynne only spent a few months of each year at the Glynne estate at Hawarden in North Wales, in the early years at least preferring the comfort of her father's various homes. Despite receiving at least one offer of marriage, Lady Glynne never remarried.[9] For support, she relied much on her brother George and her uncle, Thomas Grenville.

Lady Glynne educated her daughters in a relatively unstructured way, not untypical of the time. In 1828, she took Catherine, Mary and their governess to Paris to enjoy a glittering season of balls and parties, and to be presented to the elite of European society – but also to continue their education. Catherine was able to perfect her already excellent French (she was also accomplished in Italian). Among their other teachers while they were travelling was Franz Liszt, who gave them piano lessons.

According to Catherine's daughter, Mary, the sisters were 'brought up with infinite and most loving care and discipline, duty being always placed before pleasure. Reticence and self-control in those days were considered indispensable to good manners'.[10] Both girls were presented at Court, and both attended the coronation of Queen Victoria in June 1838. It was shortly after the coronation that the Glynne family party set off on its continental tour, arriving in August in Bad Ems, and meeting up with the Gladstones. Catherine expressed herself 'much struck by [William's] attentions to Miss Gladstone, who is an invalid'.[11]

From Bad Ems, Gladstone travelled through south Germany to Milan. His travelling companion was the Whig MP Arthur Kinnaird. Kinnaird seems to have been a salutary influence on Gladstone during their time together, not suffering gladly some of Gladstone's more irritating characteristics. Later, reviewing the trip on his return to London, Gladstone commented that there had been a

> cause for useful humiliation ... namely that the admission of one, who has I am certain ... an enlightened conscience, to the familiar intercourse of companionship in travel, had shown him the delusiveness of that gloss which I sometimes seem to wear upon my outward character, and had led him to say, and to leave unretracted, more severe sentences than have been passed upon me for a very long time if ever: as for example to express suspicions of my deliberate insincerity.[12]

In Milan, Gladstone suffered his first pangs of conscience: first, about leaving home and, secondly, about leaving Helen; or perhaps they were pangs of homesickness after a few weeks travelling. He felt 'much embarrassment as to the propriety of my leaving my family alone to seek a very problematical benefit for myself; and I was anxious to hear from home – a word or a syllable would have turned me back – but no letter came'.[13] To Helen, he wrote by way of justification:

> I shall be very anxious to hear what are your plans: and am not quite satisfied to be absent ... from you, though I had reasoned myself into the conviction that it was necessary in order to give repose to my eyes. At the same time I know how little it was in my power to do for you and consequently your independence of me.[14]

From Milan, Gladstone travelled with Kinnaird to Florence. With marriage still on his mind, he was much moved by an epitaph engraved on a gravestone in the convent of Santo Spirito. It read: 'O sweet wife! When our daughter reaches the age of reason I, having told her of the virtues with which you were adorned, will lead her to this tomb. Here, shedding tears, she may pray to God to make her like her mother'.[15] On 5 October they arrived in Rome. Again Gladstone expressed guilty concern at the absence of news from Helen: 'I am up to this time without any letter. I have compunctions on reflecting that my sister is under the escort of persons not of her own family while I am here'.[16] To Helen, now in Baden Baden, he wrote, again with a hint of homesickness:

> I hope you are comfortably settled ... and God grant that your stay ... may assist the general objects of your trip to the Continent. I have been very sorry to leave you alone: and the more so when I began to suspect that it was a phantom of advantages which had drawn me away and the strong sun of Italy, even at this season, would do my eyes more harm than the relaxation would secure them of benefits ... I sadly long for you all – a foreign land requires home faces more than one's own country. I trust in God you are making steady progress and that you may return to England wholly restored.

From Rome, the two men set of for Naples and two days later embarked on an extended tour of Sicily. Gladstone was particularly interested in comparing the volcanic activity of Mount Etna with that of Vesuvius outside Naples; his account of climbing Etna was later including in Murray's guide to Sicily. On leaving the island at the beginning of November, Gladstone described saying goodbye to the animal that had carried him throughout his trip: 'It's rather sad to leave one's mule after a service of four hundred miles without being able to like him'. The Sicilian mule comparison was one he would use over half a century later to describe the passionless way that Queen Victoria dismissed him after a lifetime of public service. Sicilian mules, he wrote, seem to have

> no sense of fatigue ... a light or a heavy load, a long or a short distance, a good or a bad load ... are all alike ... the wiry beast works in his own way ... resenting punishment, but hardly otherwise affected by it.[17]

There had been further contact with the Glynne party by letter as the two groups moved round the Continent. Within a couple of days of being back in Naples, Gladstone met up again with the family to

compare notes on their travels. From then on, they met every day or
two. On 19 November, at the opera, 'the hired boxes seem ill furnished:
to judge from that which the Glynnes had'. The next day: 'At 10.30 with
the Glynnes to the Duke Scondito's'. Two days later: 'Dined with the
Glynnes'. The following week: 'To Vesuvius with the Glynnes'. On 2
December he went to hear a sermon on the Virgin Mary at the church
of San Ferdinando: 'horrible ... The Glynnes whom I accompanied were
similarly impressed ... Dined with the Glynnes.' Catherine records the
same events from her own angle: 'Mr Gladstone dined with us, a very
agreeable evening'; 'shopped in spite of a tremendous storm of rain with
Stephen and Mr Gladstone'; 'to the church of San Ferdinando with
Mr Gladstone and heard a most extraordinary sermon'. On 3 December,
Gladstone left for Rome where he found a letter from Helen's companions that left him 'reeling'. The following day a letter arrived from Helen
herself, explaining that she had become informally engaged to the
Polish-Russian Count Léon Sollohub.

> I have felt so anxious and so timid regarding my own hopes and your share
> in them, that I have felt miserable when the days since we arrived here have
> not found this letter written ... Paris is too much a bustle ... Baden was too
> trying and damp ... Sir S. was very tiresome ... And now, dearest Willy, I
> need to ... talk to you on the subject most present to my thoughts. I would
> gladly and earnestly seek your friendship for Count Sollohub ... beyond the
> friendship which you would naturally wish to extend to your sister's chosen
> guide and friend. I long for you knowing him, because I believe you will
> swiftly appreciate his remarkable union of noble integrity with a delicacy and
> refinement of mind almost womanly. One of the first things about him that
> pleased me, was his constantly reminding me of you.[18]

Between receiving Scott's letter and Helen's, Gladstone had recorded
his misgivings, his 'first and most involuntary thoughts' about the affair:

> I cannot ... feel perfectly easy under circumstances so singular: alone, un-
> protected, in ill health: a foreigner, a Russian foreigner, a frequenter of
> watering-places, self-attested – and with a difficulty about religion,
> probably.[19]

After reading her own explanation, he felt reassured to some degree.

> From dearest Helen herself I learn better the truth of this startling intelli-
> gence: and ... become at once confident that her chosen one is worthy.

She speaks of the sacrifices to be made with the strength of a great character but with the pathos of a deeply feeling heart. Poor dear soul – does she know them yet? But I cannot judge for her. At least I cannot but see it is in no selfish spirit but in one of profound affection that she acts.[20]

To Helen, he wrote frankly: 'My beloved sister ... though I know not how to write, I still less know how to stay silent'. He was himself desperate for the consolations and comfort of marriage. He understood the need of sisterless, motherless Helen for deep affection – a need strong enough for her to contemplate life in a strange country. He knew from bitter experience the agony of waiting for approval. But his reservations towards the Count were considerable. In a letter of affectionate but thinly-disguised concern, he wrote:

I have been utterly shaken and perplexed at the idea of your removal so far, so very far from your home ... feeling most deeply for you during the delay which must intervene before you learn what course is to be taken – and feeling more deeply still how great must be the sacrifices which ... you will be called upon to make ... I wholly forbid myself to enter upon the details – I will rather seem what some might call unfeeling than awaken, where I can avoid it, your anxieties.[21]

Concerned though he was, Gladstone gave no thought to travelling to be with his sister. As she clearly had their father's provisional approval, he perhaps thought that there was little he could add to the process. In any case, there were more pressing affairs of the heart to deal with closer to home, for by now the Glynnes, too, had arrived in Rome and the social round of teas, dinners, 'church-hunting' and gallery visits resumed. In the late evening of 3 January the party visited the Coliseum by moonlight.

The loveliness with magnificence of the interior of the Coliseum itself was such as left nothing to be desired. Not only should every one see these ruins by moonlight but I think perhaps see them first by moonlight. The perfect stillness ... the actual beauty ... the distinctness of colour ... its dead repose ... the analogy between this mixture of grandeur and of ruin ... all this and much more impressed upon us: we mounted and descended, traversed, wound round ... gazed, and said little.[22]

Little may have been said, and Gladstone was perhaps wise in leaving that little out of his diary until he could tell how things would progress.

But he had, in fact, mumbled a first, faltering declaration to Catherine, who, perhaps intentionally, had failed to grasp what he was saying, and had moved away. Many years later, she still expressed regret that she had not asked him to repeat himself.

Gladstone continued to meet the Glynnes on an almost daily basis for tea or dinner, visiting art galleries, palazzi and churches – particularly when there were sermons to be heard. He gave Catherine a copy of his new book, which had just been published (but which was receiving very mixed reviews), and she loyally copied out whole passages and learnt them by heart. On a visit to Santa Maria Maggiore with its rich decorations, Catherine asked Gladstone whether he thought one could be justified in indulging such luxuries. 'I loved her for that question', he wrote later.[23] One evening Gladstone and the Glynnes joined a group of English visitors for a 'torch-light expedition among the statues'.

The night before he began packing to travel back to England with Stephen Glynne and two other companions, Gladstone approached Catherine again, this time with a letter of breathless, self-effacing complexity. Its second paragraph alone consists of a single sentence of a hundred and forty-one words. But one clear sentiment shines through the fog: 'My dear Miss Glynne ... my heart and hand are at your disposal'.[24] On receiving it, Catherine affected surprise; but neither did she say no, except for the present. Her reply was a gracious 'maybe'.

> Your letter had so completely taken me by surprise, that I feel it is almost impossible to express my sentiments by writing. Although I regard you with great esteem and friendship, you must be aware that warmer feelings are required before consenting to a proposition such as your letter contains. Is it not, therefore, due to you to say that, were an *immediate* answer required (which is only what you ought to have), it must be in the negative? Should it be of any satisfaction to you to see me we shall be at the Porta Maggiore soon after twelve. I will not enter into the feelings of gratitude I entertain for your far too good opinion, or dwell upon the compliment you pay me.[25]

The next day Gladstone departed for Civitavecchia whence the party sailed to Livorno, then to Marseilles, arriving on 23 January. Immediately on arrival he 'wrote to Rome'. Catherine had evidently asked him if she might talk confidentially about their incipient relationship to her old friend Harriet Brooke, now Lady Brabazon. Gladstone, in giving his 'hearty consent' – and, doubtless, the more people knew of the affair, the more favourable an interpretation he could attach to its progress – also stressed to her that he had no 'disposition to interfere with your free will'. Catherine had clearly also broached with him her misgivings about the risk of hurting his feelings if she decided against marriage. To this he replied:

> [Do not] do yourself an injustice by considering the pain which it might hereafter be your duty to inflict, as injury. The truth here as elsewhere is delicate and easily missed ... but true it is ... you are already my benefactress and I am your debtor for pure and delightful recollections ... for the freshness of childhood renewed, and for a hope which, though it be slender, is dearer to me beyond all comparison that any other earthly object.[26]

Compared with the dry religiosity of his previous correspondence with prospective fiancées, Gladstone's style had become quietly irresistible. Catherine certainly thought so. She wrote to her brother that she appreciated 'very much the generous feelings which are expressed in his letter to me'. She asked him to pass this sentiment on to William and to report back. By now William had already been assimilated into the private Glynne family vocabulary, Glynnese. They called him 'Già'. In Italian the word means several things: from 'already' to 'quite so'. From other documents, we know that 'Quite so!' was a favourite Gladstone exclamation, and it is probably to this readiness to accommodate other people's opinions that his affectionate Glynnese nickname of 'Già' refers.[27]

Marriage was still on Gladstone's mind as he wandered the streets of Marseilles, waiting for the mail coach to take him to Paris. In a street near the harbour, he records seeing, in a shop window,

> a formidable column of advertisements under the head 'à marier'. There were eleven separate notices, all from females, ten of them widows, ages varying from 24 to 45 and 50, no other particular mentioned except the fortunes, which in once case (of a quinquagenarian advertiser) rose to no less than 400,000 francs. What a strange picture of humanity this is![28]

Four days later, the group arrived in Paris. By the end of January they were back in London. There Gladstone began to review with some misgivings his clumsy, over-eager courtship of Catherine in the context of his inner loneliness and childish dependence, sufferings compounded

by his two previous infatuations, disasters which had made him feel
'shop-soiled'.

> Here again – yes, even a third time – it would appear that in incorrigible stu-
> pidity, I have been precipitate. And yet not perhaps to the extent that no
> suspicion of my leaning was entertained previously ... The truth is I believe
> my affections are more worthless than ever. Poured forth more than once
> and more than once repudiated they have become stale and unprofitable:
> and I am strangely divided between the pain of solitude in the heart and the
> shame of soliciting a love which I sometimes feel it is impossible for me to
> repay. I am so deadened and exhausted by what has taken place: my still
> dreams of romance have been so near my real life and their dissipation has
> brought so much devastation, at least the pain of devastation, upon it: that
> I am to one who freshly and genuinely loves, what a sacked and blackened
> country seared with recent conflagration, is to the green shady and well
> watered vales which have never know the tread of the spoiler.[29]

Had Gladstone known at the time just how many former suitors Miss
Glynne was about to confess to, he might have worried less about his
'third time lucky' approach. For now, he feared that

> a nature truly noble would probably come to the conclusion that it had noth-
> ing left to give which would be worthy of any woman herself ... worthy of
> its attachment. I offer myself therefore with many conflicting feelings: but
> this time I must suppose to be the last, were it only for shame's sake.[30]

Between February and May Gladstone sat tight, waiting for Catherine
to decide whether, on closer acquaintance, she would have him. Meanwhile, his sister Helen's dreams of engagement to Count Léon seemed
to be fading under parental pressure in St Petersburg. Perhaps the Sol-
lohubs were uncomfortable with the prospect of a daughter-in-law who
was not Russian Orthodox. Perhaps they regarded the Gladstones, rich
though they were, as 'trade'. Perhaps they had heard of Helen's opium
addiction. Perhaps the Count, as Helen's letter hints, was under the
thumb of a jealous mother. Or perhaps he was, as Gladstone suspected
at the start, simply an unreliable 'frequenter of watering-places' where
romances like these happened.

Meanwhile, back in London, William was still spending much time
with the Glynnes, but still doubtful of a happy outcome, convinced that
'what I seek is next to an impossibility'.[31] Two weeks later, he was put

out of his misery when, at a neighbour's garden party in Berkeley Square on 8 June, 'my Catherine gave me herself. We walked apart, and with an effort she said that all doubt on my part might end'. Gladstone spoke to her of the importance to him of religion in private and public life, and of his earlier calling to enter the Church. She was not deterred. She told him she had copied out many extracts from the copy of *The State in its Relations with the Church* that he had given her in Rome, and had learnt them by heart.[32] Nevertheless, he suggested that they make no announcement until the following day, after he had had the opportunity to show her his letter to Lady Farquhar of September 1835, whose religious content had apparently scared off her daughter Caroline. Catherine read it, and again said she was undaunted; indeed she 'rejoiced in it'. Gladstone breathed a sigh of relief. He had won his bride, and without needing to compromise his principles.

> It was not fear that she would view it differently, but it was the desire to fulfil an inward compact with myself, which prompted me to leave her free until she had read it: but now I freely and absolutely call her mine and have kissed her cheek![33]

The woman Gladstone was to marry was as different from the two Annes – his mother and elder sister – as could be imagined. Like them, she was kind and devout. But she was also bonny, healthy, bouncy, witty and irreverent. She would be the making of him as a human being. She was living proof that being good was not the same as being sickly.

As mottoes by which they should live their lives, Gladstone suggested to Catherine a line from St Paul to the Corinthians, and two passages from Dante's *Paradiso*, including the famous quote from Piccarda: 'In la sua voluntate è nostra pace' ('In his will is our peace') that would become for him almost a mantra and one to which he returned time and time again throughout his life.

A few days later, Catherine confided to William that she, too, had rejected, or been disappointed by, previous suitors. In his diary, Gladstone transcribed their names in continuous Greek script, within an entry written in Italian. The catalogue was impressive: Seymour, Newark, Hill, Vaughan, Egerton, Anson, Harcourt, Lewis, Mordaunt.[34] Apparently not taken aback by a list much longer than his, Gladstone expressed his admiration for her 'complete genuineness – I could not fail to become more and more attracted to her goodness'.

But there was one more romantic surprise in the Glynne household. George, Lord Lyttelton had been paying court to Catherine's beloved younger sister, Mary. The week after his engagement to Catherine, Gladstone was at the Glynnes house in Berkeley Square, discussing wedding plans with Catherine. At about 3.30 Lyttelton, who had been there for lunch,

> in a tempest of joy tottered across the room to let us know we were his brother and sister respectively. Mary was a good deal overcome and hid her head in Catherine's bosom: then they fled for a little. He for a while could not in the least control his emotions of delight – and yet he directed them towards God. He is a very noble and powerful creature. 'I never loved any other', he said, 'I never dreamed of any other' – it was true: and this gush of virgin affection bursting its banks was extremely moving. We adopted address by Christian names, agreed to be married on the same day ... kissed each the other's love.
>
> May God be with these newly betrothed. For me, I know how much of the gloss has been brushed off my ideal: but I now know enough to be convinced that not without the faithful Providence of God have I been reserved for access to a creature so truly rare and consummate as my Catherine.[35]

Mary was very close to Catherine. Before it became clear that, as a married woman, Catherine would be free to spend as much time as she wished at Hawarden, the thought of being without her sister seemed unbearable to Mary. A month earlier she had rejected Lyttelton's proposal. After Catherine's engagement, her own now became an eminently sensible move.

A double marriage was planned to take place at the Glynne family home at Hawarden six weeks later. The afternoon before the wedding, the two brides took part in a quaint ceremony of presenting gifts to elderly residents in the village. Gladstone wrote: 'Went at one to the distribution of waistcoats and bedgowns among 200 old men and widows, in the village school: a most interesting sight. Helen assisted in the distribution. Catherine and Mary sat by the door, and warmly greeted the old people as they poured their blessings and prayers upon them'. After a party tea for four hundred local children, a celebration dinner for thirty, and final discussions between both sides of the family as to the financial settlements to be made, the bridegrooms walked together on the terrace at Hawarden Castle around midnight. 'It was a fine night and we ruminated, and spoke together of our great felicity.'[36]

As the wedding party set off the following morning in twelve carriages to drive through the park, round the ruins of the old castle and into the village, William

> fought almost in vain against such a gush of delight as I had not yet experienced. Such an outpouring of pure human affection on these beloved girls ... every house was as a bower, the road arched and festooned, flowers and joined hands amid the green; and the deepest interest on every face: a band and procession of Societies at the head. The mass thickened as they came nearer to the church. From the high road all the way to the door was carpeted: the churchyard ... strewn with flowers and dear little girls with the baskets.[37]

George and William entered the church with John Gladstone, who was delighted at this aristocratic love match that more than satisfied his highest hopes for his youngest son. 'The church was full', Gladstone wrote 'and, as we walked up the aisle, the organ and a hymn began and took away what little power of resistance I had left.' Stephen Glynne gave his sister Catherine in marriage, and Henry his sister Mary. Catherine's uncle George performed the ceremony 'with great dignity and feeling'. There were many tears; even the minister uncle 'gave way in the vestry a little ... My beloved bore up pretty well: her soul is as high and strong as it is tender', William wrote.[38]

They made a handsome pair, a picture of health and energy. Both were tall and slim. Catherine was graceful and animated, with deep blue eyes, thick brown hair and a rosy complexion; William was pale and serious in expression, but bright-eyed and upright in his bearing. Despite their differences in character, they shared the same moral values and a common attitude to life: they cared only for what mattered. In Catherine, this showed itself in an aristocratic disregard for the superficial demands of so-called polite society. In William, it took the form of a sometimes reckless disregard for public opinion over issues in which he considered himself answerable only to God and his conscience.

Catherine was a good match for the young son of a merchant prince. Her family finances may have been on the brink of ruin, but her antecedents were impeccable. Catherine would be the making of her husband as a human being. She taught him how to laugh at himself and to take pleasure in the simply things of life. Gladstone had a strong sexual side to his nature, and there is no indication that this side of their relationship was anything other than mutually rewarding. Even in old age, there was a tactile element between them. His sexual relations with his wife were not something he would ever have commented on. Pregnancy, childbirth, breast-feeding, miscarriage, menopause – his interest in all these is recorded. But it would have been out of character for him to divulge details of the most intimate act of all. He did, however, confess some ten years after his marriage, that the 'plague' of impure thoughts and 'dangerous curiosity' in sexual matters, with which he had struggled since his teens, had been 'essentially enhanced' by marriage.

After the wedding ceremony, the Lytteltons set off for Hagley Hall, George's family home near Birmingham; the Gladstones began their married life a few miles away from Hawarden at the house of a friend at Norton Priory, near Runcorn. As Catherine slept that afternoon on the sofa, Gladstone watched and wrote: 'It has been more of heaven than earth today. Life cannot yield such another sight ... She sleeps gently as a babe ... may I never disturb her precious peace, but cherish her more dearly than myself '.[39] Before bed, the new couple read the Bible together; they did so again the following morning, and 'this daily practice will I trust last as long as our joint lives'.[40]

The Norton honeymoon was spent playing billiards (Catherine was particularly good), chess and whist; but 'most of all these days are very full with the study of one another in no small part – the flower of life'.[41] There was a brief trip back to Hawarden in early August 'in order to consult respecting Lady Glynne [who], no less than heretofore, seems to depend on Catherine'.[42] The following week, in the company of the Lytteltons, they set off on a leisurely trip up to Scotland. Gladstone was apprehensive as to how his wife would be received when they arrived at his family home south of Aberdeen, but he need have had no fears.

> We had a fine afternoon and auspicious approach to Fasque. Much depends on first impressions. To beloved Catherine her entrance into her adoptive family is much more formidable than it would be to those who had been less loved, or less influential, or less needed and leant upon in the home where she was so long as a queen. We found all well and the kindest of welcomes.[43]

The newly-wed Gladstones spent three months at Fasque, from August to November 1839. For the first two weeks the Lytteltons were also there. Catherine's brother Stephen, William's Oxford friend, also paid a visit. His brothers Tom and John Neilson stayed for some time with their wives. John Gladstone took the opportunity to announce to his sons his intention to transfer to them his properties in Demerara: 'This increased wealth', Gladstone wrote, 'so much beyond my needs with its attendant responsibility is very burdensome, however on his part the act be beautiful.'[44] Meanwhile, there were walks, picnics and excursions to places of interest near and far. In mid-September, Catherine began to suffer morning sickness and, eight weeks into their marriage, she confided to William that she believed she was pregnant: 'Today my darling told me what she felt, and the reason', he wrote in his diary in Italian. ('Quest' oggi mi disse la mia carissima che cosa sentisse colla cagione del medesimo.')[45] It was in many ways an idyllic time: there was rowing and shooting during the day; singing, chess and card games in the evening. And reading, always lots of reading.[46] Even Catherine's indisposition did nothing to spoil the young couple's mood: 'Catherine suffers annoyance from sickness and bears it sweetly', Gladstone recorded.[47]

But not everyone at Fasque was so happy. Helen was becoming increasingly jealous of Catherine, but was also miserable with guilt at feeling so.[48] Her own engagement had come to nothing and she was now the only one of the five siblings left single. Her brother John Neilson had married in February of that year. Her two other brothers, Tom and Robertson, had both been married since 1835. William's devotion, to much of which she had previously been able to lay claim, was now concentrated on Catherine. Helen felt very alone, and justifiably so. One clear impression that emerges from the aftermath of Gladstone's marriage to Catherine is that, from then onwards, his family focus was on the Glynnes. He did his duty by the Gladstones, and impeccably so in the case of his father. But, after his marriage, his heart lay elsewhere. Helen sensed this during the honeymoon weeks at Fasque and, fuelled by laudanum, began behaving badly. She had been spending long periods in her room and by mid-November a family crisis erupted. The details are unclear – William's diary entries, again in Italian, are enigmatic, but it would seem a maid was obtaining secret supplies of opium on Helen's behalf. Whatever the cause, it was enough for him to describe his father as 'wracked by real agony', and presumably also deeply mortified at the impression Helen's hysterical behaviour might have on Catherine. It certainly seems to have been enough to persuade William and his wife to leave Fasque sooner rather than later. Midway through the crisis, Catherine had suffered 'an attack of the heart', and, in her condition, departure seemed a sensible move. If Helen had hoped to develop a relationship with Catherine that would result in her being drawn into the bosom of the Glynne family, she had gone the wrong way about it. Catherine was a straightforward person and robust, both physically and mentally; and she had little patience with emotional fussiness in others.

William and Catherine left Fasque on 23 November for a leisurely return to Hawarden where they would spend Christmas, calling en route at many of the great houses of their acquaintances. Among the places they stayed at was Dalmahoy, the estate of Lord Morton, father of Lady Frances Douglas – now Lady Milton – Gladstone's second romantic failure. But again, he need not have worried. Catherine and the Mortons were discretion itself, and William was quietly gratified by the comparison between his wife and the woman who might have held that position.

> Catherine walked a little with Lady Milton and liked her very much. In appearance she is just as two years ago. She dresses in excellent taste *plainly*, evincing thereby a higher tact. She seems to me in all respects now the same person that she seemed then. None of the family even alluded ever so indirectly to my having been here before. They were most kind to us ... There was some awkwardness in meeting Lady Milton. She felt it too and lingered on the handle of the door when she entered. But why should she? She has nothing to regret. I have to regret a precipitancy blamable in itself though I do not believe it at all affected the issue. In other respects, I received here a sharp instruction which I believe will chasten me for my life long with respect to all objects of my desire: combined, that is to say, with what preceded it in 1835. And I say deliberately, and I think not self-deceived, that I now see how much more wisely God judged and ordered for me: Catherine and I talked over these matters for two hours.[49]

From Scotland, the Gladstones made their way down through Northumberland, County Durham and Yorkshire, arriving in early

December at Lincoln, where Catherine was reunited with Lady Glynne, who had been staying there during their long holiday. While at Lincoln, Gladstone paid a visit to his nearby constituency of Newark, 'to discharge my duties'. It was his first working day since his marriage, and he reflected, as he rode home, on the delight of having someone to come home to: 'I found this day in returning homewards the blessing of a wife who makes home after labour a living and not merely a material thing'.[50] By Christmas the party were installed at Hawarden. On his thirtieth birthday that week, Gladstone commented in his customary year-end review:

> The last twelvemonth has seen less done and more received from God ... His mercy has vouchsafed me that which I contemplated as a help towards heaven ... United to my Catherine, I now stand in the eye of God charged with a double responsibility; and ought the more to seek grace to meet it.[51]

It was Gladstone's good fortune that his 'help towards heaven' was also beautiful, warm-hearted, graceful, vivacious and resilient; she was also untidy, sometimes disorganised, often funny, always fiercely loyal, ambitious, and generally predisposed by her aristocratic birth not to pay too much attention to the rigid middle-class conventions of Victorian public life. She was the perfect foil for Gladstone. There was something of an irony that the woman Gladstone married was, in many ways, as different from the 'two Annes' as could be imagined. But, like them, she was kind and devout, and this was fundamental.

It was little short of a miracle that a man as orderly as William should enjoy his wife's 'unlimited capacity for the unexpected', and find amusement in the odd situations she found herself in: 'My wife has a marvellous facility for getting into scrapes and an almost more marvellous one for getting out of them'.[52] Despite this he always treated her seriously. Nor did her casual nature lead to indiscretion. At the beginning of their marriage, William gave her the choice between knowing all his political secrets or knowing none. If she knew all, she must maintain total secrecy. She chose to know all, and spontaneous and haphazard as she could be in other things, she hardly ever suffered a slip of the tongue. After one rare occasion when she did, he wrote her a touching note: 'Do not be vexed. I am not. It is the first time you ever made a little mistake'.[53]

Although it was undoubtedly a love match, it was practical marriage too, in that the substantial Gladstone finances were able to save the Glynnes from disaster, enabling Catherine to remain for much of the time in her childhood home at Hawarden,[54] the focal point of her rapidly expanding extended family, whose company she always preferred to stuffy formal functions in the company of mere acquaintances. As a result, however, she and William spent long periods of their married life apart, particularly in the early years. Perhaps that was a factor in sustaining such life-long mutual devotion, although Catherine found the separations trying, particularly when the children were small. The arrangement allowed William to devote more of his carefully organised time and exceptional energy to affairs of state. The success that this brought suited them both: William, because greater authority brought with it great scope for serving society; Catherine, because she was ambitious for her husband and enjoyed his being at the heart of events. In later years, visitors to the Ladies' Gallery in the House of Commons would be shown a shining patch of brass railing in front of Mrs Gladstone's favourite seat, worn bright by the pressure of her gloved hands as she leaned forward to hear her husband speak. Catherine's life became so intertwined with William's interests as to become almost inextricable from them. She had her own projects, mainly charitable and later political, but they always chimed with his.

As the year 1840 dawned, Gladstone was a well-established political figure with brilliant prospects and a wealthy, supportive father. He had a beautiful new bride and an entrée to the best circles. Soon the Gladstones would become dinner guests of another pair of newly-weds: Victoria and Albert. On his wedding night, Gladstone had written that life just now was heaven on earth. And so it was, in many respects. But every silver lining has a cloud. The cloud on Gladstone's personal horizon was his sister. Poor, unhappy Helen – isolated, unrequited and now redundant within the wider family circle – would be a thorn in William's side for many years to come.

4

Helen

In early spring 1840, Gladstone spent five days at Eton examining boys for the prestigious Newcastle scholarship, set up by the Duke of Newcastle, his first political sponsor and father of his old friend Henry Lincoln. His co-examiner was George Lyttelton, the husband of Catherine's sister, Mary. Both Catherine and Mary were now pregnant, and Gladstone, as a prospective father, had had to provide reassurance to his wife, who was beginning to feel anxious about the physical side of childbirth. The Eton interlude provided a break, an exercise he and George felt to be 'a moral relaxation, though not one in any other sense'.[1] They lodged with Gladstone's old mentor, Edward Hawtrey. In the event they had the satisfaction of awarding the medal of achievement, if not the scholarship, to young Henry Hallam junior,[2] the brother of Arthur, Gladstone's first and dearly loved best friend from Eton days.

But perhaps more important than either of these was the other question that preoccupied him. Gladstone was seriously involved in one of the major political issues of the day – the Chinese Opium War. On 8 April, as Tory MP for Newark, Gladstone stood up in the House of Commons and spoke out passionately – in his own words 'heavily … and strongly' – in support of Opposition leader Sir Robert Peel's motion of censure against the Whig government's backing of Britain's profitable (but, in human terms, destructive and despicable) opium trade with China.

Gladstone opposed both the lucrative export of the drug from British India and the hostilities that resulted from China's resistance to accepting those imports. China had introduced legislation banning incoming opium supplies, had refused provision to ships bringing the drug in, and, as a consequence, had triggered war with the British, who were intent on securing their entitlement to trade in the Chinese market. 'I do not know', Gladstone declared, 'how it can be urged as a crime against the Chinese that they refused provisions to those who refused obedience to their laws whilst residing within their territory.'[3] In a speech described as 'by far the most interesting in the debate',[4] he added:

> I am not competent to judge how long this war may last, nor how protracted may be its operations, but I can say this, that a war more calculated in its progress to cover this country with disgrace, I do not know ... Although the Chinese were undoubtedly guilty of much absurd phraseology, of no little ostentatious pride, and of some excess, justice in my opinion is with them, and whilst they the pagans and semi-civilised barbarians have it, we the enlightened and civilised Christians are pursuing objects at variance both with justice and religion.[5]

It was a noble speech, but so controversial that he felt bound to clear it in advance with Sir James Graham, who opened the debate for the Opposition.[6] The motion had been introduced in such terms that the Tories hoped critics of government policy on both sides of the House might be encouraged to vote for it. The Whig government was tottering, and the Chinese question seemed a good opportunity to push it over the edge.[7]

For Gladstone the issue was far more than a question of political strategy. For him, opium was an intensely personal issue. Certainly, in the wider context of his career, his opposition to the opium trade was a milestone in his political growth: a defining moment in the making of him as a liberal. But more poignant than that was the fact that, on the floor of the House of Commons, he was speaking from the heart, not just from the head. Personal experience more than anything else gave real conviction to his speech. For, as in many homes in Victorian Britain, opium cast a long shadow over Gladstone family life. At the time, his sister Helen – though still only twenty-six – had been addicted to opium for years, perhaps for more than a decade. Gladstone knew at first hand the personal misery and social disruption that consumption of the drug could bring in its train.

At one level, opium – usually taken in the form of laudanum, a suspension of opium in alcohol that made the drug easier to swallow – was the universal Victorian panacea. In the days before valium, librium, prozac, seroxat or even aspirin,[8] it was virtually the only effective drug for a wide range of ailments. Gladstone in fact is known to have taken it himself occasionally, not just for physical pain, but to fortify him for a long debate. If you were anxious, it calmed you down; if you were down, it picked you up. It was used for every conceivable form of physical, mental and spiritual ailment, quite apart from its recreational and creative properties. It was in her early teens that Helen was first treated with opium, probably for period pains, possibly also for hyperactivity. Her invalid mother and elder sister were unlikely to have been equal to the task of coping with a boisterous young girl such as Helen. From an early age, therefore, Helen came to experience and appreciate the 'luxurious' effects of opium on which, in later years, she would increasingly depend as a frustrated, undervalued, 'redundant' Victorian woman. It was not until the 1880s – after Helen's death – that the medical profession began to understand the concept of physical addiction (as distinct from voluntary 'habituation') as a medical problem.[9] As a result, symptoms of drug addiction that are apparent today, even to a lay person, were interpreted in the mid nineteenth century as little short of moral turpitude, the results of a wilful act of self-indulgence, which the user (as we know today is not the case) could have stopped at any time.

It is a fact of drug consumption that its effect is conditioned to some degree by the natural temperament and social attitudes of the user. A compliant nature may submit to quiet chemical sedation (and in some cases, control), and there were plenty of sad and disappointed women following that route in nineteenth century Britain. (Catherine's mother, Lady Glynne, widowed at an early age and a sufferer from depression from then on, may have been one of them.) A more rebellious nature might find its sense of injustice and frustration enhanced, and become angry under the influence of opium. Helen Gladstone was such a one. On more than one occasion during her life, her rebellious behaviour, fuelled by opium and alcohol, became so bad that it threatened to ruin her brother's political career.

The relationship between William and Helen was a complex and frustrating one. When she was small, he sought to direct her behaviour in a teasing and paternalistic way. He wrote home from Eton criticising her handwriting (she was nine at the time, he thirteen), and questioning whether time spent writing letters to him might not have been better employed.[10] At the same time, he sent her stamps, India rubbers, and laurel leaves collected from a tree in the graveyard immortalised in Grey's *Elegy*. He also trivialised her desire to learn. For example, when she expressed a wish to learn Latin, he responded: 'with regard to the dead languages ... I do not see why learning them is at all necessary for women'.[11] As she reached puberty, when her incipient sexuality may have begun to unnerve him, his criticism extended, as we have seen, to her dress sense and time management. As she entered her twenties, his irritation with Helen increased with her increased consumption of opium. In the event of a misfortune that was not of her making, his irritation was tempered with a strong measure of brotherly tenderness – as in the case of her failed engagement. But it exploded in fury when she announced her conversion to Roman Catholicism. This decision he saw as an aberration, a case of moral delusion and an integral part of the overall depravity that centred on her drug misuse.

It was just weeks after his tirade against the Chinese Opium War that Gladstone began to suspect that his sister was leaning towards Rome, as he recalled later.

> I write to you ... as the only alternative other than that of writing to my father who, as I apprehend, is either wholly ignorant or but partially informed upon the facts relating to it. It was, I think, towards the summer of 1840 that I heard, I believe from your own lips though the words were not addressed to me, that you had been attending the worship of one of the Romish chapels in London ... at the hour of divine worship. It would not, I am sure, have been consistent with your character to conceal your proceedings in such a matter, and therefore you will not be surprised, that I also became acquainted with your having done the same thing in Liverpool during your recent visit ... how often there or elsewhere I have no means of knowing. Neither will you be astonished that, with this intelligence, my mind associates other signs, such as the religious books of a peculiar nature which you possess: and which appear to have tinged your sentiments. I am however far from having the knowledge necessary ... to enable me to form any judgement upon the state of your convictions ... but there is no doubt [about] your attendance at the Romish worship. There is indeed a difference between attending as a spectator and as a participator. But when I recollect how rare from circumstances ... are your opportunities of public worship at all,[12] I am bound to assume that you have gone to be yourself a worshipper in the Papal congregations ... Is it possible that you can be otherwise than aware that the Church of Christ in

England holds the Romish worship to be replete with peril of idolatry? To stint the word of God ... to endanger the doctrine of atonement ... to tread upon the very verge of that most miserable sin by which the honour due to God is given to His once sinful creatures? It cannot be [unclear] to you that the worship of the Romish chapels in Liverpool and in London is, putting out of view for the moment all other corruptions, a schismatical worship; that their altars are ... set up in rivalry to the altars of Christ and of His commissioned servants: that the voice which issues from them is one which denies and reviles the ministry, the sacraments, the foundations of the Church ... if their worship be lawful, the Church of England is an accursed thing. It would be weak on my part were I to descend from the consideration of these awful subjects ... to describe the extraordinary feelings with which I now find myself engaged in thus addressing you: but I must say emphatically that my astonishment is ... mixed with serious alarm.[13]

He ended with a 'prayer that there may be between us such a bond of love as death cannot break'.

The big rift came in May 1842. Gladstone realised at last that his sister's conversion to Rome was real, however misguided he may have deemed it to be. He wrote her a fourteen-page letter of such excoriating censure one almost hopes she never read it.[14] It read, in part:

My unhappy sister ... your soul is staked ... You have announced yourself to have left the Catholic church and the Apostolic priesthood of this land, and to have plunged into a schism, of which I will not here stop to mark the tremendous and peculiar perils ... What you think is a church is none, I mean the Roman schism in England. What you call and think a conviction, is, like all the rest of your moral life for years, a dream ... You have acted I well know in sincerity ... and it is this very fact, which seals the proof of your deep and miserable delusion ... This delusion is not your first. It is the completion of a web, which for many years you have been weaving around you, and which by progressive degrees has enveloped all your faculties, and deprived you of true vision ... You are living, and have been long living, a life of utter self-deception. Not in religion alone – but in all bodily, in all mental habits – in all personal and all social relations.[15]

The argument between the two bounced back and forth throughout the summer. Gladstone perceived a threat to the welfare of his High Anglican friends and to his own career, all of which might be tarnished by association with her Roman Catholicism. On 12 June, he wrote to her to express his concern that

> should it please God to permit the veil to remain with you, there will not be wanting persons to draw the inference that the material result of the Catholic principles of the Church of England is union with the Romish body; and who, connecting those principles with my name, will endeavour to wound them through my sides. It will be my solemn duty to defend them to the utmost of my means from this fatal ... aspersion.

He hinted that he might be compelled to reveal her private life in order to protect his friends. This he would do by 'unfolding parts of our agonising and I trust unparalleled family history which would otherwise remain ... known only besides ourselves to Him that seeth all'.[16]

It was untrue that, in these two respects, the Gladstone family history was in any way unparalleled. Devastating though its effects undoubtedly were within families who proved unequal to the ideological challenge, conversion to Roman Catholicism was not uncommon in nineteenth-century Britain, any more than was opium addiction.[17] Indeed, there was a time when both could almost have been described as a fashion. But Gladstone was clearly threatening to expose publicly Helen's affiliation to Rome if she declined to give up her consumption of opium. That her religious convictions might have any validity he dismissed out of hand.

> You are not fit for religious discussion ... your deep malady is not religious ... the awful office that I have been discharging towards you, that of ... standing in place of your conscience, is an office of love ... hoping for the day when it may please God by whatever discipline to discharge the phantoms from your mind and restore you to the faculty of discerning common right and wrong.[18]

Three weeks later, Helen forestalled rumour and innuendo by advertising her conversion to Rome in the press. To her brother William, she wrote bravely:

> By my consent, a paragraph will be put in the C[atholic] papers this evening, to state simply that I have made my profession of faith without any allusion to the family to which I belong. Had this not been resolved upon, an offensive and falsely coloured, but most violent invective, would have become

public. Chiefly desiring to spare you pain, I write this. I presume the rest will simply copy it.[19]

Gladstone replied immediately, accepting her decision to go public with good grace – and possibly also with a measure of quiet relief that, in finding the courage to do so, she had cleared the family from any suspicion of collusion in that decision. But, quite rightly, he took her to task over her indiscriminate use of the word 'Catholic', requesting that in future she preface it with the epithet 'Roman'. High Church Anglicans, particularly in their Tractarian manifestation, also saw themselves as 'Catholic', in the original meaning of the Greek word: that is 'universal', tracing their origins back to the early period of Christianity when there was a single, undivided church from which derived a direct apostolic succession of bishops, independent of Rome. He asked that in future she should indicate the 'Roman' connection by some indication which would not necessitate a public protest on his part.

As Helen had predicted, other publications picked up the story. And, as William had predicted, where this happened it did not lead to a positive outcome. 'Conversion to Popery', wrote the *Birmingham Advertizer*.

> We regret to say that Miss Gladstone, sister of the Vice-President of the Board of Trade, has recently been admitted a Member of the Roman Catholic Church. On Tuesday week she was confirmed by Dr Wiseman, in the chapel at the Nunnery near this town, and afterwards partook of the 'sacrament of the Holy Eucharist'. The lady is described as being highly intelligent, and about thirty years of age. [She was, in fact, twenty-eight.] During her stay in Birmingham both she and her attendants resided at the Convent.

Two weeks later, the *Record* wrote in terms that Gladstone had predicted:

> We learn from undoubted authority that the report that Miss Gladstone, sister to Mr W. E. Gladstone, Deputy Chairman of the Board of Trade, has become a Papist is perfectly correct. The truth is that in principle there is no important difference between Tractarianism and Popery; and if there were not certain practical differences attending the change, we should see many of the Puseyite clergy and laity forthwith pass over the flimsy barriers that separate the two.[20]

Once the initial shock of Helen's conversion in 1842 had been

overcome – and her father, always more generous than William, reconciled himself earlier than his youngest son to accepting the new status
quo, under certain conditions – life within the Gladstone family enjoyed
an extended period of calm. The Gladstone family continued to grow.
After William came Agnes (1842), Stephen (1844) and then Catherine
Jessy (1845). But then came a major drama with Helen. It was slow to
gather momentum, but when it did, it threatened to bring scandal on
the entire family and jeopardise William's newly resurrected career.

Helen had left England in early 1845 for the Continent and the fashionable spa towns where, a few years previously, she had nearly found
happiness. Since then there had been little direct news of her. But
rumours were filtering back to the family that all was not well.

At the beginning of 1846 the Gladstone men should have had good
reason to be cheerful. After a year in the political wilderness, William
had recently celebrated his thirty-seventh birthday by accepting the
position of Colonial Secretary and returning to Peel's Cabinet. Two of
his brothers were MPs; a third, previously mayor of Liverpool, remained
prominent in the commercial and public affairs of his native city. John
Gladstone was looking forward to receiving a long-awaited baronetcy.[21]
But, behind the scenes, a domestic crisis was developing that threatened
to bring public disgrace on the entire family. The Commissioners in
Lunacy had received an official complaint that the Gladstones were ille-
gally confining Helen on the top floor of their London home at 6
Carlton Gardens. If proved, the allegation was political dynamite. It
caused so much upset that, for a while, William considered leaving
public life for good.

It is difficult to say which distressed William more: Helen's opium
addiction or her conversion to Rome. In fact, he saw these two courses
of action linked by what he perceived to be the same moral weakness.
Of all the crises in Helen's relationship with William in particular, none
matched the intensity of the crucial three years from 1846 to 1848. This
period began shortly after Helen's return to England from Germany,
following at least one suicide attempt, triggered by misery and facilitated
by opium. It ended with her well-documented 'cure' from hysteria by
Cardinal Wiseman and her temporary reconciliation to family life at
Fasque, the Gladstone family estate in Scotland, during Sir John's

declining years. These are the years when Helen was most profoundly disturbed, most heavily addicted, and when her family's treatment of her (and the immediate family by now comprised only men) was at its most extreme.

The first part of this particular drama began to reach crisis point on the morning of 9 January 1846, when the members of the recently re-formed Commissioners in Lunacy met under the chairmanship of Lord Ashley.[22] On the agenda was the question of Helen Gladstone's possibly illegal confinement on the top floor of John Gladstone's house. Henry Bagshawe, a barrister, appeared before the Commission on her behalf.[23] Bagshawe and his wife were Helen's closest Roman Catholic friends. His sister had been her companion. He was an executor of her first will,[24] of which his son, Frederick Gladstone Bagshawe – Helen's godson – was a beneficiary.[25] Bagshawe produced various letters and memoranda, on the basis of which, according to the Commission records,

> he applied for the interference of the Commissioners with a view to her release from confinement, & the restraint which she alleged was put upon her movements by her family, in the house of her father ... Mr Bagshawe explained the circumstances of his own & Mrs Bagshawe's first acquaintance with Miss Gladstone, & their subsequent intimacy ... Mr Bagshawe stated that he saw her a few days after her return [from the Continent, a month before], when she complained to him of having been pressed by her brothers, in consequence of a letter from her father, to sign a paper, to the effect that she 'was not then, & was not likely to be, in the full possession of her mental faculties'. She had also, as he stated, been urged by her brothers to submit to be placed under the care of a foreign physician (who had attended her on the Continent) as of unsound mind, & incapable of managing her property. Under these circumstances, she asked Mr B's advice. Four or five days subsequently, she stated to Mrs Bagshawe that her family still persisted in their intentions to place her under restraint as a Lunatic. Mr Bagshawe expressed his decided opinion that Miss Gladstone was of perfectly sound mind, & that she was the subject of persecution on the part of her family.[26]

Henry Bagshawe was a brave man. To take on the Gladstone family, and to suggest that their only surviving daughter Helen was 'the subject of persecution', was a courageous step bordering almost on the fool-hardy. But the Commissioners in Lunacy thought he was right to do so.

The Commission's conclusion was that the case was 'proper for an application to the Lord Chancellor for an order to visit', and they wrote immediately to that effect, addressing their letter to Tom Gladstone, as the eldest brother and therefore nominal head of the family:

> Sir, an application has been made to the Commissioners in Lunacy calling on them to procure through the powers of the Lord Chancellor ... an order authorising them to visit and examine Miss Helen Maria Gladstone. [The grounds are that] although a person of sound mind she is not treated as a free agent but is now confined as if she were insane. The application is supported by such a statement of facts that the Commissioners feel they cannot do otherwise than accede to I ... they have therefore requested me ... to enquire whether you would permit two of their number (one of whom would be a physician) to visit Miss Helen Maria Gladstone ... and form a judgement of themselves, as to the present state of her mind, and the nature of the restraint, if any, to which she is subject, with a view to report the result of their inquiry to the Board.[27]

Tom Gladstone immediately drafted an indignant reply to the effect that:

> Miss Gladstone never has been, and is not, in a state of restraint, in proof of which I need only state that at this moment she is not in Mr Gladstone's house, having gone out, attended only by her maid, about six o'clock this evening. Although no personal restraint has been used towards her [the following section in the draft letter has been deleted from the final copy], acting under the verbal instructions of her father (on whom she is entirely dependent), Mr William Gladstone and I have been compelled to discharge one of two foreign maids in attendance on her. I beg to add, on the part of my brother Mr William Gladstone and myself, that we shall be happy to afford any information on this subject that your Lordship may wish for.[28]

That same evening, William and Tom Gladstone met Lord Ashley at the Carlton Club and 'told him a good deal of the case, which staggers him'.[29] William noted in his diary for that day: 'Saw T. G. & Ashley on Helen's matters, the latter's official letter'.[30] Tom's insistence that his sister 'was not, & never had been, under restraint' was noted in the minutes of the Commission's meeting five days later, on 14 January 1846.[31] After this meeting, the matter seems to have been dropped. Interestingly, Lord Ashley was not present at the meeting when Tom's letter to him was read out. An examination of all the minutes for 1846 indicates that, except for a summer break, Lord Ashley attended all but three of sixty-three sessions. Did he miss the 14 January meeting in order not to appear to be influencing the Commission's response to Tom Gladstone's reply – or indeed to be influenced by it? Did he disapprove of being approached privately by the Gladstone brothers? Or had they, indeed, given him private information that was persuasive but could not be made public. By the standards of the time, he may not have thought the Gladstones were acting inappropriately in the treatment of their wayward, drug-addicted and suicidal sister. Lord Ashley was back in the chair for the Commission's next meeting on 4 February, when a letter was read out from Mr Bagshawe 'asking for return of correspondence & memoranda'.[32] After that, there is no further record of Helen Gladstone's affairs in the Commission's minutes. The Gladstone men had therefore avoided public disclosure.

The Gladstone response to the Commissioners was disingenuous. Helen's own maid had indeed been sacked – but she was sacked to make way for Mary, the head housemaid at Fasque. Mary had previous experience of Helen's problems. She was sent to London by John Gladstone as the family's equivalent to Grace Poole, the fictional minder of another mad woman in the attic, the first Mrs Rochester in Charlotte Brontë's *Jane Eyre*. Ironically, Brontë's novel was published in 1847, the year of Helen Gladstone's most stringent containment. The case (like the novel) illustrates the relative ease with which wealthy Victorians were able to confine or constrain their relatives, not only by lock and key but also by the use of servants. Helen's own maid was allegedly intercepted by Tom as she left the house with some of her mistress's jewellery to sell,[33] possibly to buy opium or alcohol. This may also explain Helen's note to the pharmacist Godfrey & Cooke of Knightsbridge to 'please supply my usual powder and the same again tomorrow'.[34] Helen allegedly dropped notes from her window, offering jewellery to passers-by who would pass on her messages.[35]

More importantly, John Gladstone's instructions to William and Tom as to the containment of Helen are expressed in a letter sent two weeks before the Commissioners in Lunacy became involved. Restraint of Helen – coercion even – is precisely what her father ordered. In doing so, he was implementing what William had been openly advocating for some years.[36] And if his strategy of containment and forcible drug withdrawal on the top floor at Carlton Gardens were to fail, the other alternative was to board her out, as ultimately happened. To Tom and William, John Gladstone wrote:

> The circumstances are most painful but they must be met and everything done in the hope of saving her from destruction ... it appears that nothing ... but thorough measures offer any chance of success ... The consequences ... must be ... placing her in a state of coercion ... Mary, my upper housemaid ... in whom I have great confidence ... is to take charge of her and has given me her solemn assurance that whatever [the] Doctor prescribes or orders to be done, shall be strictly adhered to, and nothing given or anyone permitted to have access to her but by his orders or permission. I wish the joiners to be got and the bed that is in the room over Helen's brought down and put in the small room that adjoins Helen's bedroom, the door from which to the passage – as well as the one from the water closet – must both be locked and secured so as there will be only one approach and that through the dressing-room where Mary is to sleep ... I have today conversed with [Mary] fully and explained the nature of the charge she is to have, that nothing whatsoever or person of any description is to have access to Helen, without either your or Tom's or the Doctor's consent ... her food and medicine is all to be directed by him and none else taken, or permitted to be given to her on any account ... she must take it at proper times; and, if postponed, the same food must be given to her. Unless such a course is adhered to, I am satisfied that all the labour will be in vain and she must be lost. Mary will be her only female attendant ... at Carlton Gardens. If further measures should be necessary from the failure of these ... you and Tom must make necessary enquiries. I believe there are those who receive persons such as her to live at board, treating them with kindness but firmness and strict adherence to rules.[37]

A week after the Commissioners in Lunacy episode, Helen left London to stay with Catholic friends at Bath. Whether she actually escaped, or was allowed to escape, is not clear. The tone of William's farewell letter to her is ambiguous. Whenever he failed to get his own way with Helen, William would create a situation in which the outcome – whatever it was – could be interpreted as fulfilling his own original design. On 17 January, he wrote to Helen after her departure that:

painful as is this course ... I cannot lament it under the present circumstances ... it seems quite impossible to induce you to conform to my father's will as a member of his household ... it is better I believe for all parties that you should cease to be such, and should betake yourself to those whom you have given your confidence in the highest and most essential matter. My belief is that this course affords the best hope of your recovery.[38]

In a particularly unkind aside, he mentioned that his wife Catherine had asked to visit Helen but he had forbidden it. Helen, meanwhile, wrote to her maternal aunt Johanna as she left for Bath, asking to be kept informed in particular of her father's health. 'May God bless him and make him far happier than I could', she wrote. 'I know how you are grieving for me ... But do not. All is in God's hands. He would not let it be, unless it were right ... I grieve more for my father and you, than for myself ... I ask your forgiveness most humbly for every action of mine ... that has offended you who from my cradle has been so kind to me.'[39]

Helen's bid for freedom was short-lived. Shortly afterwards, she was taken by the family from Bath to Fasque in Scotland, where her quarters were adapted along similar lines to those at Carlton Gardens. An additional small room was created between her bedroom and the back stairs. Here a nurse or minder would sleep. And through it the doctor had discreet access to Helen – via the tradesmen's entrance at the east side of the house – without alerting the rest of the household.[40] The arrangements for the control of her social life were similar. Sir John's instructions were clear:

As you seem determined to persevere in paying no regard to what I say to you, or indeed any to what is right and wrong, it has become necessary I should adopt a different course. I have therefore to tell you that I shall in future prevent any person who may come here to have access to you until I have previously seen them, and accounted what their objects are, nor any parcels or letters to be taken either to you or sent out of the house from you until I have previously seen them ... this may perhaps render you less ... obstinately disobedient ... The way in which you in future conduct yourself will guide my conduct.[41]

With this last sentence, Sir John was calling in a promise he had imposed on Helen at the time of her conversion to Rome in 1842, as a

condition of his agreement to it. 'When I consented to your change of
religion', he wrote, 'you gave me your solemn promise that in all your
temporal concerns you would be guided by my advice and direction.'[42]
That advice to his 'sadly mistaken, deluded child' had been comprehensive. It ranged from her account-keeping to her diet ('no pastry
allowed ... but pudding if plain'), and even the state of her teeth, and
her halitosis. The previous year, William, too, had attacked her personal
habits. This very intimate, physical approach to Helen's problems is
echoed in many of William's and Sir John's responses. They appear
inappropriate even by the less formal standards of today. The Gladstone
men were totally out of their depth in dealing with her.

Helen failed to improve at Fasque, where she spent weeks alone in her
darkened room, corresponding with other members of the household
only by note. William wrote in his diary, on 3 October 1847, that she was
physically 'utterly shattered; and although she conversed quite rationally
about others her mind quite gone in regard to herself'.[43] She talked of
'a plot to carry her off in the night', and saw people 'coming in through
the walls'. 'This is the deplorable result to which we have long been
taught to look forward.'[44] Three days later a decision was made: 'It is
determined to try total withdrawal of the Laudanum'. Helen was to be
sent to Leamington where she was to be 'boarded out'.[45] The Gladstone
family had once lived at Leamington, where Helen had been treated by
a Dr Jephson. There she was to remain in the care of a minder
appointed by Jephson, one Mrs Elliot, a woman experienced in such
cases. Her welfare was to be monitored by Elizabeth Rawson, the wife
of the vicar of Seaforth. Both of them had known Helen since she was
a child. The conditions under which she was kept appear to have
become increasingly intolerable, despite Jephson's comments to the
contrary.[46] She was forbidden visits from her beloved Aunt Johanna, her
mother's sister, and her letters to her aunt were intercepted. These conditions, and her physical treatment, were reported to Sir John via
William in a spirited exchange of letters with Mrs Rawson, who found
Helen's treatment disgraceful.[47]

The Rawsons were old friends of the Gladstone family. William Rawson had been brought to Seaforth years before by John Gladstone to run
a small local school attended by the boys of the Gladstone clan. The couple were conscientious and solicitous in all Gladstone family matters.

Elizabeth Rawson's comments on Helen's plight at Leamington there-fore have credibility. Yet her appalled response to what she found there – including a clear reference to delirium tremens and dubious, invasive, medical treatment – profoundly shocked Sir John. He refused to accept her report, and the affair caused a rift between the two families that was healed only on the old man's death-bed. Elizabeth Rawson's main report ran to fourteen pages in which she listed a number of grievances aired by Elliot, the minder. These included Elliot's lack of payment or free time; the absence of a companion or any pocket-money for Helen; Helen's heavy drinking, gluttony and her disgraceful behaviour at church – plus 'such wickedness allowed and I have no power to prevent it'. Elliot insisted that Dr Jephson had no sympathy for Helen. She alleged that he called her 'wicked, the worst case I have ever had', and countered her threats of suicide with the reply that 'she lacked the moral courage'.[48] This is in direct contrast to the tone of Jephson's own letters to Sir John.

More importantly, Elliot took Mrs Rawson to Helen's room to show her 'some surgical instruments'. The use of these she described in dis-turbing detail but the medical implications remain unclear. One possible explanation is that they were hypodermic syringes, but these could hardly be described as 'surgical' and the subcutaneous injection of opium was very new. Also, Helen was known to be an opium addict – that is why she was at Leamington – and the outrage of both Elliot and Mrs Rawson suggests something more than that. Words began to fail Elizabeth Rawson in her letter to Sir John and she concluded: 'But I shall not enlarge: the whole is too disgusting for me to write or you to read.' Helen was known to have liver and bowel problems, probably as a result of opium consumption. Yet even Dr Jephson, despite his upbeat reports on Helen's progress, confided to Sir John that there was 'another cause' of her problems that he would prefer to discuss privately when they met rather than commit to paper.[49] That cause has yet to be identified.

Sir John's response in defence of his daughter was indignant. He insisted that the surgical instruments observed by Mrs Rawson were part of the doctors' instructions for treatment of an 'internal indisposition'. In the draft of his letter, but deleted from the final copy – presumably for the sake of propriety – he stated that, in this treatment, 'internal bleeding and other relief were included, but of too delicate a nature to be spoken of by a female even to her husband'.[50] This opens up interesting avenues of speculation. Had Helen been undergoing treatment for gynaecological problems? If so, it must have added a new dimension to her life-long misery. Or was she being treated in a gynaecological manner for nervous disorders of an 'hysterical' nature. If so, this reflects an interesting aspect of Victorian medical treatment of difficult women. Vaginal leeching and use of the speculum were not uncommon treatments for menstrual and 'hysterical' disorders in the nineteenth century,[51] and there was a suspicion that the latter in particular could lead to 'the practice of solitary vice'.[52] This might tie in with Elliot's account of 'such wickedness allowed', and her reference to Helen's 'indulgence of the most debasing passion'.[53]

Eventually, Helen asked to be admitted to a convent at Leamington, where her health evidently improved. She returned to Fasque the next year, 1848, but again she deteriorated. She was sent to Edinburgh, in the care of Aunt Johanna, to be treated by a nerve specialist, Professor Miller, for clenched hands and locked jaw, assumed to be of an hysterical nature. This condition was ultimately resolved by Cardinal Wiseman's famous cure. Supported by the prayers of various Catholic women's organisations, Wiseman took a relic – a purported saint's knucklebone – and with it touched each side of Helen's locked jaw and her clenched hands. Visibly, the affected parts relaxed. It seemed like a miracle and was spoken of as such in Catholic circles in Edinburgh.[54]

After her health was restored, Helen's life entered a period of relative calm. In this same year – 1848 – she took on a new maid, Ann Watkins, who was devoted to her for the next thirty-two years. At last she had the commitment of a full-time female companion. The importance of this for a motherless, sisterless woman should not be underestimated. The worst of the crisis was over.

Back at Fasque, Helen provided comfort and strength to Sir John in his declining years as she had done during her mother's terminal illness. On 17 March, 1849, Sir John wrote to William that 'her considerate and judicious conduct has been everything I could wish. She is anxious to do everything right'.[55] In extreme old age, Sir John Gladstone became completely dependent upon his daughter, who was thereby able to liberate herself from the frustrated impotence which had so often made her ill in the past.

But she had not lost her wilful, defiant spirit, nor her ability to annoy her brother. The famous incident of the Fasque lavatory paper proved as much. Though still the MP for Oxford University, William was out of office at the time and was paying an extended visit to Fasque during the autumn and winter of 1848/49. He had been disturbing Helen's accustomed control of the household, so the incident may have been her way of retaliating. On 24 November 1848, he sent her a shocked note, marked 'secret':

> I write to you with the greatest reluctance on a most painful subject ... I have this morning seen with my own eyes that which, without seeing, I would not have believed: a number of books upon religious subjects in the two closets attached to your sleeping apartments, some entire, some torn up, the borders or outer coverings of some remaining – under circumstances which admit of no doubt as to the shameful use to which they were put.[56]

William threatened to inform their father – unless Helen gave an undertaking never again to use Protestant tracts as lavatory paper. She declined to reply. He wrote again with another deadline. She again declined to reply. He wrote again, saying that, if she didn't reply, he would assume she agreed to his demand. Apart from the battle of wills played out over the lavatory paper, it is interesting that William even knew what was going on in Helen's closet which was only accessible from inside her bedroom, and which one would have expected to have been her private domain.[57] Helen's otherwise exemplary behaviour during her father's illness – as previously during her mother's – proved that, when presented with a practical challenge, she was able to combat it successfully. Her major problem was having so few challenges to which to rise. Her handwriting indicates that she was a woman with strong organisational abilities.[58] But for most of her life she had little on which to focus them. In that respect, her plight was typical of many redundant women in upper-class Victorian society, whose lives were relegated to the footnotes while the men made history.[59]

Helen – whose inheritance was halved shortly before her father died, at William's insistence – was offered a house on the Fasque estate on Sir John's death in 1851. But she declined it and went to Rome, where she relapsed into heavy opium use and was admitted to a Dominican convent for a lengthy course of treatment. In 1855 she became a novice of the Third Order of St Dominic. She returned in 1856 to live at St Helen's Priory on the Isle of Wight, where she spent many contented years, founding St Dominic's Chapel in the priory grounds for the benefit of local Roman Catholics. She left England for good in the late 1860s after the death of her Aunt Johanna. From then on, she lived mainly in Cologne, where she died in 1880, aged sixty-five, of paralysis of the bowel, a side-effect of prolonged opium abuse.

Unmarried, unloved, unfulfilled and undervalued, Helen Gladstone has been described by one commentator as having 'found in doses of opium what she lacked in life'.[60] Yet she was a woman with a powerful mind – even William acknowledged that – and, under different circumstances, could have achieved much. Born in a different age, into a different family, under different circumstances, Helen could have found an identity and forged for herself a useful role. And, to the last, Helen resisted William's entreaties that she should return from voluntary exile on the Continent to spend her final years close to him. She had an instinctive sense that, once within his sphere of influence, he would begin again to assert it against her. She was almost certainly correct in this.

If Helen's mother, and the saintly sister Anne, with whom she was unfavourably compared, had not died when Helen was young; if she had had more close female relatives to turn to; if she had not been at the almost exclusive mercy of the Gladstone men; if any of the sisters-in-law – William's wife Catherine in particular – had made her feel welcome, perhaps Helen Gladstone could have had a role as a meaningful part of their families. Alternatively, had she been born into a less privileged class, where opportunities for female employment were beginning to appear, such as that of governess – the classic upwardly and downwardly mobile career option for women of the time, fictionalised supremely in *Jane Eyre* – she might have found an opportunity to assert herself in a more productive way.

A sad, disruptive and unfulfilled figure for much of her life, Helen Gladstone's case has a wider significance. The way in which her frustrations, torments and unhappiness were handled by the Gladstone men illuminates many of the less palatable aspects of Victorian family life. Helen's predicament, and the degree to which the Gladstone men were partly responsible for helping create the monster (which Helen undoubtedly was on occasions), speaks volumes about the condition of 'superfluous' women in the patriarchal world of the nineteenth century. Helen was strong-minded, wilful, independent of spirit and intelligent. But she lacked any useful role. Her treatment by her father and brothers, William in particular, speaks volumes about the Victorian male's need to control the female. The ways in which they did so seem, by today's standards, unkind to the point of criminality. Helen's beloved William was normally so courteous in his dealings with women of all stations and classes. Yet to Helen he often behaved atrociously. William's sense of chivalry was almost mediaeval.[61] But it required women to collude with this courtly ideal. When Helen had other ideas, she was punished. 'Trust and obey' was William's motto for her,[62] and all would be well. The older she got, the less inclined she was to do either. And yet she appears never to have wavered in her love for him, 'my principal friend', who was assured of 'my truest affection, however you may treat me'.[63]

By dying young, Gladstone's saintly sister Anne had been immortalised as the feminine ideal. If Anne, in her goodness, represented the best that William aspired to, Helen was his dark side. Helen admitted herself that she was 'naturally excitable', referring more than once to 'the violence of my mind's temper'.[64] She was the person William might have become, had he not exercised rigorous self-discipline. He saw in her what could have happened had he not contained his own the powerful emotions within the strict middle-class conventions of the day. That he had done so, while she had not, irritated him intensely.

Helen Gladstone was clearly a handful for the Gladstone men, a frequent loose cannon. Yet she retained the life-long affection of at least two women – her Aunt Johanna and her maid, Ann Watkins. In contrast, the Gladstone men – and William in particular – were by any standards misguided in their treatment of her. This is not exclusively a modern point of view; the brave Elizabeth Rawson shared it. Helen's behaviour in the troubled years 1846–48 may have threatened to wreck William's career and bring scandal upon the family as a whole. Yet the fault was not entirely hers. As Mrs Rawson insisted:

> I shall never cease to think that of all the mismanaged cases I could conceive, this is the worst; and I have not a doubt in my mind that, if your daughter

had been in other hands, and the penitent and good feelings she had had
been encouraged and good habits steadily persevered in ... she would indeed
have been a different being from what she is.[65]

Helen Gladstone could already have become an entirely different
being well before Mrs Rawsons's prediction of 1848. As early as the time
of her sister Anne's death in 1829, when Helen was fifteen, there was
another development in the Gladstone household of which even
William may not have been aware. Helen had a suitor. The interested
party was Thomas Kirkman Finlay, the son of a close business associate
of John Gladstone, and a former neighbour of the family in Rodney
Street. Thomas, who was several years older than Helen, had quite properly written to the Gladstone parents declaring his admiration for their
daughter, while conceding that she was still too young to be approached
directly.[66] John Gladstone, who could hardly be expected to contemplate
with equanimity the thought of losing his one remaining daughter to
matrimony so soon after the death of his first, was unambiguous in his
reply. 'The subject ... seems almost too ridiculous to require a serious
answer', he wrote, warning that 'unless you banish from your mind all
such ideas ... we cannot have the pleasure of receiving you here.'[67] After
a lengthy and, by his own admission, 'tedious' explanation of his 'absurd
conduct' – and clearly anxious that his own father should not hear of
the matter – Finlay apologised profusely. But not quite unreservedly. He
made a spirited defence of his 'lively interest' in Helen.

> I shall always feel it, for, young as she is, I have seen enough of her charac-
> ter to admire it and although she is too young and I neither young enough
> nor rich enough nor perhaps wise enough to allow myself to think of her in
> any other light than a person I have long known and esteemed, I can see no
> harm in expressing a wish for her welfare and happiness.[68]

With that, the matter seemed to be at an end, and Thomas Finlay
continued to be received at the Gladstone home at Seaforth. In December of that year, 1829, he chanced his luck again, however, writing to
John Gladstone:

> I think it proper at once candidly to own that I am more attached to your
> daughter than ever. At present I expect only to learn only Mrs Gladstone's
> and your sentiments (for the rest patience), which I most sincerely hope may

be favourable, but if you wish me to banish all thoughts of your daughter from my mind, the sooner I am put out of suspense the better.[69]

John Gladstone did not disappoint, and Finlay finally agreed to 'dismiss the matter from my mind'. Helen's father filed the correspondence under the heading: 'T. K. Finlay's foolish letters and my answers to them'. Helen seems never to have known of the affair. One wonders what different course her unhappy life might have taken had she found an early, even if not ideal, home for her emotions. It also indicates that, while Gladstone family dynamics may have produced conditions which encouraged difficult behaviour in Helen – and affectionate though she was, she was certainly not an easy person – she was clearly not without considerable charms.

5

Lady Lincoln

By the summer of 1849, the condition of Gladstone's sister Helen had stabilised, at least for the time being. Now aged thirty-five and miraculously cured of her nervous paralysis, she was safely re-established at the Gladstone estate at Fasque in Scotland. Here she had a real job to do as housekeeper caring for her increasingly senile father in his final two-year decline. But within the wider Gladstone circle another domestic drama was reaching crisis point, this time involving Susan, wife of Gladstone's close friend Lord Lincoln, son of the fourth Duke of Newcastle. Again it involved a difficult, headstrong woman, a severe Victorian patriarch, opium addiction and a flight to the Continent. And again it had Gladstone centre stage, this time as a hapless knight errant in the first scene of the final act of what became the most dramatic society scandal of mid-Victorian Britain.

Gladstone was out of office at the time and at a crossroads in his career. His short-lived return to the Colonial Office in December 1845 had ended with the fall of Sir Robert Peel's government the following year. While still Member of Parliament for Oxford University, he was to remain out of office until 1853. His need to find an outlet for his considerable nervous energy during this period fitted well with his vision of himself as mediaeval chevalier on a mission to rescue a noble friend's wife from the dragon of adultery, and to bring her safely home. Lord Lincoln, later fifth Duke of Newcastle, was one of Gladstone's closest friends. They were together at Eton and Christ Church, where they consolidated what was to be a lifelong intimacy. Both were serious young men with a strong sense of public duty. Lincoln is believed to have been the inspiration behind Trollope's character Plantagenet Palliser, later Duke of Omnium, whose fictional happiness and career were compromised, as Lincoln's would be in life, by a charming but flighty young wife.

Gladstone was delighted by this close association with the aristocracy but conscious as ever of his own lack of title. 'People call Lord Lincoln my friend', he wrote two years later, when they were both appointed to the Treasury, 'and he acts as such. But it is well for me to remind myself of the difference of rank between us ... Oh God, that I were better worth having!'[1] The same self-deprecating sentiment was reiterated more than a decade on. During the Lincoln divorce case, he was asked: 'You and Mrs Gladstone were friends and acquainted with her, besides knowing Lord Lincoln?' He replied: 'Yes; allowing for the difference of station, we were well acquainted with her Ladyship'. Gladstone's sense of deference to the aristocracy prevailed whatever the circumstances. To some extent, this underlines a very middle-class approach to what, in Lady Lincoln's case, was a not uncommon upper-class delicto.

Gladstone, being eighteen months older, graduated from Oxford ahead of Lincoln. When Lincoln turned down the offer from his father, the fourth Duke of Newcastle, of a secure seat as Conservative MP for the pocket borough of Newark in Nottinghamshire – he preferred to study hard for a First Class degree – he suggested the seat be offered instead to his friend Gladstone. Gladstone was on his first Grand Tour of Europe when he heard of the offer on his arrival in Milan on 6 July 1832. He accepted, and so began his political career.

At the same time that Lincoln was working for his final examinations, his father was negotiating with the flamboyantly wealthy Duke and Duchess of Hamilton to have him married off.[2] The Duke of Newcastle was a dour, debt-encumbered widowed father of ten – of whom Henry was the eldest. He had originally approached Hamilton about a possible match between Georgiana, the eldest of his four daughters, and Hamilton's only son, Lord Francis Douglas. Hamilton welcomed the prospect of closer relations between the two families, but suggested, as an alternative, a possible marriage between Lord Lincoln and his only daughter, Susan. The fathers agreed that, while they would facilitate a closer relationship between the young people, an arranged alliance was out of the question. Matrimony was something the two young people must decide for themselves. Temperamentally, the couple were very different. In the cold light of marriage, his admirable qualities of absolute probity and lofty idealism – offset against her beauty and sparkling but self-indulgent charm – would prove increasingly difficult for the other to live with. But initially their prospects seemed promising enough. Meetings were orchestrated. While the parents extolled to each other the endless merits of their respective offspring, it became clear that Henry and Suzie (or 'Toosey'), as she was known, were sufficiently attracted to each other for the relationship to be considered a love match. An engagement was announced, and, after a short delay while Lord Francis recovered from smallpox, they were married in November 1832. The bride was eighteen, the groom twenty-one. Gladstone, as a new Member of Parliament, was too busy to attend the lavish ceremony at the fairytale Hamilton palace. But he wrote, congratulating the young couple and looking forward to their closer acquaintance.

It was on 23 February of the following year when Gladstone first met his friend's new wife. 'Introduced to Lady Lincoln: much struck with her manner as well as, or more than, face', he wrote in his diary.[3] The gauche young Gladstone appears to have become quietly infatuated by bright young Suzie. In 1836, he wrote a poem to her, by then a mother of two young sons but still only twenty-two. The poem has been lost; but, in a letter to his sister Helen, William confirmed that the 'young and noble lady' to whom it refers was indeed Lady Lincoln.[4] The poem was written shortly after his failure to woo Caroline Farquhar and before a similar disappointment with Lady Frances Douglas (a distant relation of the Hamiltons). Gladstone had recently completed one of the intensive Dante reading programmes he was to repeat throughout his life. It seems not unlikely that his poem to Lady Lincoln was influenced by Dante's Beatrice, the mediaeval feminine ideal, a symbol of divine love and man's ultimate salvation. If he ever did entertain romantic feelings for Suzie Lincoln, Gladstone must have counted himself blessed in later life that she was already married when they met. The fact that she was a married woman, of course, made her the ideal candidate for courtly admiration.

This early infatuation, together with his inherent belief in the fundamental goodness of women, helps explain Gladstone's enduring conviction, in the face of overwhelming evidence to the contrary, that his friend's erring wife could and would be redeemed. But Suzie Lincoln, like Gladstone's sister Helen, of whom she was an exact contemporary, was neither ready nor willing to be saved from the wayward tendencies that made a misery of her husband's life. Petted and spoiled from infancy, she expected such treatment to continue into adult life (and, indeed, it did on the Hamilton side of the family). Except when it suited her, for reasons of expediency, to be readmitted to the bosom of her family by marriage, she remained steadfastly unrepentant, firmly and petulantly manipulating the blame for her indiscretions – or rather, their discovery – on other people. In the last dramatic dénouement, this included attaching blame to Gladstone himself for the unhappy outcome. Without his interference, she maintained, she could have been spared public knowledge of the consequences of her final elopement. Appearances were all.

The first of many of Suzie Lincoln's indiscretions came to light in late January 1837, towards the end of a tedious holiday period at the Newcastle estate at Clumber in Nottinghamshire. The Clumber household was as sober as the Hamilton home in Scotland was extravagant. Gladstone had visited Clumber for a weekend only days before. With little idea of the storm that was about to break, he hinted in his diary nevertheless that something was wrong with Suzie: 'Singing in the evening. Lady Lincoln has much of her usual buoyancy: but suffers much I believe – bravely and in secret'.[5] What Suzie was really doing in secret was conducting an affair with one of her brothers-in-law. Starved of entertainment, she had created her own diversion by embarking on a heavy flirtation with Henry's younger brother, William. A love letter to her from her brother-in-law was intercepted and handed to Lincoln. It hinted at smouldering passion. But more shocking than that: it elicited a bid for sympathy, by her, that was utterly disloyal to the devoted but humourless husband whom she openly accused of resuming marital relations sooner than she had wished after the birth of their second child. William's letter read:

> My own Angel, yesterday was the happiest day of my life or one of the happiest – those I spent with you in town are equally so. I am glad you have weaned the baby – it is proof of your love, and I hope now your chest will get strong. Don't have the leeches – the medicine you are taking will weaken you much ... I fear you will never be mine. What a cold set we are surrounded by – if I can get off going to the dinner I will, after the promise you made me. You deserve to be happy in this world and you will be happy in the next. Don't let Lincoln do it – rather incur his anger. Swear you are ill.

He made you ill after your confinement in town, beginning so soon. I have
no patience with his selfishness.[6]

Once the affair became know, the contrite young William – to whom
little blame seems to have attached – was promptly dispatched to his old
tutor, Mr Thompson, for an intensive programme of Bible reading.
Gladstone clearly knew something of the business, since he wrote both
to his father and to Lincoln's on 4 February 'in answer to an
unfavourable account of Lady Lincoln'.[7] A desolate Lincoln left for London without seeing his wife. He never trusted her again. But his tragedy
was that, despite this, he never ceased to love, forgive and be manipulated by her. In contrast, Suzie's reaction on being discovered set a
pattern for all such future crises. Determined to be the focus of attention whatever the circumstances, she avoided taking responsibility for
her actions with fainting fits, spasms, nervous prostration and self-pity
in an attempt to attract sympathy rather than the opprobrium she
deserved. It was always someone else's fault. In this she was encouraged
and reinforced by adoring, over-indulgent parents. Indeed the parents
on both sides had much to answer for in the level of interference they
permitted themselves in the young couple's marriage. Newcastle's
relentless probity and censorious attitude, even to harmless entertain-
ments by his daughter-in-law – such as archery – did much to make
Lincoln's lot even more difficult. On the other hand, the Hamiltons'
limitless capacity to condone and excuse whatever scrapes their cherished 'Toosey' became embroiled in inhibited their daughter from ever
taking responsibility for her own behaviour.

From Clumber, Suzie was transferred to London, where doctors
agreed on internal leeching as the preferred treatment for her 'hysterical'
complaints (or 'imaginary derangements', as Mr Thompson called
them). From London, the francophile Hamiltons transferred their
daughter to Paris, where they were joined shortly by Lincoln.[8] He found
his wife partially blind and unable to speak, but indicating by signs that
she believed death was imminent. After a series of melodramatic sickbed
scenes, the doctors banned him from seeing his wife for a time. Eventually a reconciliation of sorts was brokered, Lincoln persuading himself –
perhaps rightly in this instance – that his wife's medical treatment, which
included hypnotism ('that vile magnetism'), was partly responsible for
prolonging her problems.

Suzie returned to England almost a year after her flirtation with Lord William had been discovered and family appearances were restored, though not the substance of family life. By and large, it is hard to feel much sympathy for her manipulative, self-pitying ways. She had seemed genuinely fond of her husband in the beginning. But when the realities of marriage began to highlight the extreme incompatibility of their natures, exacerbated by a certain sexual robustness on the part of Lincoln, she was unequal to the challenge. On her return to the fold, Suzie described to her mother the fundamental hopelessness of the situation:

> You must know that once the flame of love is extinguished it is rarely to be rekindled once more. I did love tenderly, and would have done all, and did do all in my power to please, and in return I met with indifference, ill temper and unkindness, and though God knows I respect, I cannot love. There are words, looks and impressions which none but me can have seen, which I never would, and which I never shall name.[9]

In August of that year, 1838, the Lincolns set off an on eight-month continental tour. A month after their return Suzie gave birth to a third child, a girl they called Susan. In December that year, the Gladstones stayed at Clumber where William went shooting with Lincoln and his brother Edward while 'Catherine makes much progress in Lady Lincoln's affections'. Increasing intimacy between the two young wives – who by now were calling each other by their childhood nicknames 'Pussy' and 'Toosey' – brought a double potential benefit: Gladstone could consolidate his aristocratic connections while there was the chance that Catherine's kind and noble nature might exercise a positive influence on the wayward Suzie.

But all was not well. Despite being safely delivered of a fourth child, Arthur, in 1840, Suzie's obsessive ill health (particularly when thwarted), relentless flirtations and increasing consumption of laudanum made for a miserable domestic situation. When, in December 1841, it appeared that his wife had taken a new lover, a formal separation seemed inevitable. Solicitors were retained in case the Hamiltons might sue for custody of their grandchildren, and Gladstone was appointed one of their guardians should anything happen to Lincoln.[10] Meanwhile, a Hamilton family friend wrote to advise Suzie: 'I think you may still save yourself by a complete compliance with Lord Lincoln's wishes', which

included complete divulgence of all the facts, including her lover's identity. But he warned that time was running out and that she must decide
'between respectability and disgrace, comfort and misery'.[11] The Duke
of Newcastle also tried to exert an influence on his daughter-in-law but,
on visiting her, found, as he wrote in his diary, that 'her affections were
entirely alienated from Lincoln and that she did not anticipate a possibility of its revival'. He added: 'I am convinced that Lady Lincoln
subsists upon laudanum and other stimulants and sedatives'.[12]

In early 1842 Lincoln was writing to his father that the situation made
him too depressed 'even to dine with Gladstone', when, out of the blue,
a letter arrived from Suzie suggesting a reconciliation. By this time, Lincoln was Forestry Commissioner and Gladstone Vice-President of the
Board of Trade in Sir Robert Peel's government. The Prime Minister, to
whom Lincoln showed a copy of the letter, found it 'so becoming in
every respect, so submissive, so fully acquitting Lincoln of misconduct,
expressing such proper feelings with respect to future conduct' that he
advised his young colleague to forgive and forget. But Peel confided to
his wife that he believed the Lincolns' prospects of happiness were small.

> I am afraid from what I have subsequently heard that that there has been
> more, at earlier periods since their marriage, to make him dissatisfied with
> her conduct. I have always feared a part of her strangeness arose from the
> mind. She is now in a very excited state and has taken great quantities of lau-
> danum of late ... I only fear one thing, namely that after all, Lady Lincoln's
> letter may not be sincere.[13]

Peel was right. Her letter wasn't sincere; or, if it was, her penitence
was short-lived. After another temporary and superficial reconciliation,
Suzie Lincoln abandoned the family yet again in August 1842. Ostensibly it was to seek an improvement to her health at the fashionable new
seaside resort of Anglesea Ville near Gosport on the south coast. But
rumour had it that a Guards officer was involved. Lincoln threatened to
prevent her ever seeing her children again if she persisted in her 'wicked
obstinacy and disobedience. You have found me for eight long years
merciful and generous – you will now find me firm and inexorable', he
warned.

Within six months the affair had petered out. Suzie had left Anglesea Ville and, with the help of her mother, was gradually reintroducing

herself into polite society. On 28 June 1843, Gladstone was at Buckingham Palace for the marriage of Princess Augusta of Cambridge to a German Grand Duke and observed that, at the celebration balls, 'the Lincolns both there – and apart'. This seems to have prompted an attempt by the Gladstones to mediate between the couple. The following day Gladstone wrote in his diary: 'Another conversation with Lincoln at length'. And again, on 30 June: 'Conversation with Catherine on Lincoln's matters – and in evening with Lincoln on the result of her interview with Lady Lincoln – what a strange and woeful reverse is there'.[14] Catherine's involvement in the affair earned her warm thanks from Lincoln: 'Had you been her sister, you could not have done more'. In September, news that both her husband and son Arthur were ill provided the Countess with the opportunity to write suggesting a rapprochement. Susceptible as ever, Lincoln took her back, but his father, to whom he forwarded her letter, was appalled.

> The receipt of Lady Lincoln's letter ... occasioned quite a revulsion in me ... The sudden reception now of such a woman must either stamp your conduct towards her, thus presumed to be an innocent woman, as atrocious, or, as the weakest and most inconsistent of human beings ... She is now at liberty to do as she pleases, she may run off with a man tomorrow, and you cannot touch her.[15]

To Catherine Gladstone, Suzie wrote in early 1844: 'I am, thank God, reunited with my husband and children. Yes, dearest Pussy, we are all together again'. She looked forward to being well enough 'that I may be enabled not only to fulfil my duty but to contribute to the comfort and happiness of my home'.[16] But her father-in-law was right and within three years she was off again. A weary note in the Duke of Newcastle's diary for 14 September 1847 read: 'Lady Lincoln run away'.[17] Again a Guards officer – although a different one, this time – was said to be involved. But within two months she was again negotiating a return, trusting that Lincoln would be 'merciful to a sorrowful, sad, penitent wife'.[18] Once again the reconciliation was superficial and short-lived. By now Suzie Lincoln was desperate for an escape that would finally put an end to her marriage. And there were few other escape routes for a woman of her class at the time, other than via the arms of another man. Her choice was an unfortunate one. Horatio, Lord Walpole was a notorious philanderer and known wife-beater.[19] But despite her lover's reputation, on 2 August 1848, at the age of thirty-four, Susan, Countess of Lincoln and mother of five children between the ages of three and fourteen (Albert had been born in 1845), turned her back forever on polite society and embarked on her final and most spectacular bunk of all. Leaving a three-line note saying she had gone to Germany to consult a doctor, she escaped to the fashionable spa resort of Bad Ems, where Lord Walpole was waiting for her. The elopement triggered one of the biggest society scandals of the mid-nineteenth century and Gladstone was to be centrally involved in the resolution of the affair.

It is unclear how much Gladstone knew of the detail of his friend's domestic troubles until this point, but he was certainly always aware of the broad outline. Equally, he seems to have remained convinced to the bitter end that Lady Lincoln could be redeemed. More than five years earlier, when Lincoln was taking steps to prevent a possible move by his parents-in-law to gain custody of his children, Gladstone had written in his diary:

> Lincoln opened to me on his domestic situation: a sad tale indeed, and a speaking lesson when the contrast with what once was or seemed to be is discovered. In a long conversation, I was almost stunned by the view he gave me. May God's mercy find an issue! He has named me one of the guardians of his children.[20]

When Lincoln discovered his wife had finally gone, Gladstone was one of the first to be told. On the evening of the fateful day, 2 August, he noted in his diary: 'Lincoln came in at 11 p.m. and told us the sad news of his wife's clandestine and very sudden journey, a very terrible blow'. Two days later he 'saw Lincoln again on his great calamity. He declares this is final: but we must yet hope'. On 6 August, Lincoln brought his four boys to an early dinner with the Gladstones, who lived next door. 'Conversation with him afterwards on ... Lady Lincoln', Gladstone wrote. 'I tried to point out how laudanum goes to destroy responsibility and unfit people for punishment properly so called or for abandonment to themselves: using my sister's case as a parable.'[21] For the next two weeks Gladstone wrote to his friend regularly, sometimes twice a day, with sympathy and encouragement.

> It has pleased God to endow you with great strength of both mind and body or you could not have gone through what has been laid upon you ...

Feel for you I wish that I could with an hundredfold greater depth and truth.[22]

The extent of Lady Lincoln's indiscretion was never discussed publicly. She continued to maintain that she was abroad solely for her health and was passing her time on the Continent quietly reading books. To her mother, she wrote: 'The deed is done, I have chosen exile, solitude, exclusion, slander, in preference to living with him; this being the case, je me dois de me pas laisser abattre – je le répète, j'ai bien choisi pour mon bonheur si j'ai mal fait pour ma position'.[23] Catherine Gladstone, still believing in her friend's innocence, wrote advising her to take a female companion for the sake of appearances, and received from Rome, on 25 November, the following reply of breathtaking hypocrisy and ingratitude:

Nothing would be so annoying to me as to have a *lady appendage* – she would be terribly in my way ... the constant companionship of almost anyone would be a discomfort to me ... when out of society I infinitely prefer being alone with my books and different occupations – solitude is no hardship to me ... A thousand thanks for sending me a favourable report of my precious children, I am so pleased to think they write to you and I only wish they were with *you* dearest instead of other people whose only wish seems to be to prevent my hearing from them. I confess I think it heartless of Mrs Herbert – but she is not yet a mother or she would feel it a duty to send a report of my darlings. But I suppose her Lord and Master has forbidden her writing! God forgive her! I *can't* forgive it when I think back to former times and think of all the *professions* of regard made by all the family. I admit I do feel hurt with the silence maintained by *all* the Herberts towards me – particularly when it would be in their power to afford *so much* comfort.[24]

Gladstone was seriously annoyed at the lack of realism displayed in this letter to his wife, and sent an angry reply back. He questioned Lady Lincoln's claims to ill health, suggesting she was 'seeking pleasure under the plea of necessity'. Yet even he seems to have believed she had not yet committed the ultimate indiscretion but was simply and foolishly jeopardising her reputation. 'How little you have been able to estimate the dangers of your position', he continued, suggesting that having a female companion under the same roof would not only safeguard her reputation but also provide 'a gentle restraint to keep peril

1. Gladstone (1809–1898) as a young man. By George Richmond. (*Athenaeum, Liverpool*)

2. 62 Rodney Street, Liverpool, Gladstone's birthplace. The house still stands today.

3. Seaforth House, John Gladstone's house on the banks of the Mersey. The site is now part of Bootle Docks.

4. Helen Gladstone (1814–1880), Gladstone's sister, from a portrait at Fasque.

5. Helen Gladstone's medicine chest.

6. Catherine Gladstone, *née* Glynne (1812–1900). Drawing by George Richmond.

7. Agnes Gladstone (1842–1931). Drawing by George Richmond.

8. Catherine Jessy Gladstone (1845–1850). Portrait by George Hayter.

9. Helen Gladstone, Gladstone's daughter (1849–1925). Drawing by K. Hartmann.

10. Mary Gladstone (1847–1927).

11. Hawarden Castle, Flintshire. (*Flintshire Record Office*)

12. Fasque, Kincardineshire.

13. Group photo at Hawarden in mid-1880s. Standing (left to right) Mrs Willy Gladstone, Willy Gladstone, Mary Gladstone, William Gladstone; seated Henry Gladstone, Herbert Gladstone, Agnes Wickham (with child), Catherine Gladstone, Edward Wickham, Stephen Gladstone, Helen Gladstone. (*Flintshire Record Office*)

14. Group photo at Hawarden. Catherine and William Gladstone (centre) with children and grandchildren. Back row (left to right) Stephen Gladstone and his wife Annie; Mary Drew (*née* Gladstone) and her husband Harry; Herbert Gladstone; Helen Gladstone. (*Flintshire Record Office*)

15. William and Catherine Gladstone during their final holiday at Cannes in the south of France. (*Flintshire Record Office*)

at bay'. The peril, presumably, was the prospect of inappropriate male visitors.

I have written hard words, they are not more hard than the things to which they relate – you know me – it is for you if you like to judge me – allow as you will for the writer but, in the name of God, ere it is too late, give heed to what I have written.[25]

As rumours began to harden, and Gladstone sensed that Lincoln's patience was beginning to run out, he made a last-ditch attempt to persuade Lady Lincoln to see the error of her ways. Unbeknown to his friend, he wrote a sixteen-page letter to the errant wife, more in sorrow than in anger. It encapsulates many of the ideas on marriage, family, duty and women that were central to his personal values, and combines them with a healthy pragmatism as to what must be done now:

Without knowing or pretending to know the merits of the case, which lie in private history as between you and Lord Lincoln, I am so far aware of its present position as to be compelled to see that you are on the brink of such proceedings as humanly speaking must utterly extinguish hope of better things ... [My] justification is to be found, if anywhere, in personal attachment to those concerned, in warm remembrance of their kindness, and in an overpowering sense of ... sin and horror, for such it is and nothing less in the eyes of God ... and of the scandal and demoralisation consequent upon it to the society in which they live ... It is not for me to enter into the question whether this or that should have been done, or should not have been done, on either side – the question is what ought now to be done: and I say without scruple or doubt that, as frail human beings, we have no right to look to the right or the left away from the path of duty ... It seems to me that, in most cases of difference in this world, the parties are chiefly anxious to show ... how ill the other has behaved: but surely this is not what our Saviour and Judge will require us to prove. He will demand that we should show ... how we turned the other cheek. It is not for me to cast the balance between you, or whisper either way one word of blame ... would that I were also able altogether to avoid wounding by my words. But I say this, that in this controversy ... in which both may be wrong, and both cannot be right ... everything is lost: all hope of the future, all the sanctity and obligation of the nearest and most sacred relation; and what a picture unfolds itself from day to day before your children! those children who wish their parents but reunited ... to dwell together in love ... If that reunion shall ... fail to take place [it] will add more and more bitterness continually as their lives and your advance. I do not allude in detail to what I know Lord Lincoln's intentions to be because it is not by anything that would bear the appearance of menace that I would hope or seek to act upon you: but it is the actual position of circumstances which has terrified me into the daring ... of this representation. It has suggested itself to me, is it not dastardly to take side against the party whom sex and susceptibilities should give – and especially with women – the strongest claim to sympathy? It would be so: but this I trust and firmly believe is not siding against you – it is entreating and beseeching you to do that which, whatever the world and human pride may think of it, will be the greatest honour to you as a woman, as a wife, as a mother ... and which would save you from pain and self-reproach in the hour of death and judgement ...

   Lord Lincoln is unaware of my writing – I know his spirit yearns, while his convictions are becoming fixed in the forced abandonment of ... an idea ... for the restoration of conjugal relations between you ... True, there is difficulty in the way. What act of duty was ever done without difficulty? It is not by an easy path that triumphs over evil without us or within are achieved ... But I have said too much, perhaps both too much and too little. I desist: may God give to you the precious gift of a true judgement and a kinder heart.[26]

In June 1849, by which time Lady Lincoln had been gone for ten months, Gladstone was advised by a legal contact that there was 'new and very painful evidence raising for the first time in my mind the serious fear that Lady Lincoln may have committed the last act of infidelity'.[27] It is not clear whether this evidence was an eyewitness account of adultery being committed – such concrete evidence was later produced during the divorce proceedings – or whether the visible result of the liaison was being reported back. For, by now, Lady Lincoln was seven months pregnant. On 21 June, Gladstone consulted Peel on the subject, 'and it is a great privilege to be able to call in his aid'.[28] Two weeks later, the three men – Gladstone, Lincoln and Peel – met to discuss a strategy for locating the Countess at Naples, and for either bringing her home or establishing grounds for a divorce.

> We talked chiefly on the subject of a mission. Lincoln having said that the only persons whom he would like to send were in circumstances to render it impossible, I told him he ought to let them judge of that. He thereupon named [their close mutual friend Henry] Manning and me. I undertook to write to Manning and said it might probably be practicable for me – which Catherine approved.[29]

Other friends agreed on the need for a 'mission', and Catherine Gladstone, who still professed affection for Suzie Lincoln, continued to be closely consulted about the consequences of her husband's going abroad during her own late pregnancy. After discussing with Manning which of them should go,[30] Gladstone called at Peel's office on the morning of 11 July, 'where it had been decided to accept my offer to go to Naples. So I had to commence my preparations forthwith'.[31] The following day, Manning wrote in some relief that he was not required to lead the operation, but offering nevertheless to stand by if further help was required, and wishing Gladstone good luck on his mission: 'May you have your fullest reward in restoring a wife to herself and then to her home. I know if no act that would fill you with such joy at the last'.[32] The following evening Gladstone took the boat train to Dover: 'Catherine drove with me to the station and saw me off at 8.30'. The chase was on.

The day before her husband left, Catherine wrote to Lady Lincoln a letter of great generosity under the circumstances, but making clear nevertheless the extent to her friend's behaviour was upsetting other people's lives:

Upon the eve of seeing my precious husband leave for Italy, and so near my confinement I am weak enough to feel sorrowful and give way more than I should. I hope physical reasons have something to do with this for in truth dear I would not have it otherwise. I am pleased to show you proofs of the reality of our affection and deep interest in your welfare, thankful that my husband can make up his mind to the sacrifice and anxiety of leaving me just now in the hope that God may bless his errand. Oh may the earnest desire, the Christian and tender spirit which so fills his heart, may they have their effect upon you dear Suzie and lead you to follow his advice. What motive can he have but your good? Believe me dear it is that which activates him. Listen then to the persuasive voice which you have so often told me you liked to hear. He cannot leave you in the awful position you are in. But true and real friendship can make sacrifices and so he sets forth alone but with many prayers. Had it been possible for me to go with him I would have done so and much do feel aggrieved I cannot. He will tell you how much your children are with us – how deeply affecting it is to see them. It was only upon your birthday that Suzie was heard crying in her little bed alone – she was saying aloud 'Oh Mammy, Mammy, why did you leave us?'. She will turn pale if asked by a child who her Mama is. She loves to dwell on Mammy singing, Mammy this and that. She is greatly improved and her warm heart is still full of pretty attentions to her father. Care and sorrow sit upon his brow; no one can see him without sorrow; no night does he kneel down in prayer without praying for you.[33]

After suffering his customary sea-sickness, Gladstone landed at Calais early on the Saturday morning and set off overland for the southern port of Marseilles. 'I feel the pain of a Sunday spent in travelling', he wrote as he sped across rural France admiring the harvest, 'but on this occasion I could not doubt as to my duty.'[34] Four days later he boarded the steamer *Scamandre* at Marseilles en route for Naples via Genoa and Livorno, but left the boat at Civitavecchia on hearing of a quarantine in force at the port of Naples. He finally arrived there by road, eleven days after leaving London, and booked into the Hotel Crocelle, overlooking the bay. It was the hotel where, eleven years earlier, he had first met Catherine Glynne. The following day, 25 July, was their tenth wedding anniversary and he wrote to her:

> this place, this house ... on this day is full of its own associations. I feel myself to be beneath the roof where ... when I could not get our bell answered at dinner we were told it was because *una grande famiglia inglese* had just arrived and put the house in confusion – it was yours, and you had been guided hither to bless my life.[35]

Following discussions with British officials in the city, Gladstone established to his dismay that Lady Lincoln had given him the slip again. Passing herself off as Mrs Lawrence, travelling with her 'brother' Mr Lawrence, she had 'certainly gone north, to Milan as her first point. I decided in following her thither ... tomorrow'. Arriving at Milan on 30 July, Gladstone immediately 'set out my search for Lady Lincoln, the details of which I detailed to Catherine', and made arrangements to follow the trail to Como where, the following day, he 'set about the sad purpose of my visit'. It was a day that combined dismay and farce in equal measure.

What really happened that day was only to emerge later from the evidence collected for the divorce proceedings. It would appear that Lady Lincoln and Lord Walpole believed that the English 'milord' who was on their trail was, in fact, Lord Lincoln himself. Had they accepted any of the letters their actual visitor sent up to them, presumably they would have realised that the handwriting belonged to someone else. In one scribbled but unread note to her, Gladstone wrote:

> I have followed your steps; I have seen your passport. I have not seen you whom I have come to see; alas alas I have heard more than I sought to hear. You think it is too late. It is never too late – there can be *no* moment of your life at which it is not of inestimable consequence that you should resolve to do well. Once more I enjoin you now to see me, or to hear me without seeing me ... it is not to speak words of anger and reproof – these are not for lips as unworthy as mine. It is that I may beseech you to do something that may mitigate ... the desolation of so many hearts.[36]

Upstairs at the Villa Mancini, Lady Lincoln and Lord Walpole, alias Mr and Mrs Lawrence, were frantically packing their bags. Lady Lincoln returned Gladstone's letters unopened, declaring that Mrs Lawrence had never heard of a Lady Lincoln. Walpole, meanwhile, set off at night across Lake Como, during which trip he apparently caught a bad cold and was ill for many weeks – an outcome for which Suzie later blamed Gladstone entirely. Gladstone returned to the villa later that evening, disguised as a guitar-player. Hidden from view, he peeped over some railings to see the heavily cloaked figure of her ladyship escape by carriage into the night. It had been, for Gladstone,

> a day of great excitement, constant movement, overpowering sadness. I saw the Governor of the Province, the head of Police, the landlord, the (false) Mrs Laurence's [sic] courier, the *levatrice* [midwife]. All this I wrote fully to Lincoln in the evening except the horror reported to me.[37]

The 'horror' that Gladstone had discovered was the confirmation that Mrs Lawrence, who had by now escaped across the lake in the direction of Verona, was heavily pregnant. The next day Gladstone went in search of a Dr Balzari, who, he was told, had attended Lady Lincoln at Como, but failed to find him. Then he packed his bags again and set off across Lake Como in search of his friend's wife. 'The contrast between the ... sweet and cool airs upon the lake, with its beautiful scenery and sky, and the business I was about was really horrible', he wrote. So, too, was the discovery that Mrs Lawrence had moved on again – this time to Bergamo. At this point, Gladstone gave up. Returning to Como, he called on Dr Balzari, also visiting again the Villa Mancini where the 'Lawrences' had been staying and where Lady

Lincoln had planned to be confined. At last Gladstone 'commenced a long and painful letter to Lincoln'.[38]

Setting off on his journey home, he tried to console himself with the beauty of the scenery.

> But all the delights of travelling (and delights there must be in this most lovely region) ... are suppressed by the deadly weight of the subject which I carried home with me and now in a far more aggravated form I carry home. I have but one real comfort: a hope flows in me, nay a belief, founded perhaps on the worthlessness and brutality of the seducer in this case, that the day of penitence will come, and that then this journey though for no worthiness of mine may have its fruits.

Stopping at Lausanne two days later, he went to Holy Communion before sending another note off to Lord Lincoln. He commented sadly in his diary:

> Oh that poor miserable Lady Lincoln – once the dream of dreams, the image that to my young eye combined everything that earth could offer of beauty and of joy. What is she now! But may that Spotless sacrifice whereof I partook, unworthy as I am, today avail for her, to the washing away of sin and to the renewal of the image of God.[39]

Four days later, Gladstone was back in London,

> where I found dearest Catherine waiting for me at the station: and Willy too wakened up to welcome me. I found Agnes delicate but all thank God well: would God I had brought to them such tidings as Catherine brought to me. I ought to be most thankful for having accomplished such a journey without derangement of health or failure of strength. To some lassitude and exhaustion I must of course plead guilty.[40]

The following morning he wrote to his friend Manning to describe his journey,

> of which the labours, the interest, and the anxieties, all great, alike vanish into utter insignificance when compared with the afflicting weight of the circumstances it has revealed to me ... You will be shocked and stunned to hear that I can entertain no moral doubt whatever of the fact that the unhappy subject of our cares is within a few weeks, probably a few days of her delivery – this tells all ... The case is beyond reasonable doubt in my view: and I conceive it to be immoral in a husband to allow such matter to remain beyond the notice of the law.[41]

The mission to save Suzie Lincoln had been an enormous, chaotic and at times farcical failure. 'What novel comes up to the realities of life?', Catherine Gladstone wrote to her husband on 4 August, on hearing of the extent of the scandal.[42] But it was a project generously and sincerely undertaken. In typical fashion, Gladstone found some comfort in imposing order on the process by listing the precise details of his month-long travels in his diary.

The statistics are as follows.
Time 27 days – of which two in forced idleness at Marseilles.
Distance over 3000 miles

Of which steam about	950
Railway about	750
Posting and priv. carriage	220
Malle Poste, French	600
Italian Courier with	
Mail and Swiss about	350
Diligence	140
I was in	
Paris first time, hours	8
Marseilles	57
Genoa first time	4
Rome	22
Naples first time	14
Naples second time	20½
Genoa second	7½
Milan	18
Como first time	24
Como second time	5
Lausanne	12
Paris second time	18

I was in bed ashore 11 nights, altogether about 55 hours. In steamer 6 nights. Travelling 10 nights. With a courier and carriage I should I think have spent more time and four times as much money: though I might have gained in bodily comfort somewhat.[43]

With the fact of Suzie Lincoln's pregnancy revealed, her husband had little option but to end the marriage to ensure that the illegitimate child was never entitled to inherit the Newcastle estate – although with four legitimate sons already, this was unlikely ever to be a genuine issue.[44]

But not everyone had totally given up on Suzie Lincoln – Catherine Gladstone wondered if she might not spend a year in some sort of penitentiary, under the good discipline of someone like Archdeacon Manning, and come out a new woman. She wrote to Suzie that it was never too late to repent, a letter which prompted a chilling reply to Catherine via a mutual friend:

> Will you give her a message from me, a terrible one? She is likely to see a great deal of my children. For most things they could not be better than with her, but tell her that if she ever speaks against their mother my ghost will haunt her. When she is happy with her children, let her think of me.[45]

With characteristically loyal generosity, Catherine Gladstone's reply was simply: 'Oh, poor creature'.

Nor was Gladstone prepared to compromise his loyalty to the Lincolns by providing the main source of evidence against Suzie. Perhaps he harboured some lingering doubts as to the identity of 'Mrs Lawrence', though this is unlikely. He certainly seemed sure in his letters to Catherine. He told her that a servant at the Villa Mancini identified Lady Lincoln to him as a 'bella figura ... cappelli neri ... occhi neri ... bocca un po aperta'; and Suzie Lincoln was indeed handsome, had dark hair and eyes, and good but slightly protruding teeth.[46] Perhaps Gladstone was reluctant to be judgemental; or perhaps he simply preferred to be less involved in the divorce proceedings than would be necessary if he were the formal identifier. Consequently, a lawyer, Lewis Raphael, was dispatched to Verona in early September, accompanied by the Lincolns' former butler Joseph Asman, with the mandate to confirm that Mrs Lawrence was indeed Lady Lincoln and had indeed given birth. This was confirmed in a letter from Raphael on 24 September 1849.[47]

Lady Lincoln herself was still placing the blame for her predicament at the door of others. In December 1849, Gladstone received a letter from Lord Lincoln's solicitor apropos a letter from her

> in which she is very severe upon you as having, as she states, been the cause of all her exposure, and is also severe upon Mrs Gladstone for writing to her. You were no doubt the occasion of ascertaining her state which of course was intended to have been kept secret ... She writes ... as if she were the injured person ... It seems that Lord Walpole was at the Villa near Como when you were there, and that when they first heard of you they thought it was

Lord Lincoln, and Lord Walpole crossed the lake between two and three in the morning, caught a violent cold and was confined for some weeks. Lady Lincoln hurried to Verona and she was very seriously ill in her confinement and was not expected to live. My own impression is that her Ladyship is deranged.[48]

Gladstone replied that he was sorry Lady Lincoln felt resentment towards him as the cause of her exposure but pointed out that, had he not gone, a professional would have gone in his stead. In any case, 'not I, but the act has been the cause of the exposure ... it was not I but a Higher Power that made me the instrument of discovery'.[49]

By February 1850 divorce proceedings were under way. Gladstone recorded in his diary that he was correcting the legal detail in Lincoln's first formal plea in order to avoid counter-claims of libel. Seven years before the Wrst Divorce Act came into force, at the time the legal termination of marriage was a complicated procedure involving three stages: an ecclesiastical court, a common law court, and a Private Member's Bill in the House of Commons, then to be approved in the House of Lords. On 1 April, Gladstone was called to testify on Lincoln's behalf in the ecclesiastical court. It was a dreadful time for him. His second daughter, four-year-old Jessy, was seriously ill with meningitis, and died eight days later. He recorded rather testily in his diary that he was 'examined 3½ hours (by a most tedious process) on Lady Lincoln's wretched case'.[50] Under the circumstances, it is understandable that he should feel aggrieved at Lady Lincoln's frivolous child-bearing activity when his own dear daughter was on her death-bed. A few weeks later, on 28 May 1850, Gladstone – who in the meantime had buried little Jessy in the family vault at Fasque – was back in the House of Lords to repeat his evidence on 'poor Lincoln's divorce bill' and negotiating with other friends and colleagues what settlement his ex-wife could reasonably and decently expect.

The evidence presented in the Lincoln divorce case was incontrovertible – and, indeed, the case was not contested by Lady Lincoln. It fell naturally into three parts. The first included the testimony of those who had witnessed the Lincoln marriage and the serving of divorce papers, and who could confirm that Lady Lincoln had been out of the country for long enough (twelve months) to exclude the possibility of Lord

Lincoln having fathered her child. There then followed the riveting evidence of Noel Paovick, the servant who had accompanied Lord Horace to Ems and beyond, who stated quite unambiguously under examination that he had caught the couple *in flagrante*.

Q. Was Lady Lincoln sitting on the sofa, or lying?
A. No, lying.
Q. Was Lord Walpole sitting or lying?
A. Lying also.
Q. Did he appear apparently [sic] to be upon her?
A. Yes.[51]

Paovick, who had stayed with the couple until he was dismissed at Frascati in May 1849, was asked: 'had any alteration become visible in her person?' He confirmed that it had: 'She was rather stouter ... it was increasing'. This was the substance of the first part of the evidence. The last part comprised the testimony of two people: Joseph Asman, Lord Lincoln's former butler, and Lewis Raphael, his solicitor, who travelled together to Varena in September 1849 to establish the true identity of 'Mrs Lawrence', the fact of her having given birth the previous month, and the presence there of a former Lincoln family wet-nurse, Ellen Jones.

The central part of the evidence given to the Lords on 28 May 1850 was that furnished by Gladstone. In its reticence it confirms his intense loyalty and reluctance to be judgemental, particularly when the wife of a nobleman and friend was involved. It also underlines his enduring feelings of inferiority to the aristocracy. As regards women, it displays what could be seen as an excessive generosity towards female folly committed because of 'delicate health', 'delicate frame' or 'nervous frame'. On the other hand, one should not exclude the possibility that Gladstone's answers under examination did in fact reflect a genuine empathy with the frustrations inherent in being female in upper-class Victorian society.

Q. Have you been living in habits of close friendship with that nobleman?
A. Yes, for years.
Q. Are you also acquainted with my Lady Lincoln?
A. Yes; I have been well acquainted with Lady Lincoln for many years.
Q. You have been in the habit of visiting them as husband and wife while they were cohabiting together?

A. Yes, for many years.

Q. Is she a lady of delicate health?

A. Certainly; a person who has gone through very great suffering.

Q. I believe she underwent very great suffering when she was ill at Paris and was not expected to recover?

A. Yes, and at various times.

Q. She was a person of delicate frame?

A. Yes.

Q. She is a person of nervous frame?

A. Yes, of nervous frame, and liable to very great suffering, even at times when she has apparent health.

Q. You and Mrs Gladstone were friends and acquainted with her, besides knowing Lord Lincoln?

A. Yes, allowing for the difference of station, we were well acquainted with her Ladyship.

Gladstone was asked to confirm when he knew that Lady Lincoln had left the country, whether she had returned since then, and whether he thought she and Lord Lincoln had met her in the intervening year – clearly with a view to establishing that the child born at Verona on 2 August 1849 could not be his. He confirmed they had not met, and admitted that by July 1849 'certain rumours [were] reaching England in connection with Lady Lincoln'. He was then asked to relate the journey he had undertaken on Lord Lincoln's behalf with the support of his most intimate friends.

Q. What was the motive of your going?

A. I went quite as much, as I then believed, in the interest of Lady Lincoln as of his Lordship ...

Q. What was the immediate object of your going?

A. The character of the rumours to which you have referred were such as left no doubt that there had been unhappy indiscretions, which were capable of the worst construction. At the same time there was no disposition to put the worst construction of which they would admit upon them, and there was a strong hope that there was nothing more than indiscretion. The question was, in what light they should be viewed; whether they should be regarded as evidence of criminality, and whether a professional person should at once be sent abroad for the purpose of investigating the precise state of the case, or whether they should be regarded, not as evidences of criminality, but as simply that which at first sight they evidently were, and whether a friend of Lord Lincoln's should go for the sake of inducing Lady Lincoln, if he could obtain access to her, to place herself in a position of security.

Q. Was that the object with which you went?

A. The latter of these two was the object with which I went. There was no question or doubt at all that one of the two things must be done, and the whole question was, which should be done.

Q. Were you not authorised by Lord Lincoln rather to induce Lady Lincoln to come back – to return home?

A. Yes. I used general words, 'to place herself in a position of security'. That might be done by coming home, or by joining friends abroad, or by having any person with her whose presence would be a defence to her.

Q. Lord Lincoln's intentions did not exclude, as you understood, the hope of her coming back.

A. No, I think not. My object was to induce her to do what prudence seemed absolutely to require ...

Q. Did you, in consequence ... go to Como ultimately?

A. I found she had left Naples for Genoa. From a respectable person who keeps an hotel at Naples, and who had been formerly in her service, and had her confidence and Lord Lincoln's too, I found, on enquiring as a friend, that she had left Naples on a certain day, and had directed her letters to be addressed to her at Milan, and had left general information that she was going to baths in the neighbourhood of Milan. With this information I set out from Naples, and went immediately to Milan.

Q. From thence did you go to Como?

A. Yes. My path from Milan was no longer an obvious one; because, when I got to Milan I entirely failed to find any trace of Lady Lincoln by her own name.

Q. In consequence of something that you did hear, did you go to Como?

A. Yes. The information I obtained at Milan led me to believe that she must have gone to Como under the name of Mrs Lawrence.

Q. Did you find that a person of the name of Mrs Lawrence, or passing by that name, was living at the Villa Mancini, on the Como Lake?

A. I did ...

Q. Did you go to the Villa Mancini?

A. I did.

Q. Did you endeavour to procure an interview with the lady who lived there under the name of Mrs Lawrence?

A. I did; both by inquiries from her servants and by notes and messages addressed to herself ...

Q. Did you send in your card to her as Mrs Lawrence?

A. Yes; having failed to obtain from the courier any recognition of her as Lady Lincoln.

Q. Did you ask, when you got to the Villa, whether Lady Lincoln was there?

A. I asked first for Mrs Lawrence, and then for Lady Lincoln.

Q. What was the answer you received?

A. The answer was, that there was no such person as Lady Lincoln there.

Q. Did you write to Lady Lincoln?

A. Yes, I did. I wrote to her, and enclosed the letter in a cover to Mrs Lawrence, and used every method that suggested itself to make sure, because I was going on presumptive evidence. I had no positive information. I had not seen anyone, since I left Naples, who knew Lady Lincoln's person; that was a matter of inference.

Q. What was the answer to the letter you addressed to Lady Lincoln?

A. It was returned with a statement that the lady knew nothing of Lady Lincoln.

Q. A verbal statement?

A. A verbal statement. I made an effort to obtain a written statement, but failed .[52]

It having been established that Gladstone remained at the Villa Mancini throughout the day, he was then asked whether he noticed any preparations being made for her departure. He confirmed that he saw a carriage being prepared for flight that evening.

Q. Did you see the carriage at the door of the villa?

A. I saw the carriage ready to start, within the gate.

Q. Did you see anybody get into it?

A. No, not get into it; I saw a female figure standing ready to get into it. I was very anxious not to be observed. I did not wish to take the responsibility of anything that might happen upon an observation of me by the person most interested.

Q. Did you, whilst you were there, and whilst the carriage was there, see the figure of any lady in the house?

A. I saw the figure of a lady prepared, apparently, to get into the carriage.

Q. Was anybody with her?

A. I only saw one figure at that moment.

Q. You did not, I understand, actually see them get into the carriage?

A. No.

Q. Did the carriage drive past you in the road?

A. The carriage drove past with the blinds down.

Q. Did you see the lady sufficiently to be able to state who she was?

A. I can only say that the figure corresponded with the figure of Lady Lincoln.

Q. Could you tell whether she was with child?

A. No; her figure was wrapped up as if for travelling, with cloaks.

Q. Upon that, I suppose, your endeavours came to an end?

A. Not absolutely to an end. I went some way after Lady Lincoln the next day; but, weighing all things, and putting all things together, and the extreme undesirableness, from what I believed of the state of Lady Lincoln, of my appearing suddenly before her, I desisted and turned back ... and returned to England.

In embarking on the pursuit of Lady Lincoln, Gladstone was full of energy and enthusiasm. Faced with the stark reality of her situation, he seems to have faltered. His disingenuousness in referring explicitly to following 'Lady Lincoln' immediately after denying he was sure of her identity, and his expressions of doubt as to her pregnancy so shortly after talking to her midwife, imply cold feet when faced with the blatant evidence of sexual misconduct in a woman he had admired for so long.

Gladstone's evidence merely filled in the gaps of what was incontrovertible evidence from other sources. On 29 May 1850, Lord Lincoln, 'deprived of the comforts of matrimony' and 'liable to have a spurious offspring imposed on him', was granted a divorce. Lady Lincoln was found guilty of 'adulterous intercourse and criminal conversation' and there was a 'definitive sentence of divorce from bed and board and mutual cohabitation'.[53]

By the time her divorce was finalised, the illegitimate son of Lord Walpole and Lady Lincoln– 'my pickle' as she called him – was ten months old. He had been born at the Albergo Torre de Londra in Verona exactly a year after his mother left England and at the very moment that Gladstone was packing his bags to return home from

Como. Three weeks later, on 23 August 1849, in a sitting-room at the hotel, the baby was baptised Orazio Walpole by order of the Archpriest of San Fermo Maggiore.[54] Originally he was believed to have died. Both Gladstone and Newcastle received confidential letters to that effect in February 1850 from the Duke of Hamilton's solicitor. In fact he had been farmed out – probably with nuns at a convent near Florence where Walpole had a house. Horatio, as he became known,[55] is believed to have been educated at Heidelberg University, was made a ward of Chancery 'to avoid possession by an itinerant mother, lived and prospered'.[56]

After the Lincoln divorce, Lord Walpole had nothing more to do with his erstwhile mistress. Divorced himself by then, he lived mainly on the Continent, where the former rake gained a reputation as a misogynist. As for Suzie Lincoln – or Lady Susan Hamilton as she became, reverting to her Scottish title – after so much public exposure, the rest of her life passed in relative obscurity. She, too, remained abroad, travelling between France and Italy, visiting England only rarely. Gladstone thought he caught sight of her in the distance on Easter Sunday, 16 April 1854: 'St Andrews Wells St evening: where I thought I saw poor Lady Lincoln from afar'.[57] In 1860, she settled in Paris with few friends, little contact with her children, having little money beyond the annuities from her father and mother, who had died in 1852 and 1859 respectively. Under the terms of her divorce, she forfeited all claims to the Newcastle estate.[58] In Naples in 1862, she married her Belgian courier and long-term companion Jean Alexis Opdebeck, with whom she seems to have found a degree of domestic contentment.

The former Lord Lincoln, by then Duke of Newcastle, died in October 1864 at the age of fifty-eight. He never recovered from the pain of his wife's betrayal, and struggled – as his widowed father had done before him – to bring up a clutch of motherless children, while continuing to pursue his public duties with dedication and integrity. The scandal in no way jeopardised the family's social standing; indeed, his daughter Susan was bridesmaid to Queen Victoria's daughter, Vicky, when she married the Crown Prince of Prussia in 1858. But Lincoln's heart was broken. On his friend's death, Gladstone, as a trustee of the Newcastle estate, removed many of the sensitive family papers to Hawarden for safe keeping away from public scrutiny.[59] Catherine Gladstone wrote immediately to Suzie in Paris to inform her of his death and received a reply the following week, thanking her for the news and asking for a full account of his final hours. She clearly still saw herself as both the injured party and as a devoted mother when she wrote: 'Be assured that I have long since ceased to feel unkindly towards anyone and in the face of death I only remember that he that is gone was the father of my beloved children! and I mourn with them his death'.[60]

The Gladstones, who had often provided a temporary home for the five Lincoln children in the period after their mother abandoned them, continued to give what support they could over the years; but their influence seems to have had little effect, as Gladstone had predicted, in the face of the bitterness of their mother's abandonment. Only the second son, Edward Pelham-Clinton, made something of himself. And only he outlived his mother. He, ironically, was the infant son weaned early to facilitate his mother's dalliance with her brother-in-law. The first Lincoln son, Henry, notorious for his massive racing debts and controversial political career, died in 1879. The third son, Arthur, reported to have wounded his eldest brother in a duel, died of scarlet fever in 1870, bankrupt in fortune as well as reputation A navy deserter, he was on bail at the time after being charged with wearing women's clothes.[61] The fourth son, Albert, named after his sponsor Prince Albert, died in 1884 following a disastrous marriage and a life of debt. Young Lady Susan contracted a disastrous marriage at the age of eighteen with the notoriously unstable Lord Adolphus Vane, son of Lord and Lady Londonderry, described by Queen Victoria as having 'a natural tendency to madness'. Vane, who on one occasion violently attacked his wife and infant son, died four years later during a struggle with four keepers. After several years as an occasional mistress of the Prince of Wales, Susan bore 'Bertie' an illegitimate child in Ramsgate towards the end of 1871. She died in 1875.[62]

As for Edward, after an early career in the army, he became the Tory Member of Parliament for North Nottinghamshire shortly after his father's death in 1864. In later life he was Groom-in-Waiting to Queen Victoria and then Master of the Royal Household until the monarch's death, when he became Groom-in-Waiting to Edward VII, the father of his sister Susan's child. Throughout his life, Edward Pelham-Clinton remained in close touch with the Gladstones, remembering, as he said, their many kindnesses to the Lincoln family. In 1880, when his mother, now Lady Susan Opdebeck, returned to England, he contacted Gladstone, as a trustee of the Newcastle estate, to enlist his help in acquiring some money for his mother from the Newcastle estate, to which her legal entitlement had ceased on her divorce. His father, he insisted, would have wished such help to be made available.[63]

Suzie Opdebeck died on 28 November 1889 and was buried at St John's cemetery, Burgess Hill. The following day, Edward Pelham-Clinton – who later negotiated with the Newcastle trustees for an allowance to be made from the estate to his late mother's second husband – wrote to Gladstone:

> Remembering the great friendship you always entertained for my father, and knowing how intimately acquainted you have been with his greatest sorrows, I feel that I should be neglectful if I did not write to tell you of my mother's death which took place yesterday at Burgess Hill, near Brighton. She had been very unwell for the last four months, but the end came somewhat suddenly – however I am happy to say that M. Opdebeck writes 'sa mort à la fin a été très douce, aujourd'hui sa figure est très calme, souriante, on dirait un enfant qui sommeille'[64] – and so the end of a sad life has come at last, it is really a comfort to know that she is at rest. I am the sole survivor of what ought to have been such a bright and happy home. I think the funeral will take place at Burgess Hill, unless the Duke of Hamilton should have any wishes concerning it. What would father have wished? I wonder! I feel sure her death will carry back the thoughts of yourself and Mrs Gladstone for many years, and I am equally confident that I shall have the sympathy of two kind hearts.[65]

A few days later Gladstone wrote to his old friend Laura Thistlethwayte, who had apparently offered to defray the expenses of the funeral: 'Our poor friend then is laid peacefully to sleep. So passes beauty, glory, charm. None had more. There was a worm at the root. It is the same worm with us all. Peace be with her'.[66]

Whether the 'worm' that Gladstone identified was original sin in general, or the more specific issue of sexual misconduct, his compassion for the dead woman – despite the havoc she had wrought – is clear. There were many reasons why he chose forty years earlier to embark on his heroic attempted rescue mission: to help an old friend; to protect a good name from shame; to provide solidarity with the social class he aspired

to. Not least it was a mission that cast him in the romantic and chival-
ric role of potential redeemer of a Magdalen. But, most of all, Gladstone
understood from personal experience the immense discipline required
to control sexual desire, and was understanding of those, like the former
Lady Lincoln, who failed.

6

Fallen Women

Throughout his public life, Gladstone was no stranger to controversy. The aspect of his private life that caused the most stir – and threatened most to jeopardise his public reputation – was his forty-year crusade to rescue fallen women on the streets of London. It came at the cost of a risk to his gravitas that delighted his political enemies, providing welcome ammunition for whispering campaigns. A rhyme circulating in London at the time of the Jack the Ripper murders ran: 'Eight little whores, with no hope of heaven, Gladstone may save one, and then there'll be seven'.[1] At times, Gladstone's insouciance reduced his friends to despair. That he showed a reckless disregard for what the world thought hints at both naivety and innocence. It was perhaps to Gladstone's credit that he believed himself answerable only to his God and his conscience. It could also be interpreted as a sign of arrogance. As for Catherine, she supported him from the very beginning in his attempts to redeem the fallen women of London. She also displayed her customary indifference to any possibly adverse interpretations of her husband's activity: in her case, this which was as much a function of her spontaneous and carefree nature, as it was of her aristocratic disregard for bourgeois opinion.[2] Only rarely did she question the wisdom of any of her husband's actions.

Yet Gladstone's prostitute involvement was potentially far more explosive than even his critics realised at the time. Had they had in their possession the facts that came to light with the publication of his diaries, they would have had additional and powerful ammunition with which to attack both his personal credibility and his public career. For the truth is that, from 1849 onwards, after many of his encounters with prostitutes, Gladstone went home and privately whipped himself with a small scourge. Whatever explanation may be given as to the nature of this self-flagellation, its origin and its possible justification – and the facts are much more mundane than this hint of *le vice anglais* might suggest – it would have been a godsend to Gladstone's enemies. By honestly recording the practice in his diaries, yet wisely keeping it private at the time, Gladstone was perhaps anticipating correctly that posterity would judge his actions more objectively, and in the context of his total life more compassionately, than his contemporaries would have. There is also evidence that he kept the information from Catherine: 'How little you know of the evil of [my life] of which, at the last day, I shall have a tale to tell',[3] he wrote to her in July 1851, at the peak of his involvement with prostitutes. But it was not the evil that was the scourge, but the sexual excitement for which the scourge was a deterrent.

Gladstone's interest in prostitute rescue work began as an Oxford undergraduate. It peaked in his late thirties and early forties – a time of great emotional and nervous upheaval for him on many fronts. And it continued well into his eighties, until he eventually heeded the pleas of his long-suffering private secretary and gave it up, lest it should compromise the credibility of his campaign for Irish Home Rule. Rescue work was the main charitable enterprise of Gladstone's life. He spent on it an estimated £80,000 – the equivalent of perhaps four million pounds today. Most of that money came from properties in the West Indies that John Gladstone had made over to his four sons around the time of William's marriage. It was a noble, and an expensive, enterprise. Yet even today to mention Gladstone and women in the same breath almost invariably brings a knowing snigger, and an oblique recognition of his links with prostitutes – to the exclusion of all his other charitable activities – from people who otherwise know little of his personal life.[4]

Prostitution was a massive problem in Victorian Britain, and particularly in its capital city. Estimates as to the number of prostitutes operating in central London in the mid-nineteenth century vary widely: from the probably understated figure of 8000 suggested by contemporary police reports to a sensationalised figure of 120,000 that appeared in the press. The campaigning journalist Henry Mayhew, who chronicled the condition of the capital's underclass in the mid-century in his *London Labour and the London Poor*, inclined to a figure of around 80,000, while warning that this was probably a conservative estimate. At the time, the population of London was around two and a half million.[5] Small wonder that nineteenth-century visitors to the city from abroad, where these things were often much better managed, expressed dismay and amazement at the scale and uncontrolled nature of London prostitution.[6]

The difference in estimates may depend partly on how the term prostitute was defined. Mayhew used three categories. 'Professional Prostitutes' included 'Kept Mistresses' and 'Prima Donnas', described as 'women who are kept by men of independent means ... This is the nearest approximation to the holy state of matrimony, and finds numerous defenders and supporters'. 'Clandestine Prostitutes' included 'Maid Servants' and 'Ladies of Intrigue'. 'Cohabitant Prostitutes' was a wide-ranging group that embraced conscientious objectors to marriage, those who could not afford marriage fees, and those who declined to marry because by doing so they would forfeit an income, for example, officers' widows in receipt of a pension, and those who held property only while unmarried.[7] By comparison, a Metropolitan Police survey of May 1857 categorised prostitutes as belonging to one of three differently defined groups: 'well-dressed, living in brothels', 'well-dressed, walking the streets' and 'low prostitute, infesting low neighbourhoods'.

In a breakdown of the types of employment claimed by 'disorderly' prostitutes taken into custody between 1850 and 1860, police records show that they most frequently gave their trade as milliner (reflecting, at the very least, the fact that everyone at the time wore hats). Laundresses, shoemakers and tailors formed the next biggest groups. Mayhew queried whether these occupations lent themselves particularly to 'demoralisation' – by which he meant a tendency to moral laxity – and concluded that probably this employment profile simply reflected the absolute numbers working in those particular trades.

Again, an 1858 police survey indicates that most prostitution was concentrated in Stepney, followed by Whitechapel, Lambeth and Southwark. In 1850 the fifth most active district had been Westminster; but by the time of the 1858 survey the business there had dropped by one-third. It would be wishful thinking to suggest that Gladstone, on his nightly walks home to Carlton Terrace from the House of Commons, had single-handedly brought down the vice rate. He may, however, have helped drive them elsewhere: working girls found his presence was notoriously bad for business and his activities annoyed the madams of many a brothel.

The vulnerability of particular trades to economic fluctuations was a key factor in determining the pattern of urban deprivation throughout the nineteenth century. Whether it was the end of the 'Season' in London society that tipped dressmakers and milliners into poverty, or the cotton famines that deprived the Lancashire mills workers of their livelihood, the result was often the same. Some Victorian commentators, such as William Acton, who dedicated his medical career to the cause of state regulation of prostitution, looked for its origins in feminine weakness and the 'overgenerosity' of the female spirit. But the reality was that hard economic times meant that, for many women, prostitution was the only way to make ends meet. Many Victorian sex workers were only transient fallen women, moving in and out of the profession as family finances dictated. Sometimes, if they were lucky, they might move away from it for ever through marriage.

Before the 1834 Poor Law Amendment Act a modicum of relief was available to the poor through the provision of Outdoor Relief, a parish-based support system that enabled applicants to remain in their own homes, doing what they could to earn a living, but receiving supplementary benefits as well. The new Act overturned those provisions, establishing a workhouse regime so oppressive that only the most destitute were willing to have recourse to it. In the workhouse wives were separated from husbands, and children from parents, under conditions so dreadful that they could make even prostitution seem a lesser fate than death, if it kept the family together. The plight of the urban poor was further complicated by the new Act's stipulation that, where parish relief remained available, it was to be confined to the parish from which applicants originated, not where they had settled. This effectively meant that migrants from country to town often could make no claim for relief from their new parish; indeed they risked being removed to a parish which they, or even their parents, had left many years before. It also inhibited mobility of labour, since those with a potential claim on their home parish would be reluctant to leave it in search of better employment prospects elsewhere. It was not until 1846, when Peel's government introduced the Poor Removal Act, that they had any protection. This legislation ensured entitlement to irremovability after five years' continuous residence in a parish, a period reduced to three years by a subsequent Act in 1861.[8]

There were two distinct aspects to prostitute rescue work in Victorian England. Many philanthropically-minded people served on committees and helped raised funds for charitable initiatives. Others, including Gladstone and Charles Dickens, wanted to be out on the street, making an immediate and a personal difference. Some, like Catherine Gladstone, did both. She responded spontaneously when the moment required direct intervention and, like William, would occasionally approach prostitutes directly on the street. On the other hand, she was not above resorting to brazen extortion in her fund-raising exercises when money was what was required most. William, however, was driven almost exclusively to work on the streets. To a female co-worker, Marian Hughes, he wrote in 1841:

> People will give money to good causes but what does money alone avail if there is no action to put that money to good use. There has been so much talk for so long about doing something about reforming the character of urban life, of restoring to the Church the broken vessels of female humanity who are strewn like flotsam on the streets of our great cities. The task is vast, but I intend in my own small way, to make a real effort to come to grips with it. Women alone cannot do this work; it must be a partnership between laity and clergy, between priests and sisterhoods, between man and wife.[9]

The problem of prostitution in the capital was obvious to anyone who walked the streets of mid-nineteenth-century London, day or night (as was its companion evil, the open sale of pornography, to which Gladstone also succumbed). Indeed, young men coming up to town could buy a readily available printed guide to both sources of entertainment – prostitution and pornography. But while prostitution was rife, talking about it as a social issue was not. It was rarely discussed publicly, nor would it be for many years. As late as 1869, a campaigning journalist and 'social investigator', James Greenwood, felt himself obliged, in *The Seven Curses of London*, to begin a report on prostitution with an apology to 'the supersensitive reader, who will doubtless experience a shock of alarm at discovering this part's heading'. But he explained that it would be pointless to discuss the 'curses of London' without including prostitution.

> Doubtless it is a curse, the mere mention of which, let alone its investigation the delicate-minded naturally shrinks from. But it is a matter for

congratulation, perhaps, that we are not all so delicate-minded. Cowardice is not infrequently mistaken for daintiness of nature. It is so with the subject in question. It is not a pleasant subject – very far from it; but that it is not a sufficient excuse for letting it alone ... The monstrous evil in question has grown to its present dimensions chiefly because we have silently borne with it.[10]

Others may have borne silently with this 'monstrous evil' but not Gladstone. He was well ahead of the time in this respect. He had already been involved with serious rescue work for twenty years before Greenwood 'discovered' the evil of prostitution. He was years ahead of feminist Josephine Butler (1828–1906), who campaigned against the insidious Contagious Diseases Acts of the 1860s. This was an Act, which, ironically, Gladstone supported, that attempted to regulate prostitutes by subjecting them to regular, compulsory and humiliating medical examination.[11] Gladstone, who attempted to redeem prostitutes on the streets not only of London but also of Baden, Brighton, Corfu, Dresden, Nottingham and Milan, was decades ahead even of the campaigning journalist W. T. Stead, who in 1885 bought a young virgin from a London brothel and took her to Paris, simply to prove that he could – and paid the price of imprisonment in Pentonville.[12]

Nor was London particularly well provided with refuges to which prostitutes who wanted to give up the profession could turn for help. Before the early 1800s, there was just one institution in the capital that had as its aim the rescue of fallen women. This was the Magdalen Hospital, founded in 1758. The hospital took in nearly nine thousand women in its first one hundred years, of whom about two-thirds were 'restored to friends or relations'.[13] By the middle of the nineteenth century there were about fifty metropolitan institutions for the 'reception of the destitute and criminal, or those who are exposed to temptation', and together they could provide accommodation for about four thousand people at any one time. Most were supported entirely by voluntary contributions and by the earnings of the inmates, who were either admitted free of charge or by payment of a small sum towards their maintenance costs.[14] This was around five pounds. It was a sum frequently paid out to the institutions by Gladstone on behalf of the women he tried to place with them.

Of the fifty London reformatories noted by Mayhew, twenty-one were devoted exclusively to 'the rescue and reformation of fallen women, or such as have been led astray from the path of virtue'.[15] Ten of the institutions were connected to the Church of England, while in the remaining eleven the religious instruction was 'unsectarian and evangelical'. But, even here, class prevailed. Three houses were designed for the 'better educated and higher class of fallen women', while one provided 'shelter exclusively to those who have recently been led astray, and whose previous good character will bear the strictest investigation'.[16] Another was for girls aged fifteen or younger.

Gladstone was just eighteen years old himself when he first met a prostitute, on a pre-matriculation visit to Oxford in August 1828. He seems to have been curious but relaxed about this inauguration. 'Out at night', he wrote in his diary on 5 August 1828: 'Met a woman and had a long conversation with her. Up late. Bible as usual.' The following evening he renewed their acquaintance: 'At night met the poor creature again, who is determined to go home ... finished Book 4 of *Odyssey*.' In the next three years, he mentioned two more meetings with prostitutes, wondering on 22 July 1831 if such encounters were 'imprudent? God knows'.

It was in 1848 that Gladstone's rescue work became a serious and regular activity. He was then aged thirty-eight, and, with some friends from within the Oxford Movement, had formed a charitable lay brotherhood known as 'The Engagement'. It was based at the Margaret Street Chapel, just north of Oxford Circus.[17] Its members were committed to several undertakings, including giving considerable time and money to good causes, specifically for the immediate relief for the destitute of both sexes. Initially, the work of 'The Engagement' was concentrated on supporting the efforts of a Soho refuge, the House of Saint Barnabas. But gradually, as the work of the brotherhood as a whole petered out, Gladstone found that the rescue of fallen women was what appealed to him most. That his desire to help fallen women was genuine there can be no doubt. That his association with young and pretty ones meant he was playing with fire is equally clear. By early 1849, nocturnal encounters with prostitutes had become a regular feature of his London life and he would often return with them to their lodgings to talk late into the night. The next ten years would represent the peak of Gladstone's rescue mission.

In the autumn of 1845 when Gladstone was in Germany trying to persuade his drug-addicted sister Helen to return home, he began to draw up 'a sketch on my chief besetting sin'. At this point his prostitute work had not yet begun. The sin in question was, therefore, the 'plague' of masturbation, usually, in the early days, following exposure to pornography.[18] It was 'more than twenty years since the plague began', which meant he was fifteen years old when it started. In later years, he had found it was exacerbated by over-exertion and 'exhaustion of the mind'.

Gladstone's analysis of his condition was written on separate paper but kept in his diary, and he added to the information over the years once he began his involvement with prostitutes. Initially his sketch comprised four headings. Three of these were: 'Channels of Temptation', which included most methods of human communication, from touch to conversation; 'Incentives', under which he included idleness, exhaustion, curiosity and sympathy; and 'Chief Actual Dangers', predominantly impulsive thought. The fourth heading, 'Remedies', together with obvious solutions such as abstinence, prayer, and not looking in print shop windows, included 'immediate pain'. It was the first hint that the scourge would come to play an important part in his attempts at self-discipline.

This sketch became known as the 'Baden Rules', after the German spa town where he began to formulate them during his trip in search of Helen. It was supplemented a couple of years later with a list of the dates on which he had read pornography, marked with 'X'. Elsewhere in his diary, Gladstone explained that

> these offences are far from representing all that I had to deplore ... in regard to the particular subject: they represent the occasions on which by some act of mine I had courted evil – not those on which, when it came without my seeking, I had by infirmity and evil habit, suffered from it.[19]

He recounted occasions when he had visited bookshops ostensibly to buy political works but found himself reading pornographic poems instead. And, hinting at his future scourging, he wrote that this confession 'stings my pride a little: and perhaps ... may lead to what will sting it more'. The following year he began to whip himself to subdue unwelcome sexual stimulation after reading pornography or visiting prostitutes.[20] These occasions are marked in the diaries with the sign of a small whip.

The time when Gladstone began his serious prostitute work was a period of great anxiety for him. He was out of office. There were long separations from the warm and domesticating influence of his wife. At least while her family were young, Catherine preferred life at Hawarden Castle, and the Lyttelton home at Hagley Hall, to the suffocating regime of polite London society, for which she had little patience. The recent conversion to Rome of his sister Helen and two of his closest friends caused Gladstone much emotional upheaval. His beloved little daughter Jessy had died of meningitis; his sister-in-law Mary Lyttelton had also died, leaving twelve motherless children and a manic-depressive father. He had failed to bring Lady Lincoln back to her husband. There were financial problems, too, over to the Glynne estate, for which Gladstone wealth would be needed to redeem the situation. Together, these factors created in Gladstone an intense nervousness that expressed itself it two ways: first, a tendency to autoeroticism when most stressed; and secondly, an overpowering need, the need to be doing something worthwhile in other areas – notably rescue work.

Not all of Gladstone's potential rescue candidates are identifiable from his *Diaries*. Some are given no names at all, and he may well never have known them; others are just remembered by a surname.[21] Some are mentioned only once; others dozens of times over many years. One of the first serious cases with which Gladstone became involved was that of Emma Clifton. At this time, he had taken to patrolling outside the infamous Argyll Rooms in Great Windmill Street off Piccadilly Circus, a notorious centre for aristocratic dissipation. There, on 23 July 1850, he first met Emma, with whom he was to become much preoccupied – infatuated, even – over the coming weeks and months. The following evening he spent an hour and a half in her company before going on to a concert at Lansdowne House. A couple of days later, a Friday, he saw her again; and again on Saturday night 'and made I hope some way. But alas my own unworthiness'. On Sunday he worked on a manuscript for her, the nature of which is unclear. He had been in regular contact with a Mrs Tennant, who until recently had been superintendent of a rescue home at Clewer near Windsor (one of several that the Gladstones supported); perhaps he may have been trying to secure a place for Emma. The following Tuesday, Gladstone saw Emma again. On Thursday he sought her out once more.

Before nine I went to find E.C. but failed: after 1¼ came home ... went again at 11½ to O. Street, and again failed. Resolved to go to E.C.'s lodgings: I found her there: and left her with the resolution declared of going in the morning by my advice and with her child at once to Mrs Tennant. I therefore wrote to aid her: I hope and even think I am not deceived, while I am sure that I deserve to be.[22]

The following day he travelled to Birmingham to stay with the Lytteltons at Hagley Hall, where he took a 'walk with Catherine and told her of the proceedings of last night – which she approved and with much interest'.

After ten days at Hagley, Gladstone was back at Hawarden when on 15 August a letter arrived from Mrs Tennant which 'showed that matters had not moved with respect to E. Clifton: and after consulting with Catherine I thought it my duty to go to town'. He arrived in London at 8 p.m. but 'failed in finding E.C. for the evening, though I did all I could'. The following day was taken up with meetings involving representatives of rescue organisations who might have been able to help Clifton, including James Beard Talbot, founder of the London Society for the Protection of Young Females and the Prevention of Juvenile Prostitution. But he failed to make direct contact with his young protégée, and returned to Hawarden by train. After a summer spent mainly at Fasque, it was October before Gladstone returned again to London. Immediately he 'looked about for poor E. Clifton: but in vain'.[23]

The following day, disaster struck within the extended family. Gladstone's sister-in-law Lavinia, the wife of Catherine's brother Henry Glynne, died two weeks after giving birth to a fourth daughter. This was a highly significant event. Since there were no male heirs on the Glynne side – his older brother-in-law Stephen never married – the likelihood that the Hawarden estate might pass to the Gladstone side of the family became a real possibility. But even this momentous event failed to deter Gladstone from his campaign to save Clifton. He noted in his diary: 'At 11 p.m. Lavinia died. When I went out to look for E.C. – in vain'. Two days later he sought her out again, again in vain, but wondering: 'Could I do otherwise in common humanity?'[24] Two days later he wrote again to Mrs Tennant – the subject is not revealed but is likely have related to Clifton – before taking the train to Hawarden for Lavinia's funeral. After the funeral the family embarked on a three-month trip to Italy and thoughts of prostitute rescue work were, for the time being at least, suspended.

On his return to London, it was while scouring Shaftesbury Avenue in search of Clifton in the spring of 1851 that Gladstone met the woman who was to become another of his significant rescue cases, P. Lightfoot. Her first name has never been discovered but she was, Gladstone said, 'a singular case indeed'.[25] After working on the proofs of his translation of Farini's *Lo Stato Romano*, he went out the following night to find her but failed. The next day was a time of great turmoil, as Gladstone realised that his two friends Henry Manning and James Hope were on the brink of converting to Rome. He was dismayed at the emotional anxiety into which this plunged him and which caused him to question even the moral basis of the satisfaction he derived from his rescue work.

> Such terrible blows not only overset and oppress but I fear also demoralise me: which tends to show that my trysts are carnal or the withdrawal of them would not leave such a void. *Was* it possibly from this that thinking P.L. would look for me as turned out to be the fact, I had a second interview and conversation indoors here: and heard more history; yet I trusted without harm done.[26]

The next day he saw P.L. again. But he was increasingly ill at ease and beginning to realise that his rescue work might not always be regarded as a noble cause by the would-be beneficiaries.

> Said I thought it must be the last time: as I fear lest more harm was done than good. There seems to be little guilt, and good affections, but an ill-formed conscience, and a want of depth and strength in impressions. I was certainly wrong in some things and trod the path of danger.

Easter that year was spent at Fasque. On Easter Saturday, Gladstone tried to analyse his mixed emotions over recent events and his apparent recourse to autoeroticism, rather than the scourge, to deal with them.

> And now ends another Lent ... I am more and more convinced of the blessings of discipline. But I must write a bitter thing against myself. Whether owing (as I think) to the sad sad recent events (of the 6th) or not, I have been unmanned and unnerved and out of sheer cowardice have not used the measure which I have found so beneficial against temptations to impurity ... Therefore they have been stronger than usual in Lent; and I had no courage!

Having allowed the relationship with Lightfoot to cool for a while, but feeling guilty that she may have thought he had abandoned her, Gladstone sought her out again in May: 'Setting out about P.L. for whom it seems an obligation to inquire and if possible act'. While doing so he 'fell in with Walters [another rescue case] in evening as well as others and I hope one act of evil was stopped. But for me there is a great blank to be filled'.[27] In fact, he did not meet Lightfoot again until August 1853, by which time the intense nature of his rescue work had mellowed. 'Conduct but very middling' was his comment when they did eventually make contact. He met her again in October 'by appointment' but 'failed to see Lightfoot' in March the following year. They met briefly in April 1854, June 1856 and July 1858, but there is no indication that Gladstone's intervention had diverted Lightfoot from her trade.

'The blank to be filled', which Gladstone felt so keenly in May 1851, may have been satisfied by his association with Elizabeth Collins, whom he met on 11 June that year and with whom he was to be 'much interested' for most of that summer. Collins was very beautiful: 'bella oltre misura' – 'lovely beyond measure', enthused Gladstone, who often used Italian for expressing deep emotion. Just over two weeks after their first meeting, he saw her for an hour and a half on 27 June. On 4 July, after writing to Collins in the morning, he spoke in the House of Commons on the Ecclesiastical Titles Bill 'and went off immediately to meet E. Collins who did not come then or later in evening. Attended and spoke at the Clewer House of Mercy meeting'. He may have been intending to take Collins with him to the meeting with a view to her entering the Windsor refuge. Three days later, he wrote to her again in the morning and they met up in the evening. 'Saw E. Collins at night: and closed with advising a day visit and appeal to Catherine for advice. Finished and sent off to Catherine.'

The following day he both wrote to Collins and visited her, 'but did not advance in the matter'. On 12 July, Gladstone looked for Collins after dinner but failed to find her. After dining at Sidney Herbert's the following evening, he 'went with a note to E.C.'s – received (unexpectedly) and remained two hours: a strange and humbling experience – returned and [whip mark]'. The following evening he spent at home 'except a short time looking for E.C.' The following evening he dined with his old schoolfriend, James Milnes-Gaskell, corrected some proofs and 'fell in with E.C. and another mixed scene somewhat like that of 48 hours before – [whip sign] afterwards.' The next day he wrote to Lightfoot 'who lives at home in regular work under a person named Simpson at 25 shillings per week ... This is a great blessing'.[28]

On 19 July, he recorded seeing 'nothing of E.C. on looking', but two days later he tracked her down: 'Saw E.C. again in the same manner: and did not [whip sign] afterwards: thinking there was a change'. On 23 July, there was a formal dinner at the House of Commons for the American Ambassador. At half past midnight Gladstone left, 'the first to do so'.

> Then in a singular way hit upon E.C.: two more hours, strange, questionable, or more: followed by [whip mark]. Whether or not I have been deluded in the notion of doing good by such means, or whether I have sought it through what was unlawful I am not clear. God grant however not for my sake that the good may be done.

Gladstone and Collins next met again on 19 August, when it appeared that she had a received an offer of marriage. Respectability seemed to beckon. Writing once more in Italian, Gladstone recorded his most intimate thoughts.

> Saw E.C. again by herself; from 9.15 until 11.30. Things went partly as before. She nevertheless finds herself determined to have nothing more to do with anyone else, but to wait faithfully for Osborne; who, according to his letters, longs to marry her the moment he returns. Now there are two whom I have seen this year, who are I hope resolved to do no more evil; and I am covered with many foul stains. If God's grace has made use of most unworthy me, with how very much new guilt for me, to help these souls, may it ever be praised on their account, and glorified eternally even in my miserable self.

After this meeting, there was a gap of five months before Gladstone and Collins met again, on 26 January 1852. 'Visited E.C. and spent a long time – tea there. Matters have gone pretty well there: yet mine is a wretched part'. On 13 February, Gladstone 'met E.C. in walking home: 2½ here: ended pretty well: not so in the middle'. The news was not so good three months later, when he recorded on 7 May: 'Saw E. Collins: bad: and there must be a change'. They next met again one October evening, the day after Gladstone had recorded a success with another rescue case, A. Loader, 'who went to C.G.: lives with mother, works and looks to marry ... there is cause to hope for wretched!' He wrote in his diary that it was 'a rather busy day. In evening saw E.C. – and remained some time mainly I hope to muse but ever with shame. Afterwards P.L. who once extricated has married'.[29]

It was nearly a year, in August 1853, before Gladstone again saw Collins, 'who goes on well. But I badly'. In the autumn he saw Collins 'accidentally' (and Lightfoot 'by appointment') on a couple of occasions; but she was 'in low spirits – and no wonder'. Around Christmas time he 'put up and delivered parcel for Collins', whom he next saw on 31 January 1854 and 'who I believe goes on well: a source of real satisfaction though I must add ill-deserved satisfaction'. That was effectively the end of their relationship.

After the intense periods of activity in his mid-thirties to early forties Gladstone's rescue work became a more casual matter during most of the 1850s. But in 1859 he made the close aquaintance of a working woman of a different kind. Marian Summerhayes was a courtesan and artist's model, a person altogether more refined than the common prostitutes he had previously sought to help. Whether consciously or not, the next woman Gladstone settled on as a serious rescue opportunity was a different case entirely. In some ways, she can be seen as paving the way for his intense relationship with the reformed courtesan-cum-evangelist Laura Thistlethwayte in the 1860s. And, unlike the beneficiaries of his previous rescue attempts, in whom in many cases he maintained a benevolent but detached interest over many years, the Summerhayes affair was an emotionally charged and potentially dangerous interlude for Gladstone. For that reason it had to be short-lived.

It was on 30 July 1859 – Gladstone was forty-nine at the time – that he first met Summerhayes, whom he described from the first as 'full in the highest degree both of interest and beauty'. He was deeply smitten and sought her out on an almost daily basis. Within less than a week of meeting her, he had suggested to his friend, the Pre-Raphaelite painter William Dyce, that Summerhayes should sit to him for a commissioned portrait. On being invited to call at Gladstone's home to discuss the project, Dyce expressed himself pleased 'to comply with the wish you have expressed in a manner so handsome and complimentary to myself' but regretted he was unable to do so immediately because of other prior commitments.[30]

To expedite the project, Dyce may have resorted to the new and

exciting art of photography, suggesting to Gladstone: 'If I like your subject, which I have no doubt will be the case, some progress in the
meantime might be made by my having some photographic studies
made from her'. Further details are not known, although both Summerhayes and Dyce visited Gladstone at his home on 5 August 1859,
when photographs may have been taken. The following day, Gladstone
met Summerhayes alone regarding her picture. She was a very unusual
case, he recorded in his diary, 'and merits what I wrote of it to Dyce'.

A portrait of Marian Summerhayes was duly painted, and initially
entitled *Lady with a Coronet of Jasmine*. Dyce's fee is not known. When
sixteen years later, in June 1875, the picture was sold during a four-day
auction of Gladstone's art and china collections at 11 Carlton House Terrace, the London home he was about to leave, organised by Christie,
Manson and Woods, it fetched the handsome sum of £420. It was the
second best price of the auction.[31] It is now known as *Beatrice*. The sitter was believed to have represented Dante's idealised woman and his
guide to God in the *Divine Comedy*. 'I like this one better than any of
the many Beatrices I have seen', a Florence-based English Dante scholar
wrote to Dyce in 1863.[32] That a courtesan should model for the blame-
less Beatrice seems inappropriate – perhaps Summerhayes's coronet
of jasmine was mistaken for the coronet of olive worn by Beatrice as a
symbol of true wisdom.[33]

Having commissioned Dyce to paint Summerhayes, Gladstone continued to be obsessed with his new rescue case. When in London during
the summer, he wrote to her, or sought her out, on an almost daily
basis. When away, he corresponded with her regularly. 'The case is no
common one', he insisted in his diary. 'May God grant that all go right.
To me no trivial matter, for evil or for good.'[34] A week later, he realised
that his emotions were running away with him. 'My thoughts of Summerhayes require to be limited and purged', he wrote on 1 September
1859. But this failed to prevent his spending four and a half hours with
her one evening two weeks later, reading Tennyson's *Princess*, after
which he was 'much and variously moved'.

Autumn came and Gladstone returned to London for the season,
seeking out Summerhayes two or three times a week until December. At
this point she seems to have married, or to have been taken under the
protection of a man called Dale. Either way, from this point she called

herself 'Mrs Dale'. In April, June and August of 1860, Gladstone enquired about her in Trafalgar Square, and 'heard well of her'. He wrote to her occasionally, and sought her out from time to time, although it would appear that her rehabilitation had lapsed by 1867.

Nearly twenty years later, on 16 October 1886, at the age of seventy-six, Gladstone destroyed the letters sent to him by Summerhayes and another courtesan.

> Today I burned a number of old letters, kept apart, which might in parts have suggested doubt and uneasiness. Two of the writers were Mrs Dale and Mrs Davidson: cases of great interest, in qualities as well as attractions certainly belonging to the flower of their sex. I am concerned to have lost sight of them.

Gladstone destroyed this correspondence, as he would later destroy other potentially incriminating letters to him from Laura Thistleth-wayte. The reason was to avoid his family's being embarrassed at some future date if their content were misinterpreted, rather than because he had any sense of personal shame about his rescue activity. He had always been naive to the point of recklessness about the impression this work might have on others – being answerable in his own mind only to his own conscience and to God. When a disenchanted brothel-keeper, annoyed that Gladstone's nightly appearances were bad for business, spread rumours that he was in fact a client, he rode out the storm. When a journalist tried to blackmail him, he reported the man to the police. And when the man was later convicted, Gladstone intervened to have his sentence halved.

Clifton, Collins, Lightfoot, Summerhayes and many others: they were but fleeting figures who passed briefly across Gladstone's canvas. In themselves, they were innocent. Collectively, however, they had the potential to represent something of a threat. Time and again, his colleagues warned him of the potential damage that these women could inflict on his personal reputation and political credibility. In 1882, the Foreign Secretary Lord Granville and Lord Rosebery, who had been Gladstone's host and sponsor during the highly successful Midlothian campaigns of the late 1870s, tossed a coin to decide who should plead with Gladstone to stop his rescue missions. Rosebery, having lost the toss, made the attempt but his plea fell on deaf ears.

Eddie Hamilton, one of Gladstone's private secretaries, tried a few months later but with the same lack of success. In 1884 Hamilton tried again, reminding Gladstone that there were many 'malicious and unscrupulous persons who would give large sums of money' to persuade his police bodyguards to incriminate him. 'There is no saying to what account these persons might or might not turn such information.'[35] Hamilton finally succeeded in July 1886 by warning Gladstone that there was a conspiracy afoot to set spies on him to watch his movements and that his rescue work could jeopardise the chance of victory in the Irish Home Rule campaign. 'As I fear there *does* exist in the world the baseness you describe, I believe on the whole what you say is true and wise, and I give you my promise accordingly', Gladstone replied.[36]

There are more entries in Gladstone's diaries about prostitutes than there are about political hostesses, more recorded visits to the fallen women on the streets of London than recorded attendances at the balls and soirées of the *grandes dames* of polite Victorian society. The latter include a couple of dozen names. Most prominent among them his great friend and confidante Harriet, Duchess of Sutherland, as well as Lady Waldegrave and Lady Palmerston. The list of potential rescue cases, by contrast, runs to nearly a hundred names. That he felt entitled to operate simultaneously and openly within these two polarised milieux – often combining a grand soirée with a prostitute visit on the walk home – suggests a courage that bordered at times on folly.

Gladstone was often criticised for preferring the company of prostitutes who were young and pretty. One regular critic was fellow Liberal Henry Labouchère, the MP for Northampton, who complained:

> Gladstone manages to combine his missionary meddling with a keen appreciation of a pretty face. He has never been known to rescue any of our East End whores, nor for that matter is it easy to contemplate his rescuing any ugly woman and I am quite sure his conception of the Magdalen is of incomparable example of pulchritude with a superb figure and carriage.[37]

This was true. Rarely did Gladstone venture into the City or the East End. He concentrated his efforts mainly on the areas close to the House of Commons and his home in Carlton Terrace, specifically around Piccadilly and Soho where most of his recorded cases were located. Most common prostitutes were, in any case, young. Typically, they began sex work between the ages of fifteen and twenty. Those who worked full-time at it lived for another five years on average. But to choose prostitutes who were presentable as well as young was also common sense. They stood a better chance of being reintroduced into respectable society after a period of rehabilitation and training – probably back into the servant class to which they had often previously belonged.

That Catherine Gladstone played an important part in the rehabilitation of the women her husband picked up on the streets of London has already been mentioned. When asked one night by a companion what his wife would think of his engaging a prostitute in conversation, Gladstone replied – with some surprise at the fellow's ignorance – that it was, of course, to Mrs Gladstone that he was taking the unfortunate creature. From the very start, in 1846, Catherine was a partner in William's rescue work, although she never publicised the fact. One of their first joint rescue cases was a girl called Rebecca Ayscough from Millbank Penitentiary. A medium-term success story, she eventually reverted to her old ways after a number of years, ultimately unable – a classic behaviour pattern – to tolerate the strict rules and conditions required to embrace a new life. One of the Gladstones' early institutional successes was to help found the St Barnabas refuge in a disused workhouse in Soho. St Barnabas had links with the Anglican community at Clewer, near Windsor, which became an important asylum for London prostitutes who seemed genuinely to want to reform.

While William roamed the streets between work and home, looking for beneficiaries of his charity, Catherine was more concerned with locating places where promising cases could be housed and retrained, primarily as domestic servants. In parallel with this, she also organised soup kitchens for families in the Lancashire mill towns who had been devastated by the cotton famine that hit the country in the wake of the American Civil War. Some of the mill-workers daughters she took home to Hawarden to train as domestic servants.

Catherine willingly took in to their London residence women that William brought home off the streets for a bowl of soup and a safe bed for the night. At the same time, he honoured her commitments when she brought home a clutch of 'very clean' babies orphaned by one the of London cholera epidemics of the 1860s. One can only imagine the feelings of the Gladstones' long-suffering domestic staff at having the smart London homes invaded.

By the 1860s, with her children grown up, Catherine was operating seriously on her own behalf. Like her husband, she had enormous stores of energy and moved regularly round the country in pursuit of one deserving cause or another, public or family. Even her husband commented that he had difficulty keeping track of her movements. In 1864 she was instrumental in the establishment of the hundred-bed Newport Market Refuge in a former slaughterhouse in the notorious Seven Dials district near Leicester Square. This hostel provided temporary relief for the destitute of both sexes. Later a school was added, where the children of the destitute were taught literacy and could learn a trade. Promising musicians were trained by the bandmaster of the Scots Fusiliers. It was said that most British regimental bands at the time boasted at least one of Mrs Gladstone's boys.[38]

During the cholera epidemics, Catherine was a regular and fearless visitor to the London Hospital, comforting the sick and dying. She frequently took child survivors and orphans home with her if no other emergency accommodation could be found. She appealed in the *Times* for temporary homes for cholera orphans and raised money for an orphanage and convalescent home at Clapton. When this closed, she took a dozen boys back to Hawarden.[39] They were accommodated in an old coach house and Gladstone paid for their upkeep and education. At this time, there were still several Lancashire mill girls living and being trained in another house in the castle yard. Over the years, there were many joint and several philanthropic projects, great and small: from the establishment of free convalescent homes for the poor at Snaresbrook and Woodford Hall in Essex, and later the foundation of a home for old ladies at Hawarden, to countless individual acts of kindness. These could be quite bizarre, as when Gladstone found himself paying the outstanding livery bill for a courtesan who, at his behest, had renounced the gay life in exchange for the refuge at Clewer. The reality of having Hawarden given up to a motley crew of disorientated orphans, bemused fallen women, unemployed mill girls and abandoned grandmothers seems to have been accepted with a good grace by other members of the Gladstone family: 'I was very much amused about all the infirm people sheltered at Hawarden', Helen wrote to her father.[40]

Gladstone was always generous towards his rescue cases. He would send books of poems (Tennyson and Shakespeare were favourites), flowers and even, on one occasion, a spaniel (which he later found himself having to care for). In the early years he gave them copies of a pamphlet that Charles Dickens had written in 1849 for women taken into police custody, in the hope of directing them to a home at Shepherd's Bush, established by his friend, Angela Burdett Coutts. Entitled *An Appeal to Fallen Women*, it read:

> You will see, on beginning to read this letter, that it is not addressed to you by name. But I address it to a woman – a very young woman still – who was born to be happy and has lived miserably; who has no prospect before her but sorrow, or behind her but a wasted youth; who, if she has ever been a mother, has felt shame instead of pride in her own unhappy child. You are such a person, or this letter would not be put into your hands, If you have ever wished (I know you must have done so at some time) for a chance of rising out of your sad life, and having friends, a quiet home, means of being useful to yourself and others, peace of mind, self-respect, everything you have lost, pray read it attentively and reflect upon it afterwards. I am going to offer you, not the chance but the *certainty* of all these blessings, if you will exert yourself to deserve them. And do not think that I write to you as if I felt myself very much above you, or wished to hurt your feelings by reminding you of the situation in which you are placed. God forbid! I mean nothing but kindness to you, and I write as if you were my sister.[41]

Gladstone's desire to redeem fallen women was never less than sincere, but it had a darker side. He felt that the greater the sexual temptation they presented, the greater his virtue in resisting that temptation.[42] In the small hours of Friday 20 January 1854 Gladstone, unable to sleep, agonised over the low success rate of his rescue work and, more importantly, wondered whether his own ambivalent sexual response to the prostitutes with whom he engaged served in any way to invalidate his works of charity. The acknowledgement of his own confusion is touchingly human.

> This morning I lay awake until four with a sad and perplexing subject: it was reflecting on and counting up the numbers of those unhappy beings, now present to my memory, with whom during now so many years I have conversed indoors and out. I reckoned from eighty to ninety. Among these there is but one of whom I know that the miserable life has been abandoned *and*

that I can fairly join that fact with influence of mine. Yet this were much more than enough for all the labour and the time, had it been purely spent on my part. But the case is far otherwise: and though in none of these instances have I not spoken good words, yet so bewildered have I been that they constitute the chief burden of my soul.[43]

The results of Gladstone's 'burden' – the need for self-flagellation and other forms of breast-beating following his 'rescue' attempts – have been in the public domain since the publication of the *Diaries* began in 1964. There seems little doubt that, while Gladstone succeeded in resisting the charms of his rescue cases (in the sense that he did not succumb to them physically at the time), some encounters generated in him a powerful erotic response which he either managed to subdue, or else punished himself for later, and in private. Use of a scourge was an important tool in the Tractarian regime of self-denial; but it was emphatically not a source of further sexual stimulation. On the contrary, there is evidence that Gladstone on occasions felt too tired or depressed to use the scourge, although he felt he ought to, indicating that no element of pleasure was involved.

Catherine Gladstone is unlikely to have been aware is the degree to which his rescue work increased erotic tension in an already highly sexed man, at times to almost unbearable levels. Gladstone's sexual appetitite had been deepened, not surprisingly, by a happy marriage to a beautiful, vivacious, healthy and naturally affectionate young woman after two disastrous failed courtships. Yet he and Catherine spent long periods apart when their children were young. When they were together, Catherine was for many years either pregnant or was breast-feeding their eight-strong brood, which, by the conventions of the time, would probably have precluded sexual intercourse. The couple may have taken literally the notion that marriage was first and foremost for the procreation of children. In later life, Gladstone told his daughter Mary that the idea of contraception was anathema to him.[44] Together, these factors may have inhibited the Gladstones' opportunities for conjugal intimacy, while his enjoyment of it heightened his need.

In the winter of 1885, Gladstone dictated some notes to Charles Vickers, a colleague of W. T. Stead, the journalist whose campaign against child prostitution had succeeded in raising the age of consent to sixteen (though Gladstone would have preferred eighteen). Gladstone thought the information might be of some use to a rescue organisation with which Vickers was involved: the London Committee for the Suppression of Traffic in English Girls for the Purposes of Continental Prostitution. What impressed Vickers more than the notes – which concerned the particularly insidious evil posed by houses of procurement – were Gladstone's comments on the approach that reformers should adopt to rescue work. They encapsulated the personal philosophy that provided the background to his own efforts to redeem by kindness and respect. Vickers recalled Gladstone as saying:

> What is not generally understood by those who try to bring about reforms, whether legislative or by personal example, is that far too many well-meaning people allow religion to distort their moral sense – strange, if not impossible as such a statement may seem ... One cannot save souls by legislation alone. One cannot save souls by saying 'Thou shalt not!' It may well be that one has to revise one's view of the best means of rescuing a soul. Condemnation on the spot may be following the tenets of the Ten Commandments, but one must also realise that Christ respected the individual – to Him each one was deserving of the same consideration, and that in its turn means the same courtesies ... The whole system of legitimate courtesy, politeness and refinement is surely nothing less than one of the genuine, though minor and often unacknowledged, results of our gospel scheme. All the greater moral qualities or graces, which in their large sphere determine the formation and habits of the Christian soul before God, do apply to everyday life, though on a smaller scale. It is good breeding and manners which distinguish our Christian religion. This must most particularly apply in dealing with the outcast, as Christ himself dealt with women who had sinned. Rehabilitation must be achieved through good manners, forbearance to condemn unduly, but firm and patient inisistence on the true way of life. Failures may result despite this, alas! All too often, but neglect of this elementary but forgotten principle will far too often prevent successes which could otherwise have been achieved.[45]

By now, Gladstone was in his mid-seventies and his prostitute work was coming to an end. Opposition to the latest failed Irish Home Rule Bill meant that any opportunity was taken to vilify him, and he had promised his Private Secretary Eddie Hamilton in July 1886 that he would stop seeking out potential rescue cases in order to avoid misinterpretation. But he reserved two rights: first, to maintain contact with existing cases whom he did not wish to abandon; and, secondly, not to turn away anyone who came to him for help. He insisted that his efforts had had some success: he claimed twelve unnamed women had been completely rehabilitated in the past three years alone.[46]

It would be another four years before Gladstone ceased his rescue work completely, by which time he was in his eighties and shortly to become Prime Minister for the fourth and last time. Even then he remained in correspondence with various of the Houses of Mercy to which he had given moral and financial support over the years. But he regretted that his early lack of experience had produced a lower success rate with fallen women than that which he believed he could have achieved with the insights he had gained since. He wrote to Vickers:

> My real failure was that not until much later in life did I fully realise that many of these unfortunate women dreaded a return to normality. It was not only that they dreaded the finger of scorn pointed at them, but they actually felt a sense of shame in mixing with decent people. Only by showing them that decent people could be human, lively and gay and had emotions like themselves could they believe that they were not a race apart.[47]

Gladstone, like many socially concerned individuals of his day, believed that prostitution was caused by male depravity preying on female poverty. That poverty had many possible causes: unprovided widowhood, unmarried motherhood, rejection by step-parents, economic downturns, starvation wages; and all these factors were exacerbated by urban deprivation. In trying to help fallen women of any station, Gladstone saw himself as a mediaeval knight, attempting to save damsels in distress from the dragon of male incontinence. This was as true of his attempt to bring home Lady Lincoln as it was of his attempts to rescue prostitutes. Gladstone's Oxford friend, the journalist Martin Tupper, commented that, even as an undergraduate, Gladstone was

> in his religious outlook moved more by a broad humanity than by dogma. He is insistent on the need for more compassion for the sinner, and he could not, he said, bring himself to regard even the most consistently erring woman as other than one of God's creatures, for whom salvation was not only possible but an absolute necessity for which every Christian should fight. The Magdalen was in some ways a figure for which he has the greatest reverence.[48]

7

Daughters

A father's relationship with his daughters is one of the most important relationships in his life, and theirs. However cordial his relationship with his wife, it is in his visceral response to his daughters' interests that his expectations, prejudices and protective instincts towards women find their clearest expression. In the case of a politician like Gladstone, those paternal feelings subliminally influenced legislation on major issues like property, divorce, contraception and female suffrage – issues that affected all the daughters of the nation.

Gladstone was present at the births of all his children. From the start, he was determined to be a thoroughly involved father. When his first child, William, was born, on 3 June 1840, Gladstone made extensive notes of the experience:

> The whole day was consumed in a slow but favourable labour. Till 11 the pains were slight – till 3 quite ineffectual. About 7 ½ they began to assume the expulsory character. Praise and thanks be to God for his mercies to her & for the fortitude he gives her. This is to me a new scene & lesson in human life. I have seen her endure today – less than the average for first children, says Dr L[ocock], yet six times as much bodily pain as I have undergone in my whole life. 'In sorrow shalt thou bring forth children' is the woman's peculiar curse, and the note of Divine Judgement upon her in Adam: so 'she shall be saved in childbearing' is her peculiar promise in Christ. How many thoughts does this agony excite: the comparison of the termination with the commencement: the undergoing of another for our sakes: the humbling and sobering view of human relations here presented: the mixed & intricate considerations of religion which may be brought to bear on the continuation of out wayward race ... at 11¼ all was happily ended by the birth of a vigorous little boy. Catherine's relief and delight were beyond anything. She has been most firm and gallant, although not only Lady W[enlock] and Lady B[rayrooke] (the only friends who have been in the house) but Dr L[ocock] encouraged her to scream ... [The child] gave a faint chirp immediately on

issuing into the world ... He was declared to be extremely like me: with Catherine's mouth: he opened his eyes & looked deliberately at the nurse ... as much as to say 'What are you about'?[1]

When the second child, Agnes, was born on 17 October two years later, Gladstone recorded the process in less detail but with just as much enthusiasm and tenderness:

Catherine bore the last pain with perfect fortitude and I could not but observe how exceedingly beautiful she looked while this suffering so severe but without bitterness was upon her ... she has the higher gift of elevating this anguish, the burden of her womanhood, into a discipline of assimilations to her Lord. So likewise was her sense of the reward keen and strong: for she said within an hour she was ready to go through the same again for such another daughter.[2]

As more and more children were born, and Gladstone was increasingly *au fait* with the process, the reports of his children's arrival in the world became sparser. When the last child, Herbert, was born on 7 January 1854, Gladstone was *blasé* enough to record that, when he was called home for the birth, 'I had a dinner party going on at the moment: but F[rancis] Lawley stood in for me'.[3] But he maintained a close interest in all aspects of childcare, including breast-feeding and weaning, on which he corresponded with Catherine's sister, Mary.

Gladstone was a fond, firm and, by the standards of the day, fair father. He was often apart from his children, since Hawarden Castle remained the young family's base, and affairs of state kept him in London – possibly more than was strictly necessary. But there is no doubt that he missed his children when he was away: 'We have been much separated from you this year ... but such separation will soon I hope be at an end and will have on both sides the effect of making us the more glad to be together'.[4] They missed him, too. 'It is so odd to think we have not seen you since you have undertaken your new office', Helen wrote to her father in 1868 after he failed to return home from Downing Street for the first Christmas of his first premiership.[5]

When he was at home, Gladstone was no heavy-handed father. He encouraged his children to express their views openly, to the extent that visitors to Hawarden were 'half-startled and half-shocked by the freedom of criticism that reigned in the family circle'.[6] On the other hand, while dissent was encouraged, bad behaviour was not and was 'broken' if necessary. On 28 September 1847, Gladstone noted: 'A painful office to discharge – that of whipping Willy, for a kind of unruly attention with [his tutor] which was really becoming formidable to him'.[7] But, generally, Gladstone took great delight in his children. Seaside holidays in Wales helped to make up for his absences, and the older children often accompanied their parents on trips abroad. When they were together, Gladstone would teach them arithmetic, history, geography and languages both classical and modern. They would sing together, play cards and charades, go for walks and have snowball fights. Except when they were ill, in which event he was as attentive as any good parent could be, they rarely caused him any problems: 'No mercy of God is more wondrous to me than the absence of sorrow or anxiety about my children'.[8] But Gladstone also expected much of his children, particularly of his unmarried daughters, as his own generation had of his spinster sister, Helen. Marriage, of course, exonerated girls from all prior calls on their time on which, thenceforth, a husband could rightly make first claim.

For Gladstone, family was one of the three fundamental 'building-blocks' of the greater community. The other two were church and municipality. The union of families, he believed, was 'the basis of ... national felicity'.[9] That he achieved this within his own family and with his own daughters is beyond doubt. The question is, rather, to what extent he held them back in the process. Personal devotion to the patriarch, combined with the thrill of operating at the heart of perhaps the most exciting political family of the nineteenth century, made it difficult for sons and daughters alike to break away. In a letter to Hallam Tennyson on 8 October 1892, following the death of his father, the Poet Laureate Alfred, Lord Tennyson, Gladstone expressed his admiration at Hallam's 'filial career'. Hallam had spent a lifetime supporting the deeply sensitive Tennyson and protecting him from criticism. He had been, Gladstone wrote, 'a much more fine Aeneas than the original', recalling the eponymous hero of Virgil's epic poem, who carried his ageing father Anchises on his shoulders to safety as Troy burned. A 'filial' career was what Gladstone expected from his own children, and most of them would oblige.

One who could not was Catherine Jessy, the Gladstones' second daughter. In April 1850, Jessy became seriously ill with meningitis. After several days of hope and despair in equal measure, and with her parents in almost constant attendance day and night, Gladstone faced up to the awful possibility that his darling daughter might not survive. He talked about it to Willy, his eldest, then aged ten: 'I was obliged to put it gently into his mind how likely it is that he may no more return to Jessy'.[10] Gladstone returned home

> and found Jessy in a state almost hopeless ... Catherine perceived through a mother's divining instinct that her darling had begun to give way in the deadly struggle ... As the evening wore on all the signs grew worse, and our hearts again very sick yet I trust neither of us are [sic] so blindly selfish as to murmur at the Lord's being about to raise one of our children to Himself. Dr Locock's last visit left us no hope. [We] sat in the room of death and watched the beloved child in her death struggle, powerless to aid her.[11]

Jessy died, at the age of four, in the early hours of 9 April. Gladstone, usually so controlled, was overtaken by such a paroxysm of grief that for some time the household feared for his sanity. But, after a few hours, he regained his composure – superficially at least. He made plans to take Jessy's body back for burial in the vault of the family church at Fasque, chose an inscription for her tomb, and began to write a long appreciation of his 'splendid girl'. Travelling north by train with the little coffin, he closed the carriage blinds so as 'to have no other company than the thought of her who seems incessantly to beckon me and say "come, Pappy, come"; and of the land whither she is gone'.[12] 'The life of a child removed, transplanted into Paradise, at four years old, can but have been little marked', he wrote in his appreciation of her.

> Yet this is a deep saying: 'he is fully great who is great in love'. Now that is just the description of our little Jessy. She was great in love: and that which made her hard to part with, made her meet to go, to go to the home of love, to be folded in the arms of Love Almighty and Everlasting.[13]

Jessy was too young for her education to have been an issue; but, had she lived, she would have been taught at home like her three surviving sisters. While Gladstone's sons were sent away to school, the girls were educated, as their mother and aunts had been, by a series of governesses and visiting tutors. Of these there were several between 1847 and 1865, when the youngest, Helen, turned seventeen and was ready for presentation at Court. When Gladstone was at Hawarden, or the girls with him in London or travelling abroad, he would often take their lessons himself, particularly in Latin, Greek, Italian and Religious Studies. He would also set them little tests, sing with them and play charades. That the girls were educated at home was less of a statement than a convention. Primary education was not, in any case, obligatory for either boys or girls until the Elementary Education Act of 1870 established school boards with the power to make school attendance compulsory between the ages of five and thirteen.

As on many aspects of women's issues, what Gladstone thought of equal educational opportunities for both sexes is not entirely clear. He appears not to have become involved with George Lyttelton's work in promoting female education.[14] However, he twice read the feminist writer Mary Wollstonecraft's work, *A Vindication of the Rights of Woman*, once in May 1849 and again in January 1864, when he made some notes in the margins of his own copy. On the fly-leaf Gladstone wrote: 'The intention is good, and it contains many or some good things; but it aims by far too much at effacing in practical life distinctions which God, and nature his instrument, have made indelible'.[15] Gladstone referred to the work as 'Mrs Godwin's Wrongs of Woman' – rather unfairly, since Wollstonecraft married Godwin five years after the book was published. In it, she warned that society was wasting a valuable asset by restricting women's contribution. She argued that women should be allowed to vote and encouraged to pursue a range of career options, including politics. In the penultimate chapter of the book, on 'National Education', Wollstonecraft made a powerful case for educational equality not only between sexes but between social classes as well, rich and poor, all obliged to submit to the same discipline, and even to wear the same uniform. But most of all she championed coeducation.

> To improve both sexes they ought, not only in private families, but also in schools, to be educated together. If marriage be the cement of society, mankind should all be educated after the same model, or the intercourse of the sexes will never deserve the name of fellowship, nor will women ever fulfil the peculiar duties of their sex, till they become enlightened citizens ... nay, marriage will never be held sacred till women, by being brought up with men, are prepared to be their companions rather than their mistresses ... Were boys and girls permitted to pursue the same studies together, those

graceful decencies might early be inculcated which produce modesty without those sexual distinctions that taint the mind.[16]

Though he expressed himself uncertain of the merits of 'this scheme of educating boys and girls together', Gladstone wrote in the margin that Wollstonecraft's section on co-education 'on the whole I think ... the best in the book and some hints in it are worth consideration'. How much serious consideration he personally gave to questions of equal opportunity of education, let alone co-education, remains unclear. For example, a quarter of a century after his comments on Wollstonecraft, Gladstone, then aged eighty, gave an address on 17 July 1890 to the young ladies of Burlington Hall at their annual speech day. Mrs Gladstone had been invited to present the prizes. He spoke of the enormous educational changes 'to your advantage' of the previous sixty years. But he also expressed a personal warning. Anything which altered 'the Almighty's establishment for our constitution and capacities', which served 'to draw woman out of her sphere and expect her to exchange it for the sphere of a man, or to act in both, with the presumption that she can act in both ... with equal efficiency', this was 'a matter which in my most sanguine anticipations I do not think will succeed'. The universities of Oxford and Cambridge had opened their doors, however, providing opportunities 'totally unknown to your mothers and grandmothers'.[17] He wished the young women happiness, while clearly retaining doubts as to whether higher education was the way to achieve it. Throughout his life, Gladstone 'made it clear that to him personally the invasion of the university by women students was distasteful'.[18] That being the case, there was little reason to provide more than a decent smattering of accomplishments for his own three daughters, unless, as in the case of Helen, it was actively sought.

Of all the Gladstone siblings, the life of the eldest daughter Agnes is the least reported. This is partly because it was the least unusual, but also because she was the only one of the seven siblings who made a separate – if conventional – married life and family home for herself. Agnes was as beautiful as her mother but lacked Catherine's spirit. As a young child she was very good. 'Agnes has a gentleness which is very fascinating and makes her easily ruled', Gladstone wrote of her on New Year's Day 1848, when she was six. This was a compliment, but a qualified one, since one fears it may partake of *slight*ness in the texture of character: and since her illness her obedience has been less than perfect. When I remember that it came after a great battle, and that she was a very *proud* child, I have no fear but that she will have substance enough: and there is little else to be anxious about for she is a most loving and docile child, loving to God as well as to us; and she never *sulks*.

Not long before, Agnes had been suffering from erisypelas, a serious skin infection which can cause septicaemia. Erisypelas was a recurrent complaint within the Gladstone family, and a serious one in the days before antibiotics had been developed. For weeks Agnes had been close to death. The family were on a summer holiday at Fasque at the time, and Gladstone was not too proud to share the nursing of Agnes equally with Catherine, who praised her husband as 'the best helper anyone could be blessed with'.[19] Gladstone never shirked the physical side of family intimacy. He cared for his sick children whenever he could (though always deferring to their mother's superior wisdom) and was particularly caring of Catherine herself after childbirth.[20]

Gladstone's mother Anne had died at Fasque of the same disease as Agnes was now suffering, almost twelve years ago to the day. So great was Gladstone's distress at the prospect of losing yet another daughter, 'the struggle of death and childhood is fearful',[21] and so great his relief at Agnes's eventual recovery, that he wrote an inscription for a window in the Fasque family chapel, giving thanks for the survival of his daughter 'snatched almost from the jaws of death'.[22] He would remember the anniversary of her survival for many years in his diary.

Agnes was the only daughter to accompany her parents to the Ionian Islands, where, for a few months in 1858, her father was Lord High Commissioner Extraordinary. Her mother had suffered a nervous and physical breakdown following the lingering death of her beloved sister Mary Lyttelton just a few months earlier; she was also menopausal.[23] The foreign posting was partly intended to help Catherine recover her spirits.[24] Agnes was sixteen at the time and attracted the serious attention of one of Gladstone's secretaries, Arthur Gordon, aged twenty-nine, the son of Lord Aberdeen. But Gordon was an unreliable member of staff and Gladstone had him replaced. Whether Gordon's infatuation with young Agnes – to whom, to Gladstone's annoyance, he had even proposed marriage – played a part in his dismissal is not recorded.

At the age of twenty-nine, Agnes announced her wish to train to become a full-time hospital nurse. It should not have appeared an unusual plan, considering how much time she and her mother spent visiting and tending to the sick in the course of their voluntary charity work. But it brought forth an hysterical opposition from Catherine. She declared Agnes far too young for that sort of work. Voluntary nursing was one thing; but she may have thought professional nursing would spoil Agnes's marriage prospects. It was a strange and perhaps even hypocritical response, but Agnes accepted it with good grace like the docile daughter her father knew her to be. Two years later she became engaged to Edward Wickham, then Headmaster of Wellington and later to become Dean of Lincoln. At thirty-one, she was the first of the Gladstone children to break out of the immediate family circle and the only one to do so completely.

This time, Gladstone was delighted with her suitor. 'He is excellent', he wrote in his diary on 6 September 1873 after a private meeting with the young man at Hawarden. It was in Wickham's favour that he was a priest. Gladstone's second son, Stephen, who had been ordained in 1868, became rector of Hawarden the year before Agnes's marriage. Before he took up politics as a career, Gladstone's own ambition had been to enter the Church. To have one son and one son-in-law in holy orders was a source of great vicarious satisfaction to him. Two years after her marriage, Agnes gave birth to a daughter and William and Catherine became grandparents for the first time. The Wickhams remained close to the Gladstone clan throughout their lives but, after her marriage, Agnes was never subject to the same demands as her unmarried sisters, nor expected to be so.

Agnes's marriage in 1873 left Mary and Helen at home. They were then aged twenty-six and twenty-four respectively. Of all Gladstone's daughters, Mary was the most malleable, the sweetest. From a child, she had expressed a hope to be a support and consolation to her father in his old age. Aged ten, she wrote for his forty-seventh birthday: 'I hope, dear Papa, that if, please God, I am alive when you are old, I trust I shall be your hope and comfort'.[25] She was not to be disappointed.

In his 1848 New Year's Day memorandum on his 'great treasures', Gladstone described the month-old Mary as displaying 'a very placid, and I hope sweet (for it is not a dull) temper; and a great susceptibility to musical sounds in the most unequivocal way'. It was a prescient comment. Music was to play an important role in Mary's life; she once even played the piano for Franz Liszt, as her mother had done before her.[26] On Mary's first birthday, 22 November 1849, Gladstone added that she was 'the quickest and most forward of all the children at her age ... She has, thank God, great health, is like her Aunt Mary [Lyttelton] ... and it seems as if Agnes and she were Catherine and Mary over again.' 'She is the most womanish of all the daughters', he commented on her ninth birthday.

Jessy's early death meant Gladstone's second daughter held a special place in his heart forever; but she was gone. Eldest daughter Agnes would be taken away by marriage. Helen, the fourth and youngest, would steal a measure of freedom for herself almost while no one was looking. It would be on Mary, his third daughter, that the responsibility for helping the Gladstones parents would fall for many years. In many ways, it was the making of her. As a girl, she had little self-confidence, and suffered from the often austere regime practised by the Gladstone governesses. She claimed they treated her 'from ten to seventeen as half-witted, so I grew up as a non-entity. I have never outgrown it'.[27]

Although she was presented at Court, in the normal way, at the age of seventeen, Mary continued to lead a protected life within the extended family and under the towering shadow of her formidable father. A shy girl with a pronounced inferiority complex, she had few suitors, and dramatically misunderstood the intentions of young Arthur Balfour who was, in fact, courting her cousin May Lyttelton. It would be fourteen years after the Balfour disappointment before Mary again dared to commit her affections. In the meantime, she found solace in music, religion and art. Her friendship with the Burnes-Jones circle reinforced Gladstone's earlier association with and admiration for the Pre-Raphaelite artists and it was he who was responsible for baronetcies being given to Frederic Leighton and John Millais. 'Clever, inconsequent Mary – fully occupied with her music and her many friends', was how one eminent biographer described her.[28] But while it may have been her father's fame and eminence that helped bring artistic friends towards her, 'it was her own personality that retained them'.[29]

Mary was a shy girl of twenty-one when her father began his first term as Prime Minister in 1868. But when Gladstone entered Downing Street for the second time in 1880, she was thirty-three years old and confident enough to immerse herself in political life. At first she was daunted at the prospect of her father being back in power. To her Lyttelton cousin Lavinia, she wrote:

> Isn't it dreadful to think of it beginning all over again ... it makes me sick to think of, but I suppose one ought not to let those sort of things weigh at all. And of course I do feel that Heaven has called him back to this post, and I like to think of the whole world recognising what he is.[30]

From 1880–85 Mary acted as one of Gladstone's private secretaries. During the second half of the 1870s, when he was out of office, Gladstone had kept no official secretaries – partly as an economy measure – and drew heavily on his children's support during this period in answering the thousands of letters he continued to receive. It was a practice he continued when he returned to power: 'I have tried almost all my children [as private secretaries] and never with a failure', he wrote on 3 July 1886. During his second and brief third administrations Mary acted as Gladstone's political hostess – a role in which she was often supported by her Lyttelton cousin Lucy, Lady Frederick Cavendish.

As well as being a fond father, Gladstone was also a favourite uncle to the twelve children of his Lyttelton in-laws, particularly after the death in 1857 of their mother Mary, Catherine Gladstone's younger sister. Their father, George, suffered from manic-depression. In 1876, following the death of his daughter May, he committed suicide by throwing himself down the stairwell of his London home, the very day before doctors were to decide whether he should be committed to an asylum.[31]

Of the three surviving Lyttelton girls – Meriel (born 1840), Lucy (born 1841) and Lavinia (born 1847), it was the middle one to whom the Gladstones were closest. Aged sixteen when her mother died, Lucy spent much of her time after that at the Gladstone homes at Hawarden and Carlton Terrace, London. She was able to return this hospitality later in life when, as Lady Lucy Cavendish, she provided regular lodgings for the Gladstones at her own London home, just five doors down from their old house. Lucy, who in later life was a staunch Liberal activist and campaigner for women's education, married Lord Frederick Cavendish, the younger brother of the Marquess of Hartington, later

Duke of Devonshire. Gladstone had groomed Cavendish for high office more than he had his own sons. In 1882, at the age of forty-six and within hours of reluctantly taking up an appointment as Irish Secretary under the Gladstone administration, Cavendish and a colleague were stabbed to death in Phoenix Park, Dublin, by members of an Irish nationalist splinter group. On receiving the shocking news back in London, Lucy's first reaction was to call for Gladstone. Her second thought was that, since he had persuaded her husband to take the post, the news might kill her uncle.

> But then Uncle William himself came in with Aunt Pussy [Catherine] – I saw his face, pale, sorrow-stricken, but like a prophet's in its look of faith and strength. He came up and almost took me in his arms, and his first words were, 'Father, forgive them, for them know not what they do'. Then he said to me, 'Be assured it will not be in vain', and across all my agony there fell a bright ray of hope, and I saw in a vision Ireland at peace, and my darling's life-blood accepted as a sacrifice ... to bring this to pass.[32]

It was the moral and practical support provided by Lucy and her sisters, notwithstanding Lucy's bereavement, that enabled Mary to settle in at Downing Street. But she was soon complaining that it was

> rather appalling finding myself this time so much in the position of a 'political intriguer' ... People ... write me heaps of letters, suggestions, questions, things to mention if possible to 'The Dictator' as [Home Office Under-Secretary] Lord Rosebery calls him ... Just now I was saying to Papa I would retire to another table at the breakfast and he answered I was not to as Lord Rosebery would be disappointed. Mama said: 'Oh no, he only uses her as a *pis aller* [last resort] when he can't get our ear'. Papa was amused.[33]

Amused Papa may have been, but the exchange confirmed Catherine's occasional irritation at the thought of Mary's having any influence at all within the Gladstone circle. Even towards the end of her father's six years in office, Mary still felt that her life was 'a worse whirl than anybody's, and my head swims with the number of things to answer and dovetail. Sixteen notes per diem and everything pulling at me at once and all the time Mama thinking I have nothing to do'.[34]

In later years, her sister Helen who was to experience the same feeling, that Catherine undervalued the work her daughters did. Nevertheless, for the time being, Mary was delighted with the enormous privileges that came with her father's prime ministerial duties. Her new life gave her access to an exciting world of intellectuals and artists, for whom her unmarried status was a matter of total indifference. Her self-confidence blossomed as a result in proportion to her sense of self-fulfilment. She found herself turning down romantic approaches, including one from Hallam Tennyson in 1883. Hallam suggested that she must marry someone, sometime, but Mary replied that she thought it very unlikely. She seemed reconciled to enjoying the considerable benefits available to the daughter of an incumbent Prime Minister, spinster or not. Again this was not always a comfortable position for the ageing Catherine. In 1880, for example, she expressed a wish to accompany Gladstone to Scotland. Gladstone insisted that he would be living *en garçon* – as a bachelor – and that Catherine's presence would be inappropriate. But Mary was going; again, Catherine was hurt.

Gladstone resigned in 1885. He returned to Downing Street in 1886 for a few months, but after that he was away from the centre of power until 1892. Coincidence or not, 1886 was the very year that Mary Gladstone fell in love again, at the age of thirty-nine. The object of her affections was the Hawarden curate, Harry Drew: handsome, penniless and nine years younger than Mary. Initially the Gladstones were taken aback at the prospect of losing their principal helper. Even Agnes described Mary's marriage as meaning their mother would be 'without her front tooth'. There were those, however, within the extended family who felt Mary's new status changed little, that she was 'just as much Mr Gladstone's daughter and as little the Rev. H. Drew's wife as ever ... and I think it may remain so to the end'.[35] Mary herself described her marriage as a 'White Burial ... of awful overwhelming change', giving up her envied social and political status and reinventing herself as the humble wife of a poor country curate. But, in the event, she embraced her new role with vigour and enthusiasm. Religion had always been as important to her as politics. Just six weeks after the wedding, she wrote to a friend that she did not remotely miss the old exciting life 'and feel increasingly the wonderful snuggery and serenity of married life'.[36]

Mary's marriage left the senior Gladstones with a problem. In 1886, William was seventy-six years old and had just completed the third of his four terms as Prime Minister. He was out of office but had recently been returned unopposed as Liberal MP for Midlothian and Leith. It would be six years before, reluctantly, he would return to Downing Street for a final term. But there was plenty of work to be done in the meantime on the sidelines. At Hawarden and in London he needed private secretarial support. Both Agnes and Mary now had family duties that excused them. It was time to call on Helen.

When the Gladstones' fourth daughter was born in August 1849, they named her after her aunt, marking a period of relative harmony in the relationship between Gladstone and his sister after the turbulent preceding years. By then the older Helen had overcome her opium addiction, for the time being at least, and was installed at Fasque, running the household for Sir John, an increasingly senile patriarch. It was a lonely and depressing but worthy existence for Gladstone's spinster sister.[37] The absence until then of a new-generation Helen had been an ongoing source of tension between Gladstone and his father. Sir John had resorted to naming one of his ships after his daughter to soften the slight of her having no namesake among her many nieces.

Helen was a 'very plump and full grown child ... I thought promising in appearance', and she thrived. Her father was away from home for most of her infancy; but, on returning to Hawarden on Christmas morning 1852, he found young Helen not only thriving but developing the same preoccupation with orderliness that was so much part of his own character.

> It was a great treat on this of all days to find myself by force with my wife and children. I found Lena [Helen] the very picture of health and much come on in intelligence. Her habit of order is something strange. She had moved a chair to look at some things. We all left the room and left her in pitch dark. She began to cry loudly. When we returned and asked the cause, she said amidst her tears, 'I can't get the chair put back'.

Helen's early love of order would stand her in good stead. In this, as in many things, 'she was said to resemble her father more than any of his other children'.[38] For the time being, however, she – like Mary – led a cloistered existence in the shadow of their father, who noted with satisfaction 'the steady force of religion that works upon her'.[39] Helen was certainly quieter than Mary, but definitely no less clever, and certainly less daunted by the inhibiting effect of strict governesses. But it was

Mary who, after a visit to Cambridge, and perhaps sensing that her younger sister might have the chance to do something extraordinary, suggested that Helen might go to what became Newnham College, Cambridge. Nora Sidgwick, the sister of Arthur Balfour, would be her tutor. Helen had 'a keen desire to study, but no intention of reading for examinations'.[40] At twenty-eight, she was much older than the average undergraduate, but she wondered whether the move might help break down prejudice against the higher education of women: 'The fact of a daughter of Papa ... being sent here ought to have a good influence'.[41] And this seems to have been the case. A fellow-student commented, that, although (or perhaps because) she was older, Helen was 'kind and sympathetic and helpful' to others.[42] But, more importantly, the college itself acknowledged that it owed

> much to Helen Gladstone and not only on account of her personal qualities. In those days ... university education for women had not fully established itself as a natural thing for those who desired it, and was looked askance at by many, and to break down prejudice it was useful that a daughter of Mr Gladstone should enter the college.[43]

Despite Gladstone's views on the higher education of women, there seems to have been no parental opposition to Helen's move to Cambridge. Gladstone missed her: 'I lost good company', he wrote when she left, 'but Mary is all-sufficing in point of society'.[44]

Helen studied at Cambridge from 1877 to 1880 but without taking final examinations (or Tripos). Women were not permitted, in any case, to take full degrees until 1920; they could sit the same examinations as men but received only a certificate. Gladstone visited his daughter at Newnham in 1878, using the opportunity to catch up with various academic acquaintances. He also planted a tree at the college, which was uprooted by Tory activists.[45] He donated another Hawarden-grown oak in its place.[46]

Cambridge was the making of Helen: 'You see the change in her at once and I really think it has stimulated her interest in everything', Mary wrote.[47] After completing her studies, Helen was invited to become secretary to the Principal of Newnham, a post she held from 1880–82. Gladstone had no objection whatsoever to this appointment. In response to a letter from Helen asking for his opinion, particularly on the thorny question of whether it was quite proper to take a salary from the college, he wrote:

> Your plan ... promises to give definite shape and body to your life ... As to your earning money, that forms, I think, no objection. The real question is what to do with your money, earned or unearned.
>   The two serious points are: 1) the qualified subordination in which you will stand to Mrs Sidgwick and 2) the independence of your position in regard to religion ... Both these I do not doubt you have considered and will consider. You are quite competent to do it and I think you are the only person competent.[48]

Helen's gratitude to her father was great. On 2 September 1881, she wrote to him:

> If in my path of duty ... I am ever able to do any good, it will be owing to you in a degree far greater than you have any idea of. I am sure you do not know what a spur and strength you are to your sons and daughters ... In my own particular work it is always the greatest satisfaction to know that I have your full trust and consent.[49]

When Helen became Vice-Principal of the college's North Hall two years later, her father approved the appointment without reservations: 'Saw Helen on her view at Cambridge and freely asserted to her taking charge of the North Hall', he recorded in his diary on 13 January 1882. Helen's students remembered her as a deeply religious woman, sincere, simple and sympathetic.[50] She showed 'earnestness, eagerness and high spirits', but her real interest was in her work and 'in her students collectively and individually'. She was someone to whom 'when one was in trouble one could go ... and put it in her hands and it would be all right'.[51] But she never forgot who she was: 'One could not be ten minutes in her company without knowing that *he* was her father. Indeed I think one of the things that kept her such a very "unmarried" person was her ingrained attitude of daughter', one student wrote.[52]

A number of Helen's students were American. In December 1886, she wrote to her father, recalling one in particular whose touching experience back home she thought would encourage him in his relentless campaign for Home Rule for Ireland.

> I must tell you an incident about the feeling for Home Rule and you among and poor Irishmen in America.

My American student went home in the summer. Her father told an Irish working man that she had been to England. Had she seen Mr Gladstone? (Luckily she had. I introduced you to her in Downing Street.) Then might he see her to shake hands with her? So she was fetched. Might he bring some other men to see her? Yes. So later, quite a large number of the roughest, poorest Irishmen came to shake hands with her, just because she had seen you.[53]

That same year, at the age of thirty-nine, Helen was offered the post of Principal of the new Royal Holloway College for women in London. Her first reaction was to refuse point-blank. To the board of trustees, she wrote:

> I feel very much the honour that you do me ... but my duty seems to be so clear that I have no hesitation in at once declining it. If my circumstances had been the same as ... before, it would have been only right to consider seriously and carefully before answering ... But since the marriage of my sister last February, home duties have become so pressing that I have felt obliged ... to make arrangements for being a great deal at home, with the very possible prospect of returning home altogether next year ... I have troubled you with this explanation because I should be *very* sorry if I seemed to refuse so honourable and so important a work without serious reason.[54]

The conventional view has been that it was paternal pressure that prevented Helen from accepting the post. But her correspondence with friends at the time reveals that the reality was much more complex. First, Helen felt she had been given the job at Cambridge, where she had a wide network of people to rely on, only because of her father's name and personal contacts. Secondly, she had no training in educational theory and was unsure whether her management skills would be adequate for a major new project like Royal Holloway. She was also worried lest the Gladstone name was being courted for publicity purposes. She liked Cambridge much more than London, and preferred to operate within an institution where she believed knowledge was acquired for its own sake, rather than in a training college that prepared young women for examinations.

It was also true that her job as a Vice-Principal at Newnham was less demanding than the new one would be, and gave her the flexibility she needed to take time off when her father needed her secretarial support or her mother her company. And she had a strong sense of the duty she owed as the only remaining spinster daughter. She spent five weeks agonising over whether to accept the Royal Holloway position. But at no stage did Gladstone put any pressure on her. On 2 July 1886, she wrote from Hawarden Castle to her Newnham colleague and friend Nora Sidgwick (feminist, suffragist and later the college's principal):

> I want to consult with you as soon as possible about this wretched Holloway business ... You know about the offer and my prompt and absolute refusal. Then came a telegram from my Father ... desiring me to leave it open for consideration, and then a long and splendid letter from him, not arguing *for* acceptance forthwith but *against* rejection forthwith, and especially against the idea that home duties should either make me refuse Holloway or give up Newnham altogether next year – and my Mother wrote in the same way. Now this doesn't alter my view: that home needs make it my absolute duty to be – 1) where I can take a very frequent part in my home life and 2) in such a position that I can retire altogether if need be at pretty short notice. These two conditions are I think fulfilled ... by my work at Newnham. And they would be emphatically not fulfilled if I were to undertake Holloway. Whoever goes there must give herself up for a few years, body and soul, till the thing is either well started, or till she has shown that she at least cannot start it. She must give absolutely the whole of her energies, she must not be considered responsible for home duties or any duties outside the College business. You know I never get an *entire* holiday now except a few days now and then, as home life always has its duties. At present this doesn't matter because my College work is light and besides my home life and work is more delightful than other people's holidays.
>
> However, I must obey my parents as best I can, and so must try to consider the many different points of the business ... Of course I want to do right, but right seems to me to be at home or where I can reach home – then home rises up and says that's no argument I ought to consider.[55]

'Home' had done more than that. After his initial urgent telegram,[56] advising Helen not to dismiss the Royal Holloway offer out of hand, Gladstone wrote a touching letter to his youngest daughter, in which a father's sense of pride at a daughter's independent achievements bursts out.

> First, I had a thrill of delight upon this signal manifestation, this tribute to the work you have done, and the capacity you have shown for such work in a special and very important department. Secondly, a strong hope that it

might be found possible for you to proceed onwards, by acceptance, into a yet larger field of service to your fellow-creatures. Thirdly, a sense that the matter could not be settled without much consideration ...

We find that ... an excess of generosity, and a lofty regard to filial duty had induced you at once to refuse this remarkable offer ... It would not only be erroneous, it would be *wrong* were you to allow your feelings to baulk the purpose of your life. *Your* life has a distinct purpose. After all we have heard and seen, there can be no doubt that you have upon you the marks of a *distinct vocation*. That call is from on high and I really do not think you have a right to overlook, or not to follow the marks of it ... Were you an only child, the case might be different ... but there are seven, of whom four are married, and of whom at present all ... are actually planted at Hawarden ... It is evidently a case for division of labour ... it seems probable that vacations ... would enable you to take your fair and your full share.[57]

Helen replied that she was 'very deeply touched' by her father's reaction; but she repeated again her reasons, including the very private one that may, in fact, above all others have been at the centre of her reservations. She voiced her 'dread of leaving work which I have tried and succeeded in, for work which would really be entirely different and in which my capacity is quite untried'.[58]

Gladstone's perception of her work as a vocation and therefore worthy of support was endorsed by Nora Sidgwick, who replied to Helen that, in her view, a career was as valid a vocation as matrimony.

About home duties – I do not, of course know all the circumstances – but I do not think the question of a woman's obligation to her parents is so clear as you do. Most people think it would be absurd under ordinary circumstances to remain unmarried for the sake of parents ... I cannot myself see that marriage is from this point of view so entirely different from other callings in life ... each case must be decided on its own merits ... it resolves itself I think into a question of where you can do the best work.[59]

Through the early hours of Friday 23 July, Helen Gladstone drew up a list of the pros and cons of the situation. By half past two in the morning, she had virtually decided against Holloway, but stressed, 'It is not a question simply of sacrifice'. Before the die was finally cast, she wrote a joint letter to her sister Mary, brother Stephy, widowed cousin Lucy Cavendish, sister Agnes's husband Edward Wickham, and Edward Talbot, the husband of another Lyttelton cousin, Lavinia. In it she aired the problem for the very last time, and asked for their advice and a commitment to take on themselves the responsibility of supporting the elderly Gladstones, leaving her free to continue her career. If she went to Holloway, she wrote:

> I must not be *counted on* for any home duties whatsoever in term time, and must have *complete* holiday for parts of the vacation. My parents' strong wish makes it clear that I must not give up the educational line at present ... I am not much use to my father while I am in office ... but out of office, if he has no secretary, it may be different. I am not of any use to my mother at any time,[60] but at least I am available (even while at Newnham) for helping in all special society things, in all times when she is not well, and in all times when her duties take her elsewhere and she wants someone to be with my father. She knows I can come up to London any time she sends to me, which prevents her feeling that she has no resource.
>
> My parents do not wish me to consider them at all – at least each does not wish me to consider him or her. But that they are generous does not relieve me of responsibility: ought I to cut myself off from the power of being so far useful to them? Even if you would say yes in an ordinary case, is it the same thing when the parents (both great in their different ways) are people who have given and are giving up their lives for other people, and who though still healthy and young in spirit *are* seventy-four and seventy-six and, therefore, may very possibly become more or less infirm?
>
> To me it seems that, under my home circumstances, it is stretching a point even to stay at Newnham – but to undertake Holloway is *wrong*. But ... that is an opinion only ... and may be mistaken. And if the relations and friends to whom I ought to be able to look for careful and faithful advice think differently, it will be likely that I *am* mistaken, and I shall be prepared to consider my home duty objection is removed ... But they must be definite and explicit – so will you please send me *Yes* or *No* or *Decline to say* to this question: *Do you consider me quite free to undertake Holloway, so far as home duties are concerned?*[61]

Helen Gladstone never went to Royal Holloway. Shortly afterwards, her father made a substantial donation to the Newnham College Building Fund.[62] Helen stayed on at Newnham for ten more years until her father finally retired in 1894 and she returned full time to Hawarden as his secretary and companion in 1896. Hers was a poignant case of a career cut off as it approached its peak. But it was never Gladstone who held her back. It was her own – and possibly her married siblings'

– sense of a spinster daughter's role that made her choose duty over self, not her father's sense of entitlement.[63]

Working as his secretaries, full- or part-time, brought Gladstone's daughters into immediate contact with the major social issues of the day, many of which contained an element that today would be called feminist. As well as education, these included prostitution control, the age of consent, divorce, contraception and female suffrage.

In 1864, when he was Chancellor of the Exchequer, Gladstone fully supported the Liberal government's introduction of the first Contagious Diseases Act. He appeared to find no contradiction between the compassion with which he treated his own rescue cases and this draconian legislation, which forced suspected prostitutes to be examined and treated for venereal disease. He also backed two similar Acts, passed in 1866 and 1869, which extended the jurisdiction of the Act, which was aimed at protecting the health of soldiers and sailors in garrison towns and ports. And in 1871 he resisted the repeal of those Acts. In this, he was a serious disappointment to the leading repeal activist Josephine Butler, who campaigned for female rights on the dual platform of 'votes for women, and chastity for men'. Even in 1882, Gladstone thought Butler misguided, though he admired her greatly as a person.

> I am not sure that ever during my life I was so impressed, in a single conversation, with the fine mind, and the noble, pure and lofty character of a woman. She seemed to me one who wherever she goes, must win her way and carry all before her ...
>
> I can understand differences of opinion as to the soundness of her judgement in the line she had taken. At the same time it is indubitable that she was pursuing a purpose she believed to be one high morality. In that view she is sustained by some very great authorities.[64]

Gladstone believed that the extreme demands made by early campaigners against the Acts had been counter-productive. Their opposition had caused the failure of previous government plans to introduce a new Bill that would have mitigated existing regulations, retaining 'only one of two which were thought useful. These the adversaries of the Acts would not tolerate: and thus it was that the measure fell to the ground'. This argument – that a measured and incremental approach to reform was more successful in the long term than dramatic gestures – was one that would also inform his attitude to the introduction of female suffrage.

The Contagious Diseases Acts were finally repealed in 1886, partly as a result of Stead's exposé of child prostitution in the *Pall Mall Gazette*. Gladstone, who found sensationalism distasteful, read the reports 'reluctantly' at the request of a female acquaintance. Suspecting that the scandal – while justified – had been exploited to boost the paper's circulation, he expressed himself 'not well satisfied with the mode in which this mass of horrors has been collected, or as to the moral effect of its general dispersion by sale in the streets'.[65] But he was clear where he stood on the related issue of raising the age of consent, a child prostitute protection measure provided for in the impending Criminal Law Amendment Act. He wrote on 31 July 1885 to John Morley, who had asked

> whether I object to its being known that in my opinion the protected age might properly be advanced beyond sixteen in the Criminal Law Amendment Bill. I cannot consider that much weight is due to my judgement in this matter, as compared with that of others. But I have considered it as well as I could, and I personally should have been glad if the government has found it consistent with their views to name eighteen, rather than sixteen, as the protected age.[66]

In the wake of the 'maiden tribute' campaign, the Bill, which had failed twice during Gladstone's time in power, was passed and the age of consent raised to sixteen.

As to the troubled question of divorce, Gladstone was touched by three high-profile divorces in his life: the Lincoln, Dilke and Parnell cases. He gave evidence for his friend Lord Lincoln, whose errant wife he had failed to redeem. He supported, in a qualified way, the political rehabilitation of the Liberal MP Charles Dilke, who was named as a co-respondent.[67] And he refused steadfastly to be drawn into condemning the behaviour of Irish Home Rule activist Charles Parnell, whose long-term adultery with Katherine O'Shea (whom he married after her divorce) had been an open secret. Gladstone's critics pointed out that he had been keen to use Mrs O'Shea as a go-between to Parnell and hinted at hypocrisy. But, while he could be priggish, Gladstone was rarely judgemental. 'Because a man is called leader of a party, does that constitute him a censor and a judge of faith and morals? I will not accept it. It would make life intolerable.'[68]

Yet Gladstone remained personally opposed to the idea of divorce throughout his life. In 1857 he opposed Palmerston's Divorce Bill, calling it an 'ill-omened document'. The commission established to enquire into the law of marriage had 'not only not sounded the depths of this very great subject, but they can scarcely be said even to have attempted an investigation of its social, much less its religious, aspects'.[69] As late as 1889 he was still fulminating against it. In December 1888 he reviewed the book *Divorce* by an American novelist, Margaret Lee, for the periodical *Nineteenth Century*. (The book was published in the UK as *Faithful or Unfaithful*.) 'The greatest and deepest of all human controversies is the marriage controversy', he began.

> It appears to be surging up on all sides around us ... It is in America that, from whatever cause, this controversy has reached a stage more developed than elsewhere ... Many a reader on this side of the water will be startled when he learns that ... in Connecticut one marriage is dissolved in every ten, and in ... California one in every seven ... I understand that the experience of America as well as this country tends to show that divorce is largely associated with that portion of communities that is lacking in solid and stable conditions of life generally ... We must be aware of all sweeping and premature conclusions. But it seems indisputable that America is the arena on which many of the problems connected with the marriage state are in the course of being rapidly, painfully and perilously tried out.[70]

Gladstone added that it was 'with great gallantry' that the author of *Divorce*, Margaret Lee, had

> ventured to combat in the ranks of what must be taken nowadays as the unpopular side, and has indicated her belief in a certain old-fashioned doctrine that the path of suffering may be not the path of duty only, but likewise the path of glory and of triumph for our race.[71]

A few months later, possibly as a result of the appearance of this review in *Nineteenth Century*, Gladstone was invited to submit a paper on 'The Question of Divorce' to the *New American Review*. He wrote that, since the Divorce Act of 1857,

> the standard of conjugal morality has perceptibly declined among the higher classes of this country, and scandals in respect of it have become more frequent. Personally, I believe it to be due in part to this great innovation in

16. Lady Susan Hamilton, later Countess of Lincoln. Portrait by Sir Francis Grant at Brodick Castle, Arran. (*National Trust for Scotland*)

17. Harriet, Duchess of Sutherland (1806–1868). Portrait by F. X. Winterhalter. (*Private Collection; image courtesy of Scottish National Portrait Gallery*)

18. Queen Victoria (1819–1901), 1854. Photograph by B. E. Duppa, with portrait of Prince Albert. (*Royal Archives*)

19. *Lady with the Coronet of Jasmine* by William Dyce. A portrait of Gladstone 'rescue' case, Marian Summerhayes (later Mrs Dale), 1859. The portrait is also known as *Beatrice*. (*Aberdeen Art Gallery and Museums Collections*).

20. Laura Thistlethwayte (d. 1894). (*Robin Thistlethwayte*)

21. Women listening to Gladstone at a meeting at the Corn Exchange, Manchester, 1868.

22. Plate of William Gladstone, 1880s. (*Flintshire Record Office*)

23. Plate of Catherine Gladstone, 1880s. (*Flintshire Record Office*)

24. A London prostitute, from the *34th Annual Report of the Female Mission to the Fallen* (1892).

25. Olga Novikov (1841–1908), from *The MP for Russia* by W. T. Stead (1909).

our marriage laws, but in part only, for other disintegrating causes have been at work.[72]

These 'other disintegrating causes' at which he hinted are likely to have included birth control, a practice Gladstone abhorred. On 23 October 1888, Gladstone received from an American physician, Henry Sterling Pomeroy, a copy of his newly-published *Ethics of Marriage*. Pomeroy had asked if Gladstone would write a preface for his next book. Gladstone declined; but, on reading the text, he was appalled to discover the apparent extent of birth control in America. At the time, Mary – by now married but not yet a mother – was largely responsible for sifting through the books that were sent to him.

> I was at the time acting at Hawarden more or less as his Secretary; a volume was sent to him from America dealing with the complicated question of birth control. The daily postal arrivals were often to be counted in hundreds; it was my custom specially to look over the books that were sent to him. On this occasion, after reading this treatise, I sent it down to him with a note of explanation, telling him that views generally held and practised in America were by no means confined to that continent, but were prevalent in Europe and in England.[73]

In that note, Mary made it as clear as possible how very conservative her personal view was on 'the American sin' – she managed to avoid giving contraception its proper name – and looked to her father for guidance.

> Dearest Father, I saw that a book called *Ethics of Marriage* was sent to you, and I am writing this to ask you to lend it to me. You may think it an unfitting book to lend, but perhaps you do not know of the great battle we of this generation have to fight on behalf of morality in marriage. If I did not know that this book deals with what I am referring to, I should not open the subject at all, as I think it sad and useless for any one to know of these horrors unless they are obliged to try and counteract them. For when one once knows of an evil in our midst, one is partly responsible for it. I do not wish to speak to Mama about it, because when I did, she in her innocence thought that, by ignoring it, the evil would cease to exist. What is called 'the American sin' is now almost universally practised in the upper classes; one sign of it easily seen is the Peerage, where you will see that among those married in the last fifteen years, the children of the large majority are under

five in number, and it is spreading even among the clergy and from them to the poorer classes.

The Church of England Purity Society has been driven to take up the question, and it was openly dealt with at the Church Congress. As a clergyman's wife, I have been a good deal consulted, and have found myself almost alone amongst my friends and contemporaries in the line I have taken ... everything that backs up and strengthens this line is of inestimable value, and therefore this book would be a help to me ...

It is almost impossible to make people see it as a sin against nature as well as against God. But it is possible to impress on them the physical side. [Three eminent physicians] utterly condemn the practice and declare the physical consequences to be extremely bad. But they have little influence. If I quote them, the answer always is: 'They belong to the past generation – they cannot judge of the difficulties of this one'.

I would not have dreamed of opening the subject, only that, as you are reading the book, you cannot help becoming aware of the present sad state of things. It is what frightens me about England's future. I suppose it was a sign of decay in the Roman and Greek empires.[74]

The following day, Gladstone summoned Mary to his study at Hawarden Castle, as she later recalled.

A message shortly after reached me, requesting my presence in the Temple of Peace. Never as long as I live shall I forget the sight that met my eyes as I entered the room. My father was standing in an attitude of profound dejection by the fire, his head bowed, his face tragic. 'Mazy dear,' he said, 'you have dealt me one of the greatest blows of my life.' He then spoke most seriously and solemnly of the perils that beset the subject. 'If I were only twenty years younger,' he said (he was then eighty-four), his eyes flashing, his whole frame upright and alert, 'I would fight. I would head a crusade ...' and words to that effect.[75]

If this interlude establishes Mary as conservative, it also endorses the quality of her relationship with Gladstone. Few daughters, even in the twentieth-first century, would feel comfortable discussing contraception with their fathers. For Gladstone to have done so was no mean feat by the standards of any age.

As far as the issue of female suffrage was concerned, Gladstone had no sense of urgency. The impression is that votes for women was an issue he hoped would be dealt with by those who came after him.[76] He repeated often his recognition of the importance of the 'Woman Suffrage' issue, and the need for a lengthy and considered debate. But he also exploited that very importance as a reason for never supporting an appropriate amendment to the various items of reform legislation with which he was involved. At the time of his government's 1884 Franchise Bill, which extended the voting privilege to additional categories of men, he argued that to include women would be to overload the draft in such a way that the House of Lords would have an excuse to reject it. In this conservative move, 'belief merged happily with wisdom'.[77] Others have suggested that an additional factor in Gladstone's decision was his fear that enfranchised women would vote Tory.

On 13 May, shortly before the House of Commons voted on the 1884 Franchise Bill, Gladstone wrote to Sir Charles Dilke, President of the Local Government Board:

> The question as to the votes of members of the government on Woman Suffrage is beyond me ... The distinction [seems] to me as clear as possible between supporting a thing in its right place and thrusting it into its wrong place. To nail on to the Extension of the Franchise, founded on principles already known and in use, a vast social question, which is surely entitled to be considered as such, appears to me in principle very doubtful. When to this is added the admirable patent, nay the fair argument, it would give to the House of Lords for 'putting off' the Bill, I cannot see the ground for hesitation.[78]

Ten days later, a Cabinet memo confirmed that he felt the 'Woman Franchise' issue was too time-consuming and divisive to be allowed to endanger the Bill. The following month, in response to a letter from William Woodall, the MP responsible for moving the women's suffrage amendment, he courteously but firmly reiterated his arguments against it:

> In acknowledging the receipt of your letter, let me say that I am very sensible of the kindness of its tone, of the singleness of your motives, and of your thorough attachment to the Franchise Bill, of the weight due to the signatures you have placed before me, and of the just title which your subject possesses to full consideration at the proper time.
>
> But the question with what subjects ... we can afford to deal in and by the Franchise Bill, is a question in regard to which the undivided responsibility

lies with the government, and cannot be devolved by them on any section, however, respected, of the House of Commons.

They have introduced into the Bill as much as in their opinion it can safely carry. The introduction of what it cannot safely carry endangers a measure which the heart and mind of the country alike desire. Assent to such intro-duction would therefore on our part be a breach of duty to the Bill and to the nation.[79]

The Bill failed in the Lords anyway, at the first attempt. It was passed the following summer after significant negotiations with the Tories on the question of the distribution of parliamentary seats. But even once it was secured – and securing its passage was a pivotal argument in Gladstone's not including a female suffrage amendment – he took no steps even to stimulate party debate of an issue he claimed was so important. Despite this, the thorny question of female suffrage would not go away. It even came to blight Catherine Gladstone's only, and short-lived, independent foray into the political arena.

For much of their lives, Catherine was easily as popular as William with the people of Britain, 'her own commemorative plate next to her husband's on many a sideboard'.[80] Yet, despite her decades of experi-ence as a political wife, she had never participated personally in political activities until 1887, when she reluctantly agreed to become president of the recently established Women's Liberal Federation. It was a deci-sion made out of loyalty to William rather than personal preference. Her forte was hands-on charitable activity, vigorous fund-raising, or – in later years, when the children were grown – being at her husband's side on the campaign trail. Committee work and addressing large pub-lic meetings were not what she did best. She soldiered on as president until 1892, however, when her position was made untenable by the ques-tion of Women's Suffrage – and, specifically, her need to remain non-commital in order not to compromise her husband's position. The aims of the federation had been to promote liberal values in the family and the home, not to engage with the female suffrage issue one way or the other. As Catherine explained to the federation in her res-ignation letter, this 'bye-question' was not part of the association's original remit. The letter, its style suggests, was drafted for her by her husband.[81]

Mrs Gladstone's personal opinions are not favourable to the proposals now made with respect to woman-suffrage. But, having accepted the honour of the Presidentship of the Women's Liberal Federation, she has always thought it right to maintain a position of strict impartiality on this subject and she refrained from signing the Declaration of August 1889 against the Suffrage ...

She considers the Resolution of the Council in March 1890 to have been open to objection in tending to commit the Federation in its collective character: but she has not been disposed to make this action of the Council the occasion of any positive steps.

Any new Resolution aggravates this difficulty, especially if it should be adopted by a body larger and more representative than the Council. She would feel bound to record her opinion that such a Resolution seems difficult to reconcile with the impartiality of the association. If the question is one of free individual action, how can it be appropriate ... to instruct the members upon it.

Mrs Gladstone ... has been governed all along by the reflection that the proper and principal object of the Federation is that active promotion of liberal interests in which all are agreed; and it would be unfortunate to allow that object to be set aside, or the prosecution of it hindered or any scandal to occur, on account of the feeling of its members ... on what is in relation to the main purpose of the association a bye-question ...

If important, contentious matters, probably requiring time, are to come before the approaching assembly of delegates, it would be inexpedient for her to appear in the chair for a few minutes as she has sometimes done, since her retiring might be subject to groundless interpretations.[82]

Catherine had already declined to support a March 1890 resolution by the council of the federation in favour of female suffrage since 'such a resolution seems difficult to reconcile with the impartiality of the Association'. Her resignation was accepted.

Catherine had only recently stepped down from the presidency when, in September 1892, Gladstone received, shortly after its publication in Leipzig, a copy of Adèle Crepaz's book, *Die Gefahren der Frauen-Emancipation* (*The Dangers of Female Emancipation*). Crepaz was opposed to social and political equality for women as premature. She argued that, while the enormous progress made in women's rights over the previous century had 'tended to the culture and ennobling of their sex, and must serve to keep it from ... empty, vapid lives', there was now the danger of the movement's 'shooting beyond the goal'. The movement now threatened to turn women 'from what ensures not only their own happiness and well-being, but also that upon which the welfare of the whole human race is grounded'.[83]

Gladstone approved her sentiments, confirming that he, too, thought the time not yet right for female suffrage. On 3 October, he wrote to Madame Crepaz from Downing Street:

> I recently found that I had had the honour to receive, possibly from yourself, your tract on the *Frauen-Emancipation*. The German type is somewhat trying to my failing eyesight, but I could not resist at once reading it; and having read it I cannot resist offering you more than a merely formal acknowledge-ment. And this is not merely because my mind inclines strongly to believe in your foundation-arguments: but because, apart from mere concurrence in this or that special remark, it seems to me by far the most comprehensive, luminous and penetrating work on this question that I have yet met with. My great grief is this, speaking for my own country only: that, while the subject is alike vast and profound, it is commonly treated in the slightest and most superficial, as well as sometimes in the most passionate manner. In such a region it is far better, as between opposite risks, to postpone a right measure than to commit ourselves to a wrong one. To save us from this danger what we want is thorough treatment: and you have given it the most thorough treatment that I have yet seem applied to it. You have opened up many new thoughts in my own mind, but I cannot follow them out. I only wish the trea-tise had been open to my countrymen and countrywomen in their own tongue.[84]

The following year his wish was answered, and the treatise appeared in an English translation by Ellis Wright under the more anodyne title, *The Emancipation of Women and its Probable Consequences*. Gladstone's letter to Crepaz appeared as a foreword, including his postscript: 'For this as well as other subjects, I deeply regret the death of J. S. Mill; he had perhaps the most *open* mind of his generation'. There is an irony here. It was Mill who had attempted in 1867 to amend Tory Benjamin Dis-raeli's Reform Bill by suggesting that the word 'person' be substituted for the word 'man'. At a stroke, this would have extended suffrage to women on the same terms as men. It was a factor in Mill's losing his place as Lib-eral MP for Westminster at the next general election. He declined offers of other constituencies, and never returned to Parliament.

Perhaps the clearest expression of Gladstone's ambivalence towards the issue of female suffrage came in a letter to Liberal MP Samuel Smith on 9 April 1892. Gladstone hoped the House of Commons would reject Smith's Woman's Suffrage Bill due to be presented in two weeks' time. Ostensibly, Gladstone's objected on the grounds that the Bill excluded married women who, he said, were 'not less reflective than their unmarried sisters and who must ... be superior in another great element of fitness, namely the lifelong habit of responsible action'. But he had another point to make: the absence of a clear demand for the vote by women as a whole. Within his knowledge, he said, there had never been 'a case in which the franchise has been extended to a large body of persons generally indifferent about receiving it'.[85]

It was a fair point. From the vantage ground of the twenty-first century, it is easy to overlook the fact that many prominent and educated women actively opposed votes for women. An article entitled 'An Appeal against Female Suffrage', which appeared in *Nineteenth Century* magazine in 1889, was signed by 134 prominent women including the Lyttelton sisters, Lucy Cavendish and Lavinia Talbot. They protested strongly against the proposed extension of the franchise to women, calling it 'a measure distasteful to the great majority of the country, unnecessary, and mischievous both to themselves and to the state'.[86]

Another, unlikely, signatory to the anti-suffrage statement was social reformer Beatrice Potter (later Webb), who insisted that being female had never held her back in life. Nor did Gladstone want to hold women back as such. As he told Smith, he was not arguing that women could not, nor should not, discharge with complete competence duties previously the exclusive domain of men. But such a change was likely to have a major impact on public and family life in a way he did not welcome.

> I have no fear lest the woman should encroach upon the power of men ... The fear I have is lest we should invite her unwittingly to trespass upon the delicacy, the purity, the refinement, the elevation of her own nature, which are the present sources of its power.[87]

In his attitude to women's rights, Gladstone remains something of an enigma. On the one hand, it was his governments that passed the Married Women's Property Acts. This legislation enabled wives to keep the assets they brought with them to the partnership; it gave certain categories of woman the right to vote in local elections; and it enabled them to sue for divorce under certain limited circumstances. Yet Gladstone vehemently opposed the Divorce Act of 1857 that gave women an even greater say in controlling their own personal destiny. Gladstone supported the draconian and invasive Contagious Diseases Acts; but he was the very soul of kindness to the fallen women adversely affected by those Acts. He believed women to be morally superior to men; indeed it was to this higher level that he hoped to restore his Magdalens. Yet he apparently thought women intellectually weaker than men and thus unable sensibly to control their personal destiny. Why else would he fear that women's being enfranchised, and enabled to play a greater role in public life, would jeopardise their purity? And clearly he never for a moment entertained the possibility that some prostitutes were sensible, empowered women, making the supreme sacrifice of selling their bodies in order to feed their children, in the absence of responsible men. Gladstone was no supporter of university education for women; yet he was totally supportive of his own daughter's 'vocational' academic career.

With most issues with a feminist element – divorce, contraception, higher education, suffrage, Gladstone understood the way things were going. In his heart, he probably felt that if equal rights and self-determination were what women wanted, justice required that they should be given them. But, as Gladstone's revered St Augustine said, when he prayed to God for chastity, not yet.[88]

8

Harriet, Laura and Olga

The closest female friend of Gladstone's middle years was Harriet, Duchess of Sutherland, a grand society hostess and Mistress of Robes for all Queen Victoria's Whig governments until 1861. The Sutherlands were among the richest and most powerful Whig families of the day, and being taken under Harriet's wing helped smooth Gladstone's entrée into Whig circles. Gladstone's relationships with the women in his family, and his female in-laws on the Glynne side at least, seem never to have been less than cordial – except in the case of his sister Helen. But he seems also to have always needed something extra, a friendship beyond the ties of kinship. In the early days at least, Catherine was mainly at Hawarden, and much preoccupied with the requirements of her own children and of the young Lytteltons, the children of her sister Mary at Hagley Hall near Birmingham. Also, although she revelled in feeling herself connected with the centre of power in the country, Catherine had little time for polite society, salons and 'drawing-rooms'. Gladstone, on the other hand, once he had overcome the initial reservations bred into him as a boy, reservations reinforced in him by his austere elder sister Anne, came to enjoy salon life. His behaviour seems to have been almost universally impeccable.[1] It was perhaps precisely because he found amongst high society ladies an innocent frisson not available at home that he felt able to indulge it with impunity.

Gladstone had known the Duchess of Sutherland since the early 1840s, but only superficially. A grand-daughter of the famous Georgiana, Duchess of Devonshire, Harriet was 'large, boisterous and charming'.[2] She was only a couple of years older than Gladstone. Having been launched into society just before her seventeenth birthday, however, she married her cousin George Granville Leveson-Gower, heir to the Marquess of Stafford, soon afterwards. She quickly established herself as a formidable Whig hostess, whose standing increased further in the 1830s when her father-in-law died within months of becoming Duke of Sutherland. Despite her wealth and influence, the new Duchess of Sutherland was also an active philanthropist with a religious approach to public life. In this respect she was the ideal hostess to smooth young Gladstone's path into liberal politics through the contacts she helped him forge at her many soirées and country weekend parties. It was at one such house party in 1853 that they became close.

Gladstone was taken ill on a visit to the ancient Sutherland seat at Dunrobin Castle on the Moray Firth in the autumn of 1853; through this illness he came fully to appreciate fully the Duchess's human – and very feminine – qualities. Hardly had they arrived at Dunrobin on 3 September when Gladstone was struck down by 'an apparent return of my erysipelatous inflammations'. The condition, which kept him in constant pain for days, was treated by the Duke's physician by hot poulticing of the sore and deep lancing of the wound. It was the longest illness he had suffered since having scarlet fever as a child.[3] While he was ill (though Catherine was also in residence), the Duchess came and read to him, 'full of the utmost kindness and simplicity'.[4] Her kindness cemented a grateful affection that was to endure until her death. It was surely their relationship that prompted his comment: 'Friendships with women have constituted no small part of my existence'.[5]

The Duke of Sutherland died in 1861, after which the Duchess retired from her post as Mistress of the Robes. But she was an intelligent and resourceful woman, and continued to be a powerful Whig force even as Dowager Duchess. A little older than Gladstone, the undemanding solace, support and advice she provided may have recreated to some degree, in Gladstone's mind, the relationship he had enjoyed with Anne.

During the parliamentary sessions of 1862 and 1863, Gladstone spent many weekends at the Sutherland estate at Cliveden, and at their London home at Stafford House. An enthusiastic supporter of Italian reunification, he persuaded the Duchess to play a leading role in entertaining the Risorgimento hero Garibaldi on his visit to London. Garibaldi was reportedly the only person ever allowed to smoke cigars in her private sitting-room. The Duchess's sudden death in October 1868 – just shortly before he became Prime Minister – left Gladstone devastated. He had lost the warmest and dearest friend, surely, that man ever had. Why this noble and tender spirit should have had such bounty for me and should have so freshened my advancing years, I cannot tell. But I feel, strange as it might sound, ten years older for her death ... None will fill her place for me.[6]

At her funeral, at Trentham in Staffordshire, Gladstone was one of the pall-bearers for 'my very dear friend, whom I hardly yet can believe to be dead, so inaccessible to the last enemy appeared one who lived so intensely'.[7] The death of the Duchess created a void in Gladstone's life.[8] Into that void stepped Laura Thistlethwayte.

Laura Thistlethwayte had neither Harriet's intelligence nor her political acumen. Far from it. But she had other qualities that Gladstone found intriguing and beguiling. Like Harriet, she was beautiful. In addition to this, she was a woman with a history. Previously a friend of (amongst others) Gladstone's friend Lord Lincoln after his sad divorce, and of Arthur Kinnaird (Gladstone's companion during his Italian courtship of Catherine Glynne), Laura had graduated from prostitute to courtesan to respectable – though unhappy – married woman and, by the time Gladstone came to know her, part-time evangelist. As such, she embodied many characteristics of the redeemed Magdalen that Gladstone found so attractive. Did she decide to set her cap at him because she knew that fallen women, especially redeemed ones, were his weakness; or because he was Prime Minister and therefore a potential 'good catch'? The probable answer is both. He was kind as well as naive, qualities that she exploited to the full.

The exact details of Laura Thistlethwayte's early life are unclear.[9] In later life Gladstone tried without success to trace a record of her birth. According to her marriage and death certificates, she was born on 18 October 1831. In truth, it may have been a couple of years earlier. And she may also have shaved another year or two off for Gladstone, who referred in one letter to the 'quarter-century' age difference between them. Either way, she was at least twenty-two years younger than Gladstone, and therefore about thirty-six years old compared to his fifty-eight when their relationship reached its peak of intensity.

She had been born in Ireland, probably in County Antrim, though in later life she would claim it was Dublin.[10] Her parents were Laura Jane Seymour, an illegitimate daughter of the notorious third Marquis of

Hertford, and Captain Robert Henry Bell, a bailiff on the Marquis's Antrim estate. Her maternal grandfather had a reputation for gambling and debauchery. He was satirised by Disraeli as Lord Monmouth in *Coningsby* (1844) and by Thackeray as Lord Steyne in *Vanity Fair* (1847–48). Laura's wayward early years may be explained by a reckless streak inherited from her grandfather, just as Lady Lincoln may have owed hers to her own notorious maternal grandfather, William Beckford.

At a very early age, possibly as young as thirteen, Laura left Antrim for Belfast to work as a shop girl and part-time prostitute. She became the protégée of a Belfast publican who wanted to marry her, thirteen being then the age of consent. After a brief appearance on the stage, she left for Dublin where, then aged about fifteen, she earned enough money to finance a smart carriage and became involved, amongst others, with William Wilde, Oscar Wilde's father. She is also said to have had lucrative contacts with the viceregal court at Dublin Castle around 1846. It was also perhaps there that she first became acquainted with Lord Lincoln, then Chief Secretary of Ireland, at Dublin, although the thought of his being a client defies imagination. But Lord Lincoln was a deeply unhappy man at the time because of his wife's extra-marital antics that ended with their very public divorce in 1850; and he may have welcomed any female warmth of an uncomplicated kind.

By 1850, Laura was back in London and established in a day job as a sales assistant at Jay's Mourning House in Regent Street. There, in May of that year, she attracted the attention of Maharaja Jung Bahadur, the Prime Minister of Nepal, who was in London on a state visit. He reportedly spent a quarter of a million pounds on her, also setting her up in a London house; and, when he moved on to Paris, she followed at a discreet distance. When the Maharaja returned home, Laura stayed in Paris alone for a while before returning to London, where her beauty, vivacity, wit, recklessness – and outstanding skill as a horsewoman – endeared her to many a rich friend. These may have included Louis Napoleon – later the Emperor Napoleon III, and perhaps also her own half-uncle, the fourth Marquis of Hertford. The name of artist Edwin Landseer was also linked with hers: she is said to have helped Landseer sculpt part of one of the lions for Nelson's Monument in Trafalgar Square.[11]

Among her other clients was the wealthy young Scots Fusilier officer, Arthur Thistlethwayte. When Arthur was posted away to the Crimea, he bequeathed Laura to his brother, Captain Frederick. By the time Arthur died at Scutari in 1854, Laura and Frederick had been married for two years. There were hints that some great crisis had propelled her, a successful working girl aged only just twenty, into such an early marriage; and that the marriage, which started disastrously, was 'a compact extorted by violence'. Intimations of sexual coercion, unwanted pregnancy and abortion are all left hanging in the air. After a honeymoon on the Continent, much of it spent gambling, the couple returned to London, living first at the home of her half-uncle, and then at their own house in Grosvenor Square, where Laura lived until after her husband's death in 1887.

After her marriage, which remained childless, Laura's behaviour seems to have been beyond reproach. This encouraged her admirers to forgive her youthful indiscretions, if not her detractors, who made gaining access to polite society something of an ongoing challenge. But she was an ambitious woman; and, possibly as a way of gaining greater social respectability, she began to devote much or her time and considerable energy to evangelical preaching. Her success was mixed. Her presence on the podium – she had, after all, once been an actress – and her beauty, even in middle age, never failed to impress audiences and congregations; the content of her preaching made less of an impact. Gladstone himself, after attending one of her meetings one Sunday in 1865, commented: 'In afternoon heard Mrs Thistlethwayte at the Polytechnic. I do not much wish to repeat it'.[12]

Laura had been married to Captain Thistlethwayte for twelve years when she first made Gladstone's acquaintance in 1864. It was the death of their mutual friend Lord Lincoln, by then the fourth Duke of Newcastle,[13] that brought them together. In early 1865, Gladstone 'sat above an hour with Mrs Thistlethwayte: to speak of the Duke of Newcastle: but much also of religion, and some of herself'.[14] Later, Gladstone recalled admiring the fact that Laura made no attempt, at that point, to exploit the situation to create a greater intimacy between them: 'The modesty (so to call it) struck me with which, when I rather thrust open your door (I fear) after our friend's death, you did not hasten to call me in; it struck and pleased me'.[15]

By mid-1866, Gladstone's open partiality for Laura was already beginning to cause a stir in political circles. Lord Carnarvon, then Colonial

Secretary, complained that Gladstone seemed to be 'going out of his mind ... [His] latest passion is Mrs Thistlethwayte. He goes to dinner with her and she in return in her preachments to her congregations exhorts them to put up their prayers on behalf of Mr Gladstone's Reform Bill'.[16]

But it was the death of the Duchess of Sutherland, coinciding as it did with Gladstone's first premiership, that provided Laura with an opportunity she might not have felt able to exploit had Harriet still been alive. In the summer of 1869, Gladstone was having dinner with the Thistlethwaytes when Laura 'promised some personal history'.[17] Sadly, no copy of Laura Thistlethwayte's 'autobiography' remains. But her promise of greater intimacy marked a step-change in their relationship. Her ensuing autobiography, which Gladstone clearly found at times less than coherent, came to him bit by bit over several months. A cynic might interpret this as a tease on Laura Thistlethwayte's part, a way of drawing out and sustaining his interest in her sad story for as long as possible, in order to extract from it the maximum sympathy. Certainly, on more than one occasion, Gladstone asked to be given the full text so that he could read it in its entirety in one go. But he was refused. The courtesan in Laura was skilled in building up the tension by dropping only one veil at a time. Gladstone seems to have been totally oblivious to the web that was being spun round him.

He received the first instalment from Scotland in September 1869. A few weeks earlier, Gladstone had written to Laura from Walmer Castle, encouraging her to reveal all about her early life. 'If you will send me your work ... I shall read it with great interest; only I pray that, if it relate to yourself, you will send it all at once, or as much of it as you can, for I shall be impatient if it come in morsels only.'[18] But it was clearly Laura's preference that he should receive her autobiography in instalments. A month after receiving the first instalment, he wrote: 'I think you must decide between morsels and the whole. I told you morsels would tantalise, and they do'.[19] Laura's seduction strategy seems, so far at least, to have been working. Amongst other things, Gladstone's sympathy for her early life in Ireland seems to have been awakened: 'I am ... struck in no ordinary degree with the incidents ... of such a childhood ... and girlhood.'[20]

In the autumn of 1869 Gladstone appears somehow to have offended

Laura Thistlethwayte. One cannot but feel that a woman of her experience would have been made of sterner stuff than to be genuinely offended by anything much. Whatever the rights or wrongs of the perceived slight, Gladstone apologised. 'I have long believed that I was for many purposes the stupidest of men and I am confirmed in it by your last letter which represents you as unhappy and me as angry.'[21]

A week later, a coquettish Laura was raising the stakes. She asked Gladstone whether he had not realised her feelings for him when they met to talk about their dear dead friend Lord Lincoln. He replied: 'In my ragged letter of yesterday, I did not get through my answer to your question: "Had you no knowledge of all this when you came to see me?" Yet it may be short – No! ... I did not then know you as I know you now through your tale, and what accompanies the tale.'[22]

'Under the conditions ... with which life was given to you, you were sorely tried with storms commonly reserved for later life', he wrote. Four days later, having received instalments eleven to thirteen of the autobiography, he commented:

Could you really think the perusal of this last dreadful sketch ... could arouse in anyone ... had some stranger accidentally found it by the roadside, any other sentiments than these two: first a strong affectionate sympathy, and secondly a sickening indignation ...

I will make one remark. What you describe as a great and heavy sin of the child in the impulse of self-destruction did not, in my view, merit such a description. It was a natural recoil from unnatural evil in a creature too young to comprehend definitely the responsibility of this treasure and burden of life. Am I not right? I could tell you several things on the subject of self-destruction.[23]

This exchange clearly breached a defence in the relationship between Gladstone and Laura, a development towards which she had steadfastly been working. The very next day, Gladstone was writing to her as 'Dear Broken Reed' and 'Wounded Spirit', doubtless echoing her description of herself received in the meantime. From now on, he was to refer to her as 'Dear Spirit' in their correspondence for some considerable time; indeed, until her attentions and gifts threatened to become a public liability.

It is difficult to avoid this impression that a gullible Gladstone was being manipulated by a skilful ex-courtesan. The drip-fed life-story, the constant appeals for sympathy, even the conspicuously 'averted gaze' of the photograph she sent: all these were designed to bind an unsuspecting and well-meaning confidant into the web of a clever woman. Laura's story of childhood unhappiness, deprivation and early prostitution continued to unfold. By mid-October 1869, Gladstone had reached the seventeenth instalment of her tale.

> It is like a story from the *Arabian Nights*, with much added to it. And yet we have only encountered the tale of fourteen years! The poor dear child has suffered how sharp a winter within doors, before she was driven out upon the wide and wild expanse of life.[24]

In response to an apparent admission of sadness on Laura's part, and possibly to pre-empt the development of inappropriate intimacy, Gladstone replied:

> I must ask you, *why* are you sad? And with a friend's privilege to ask, also can I remove any of your sadness? I have given you nothing. Glad should I be if I could. You will give me only that which can be given while Faith and Honour can look on, and all that I may surely accept, and I do.[25]

In her next letter, Laura was clearly sulking, having again taken apparent offence at some note of levity from Gladstone, who was mortified. On 20 October, he wrote:

> I *hate* myself, when any word of mine carelessly or causelessly uses gives pain; I cannot be at ease until the pain is gone.[26] ... Do send me the naughty letter back that I may see *how* bad it was ... you would excuse anything if you could only see the daily mass of my duty-letter business, which exhausts the brain and makes me often hardly know what I write.

The following day, he wrote again from Hawarden Castle, one of many turgid letters attempting to unravel some problem, real or imagined, presented by Mrs Thistlethwayte:

> Dear Wounded Spirit,
> For twenty-four hours I have suffered the pain of parting; and very sharp it is. For I think the inner feelings of a woman most sacred; most of all in a case such as that between us ...
> Before this ill-starred episode began for me, I had (as I found) much more to say about my recollections and impressions of you, and about myself in regard to you. But I fear I must not now continue. To find fault I have ...

lost my title: something I wanted to say strongly in the other sense, but not beyond the truths, would now seem officious and fulsome ... I wait then until you see yourself, or infer from what I write ... the *aim* of the words that have pierced you and ... me through you ... Then the ice will melt, the wound will close, and you will be very patient with me while I try to give you further peeps into my unintelligent self.

The following day's post put him out of his misery.

Thanks, dear spirit, wounded no longer. There the letter was ... and the sight ... took a real weight off my mind and heart; that pain of paining, which I hope when it comes, will always be sharp to me, for there can be no sadder proof of deadness, utter deadness of nature, than insensibility to the pain we have ourselves inflicted.

In the same day's letter, Gladstone took the opportunity to warn Laura that he might not be what he appeared, and that she should not expect of him more than circumstances enabled him to give.

I will conceal nothing, falsify nothing ... but *make sure* that you know me. Do not take me upon trust. I have not sought to deceive you, but I am a strange mixture of art and nature. All this is egotism, but it is also duty ...

You must also learn to know the circumstances of my life; how my country is my first wife, and the exacting one, and how unequal I am in all things to doing what I ought to do, and being what I ought to be. You do not know the ill consequences of the exhaustion following on mental strain: how it disturbs the balance, to what dangers it opens the doors.

According to the Baden memorandum on avoiding sexual temptation, which Gladstone drew up in October 1845, 'exhaustion' was one of the main common triggers. Mrs Thistlethwayte is unlikely fully to have understood Gladstone's meaning. She was more concerned with revealing more and more details of her unfortunate childhood, and thereby gradually stoking the emotional tension until she felt sufficiently emboldened to declare her love for Gladstone. Gladstone didn't rise to the bait immediately. His initial response to her letter was muted, perhaps even a holding manoeuvre.

You have, with an unflinching courage, a tender delicacy and an unquestioning reliance, chosen to withdraw for me the curtain from your life and history. No stronger appeal can be made by a woman to a man, if man he be. It moves me.

It was not until the following day that he addressed the matter directly, apologising that 'yesterday, although I wrote much, I did not touch the *core*'.

> It is difficult: let me try to do it now, and gently. The word you have (on paper) spoken is a great, deep, weighty word. Are you sure you are disposing of nothing, but what is yours? You will remember what you wrote, well and worthily to me: 'Let not ... interfere or mar thy daily duties, and love to her your wife.' These expressions are just and true; and they have not one edge but two. You will understand: you will ponder: you will pray.

Laura must have brought up the subject of destroying their correspondence, since Gladstone continued:

> As to keeping, and burning. The story, and the letters of the same period, are locked up alone, and together. I think burning dangerous. It removes a bridle: it encourages levity in thought. Why should not human beings retain the means of calling themselves to account?

It was a noble sentiment; but not one to which Gladstone adhered in this case. In February 1893 he burned the earlier letters from Laura Thistlethwayte, lest their content should be misunderstood. He is also known to have destroyed his correspondence with two other courtesans, as well as one particularly acrimonious exchange with his sister, Helen.

By this time, Gladstone had reached instalment twenty-three of Laura Thistlethwayte's saga, which apparently dealt with her early days as a fashionable London courtesan.

> I cannot describe to you how, while the interest of your story continues in full ... it has in xxi–xxiii become astonishment, bewilderment! ... At present I think what presses on me is the query – *is this then the story of your London life?* ... you did not then know your own feelings. I am quite certain that ... you were self-deceived. Perhaps you *are* ... you did not know the meaning, or the full meaning, of much of the admiration. Perhaps you still have the same fault of looking at things in one of their aspects, without others.

Gladstone sought to reassure the attention-seeking Laura that she was different from other women he had met. On 25 October, he wrote:

> You were never to me simply a common acquaintance. Friendships with women have constituted no small portion of my existence. I know the meaning of the words 'weakness is power': real weakness is real power ... your tale

got within my guard. In addition to that, came the letters. I think perhaps too much about all this. But *no* creature could read any parts of your narrative without sympathy, nor some parts, as I said, affectionate sympathy.

In a postscript to this letter, Gladstone added: '*Why have you never asked me any question, except one?* Prepare plenty.' He also enclosed some photographs of himself: 'Be not angry', he wrote in a postscript: 'I thought they would have a good repelling effect.' They failed.

That day, Gladstone wrote Laura two letters from Hawarden Castle. The second was in response to her account of events in her life in the year 1850. At the time she was about nineteen, had recently arrived in London from Dublin, and was about to come under the 'protection' of the vastly wealthy Nepalese Jung Bahadur, whom she would follow to Paris that autumn.

> It may interest you to note the contrast between your year 1850 and mine. It was my saddest. The great Church controversies of that year ... tore me to pieces, for in them as in other things I lived intensely.[27] In March and April I saw a most beloved little daughter [Jessy] droop and die of brain disease ... and in September when you left for Paris I was making ready to go off to Italy in much alarm about the health and even life of another yet younger one,[28] spared to us, and now among very many blessings.

Back in Carlton House Terrace, Gladstone wrote again to Laura two days later, addressing the matter of some gifts that she had sent him during the summer and which she refused to let him return.

> I propose now a compromise. I will take and keep the ring, if you will let me return the others. A ring is a bond: and in it I will have engraved: 'L.T. to W.E.G.' and have the round (it is now strictly round) made the least touch more oval to fit a finger. Is this not a fair proposal?[29]

In the event, Laura agreed to her name being engraved on the ring with a simple 'L'. The mizpah, or friendship, ring can be seen in several pictures of Gladstone from this date, including portraits by Millais. The following day, in another letter, Gladstone revisited his desire that Laura should come to know more about him.

> It would not be well that I should say much about myself without guidance from you. It would all degenerate into egotism, vanity and subtle forms of selfishness. But if you by questions guide me you shall allow the innermost

that is in me as far as words can tell it, only be patient and very indulgent in the construction of them. Much do I need that ...

Very sacred, something awful, too, are the words you have uttered to me. I wish to feel their weight – and to do in regard to them as I would be done by; to treat of them if God guide me, with a single eye to your honour, weal and peace. I have not marked, and need not mark, letters as 'private' – the subject in that respect tells its own story.[30] But I can hardly tell how we are to get through all that is to be said when we meet, or (if you prefer it) when your tale is done.

Writing to Laura two days later from Downing Street, the Prime Minister wondered whether she might prefer to use an alternative word to 'love' in describing her relationship with him. 'Do not think the weighty word pained me. Its dangers, if there are any, do not lie on that side. But I wonder what is the one you would substitute for it.' As to her professed shyness, 'surely after all those letters it will not return', Gladstone wrote. He returned to the theme in his next letter.

Can you not understand my being troubled by the weighty word? There could be no trouble were it received with *indifference*. But considering what you are, and that I cannot be indifferent about it, I ought to be troubled: full of anxiety, care and hope.

Laura had sent Gladstone a photograph of herself – perhaps the one that illustrated her *carte de visite*, showing her sitting demurely at a writing desk. 'I cannot forgive your photograph for not showing the eyes', he added in a postscript. This was a bold remark at the time, when the 'averted gaze' was the proper look for a respectable woman.

The nature of the relationship between Gladstone and Laura Thistlethwayte, and her racy past, may at this stage have become a subject of public conjecture. Gladstone wrote:

Do though too firmly believe that no rumour, no supposed notoriety, would have made me dream you are capable of what was bad and base ... It is the weak and helpless ... who almost covet to find weakness and helplessness in others that ... may not be too far above their own level.[31]

By now, despite nearly three months of increasingly intimate correspondence, Gladstone and Laura Thistlethwayte had not met again before their relationship moved up a level. In early November 1869, Laura invited him to spend a weekend at Boveridge, the Thistlethwaytes' rented house near Cranborne in Dorset, where their mutual friend Arthur Kinnaird was also to be one of the party. Gladstone was in two minds.

> It will never do that months should lapse, after the end of your tale, and before we meet upon it. But I ask you: suppose I went to Boveridge in the company you propose, which I might very well do, how much time do you think would be ours for quiet conversation ... If I go, it must be alone, without a servant, and there would be a little time: but very little! [32]

In the event, he did go. And apparently he made no secret of it. The Earl of Derby commented in his diary:

> Strange story of Gladstone frequenting the company of a Mrs Laura Thistlethwaite [sic], a kept woman in her youth, who induced a foolish person with a large fortune to marry her. She has since her marriage taken to religion, and preached or lectures. This, with her beauty, is the attraction to G. and it is characteristic of him to be indifferent to scandal. But I can scarcely believe the report that he is going to pass a week with her and her husband at their country house – she not being visited or received in society. [33]

The Boveridge house party took place on the second weekend in December. On the Saturday afternoon, and again at night, Laura came alone to his room. She came like some Pre-Raphaelite heroine, with 'her hair let down ... it is a robe. So Godiva, "the rippled ringlets to the knee"', Gladstone wrote in his diary, quoting Tennyson. That was all he wrote. Until this point, Mrs Thistlethwayte's intentions towards Gladstone might have been given the benefit of the doubt. Boveridge made it clear that he had been playing with fire.

On his return to London, Gladstone developed a nasty cough (Laura had one, too), and was 'obliged to keep to my bed but [it] need not prevent me from thanking you for your letters', he wrote to his hostess.

> On the journey to London I thought of you all the way while [I] *made up* for sleep ... It is true we did not make so much progress in our conversations at Boveridge as might have been expected ... Why was it? The opportunities were perhaps not long enough: and for my part I was I think too well pleased with your trust in me to ... disturb the silent compact. [34]

On the subject of her autobiography, he explained that he was still unable fully to 'take in the whole effect of your disclosures of character history and the state of your mind. I sometimes feel spell bound by them; and I should like to have days and days to think them over, in all their meaning, before I could fully comprehend them or know what calls upon me grow out of them'. On the appropriateness of her declaration of love, he was equally uncertain:

> It may be long before I can resolve and satisfy my own mind on the question how I ought to have replied to you when you enquired of me whether I wished you to recall the weighty word. I *dared* not have asked you to speak it: I *could* not ask you to unsay it, when I saw how high and generous and uncorrupt a meaning it bore in your conception (this of course I saw at once) and felt that the only doubt was whether the reception of it by me could be in any manner worthy of its utterance by you. It was however and is to me a mystery and a marvel, out of which I have not found my way, and from which I am perhaps selfishly unwilling to be extricated, come what may of it, whether in this tumult of my life I may or not be able to arrive at a clearer comprehension of relations and duties in the intimacy ... between us, it will never be a subject of less than pleasurable care to me as long as you ... can tell me that I *have not done* and *am not doing* you harm.[35]

This was Gladstone's roundabout way of saying he hoped nobody got hurt. In his case, it was surely genuine; but even he must have sensed danger by now. Now that her life-story was approaching its conclusion, it was a convenient point at which to step back from the brink.

> I have been much with you in thought at Boveridge since coming away ... I wonder whether again, and when, I shall be in those rooms which were my home. The time coming on is a time when I shall cease to be able to give you signs of recollection, and can only ask you to believe, and I know you will believe, in its unfailing permanence. Bear with me one moment in reminding you of that on which we were agreed: that it is not wise to expose to the observation of others that which we know beforehand it would not be possible for them upon such observation to understand aright ... Remember me kindly to Mr Thistlethwayte and may I remember him as faithfully and honourably as you remembered another.[36]

Laura sent flowers from Boveridge for his sickbed, and Gladstone reminisced about 'a little group of images that dwell in my memory: L. driving, L. riding, L. in red, L. in red and black as she walked on Sunday. All these pictures are pleasant. I could expand them in detail'. He also seemed concerned again about her reputation; the sub-text may have been that his wife had become uncomfortable about her husband's friend.

> One word about the world. I do not mean to speak of you to others except with your approval and permission. Weeks ago, I could not help saying to my wife that from what I had lately heard I was certain you had been misconceived. Without entering into details, I should like your *leave* to say this more definitely to her: because I do not like that any such misconception respecting *you* should linger however faintly in such a pure and generous mind as hers. Will you let me, trustful Spirit?
>
> One word more, as post hour draws close. I well and thoroughly understood your question about the withdrawal of the weighty word and took it for what it was – a distinct proof of an unsparingly high unselfish feeling, and nothing else ... To say 'recall it' was beyond my power. But if I found it was working against your health and peace, and driving the sunshine of God's presence from your soul, then indeed I ought to ask and strive for power to say 'recall it'. Till then, or till I find in my poor self some equally strong reason, I cannot, I shall not.[37]

Over the New Year period, Gladstone wrote to Laura from Hawarden. The main topic was the public perception of their friendship, and what he could do to help re-establish her social standing – presumably as the grand-daughter of a marquis. On 3 January 1870, he issued a gentle warning.

> I will try to explain how it is that people have been led to talk. I was known to have been for some years, your acquaintance. It is now surmised that the cords are drawn closer, and are those of friendship. This I can never deny, conceal, or shrink from avowing, unless I descend to the depths of folly as well as meanness. But then, not to mere gossips, but to those amicable interested it is quite right that I should be able to hold up high your name and fame.[38]

He suggested trying to trace her family background, for which he would need her date of birth. One reason that this search proved fruitless may have been that she gave her age on marriage as two years younger than she was. In the meantime, he was impatient for the final instalments of 'your Tale', the pity of which 'grows and grows. My wish to have it all before me comes from this that I wish to appreciate fully its extraordinary character, and to see what lessons or suggestions grow out of it for me'.[39]

Three days later, the conversation again turned relentlessly back to the question of 'the weighty word'. By now even Gladstone must have been becoming exasperated.

> You asked me whether I had desired that you should recall the weighty word. I answered *that* (perhaps because I am too, too covetous) was beyond my power to ask. But *you* would be the first to say that you would limit it, keep it within the bounds prescribed by honour and pre-existing duty, and you could even teach me this, were I not sensible of it.

As the autobiographical revelations came closer to the present day, Gladstone also found himself called upon to offer guidance on Laura's unhappy marriage. Frederick Thistlethwayte was a gentleman of considerable means and not inconsiderable eccentricity. He was known for summoning his servants by firing a pistol in the air. (One August day in 1887 he shot himself in the head – possibly by mistake – and died fourteen hours later.) A question mark still hangs over the circumstances of his marriage to Laura, who had previously been involved with his brother. But Gladstone wondered whether the apparent respect he had gradually developed towards Laura over the years together might not help to soften her heart, if she let it.

> How strange it is ... On the one side a compact extorted by violence; followed by caprice and outrage almost to the death ... On the other side ... the great and formidable change in the sort of character which it was given to you to promote ... the corresponding change in conduct which has substituted honour, confidence, affection towards you for their 'loathsome opposites'; the high and ennobling nature of the ... union itself; the strength of maternal yearning. Is it *hopeless* that all these should act upon the bitter wintry frosts which originally cast your wifehood in a mould of ice? Does your vocation include this possibility? Has the recoil, born of the horrors of the case, been once for all?
>
> Forgive me, dear Spirit, if I have gone too far ... What I have now written has grown in my mind out of all I have seen, and all I have read, taken together ... I shall keep it for a few days to review it ... before presuming to send you these thoughts which I hardly dare to utter myself in whispers. But considering the place of honour, and knowledge, and more, which you have given me, even my whispers ought to be at your command.

After Boveridge, the relationship between Gladstone and Laura Thistlethwayte entered calmer waters. Their correspondence was still frequent; and to no one but Catherine does he appear to have written so often. And she continued to use a coded, double-envelope system which ensured that the content of her letters, if not their existence, remained secret from his private secretaries. But there was none of the previous intensity that had characterised their friendship during the period while she was revealing her life-story. This is not to say that Gladstone was unmoved by her physical attractions. He would continue, throughout the 1870s, to mark his diary entries with 'X', signifying temptation, after some meetings with her.

In early 1870, Gladstone had embarked on the second year of his premiership and it was three months before he wrote again to Laura, who appeared to have complained that she had become 'dead' to him. How could that possibly be, he replied; he was simply an old man with a job to do. And there was the question of protecting reputations. 'Place yourself in my position', he wrote. 'Become for a moment, me. What would you think and feel?'

It is difficult to repel ... the attachment of a remarkable ... soul, clad in a beautiful body. No matter that the attachment is upright. Whatever be the intention that it shall ever remain so, and if that intention be nobly fulfilled, still the hold taken is deep. Should I not beseech her to have a care? It may be that so doing looks to her like indifference. But then, like much else in this world, it will seem the very reverse of what it is ...

Who and what am I? A man who in December last year made up his tale of three score years: and, though the fire burns in me yet, forty of those years at least have been so laborious, that ... at no time could I be surprised if a sudden summons came. But suppose it will be the will of God to leave me here yet a good while ... my profession involves me in a life of constant mental and moral excess. I must before long endeavour to escape from it to ... the happy mellow of sunset. But your sun is yet mounting in the sky. Even in the body, your youth is not yet ended: and the quarter of a century, that separates your years from mine, is for the mind a life-time ...

Certainly we neither of us are of everyday composition: and our coming into contact affords matter for musing. But the mark, which that contact has made, cannot be washed out like the wave-print on the shore. Remain it will: may it remain for good.[40]

Or, in other words, he hoped they could still be friends. And so it was. Laura was delighted with his response and docketed his letter: 'This

letter gave me new life, more feeling in it. Oh, my Life!' It encouraged
her to write far more than he, given that affairs of state needed also to
be dealt with, was able to respond to. And she continued, despite his
asking her not to, to send him expensive presents.

Nevertheless, it was nearly a year before Laura received the next letter
from him,[41] on which she wrote: 'These first words of welcome being the
only kindness received by *me* for over a year. Oh! What I have suffered.
Thank God I can never again suffer *as I have done* ... He can *care* for
nothing of mine, for nothing from me. Oh how madly I love!' Ten days
later Gladstone wrote to her again, and once more he tried to persuade
her to salvage her marriage.

> The truest steps towards completeness of life for you would be any step that
> could be made *towards* a fuller communion in your married life ... Could
> not some ties be drawn closer? ... It would be a comfort to me ... had I been
> able to move you in this direction![42]

Towards the end of April 1871, Laura announced her intention to
travel abroad, and this seems to have been a critical moment of some
sort: 'Saw Mrs Thistlethwayte, who goes on Monday. It was the climax
of our communications'.[43] But by the autumn she was back, and clearly
intent on manipulating her relationship with Gladstone back to its previous intimacy with further details of her personal life. In response, a
bemused Gladstone wrote to her on 21 September 1871: 'So it was only
two years ago that you became at last a woman? I thought but a small
part of the experience contained in your narration had made you one
fully long years before'.[44] Clearly, with her history as a prostitute, Laura
could not have been referring to her loss of virginity, as Gladstone seems
to have surmised. He was clearly – and perhaps wilfully – missing the
point. Like many a man before and since who has forgotten an anniversary, Gladstone failed to register that it was almost exactly two years earlier that Laura had first declared her love for him; and that it was through
that 'weighty word' that she 'became at last a woman'. The following
year, Laura decided to go on another extended foreign trip without her
husband. Gladstone commented: 'It is well for me that she goes'.[45]

In 1874, when Gladstone's first premiership was coming to an end,
Laura seems to have had some qualms about the possible effect on Gladstone's reputation of their relationship (or perhaps she was just raising

the temperature again). 'If you are likely to receive harm from me, you must decide that we never meet alone', she wrote.[46]

By this time, however, there was another female interest on the Gladstone horizon. The previous year, he had made the acquaintance of the Russian Olga Novikov on the occasion of her first visit to London from her native Moscow at the age of thirty-three.[47] From 1876, Olga Novikov was a woman with a mission. That mission may, or may not, have included trying to beguile Gladstone, But if it did, the fault was hers, not his.

On 22 February 1873, Madame Novikov had sent Gladstone a translation of a pamphlet by her brother, Aleksander Kiréev, which discussed the links between the Eastern Orthodox Church and the Old Catholics of Western Europe. Gladstone promised 'to distribute with care the copies of the "Russian view" which you presented to me yesterday ... I know how well it deserves the attention of all who are wisely interested in the religious questions of the day'.[48] Following this, there was a flurry of letters over the next few weeks and months from Madame Novikov, who gushed: 'No matter where I am, [I] always remember the charming moments I owe you'; 'How I wish you were somewhere within my reach'.[49]

Olga Novikov's Anglo-Russian credentials were impeccable. She was also 'clever, well-read with a great knowledge of European affairs' according to Gladstone's son Herbert.[50] Herbert also described her as 'physically extremely unattractive'.[51] Olga's brother Nicholas Kiréev was the first Russian volunteer killed fighting in Serbia against the Turks in the Russian-Turkish War that began in 1876 and it was this that triggered her political involvement.

Gladstone's interest in Madame Novikov was primarily as a source of authentic information about Russian affairs, particularly in respect of the union of the Eastern Orthodox Church and the Old Catholics of the West. (Another of Olga's brothers was Secretary of the Russian Society of Friends of Religious Enlightenment.) But it was with the beginning of the Russian-Turkish War, which polarised political opinion in Britain, that she became more interesting to him. At its simplest, in the absence of any clear British interest in the Eastern Question, Disraeli favoured Turkey while Gladstone was for Russia, particularly in view of the Turkish atrocities against the Bulgarian Christians. Madame Novikov was politically quiescent in the early 1870s, wintering at Claridge's – where her salon was said nevertheless to be 'one of the most brilliant in London' – and returning to St Petersburg and Moscow in the spring.[52] It was around the time of her brother's death in 1876 that she and Gladstone renewed their acquaintance at a soirée given by Laura Thistlethwayte for the Russian Ambassador. Gladstone's pamphlet on the Bulgarian horrors seems to have been written partly in response to this personal experience of hers.[53] 'In writing this pamphlet, he was not merely discharging a great duty, a duty he owed to outraged humanity, he was also satisfying his chivalrous nature by supplying the best of all balms to the broken heart of Nicholas Kiréev's sister.'[54]

A copy of the pamphlet was sent to Madame Novikov from Hawarden, accompanied by a letter from Catherine Gladstone.

> My husband, overwhelmed at this moment with business, wishes me to write and express to you our sincere sympathy with you in your great loss; indeed we know what is it to lose a precious brother ... You will ... have read the answer to your question as to Bulgaria in my husband's pamphlets in the newspapers. England is at length roused from her lethargy; indeed it is terrible what has been going on.[55]

Gladstone's pamphlet had demanded Turkish withdrawal from the 'province they have desolated and profaned. This thorough riddance ... is the only reparation we can make to the memory of those heaps on heaps of dead [and] to the moral sense of mankind at large'.[56]

Gladstone's interest in Olga Novikov may have been strictly pragmatic, but his enemies thought otherwise. Disraeli called her the 'MP for Russia in England'; she was accused of being an agent for the Tsar, sent specifically to seduce a gullible Gladstone, and 'an extremely accomplished whore'. Rumours that she was Gladstone's mistress are so ludicrous as not to warrant analysis, except that they reflect the lengths to which his adversaries would go to defame him. On being alerted in January 1877 to a report that was circulating that he had written compromising letters to Olga, Gladstone replied that the extract sent to him appeared 'to embody one of those vulgar intrusions into private life which are commonly attended with unscrupulous rashness in assertion. That any correspondent of mine on the Eastern Question is in possession of such letters ... is entirely false'.[57]

It is true, however, that Madame Novikov asked unsuccessfully to be allowed to use the private double-envelope system permitted to Laura Thistlethwayte (who was said to have been jealous of her). And she requested from Gladstone more inside information than he was prepared to supply, as he made clear in a letter written to her in Moscow on 8 May 1877. She remained gracious. 'You are fighting again a noble and grand battle in the history of the world', she wrote back. 'May God keep and prosper your heroic efforts.'[58]

The journalist W. T Stead, who acted as Madame Novikov's agent and collaborator in Britain, believed that an Anglo-Russian entente was essential for the future of Europe because 'when Russia and England are at cross-purposes there can never be peace and liberty in the East'.[59] In this her role was essential: 'In Moscow she stood as the representative of Mr Gladstone's England ... In England the important thing was to convince the leaders ... that the Russians intended fair play'.[60]

Gladstone's stance earned him much hate-mail. This included letters expressing 'a fervent wish that Mr Gladstone's wife and daughters might speedily be subjected to the same extremities of suffering' as documented in Turkish counter-accusations of outrages committed by Russian Cossacks on Turkish women and children.[61] Notwithstanding this, Gladstone and Madame Novikov continued to correspond or meet – on one occasion in Paris – every few months. In 1880, Gladstone wrote a review of her book, *Russia and England from 1876 to 1880*, which appeared in the magazine *Nineteenth Century*.[62]

Olga Novikov never got under Gladstone's skin the way Laura Thistlethwayte had done. But she provided an alternative female correspondent to the extent that Laura became jealous. By 1876 communications with Laura had shrunk to three postcards. On 25 June, he recorded: 'Wrote ... to Mrs Thistlethwayte: this closes a correspondence affording much matter of reflection'. By comparison, Gladstone's correspondence with Madame Novikov was becoming quite extensive, certainly more extensive than Gladstone's diary entries imply. These entries total twenty-four for the twenty years of their acquaintance and that includes meetings as well as letters. In her reminiscences, Madame Novikov mentions having received around 150 letters from Gladstone until their final meeting in 1893.[63] But the idea that she was more than a well-informed source of interesting information seems fanciful.

Meanwhile Gladstone's offer of continuing care for Laura's welfare – and his recklessness in ever having made such an offer – were thrown into relief by the Padwick affair of 1878. Based in Paddington, Henry Padwick was a well-known horse owner, gambler and money-lender. Laura's husband was refusing to honour the substantial debts she had incurred as a result of her lavish entertaining and 'munificence'; and Padwick was threatening to take him to court. Gladstone was seriously embarrassed at being a recipient of much of this 'munificence', and tried, but without success, to return to his friend the many presents she had given him over the years. He was particularly alarmed to receive a subpoena to appear as a witness in the case, which, as he explained to Laura, could be disastrous for him.

> The witnesses would probably be asked whether they had partaken of your hospitality – I should have to reply yes; especially at luncheons from time to time where I used to meet some greatly esteemed friends ... I would probably be asked who were the guests I had met at your table. It would be offensive to me to detail their names as if charging them with something discreditable.[64]

Fortunately for Gladstone, the matter was settled out of court. But he was so daunted by what might have happened that he never again addressed Laura in writing as anything other than 'Mrs Thistlethwayte'. The days of 'Dear Spirit' were over; and henceforth it would be largely she who initiated their correspondence. But they remained friends. In later years, when the former Lady Lincoln returned to England, Gladstone sought – and received – Laura's agreement to take Suzie under her wing. Laura had been close to Lord Lincoln from the Dublin days when his marriage to Suzie was in its death throes; yet she seems also to have felt compassion for the 'bolter'. 'You have evidently been most kind to her', Gladstone wrote to Laura, 'and she is grateful in proportion.'[65] Perhaps Laura – a fallen women who had found in marriage a spurious respectability – felt some affinity with Suzie, a respectably married woman who had fallen from grace. When Laura fell ill in January 1882, it was Suzie who nursed her: 'a most available and kindly nurse', as Gladstone described her.[66] By the early 1880s, Laura had taken possession of Woodbine Cottage in Hampstead. Gladstone dined there with her and her husband on New Year's Day 1884. In July of the following year, she reminded him that they had known each other for over twenty years, to which he replied:

> How little I have used those twenty years in friendly office. They have been marked by your confidence and kindnesses; on my side, how near they are to a blank so far as regards any return that might be worth remembering for good ... I had always hoped to be of some use, but I am afraid even your charity and kindness can hardly think the hope has been fulfilled![67]

The relationship remained close. On 21 July 1886, Gladstone wrote to Laura: 'Well, as to authentic news? We have resigned'. At this point, the only other person who knew that was Queen Victoria.

In May 1887, just weeks before Captain Thistlethwayte's fatal accident, Catherine Gladstone was at last introduced to the woman who had been her husband's close acquaintance for so long. Together they visited on a number of subsequent occasions. On Frederick Thistlethwayte's death, Gladstone wrote to Laura to say that he was thinking of her and 'of this great transition of life that must be before you. I have hope that some of your younger friends may gather round you. [He was seventy-seven at this point, she around fifty-six] ... My anticipation, as well as wish for you, is that so far as temporal affairs are concerned, he will have left behind him everything straight – well adjusted and easy. He always seemed to be one who so well understood his concerns ... my wife joins me in all my feelings'.[68]

Six years later, on 25 February 1893, Gladstone burned his box of Mrs Thistlethwayte's older letters. 'I had marked them to be returned but I do not now know what would become of them. They would lead to misapprehension: it was in main a one-sided correspondence: not easy to understand.' He also returned the manuscript of her autobiography, adding: 'in view of my years, it is better lodged with you than me'.

9

Victoria

It was a mixed blessing for Gladstone when, at the age of eighty-two, he achieved a triumphant return to the premiership for a fourth and final period of office. Catherine, ambitious as ever, was keen for him to return to the centre of power, but personally he was less than enthusiastic. He agreed to take the job only because there was no one else in his party who could do it. Queen Victoria was less than delighted. Victoria's opinion of Gladstone at this time has entered history as typical of the animosity that characterised the latter part of the relationship between the sovereign and the statesman. But is far from being the whole story.

It is true that Victoria complained that Gladstone addressed her as if she were a public meeting. Gladstone, on the other hand, grumbled that the Queen treated him like a common tradesman. She called her Prime Minister mad and wicked, 'wild and incomprehensible';[1] he insisted the Queen was enough to kill any man. The tension that existed between these two great icons of nineteenth-century Britain has achieved cliché status with time. But their relationship was not always so fraught. Nor was their dislike always mutual. Indeed for Gladstone, a fervent royalist, his failure to achieve a close relationship with the Queen was more a source of sadness and frustration. In the early years, particularly when the Prince Consort was still alive, they got along tolerably well. The real disintegration began in 1874, when Benjamin Disraeli took over from Gladstone as Prime Minister. For Disraeli, Gladstone was an impetuous, pompous, long-winded hypocrite. Gladstone thought his political archrival a dishonest flunky, the 'artful dodger' of contemporary politics. But it was Disraeli who won the heart of the woman he called his Faery Queen; and who spent six years in government charming Victoria into believing she was, in fact, a Tory. This was the cross Gladstone would have to bear when he returned to power after Disraeli in 1880.

Yet Gladstone and Victoria shared many fundamental values. Duty, honesty, integrity, morality, order, a sense of family and a sense of nationhood: these were equally important to both of them. Both were also opinionated, nervous, excitable and stubborn; and both demonstrated at times an obsessive, controlling streak. Both their marriages, though of differing duration, were happy; both had strong affinities with the opposite sex, although they remained uncomfortable with the demands of so-called polite society. There were family links, as well, that bound them. Catherine Gladstone's sister Mary was married to George, the eldest son of Sarah, Lady Lyttelton, a favourite royal lady-in-waiting, and later supervisor of the royal nursery. Gladstone's great friend and confidante Harriet, Duchess of Sutherland, was Mistress of the Robes under all Victoria's Whig governments until 1861. All these factors made the falling out between Victoria and Gladstone in later years that much more surprising.

Victoria also liked Catherine Gladstone. At the time of Gladstone's final retirement in 1894, it was the Queen who comforted a sobbing Catherine when she and William took their official leave of the sovereign for the last time at Windsor Castle. She accepted Catherine's tearful reassurance that her husband had acted at all times with the Queen's interest at heart. As a young princess, Victoria had first met Catherine and Mary Glynne, who were a few years her senior, on a visit to the Glynne family home at Hawarden Castle with her mother, the Duchess of Kent, in 1832 – long before Gladstone came on the scene. She met them again three years later at York where, as she reminded Catherine in old age, 'I saw the two very beautiful Glynne sisters, and have not forgotten it'.[2] The sisters, recently presented at Court, also attended the Queen's coronation in 1838. Victoria and Albert married a few months after Catherine and Mary wed William and George in 1839; and the young wives – and soon, young mothers – found much to gossip about at dinner parties and card tables at Buckingham Palace. Catherine was invited to bring the little Gladstones to play with the royal children at Windsor. Throughout their fifty years' acquaintance, Catherine and Victoria exchanged affectionate, if inconsequential, letters about children, betrothals, weddings, fashions and the like. But these letters became fewer after the death of the Prince Consort, and fewer still after Disraeli became Prime Minister.

If the Queen recalled exactly her earliest meeting with Catherine, the first time that she met her future Prime Minister was, by comparison, an unexceptional experience. Neither mentioned the other at all in their journal entries. Their first encounter was on 28 May 1834, when Gladstone merely wrote in his diary: 'At the Drawing room – 3¾ hours; 2¼ to 6, nearly'.³ The 'drawing room' in question was an event hosted by Queen Adelaide at St James's Palace to celebrate the birthday of King William IV. Gladstone and Victoria met again a year later, on 4 May 1835. Gladstone recorded his visit to the home of Victoria and her mother, the Duchess of Kent, without enthusiasm or comment: 'at Kensington Palace in evg. – What am I, to walk there?' On Victoria's accession to the throne in 1837, Gladstone visited St James's Palace on 14 July to present the Oxford University address, briefly noting that he 'went up with Oxford Address: an interesting occasion'.⁴ Nor did Victoria mention him in her own journal, remarking only that the event was well attended, the room very hot, and her Garter mantle of blue velvet lined with white silk, and that Prime Minister Lord Melbourne, who read her speech, was 'distinguished by so much good feeling'.⁵ On the first recorded occasion when the Queen invited the young Gladstone couple to dine at Windsor Castle, she commented again on Catherine's charm – but said nothing about her husband.

Although their first impressions of each other were unspectacular, the prospects seemed set nevertheless for Gladstone to become a modest royal favourite. The young Queen was fond of William's wife; and her husband, Prince Albert, was fond of Catherine's husband. Albert, whose opinions were to define Victoria's actions for the rest of her life, both admired Gladstone's moral character and enjoyed his acquaintance. The two men corresponded regularly, exchanging cuttings from various, often obscure, continental journals. Albert chose Gladstone's eldest son, Willie, to travel to the Continent with the Prince of Wales in 1857. And the memory of Albert's preferences lingered on. As late as September 1868, seven years after the Prince Consort's death, the Queen was still echoing her late husband's opinion in her journal and writing positively about Gladstone after a dinner at Balmoral: 'He is very agreeable, so quiet and intellectual, with such a knowledge of all subjects, and is such a *good* man'. Albert had clearly identified sterling qualities behind Gladstone's sometimes offputting exterior – and probably the same was true

in reverse. But credit must also be given to Catherine's efforts at tutor-
ing her husband in how to handle Victoria. When he was visiting the
Queen at Windsor in October 1862, Catherine wrote to her husband that
she hoped he could be a comfort to 'that darling Queen'. 'You will take
in that this is nearly the anniversary of our visit, when all was still
bright ... Now, contrary to your ways, do pet the Queen, and for once
believe you can, dear old thing.'[6]

At the beginning of their relationship, Gladstone appears to have been
someone with whom the Queen felt comfortable. His family credentials
were impeccable, the Prince Consort approved, and Gladstone, like the
Queen, was still, at this stage, politically conservative. One of the com-
plications of their relationship was to be that the Queen became more
conservative with time, while Gladstone became more radical. But in the
early days, at least, she was at ease with him. She had grown out of her
penchant for raffish old men like Melbourne, her first mentor on
becoming Queen. Disraeli had not yet begun to weave his spell. Gladstone, with his cultivated tastes, measured views and delightful young
wife, seemed in harmony with the atmosphere at Court. Yet, even before
Disraeli's influence began in the mid-1870s to change things dramatically and permanently, there were early warnings of a subtle change in
the popularity of the monarchy at the very time when Gladstone's public standing was growing. On 14 December 1861 Prince Albert died, a few
months after the Queen's mother. This should not in itself have altered
her feelings for her then Chancellor of the Exchequer: Victoria always
considered what Albert would have done to be the grounds for her own
actions. And the Queen expressed herself 'touched and gratified' by a
speech that Gladstone gave at Manchester the year after the death of the
Prince Consort, which 'well described the love that bound and binds the
poor, broken-hearted Queen to that adored and perfect Being who was
and is her All – but without whom life is utter darkness'. She added that
'Mrs Gladstone who the Queen knows is a most tender wife – may – in
a faint measure picture to herself what the Queen suffers'.[7]

With Albert's death began a protracted mourning that kept the
Queen out of public view for much of the next twenty years. But, for
the rest of the world, life carried on.[8] This coincided with a steady
increase in Gladstone's popularity. He was Chancellor of the Exchequer
almost continuously from 1852 to 1866, and Prime Minister from

1868–74; he followed Disraeli back to the premiership again in 1880, a post he assumed yet again in 1886 and, finally, in 1892. It was during Victoria's semi-retirement that Gladstone emerged as 'the People's William'. He began to discover his popular appeal in early 1862, when he travelled to Lancashire to establish the impact on the region's cotton-processing industries of the American Civil War, and the attendant drop in exports of raw cotton to Britain. It was, in effect, the first time that he had been outside the rarefied atmosphere of the capital on office business, and he found himself exposed to the feelings of the ordinary British working man. As he proceeded on to what proved to be a triumphal visit to Newcastle, he found a wider audience than he had ever known. He sensed that the people of England were eagerly waiting for him to speak to them. His sympathy reached out to them, they responded – and in the process Gladstone found his voice. An insecure person by nature, it would be surprising if the reclusive Victoria had not resented the nation's growing affection for Gladstone.

Despite this, their personal association remained cordial enough. When Gladstone became Prime Minister for the first time in 1868, the Queen offered the use of Abergeldie Castle, a tower house two miles east of Balmoral, for an autumn holiday. And the family links remained close. Catherine and William visited Windsor Castle in 1870 with their eldest daughter, after which the Queen wrote that she 'thinks Mr Gladstone will not be displeased at her saying what a charming girl Agnes is'.[9] Gladstone replied that 'the recollection of Your Majesty's kind words about his daughter will be to his wife and himself a lifelong pleasure'.[10]

That same year the Franco-Prussian War broke out and Victoria, whose eldest daughter Vicky had married the Prussian Crown Prince Frederick (who finally became Emperor of Germany in 1888),[11] was impressed at the Gladstone's discreet, non-partisan stance on the conflict, finding him 'most prudent and yet civil and kind for he has managed to say nothing yet to be very full of sympathy'.[12] Yet still her claims of ill health and bad nerves continued to keep the grieving widow away from public view. As early as 1852, when Albert was still alive, she had insisted that women were not fitted to reign if they were also expected to be good, feminine, amiable and domestic. In the summer of 1871, ten years after Albert's death, she was still complaining that too much was expected of her, being a woman. Asked to stay in London until the Prorogation of Parliament, she insisted that she was being exploited by her ministers for party political purposes, and that this must stop.

> She has opened Parliament this year and the fatigue and trouble of Princess Louise's marriage, held all her Drawing-rooms, Investitures – councils – received all the Royal Visitors who came, held two Reviews, and went to two public breakfasts, besides opening the Albert Hall and St Thomas' Hospital. All these have been done in one year & the Queen would really ask what right anyone has to complain.
>
> [The Ministers] should also plainly state that the Queen cannot undertake any night work in hot rooms and when much talking is required, nor any residence in London beyond two or three days at a time as the air, noise and excitement make her quite ill, cause violent headaches & great prostration.
>
> It is really abominable that a woman, a Queen, loaded with care and anxieties, public and domestic which are daily increasing should be unable to make people understand that there are limits to her powers.
>
> What killed her beloved Husband? Overwork and worry . . . and the Queen, a woman, no longer young is supposed to be proof against all and to be driven and abused until her nerves and health will give way with this worry and agitation and interference in her private life.
>
> She must solemnly repeat that unless her ministers support her . . . she cannot go on & must give her heavy burden up to younger hands.
>
> Perhaps then those discontented people may regret that they broke her down when she might still have been of use.[13]

Gladstone would have been the first to sympathise with nervous prostration – from personal experience he knew its devastating effects well. But the Queen was ill-advised in pleading overwork to one who worked as hard as he or to hide behind her gender. To the Queen he replied that he was

> deeply sensible of the arduous nature of the charge to which Your Majesty has been called, and of the many limitations which such a charge imposes on the freedom of a Sovereign while large numbers of her subjects are free of them. He will venture to add that he never personally receives Your Majesty's gracious courtesies without a sense of regret that he should himself occupy any portion of the time and care which he knows to be so precious.[14]

Privately, Gladstone was writing to Henry Ponsonby, the Queen's Private Secretary, that he was 'surprised and sorry, that the Queen should think that we have had really in our minds, during this deplorable business, the benefit of the Government'. Personally, he was more concerned about the consequences of the monarch's reluctance to carry out her royal duties to the extent that the public expected. The twin clouds of revolution and republicanism that hovered over the Continent can hardly have been far from his mind. And he, who held himself answerable to his Maker for every minute of every day, will have felt little sympathy with the Queen's self-indulgent reluctance to do what the country was entitled to expect. 'Upon the whole I think it has been the most sickening piece of experience which I have had during near forty years of public life', he wrote. 'Worse things may easily be imagined: but smaller and meaner cause for the decay of Thrones cannot be conceived ... it is like the worm which bores the bark of a noble tree and so breaks the channel of its life.'[15]

As to the female dimension she claimed for her incapacity, Gladstone had written privately two years previously to General Charles Grey, her then Private Secretary, expressing his concern to establish the simple truth about the Queen's health – no easy matter, when his own opportunities of observation were limited, and when the Queen's physician, Sir William Jenner, seemed to be taking 'a narrow and unwise view of the case'. 'Will lies at the root of many human and especially of many feminine complaints',[16] he warned, echoing the attitude he had adopted with his younger sister, Helen. Gladstone told Grey he planned to meet Jenner to tackle the matter of the physician's over-protectiveness of the monarch and the possible self-fulfilling nature of this treatment: 'For fanciful ideas of a woman about her own health, encouraged by a feeble-minded doctor, become realities [with the effect of] producing in a considerable degree the incapacity which but for them would not exist'.[17]

Although her public might, with some justification, expect the Queen to rally after a dozen years of widowhood, few were brave enough to tell her so. John Brown, her devoted Highland servant and Prince Albert's former ghillie, may have been an exception. But at the same time, the debilitating symptoms of grief of which she complained – bad nerves, irritability, insomnia, headaches, suffering from the heat, fatigue and crises of confidence – were and are typical for many women of her age, widowed or not. Not even Victoria herself seems to have grasped that particular nettle. Whatever else she was, the Queen was clearly menopausal.

But there were more pressing issues of public concern. In 1871, the threat of republicanism raised its head. Victoria was aware of the excitement caused in the country by radical MP Sir Charles Dilke's short-lived parliamentary flirtation with the subject. She expressed her concern to Gladstone and asked him to stamp out even the merest flickering of an anti-monarchy movement.

> The Queen is aware that Mr Gladstone made some allusion to this Speech at the Mansion House and expressed his preference for the Institutions under which this Country is governed to a Republic, which Sir C. Dilke prefers. But if the Queen understood the meaning of Mr Gladstone's remarks on the subject, he intimated that the question was one which was open to discussion ... She did not for a moment doubt the sentiments of the Cabinet on the subject and only wishes that they should be expressed, for Mr Gladstone may feel assured that a large section of his supporters in Parliament and out of it view with abhorrence the revolutionary theories now promulgated, and naturally look to him and to his Colleagues for some very decided expressions of their condemnation of such opinions.[18]

Gladstone, ever the ardent, reverent monarchist, was eager to reassure her. But this matter, in turn, paled into insignificance with the news of the sudden illness of the Prince of Wales at Windsor – almost exactly ten years to the day since the death of his father, and probably from the same cause: typhoid fever. Local plumbing systems were again held responsible at a time when one man in three died from an infectious disease. Indeed, after the Prince's recovery, Charles Kingsley – as Dean of Windsor – gave a thanksgiving sermon in the Chapel Royal that focused heavily on the evils of poor sanitation. By the week before Christmas, however, the Prince was on the road to recovery and plans were being laid for a service of thanksgiving for his safe delivery. It was the perfect opportunity to deflect republican feeling, and enabled the Queen to appear again in public without seeming to have been forced to do so.

Early in 1872, the Queen wrote to Gladstone of her plans to take 'a run across to Baden', incognita, to visit her dying sister-in-law, Princess Hohenlohe-Langenburg. The Princess was the widow of Victoria's half-brother Feodore, the younger son from her mother's first marriage to

Emich Charles, Prince of Leiningen. The Princess was Victoria's only
near relation 'besides her own Children and her Brother in law and Sister in law the Queen has left in this World'. The Queen felt it 'a duty as
much as a great wish to see her once more – for her attacks of illness
are of a nature to cause serious alarm'.[19] Gladstone, despite sharing the
Queen's sense of commitment to family, was nevertheless surprised at
this display of energy by a woman who, only months earlier, had
expressed herself too weak to stay in London until the end of the parliamentary session. But, after some initial objections, he agreed. The
subsequent death of Princess Hohenlohe later that year provided some
justification for Victoria's course of action, without the royal feathers
having been ruffled.

In July of the same year, the Queen and Gladstone again returned to
the vexed question of trying to find suitable employment for the Prince
of Wales: something that would both absorb the latter's interests and
energies, and provide a good training ground for a future monarch. The
Queen fancied a post for him in some government department in England. The Prime Minister repeated time after time that such an
appointment was not possible; the Queen, still holding to the notion of
royal prerogative, insisted again and again that it was. The subject
remained a source of continuing disagreement between them. It also
triggered another issue of typical Gladstonian insensitivity: the question
of the Queen's possible abdication. For Victoria to threaten abdication
was one thing: she did so five times in 1878–79 alone, in frustration at
the Disraeli government's handling of the Eastern Question. But that
Gladstone should recommend abdication in favour of the Prince of
Wales was both reckless and naive. He did so in 1891, on the occasion of
the engagement of Victoria's grandson, the future King George V, to
Princess Mary of Teck, and again at her Diamond Jubilee in 1897.

The question of royal prerogative remained an unarticulated source
of irritation between Victoria and Gladstone. Walter Bagehot, the
nineteenth-century British constitutional writer, described the monarch
as having three rights: 'the right to be consulted, to advise and to
warn'.[20] Victoria wanted more than that. For her, the royal prerogative
comprised, rather, 'the right to instruct, to abuse and to hector'. The
Queen did not see herself as a non-executive constitutional monarch
in Bagehotian terms, but as an integral part of the policy-making and

decision-making process of government. One famous example of this use, or abuse, of power occurred when she had the Prime Minister, Lord John Russell, sack Lord Palmerston for failing to keep her informed in advance of foreign policy matters. Her reasons were outlined in a royal memorandum.

> The Queen requires, first, that Lord Palmerston will distinctly state what he proposes in a given case, in order that the Queen may know as distinctly to what she is giving her royal sanction. Secondly, having once given her sanction to such a measure that it be not arbitrarily altered or modified by the minister. Such an act she must consider as failing in sincerity to the Crown, and justly to be visited by the exercise of her constitutional right of dismissing that minister. She expects to be kept informed on what passes between him and foreign ministers before important decisions are taken based upon that course; to receive the foreign despatches in good time; and to have the drafts for her approval sent to her in sufficient time to make herself acquainted with their contents before they must be sent off.[21]

Palmerston failed to do all this, and Palmerston was dismissed. The Queen was to repeat the argument – that no foreign policy matters must proceed without her knowledge – a few years later, when complaining about Gladstone meeting various European heads of state on an unplanned visit to Copenhagen during a private cruise to Norway.

When Gladstone was in government, he did his best to shield the Queen from the consequences of her non-constitutional onslaughts, bearing the brunt of her outbursts with discretion and patience. He wrote to her after every Cabinet session, every evening after a Commons session, and up to six more times a day during times of crisis in response to her letters and telegrams. However, on one question of royal prerogative – exemplified in her relentless request for a government post for the Prince of Wales – he remained immovable.

In 1873, the failure of the Gladstone government's ambitious Irish University Bill, which would have enabled Protestants and Catholics to study together at Dublin University, threatened to bring the administration down. But Disraeli's reluctance to form a Tory government kept Gladstone in power, though the Liberal Party's days of easy dominance were numbered. The Queen's anxiety over Gladstone's possible departure from political supremacy manifested itself in concern for his health once he did, in fact, albeit temporarily, return to power.

Above all, Victoria did not willingly embrace change. Throughout their pre-Disraeli acquaintance, communications between the Queen and Gladstone continued to mix the political with the personal. She sent a telegram of condolence on the death of Catherine's brother, Henry Glynne, rector of Hawarden and husband of Lady Lyttelton's daughter Lavinia. And that summer, when both were at Balmoral, William wrote with news of his daughter Agnes's betrothal.

> Your Majesty's extreme kindness on all occasions to Mr Gladstone and his family emboldens him to apprise Your Majesty in his wife's name and his own that their eldest daughter Agnes has just engaged herself to be married to Mr Wickham, a clergyman of the highest character and considerable distinction at Oxford, who has recently been appointed to the Headmastership of Wellington College. There appears to be every prospect that this union will be a happy one.[22]

Victoria was delighted. In reply, she wished the Gladstones sincere joy of the engagement. 'May she be as happy as she deserves to be and may this hope in some measure make up for the loss the Queen feels sure she will be to himself and Mrs Gladstone.' She offered her warmest congratulations to Agnes 'whom she has known from childhood, and in whose welfare she will ever take a sincere interest'.[23]

The following day the Queen sent an Indian shawl as a wedding gift for Agnes, 'who was a playfellow for our eldest girls',[24] and with it a book for Gladstone himself. Agnes was married at Hawarden a few months later. When details appeared in the press of private comments made at the wedding reception concerning the Queen's kindness to his daughter, Gladstone was mortified. But the Queen was all graciousness, reassuring him that there was 'nothing in his speech on the occasion of the late interesting family event at Hawarden to which she could take the very slightest exception. He only stated the truth as regards herself and his dear daughter'. But, perhaps with an eye to the protection of her own privacy from the prying eyes of the press, she added: 'she does think it very hard and very wrong that a family party of a comparatively private nature should have every detail published in the Papers'.[25]

Such family intimacy was under imminent threat. In February 1874, the Liberal Party was defeated in a general election and Benjamin Disraeli was called on to form a Tory government. In their final exchange of letters, the Queen approved Gladstone's honours list, adding that 'she wishes to record her offer to Mr Gladstone himself of a mark of her recognition of his services – which however he declines, from motives which she full appreciates'.[26] The People's William continued to decline an honour to the end of his life.

In the first phase of their relationship, until his departure from government in 1874, Victoria had accepted William Gladstone's strange ways, trusting in his integrity and in the anchor provided by Catherine. But for the latter part of their half-century's acquaintance, she found him hard to abide. While still not doubting his sincerity, she often described him as 'mad' or 'wicked' when his policies failed to agree with hers. Towards the end of their lives, when Gladstone was returned to power for the very last time of all, in 1892 – at the age of eighty-two – with a majority of forty, including seventy-two Irish Nationalists, Victoria was totally outraged at the thought of having to tolerate him yet again as her Prime Minister. She wrote to Lord Lansdowne, then Viceroy of India.

> She feels more than ever at this painful, anxious moment when, by an incomprehensible, reckless vote, the result of most unfair and abominable misrepresentations at the elections, one of the best and most useful Governments has been defeated, how important it is to have so able and reliable a Viceroy in India. The Queen-Empress can hardly trust herself to say what she feels and thinks on the subject ... the danger to the country, to Europe, to her vast Empire, which is involved in having all these great interests entrusted to the shaking hand of an old, wild, and incomprehensible man of eighty-two and a half, is very great! It is a terrible trial, but, thank God, the country is sound, and it cannot last. The Gladstonian majority is quite divided, and solely depends on the Irish vote.[27]

Over the fifty years of their acquaintance, the Queen and Gladstone fell out over many issues, both great and small. They disagreed about a useful role for the Prince of Wales, then as now a vexed question. They argued about the conflict between royal prerogative and parliamentary power, particularly as it manifested itself in the appointment of ministers. She felt that information about affairs of state was sometimes wilfully withheld from her, as indeed it was. They were at variance about issues as wide-ranging as the strength of the armed forces, and the cost and inconvenience of entertaining foreign heads of state – to many of whom, it must be said, she was directly related. The state of the railways, the prospect of women studying medicine, her unflattering new image on the coinage, plans for recruitment by examination to the Civil Service, the Egyptian question, church patronage: all these areas of contention and complaint tested their relationship. Most testing of all, however, were the two great issues: Ireland and Empire.

Victoria's stand on Home Rule for Ireland was simple: she opposed it totally. For Gladstone, on the other hand, achieving devolution and peace for the island was the burning ambition of the latter part of his career. When he returned to government in 1886, all those invited to join the new Cabinet were required to read Gladstone's memorandum, advocating the feasibility of Home Rule, before accepting a post. Acceptance thus gave tacit approval to the policy. The memorandum read as follows.

> I propose to examine whether it is or is not practicable to comply with the desire widely prevalent in Ireland ... for the establishment of a Legislative body to sit in Dublin, and to deal with Irish as distinguished from Imperial affairs; in such a manner as would be just to each of the three kingdoms, equitable with reference to every class of the people of Ireland, [and] conducive to the social order and harmony of that country, and calculated to support and consolidate the unity of the Empire on the combined basis of Imperial authority and attachment.[28]

That Gladstone's first Government of Ireland Bill was defeated in the Commons a few months later, and brought the administration down with it, consoled the Queen. A sense of 'I told you so' satisfaction oozes from Victoria's letter to Gladstone on 31 July 1886, the day after he came to offer her his resignation.

> On the occasion of Mr Gladstone's visit yesterday, the Queen did not like to allude to the circumstances which led to his resignation – but she would like to say a few words in writing. Whatever Mr Gladstone's personal opinion as to the best means of promoting contentment in, and restoring order to Ireland, the Country has unequivocally decided against his plan and the new Government will have to devise some other course – in due time. Mr Gladstone when he took Office in February, explained to the Queen his intention of 'inquiring' as to what could be done as well as his proposed mode for doing so; upon which the Queen said she feared he would never carry it – and he replied 'it is forty-nine to one that I shall not carry it'. This has come true. But what the Queen is now anxious to say is – that she trusts that this being the case, both in and out of Parliament, he will do what he can to aid

those who will have the difficult task of trying to propose measures which do not present the objections to any of those, calculated to promote Home Rule. She trusts that his sense of patriotism may make him feel that the kindest and wisest thing he can do *for* Ireland is to abstain from encouraging agitation by public speeches which though not so intended by Mr Gladstone may nevertheless increase excitement and be construed as supporting violent proceedings to those who do not hesitate to defy the Law.[29]

Victoria's smugness was relatively short-lived. Seven years later Gladstone was back in power and another Irish Home Rule Bill was on the books; indeed it was approved by the Commons, only to be defeated by the Lords.

Gladstone's 1886 memorandum on Home Rule for Ireland mentioned consolidating the unity of the Empire as one of its objectives. But Victoria is unlikely to have been fooled. One of the first things Gladstone had done when he last came back to government in 1880 was to address the question of redirecting colonial power back to the nations concerned. He was not hostile to the basic concept of colonisation, and accepted it in other nations. But he questioned its usefulness, and sought no expansion of the British imperial responsibilities he had inherited from Disraeli. His main area concern was to maintain stability within the existing Empire and where possible devolve local responsibility – and some local costs – on to the colonies. He believed India contributed little to the strength of the Empire but much to the effort required by government. He wrote to the Viceroy of India, Lord Ripon: 'We have undertaken a most arduous but a most noble duty. We are pledged to India, I may say to mankind, for its performance, and we have no choice'.[30] Ripon had been appointed almost immediately Gladstone returned to government, with a clear mandate to begin dismantling the Tory imperialist structure in India. Gladstone told Ripon:

There is a question to be answered; where, in a country like India, lies the ultimate power, and if it lies for the present on one side but for the future on the other, a problem has to be solved as to preparation for that future, and it may become right and needful to chasten the saucy pride so apt to grow in the English mind towards foreigners, and especially towards foreigners whose position has been subordinate.[31]

It would be wrong to attribute this type of 'saucy pride' to Victoria:

her affection for India in general was as great as her personal generosity to Abdul Karim, the 'Munshi', the Indian servant of her later years. But it did nothing to endear the Prime Minister to the Queen that he should regard it as a chore – albeit a noble one – to continue administering the territory over which Disraeli had made his Titania the Queen Empress.

Even at their most contrary, the relationship between Victoria and Gladstone in the earlier years had displayed an intimacy that the coming of Disraeli would totally destroy. And the Queen could be very contrary. On one occasion she summoned Gladstone to Osborne, and then took days to receive him. In the summer of 1872, she invited him to Balmoral. Shortly after her invitation they fell out again over his persistence regarding a role in Ireland for the Prince of Wales – a plan that Victoria had resisted from the start with equal determination. In a sulk, Gladstone wrote to her from Hawarden that he was 'not aware whether as matters now stand it will still be Your Majesty's desire to see him' at Balmoral. He would assume, 'unless he hears to the contrary, that Your Majesty has no occasion to command his presence'.[32] Her Majesty replied with some exasperation that she was

> very sorry not to have been able to agree with him on the important subject of employment for the Prince of Wales – but ... after repeatedly considering the question she cannot conscientiously advocate what she is thoroughly convinced is not practicable and which the Prince of Wales himself is entirely against. The Queen would be very glad if Mr Gladstone had found it convenient to come over for two days early next week to Balmoral – but if there is nothing very special to communicate the Queen hardly likes to urge Mr Gladstone to put himself to the inconvenience and fatigue of coming over.[33]

In many ways, the Queen and Mr Gladstone were well matched in contrariness. In Opposition, from 1874–80, Gladstone saw very little of the Queen. The letters and small gifts he sent were acknowledged by her Private Secretary, Henry Ponsonby, rather than by the Queen herself. On the few occasions that they met, William found her uneasy and restrained. She seemed to have become strangely apprehensive of Gladstone and, within a year of her change of ministers, even Disraeli diagnosed her solicitude for his own health as occasioned not so much from love of him as dread of someone else. Victoria worried over Disraeli's health, as she once had over Gladstone's; he flattered her literary vanity by introducing his comments on books with the preface 'We authors, Ma'am ...' She sent him snowdrops and primroses (on his death, she sent wild primroses for his coffin); and in 1877 he made her Empress of India. With that began a change in her that Gladstone was beyond reversing when he came back to power. It cannot have helped that, the following year, Gladstone attacked Disraeli's imperialism.

Just as she continued after Prince Albert's death to act as she thought he would have advised, so, too, after Disraeli's departure, she continued in the mind-set conferred by a man who had converted a mere Queen into Victoria Regina Imperatrix. Disraeli played upon her political vanity by supplying her with all the gossip. Gladstone felt this to be beneath him. Playing on her perception of royal prerogative, Disraeli made her feel that her views were important to the government – although the reality was that their impact remained the same. He also succeeded in persuading Victoria that the values of the Tory Party were Victoria's own; this, like Albert's earlier legacy, was to prove impossible for Gladstone to dislodge. After all, Disraeli had enhanced her status dramatically, and in a way that fed her instinctive desire for the exotic. As the Queen grew into the role of Empress, her style changed. She began to reinvent herself into something more magnificent, and the change that Disraeli had wrought carried on to the end of her life. The consequences of that change were to be devastating for Gladstone when he returned to power.[34]

By sharing with her the gossip surrounding matters of state and the detail of Cabinet sessions, Disraeli had persuaded the Queen that she exercised more power than in fact she did. By persuading her that his policies were those of which the dear departed Prince Albert would have approved, he convinced her that the interests of the Crown matched those of the Tory Party. By elevating her status to that of Queen Empress, he raised her expectations to a level that the more prosaic Gladstone could not hope to match. Gladstone had, in 1878 – just one year after her proclamation as Empress of India – campaigned against Disraeli's imperial policy. And, in 1880, when Disraeli was defeated, the Queen was desperate that Gladstone should not become her next Prime Minister. She thought she had a choice. But soon enough she realised the limits to the notion of royal prerogative. She had no power to prevent his appointment. But Disraeli had destroyed forever her confidence in Gladstone, whom she held responsible for her favourite's downfall, since 'the incessant thunder of his criticism since 1876 had done more than any other single factor to bring down the government', as if that were not the *raison d'être* of Opposition parties everywhere.[35]

When she summoned Gladstone to ask if he would form a government in 1880, she remarked with some satisfaction to Disraeli that maybe Gladstone would not last very long since he looked very old, very ill and very haggard. As it happened, it was Disraeli that died within the year, while Gladstone survived for another nineteen. But the Queen remained a cross Gladstone had to bear. Even after Disraeli's death, she remained in active consultation with the Leader of the Opposition, Lord Salisbury. Meanwhile, Gladstone, walking in the grounds of Hawarden Castle with Lord Rosebery early in 1882, halfway through his second premiership and a year after Disraeli's death, commented that the 'Queen alone was enough to kill any man'.[36] When he resigned his second premiership in 1885, Gladstone, who by now had come out as the open champion of Home Rule for Ireland, noted that 'to me personally it is a great relief, including in this sensation my painful relations with the Queen, who will have a like feeling'.[37]

There was an additional factor that exacerbated Victoria's antagonism to Gladstone in the mid-1880s: Sudan and General Gordon. Victoria persuaded herself that the death of Charles Gordon (who had grossly disobeyed government instructions not to engage in local fighting) was solely the result of Gladstone's prevarication over whether or not to send timely reinforcements to Khartoum. The issue was hotly contested at the time. On 5 February 1885, Victoria sent an open (*en clair*, so anyone could read it) telegram to Gladstone: 'These news [sic] from Khartoum are frightful and to think that all this might have been prevented and many precious lives saved by earlier action is too tearful.'[38] Gladstone's reply, sent the same day, was quietly excoriating. The second paragraph of his lengthy diplomatic reply read:

> Mr Gladstone does not presume to estimate the means of judgement possessed by Your Majesty, but so far as his information and recollection at the moment go, he is not altogether able to follow the conclusion which Your Majesty has been pleased thus to announce.[39]

Benjamin Disraeli died in 1881; John Brown in 1883. For a time,

perhaps tempered by a growing sense of mortality, there was a temporary softening in Victoria's personal attitude to Gladstone, with repeated
enquiries as to his health, even though politically they remained divided.
But that autumn another event occurred, again typical of Gladstone's –
doubtless unwitting – lack of sensitivity to the Queen's perception of
what was proper.

If Disraeli became the Queen's champion, Gladstone had become the
people's champion. And if the idea of the 'People's William' was not
enough, the idea of the 'Empire's William', as it may have appeared to
the Queen in 1883, was intolerable. What happened was that an
exhausted Gladstone decided to take a few days' rest on a trip around
the British coast on the *Pembroke Castle* as the guest of Sir Donald Cur-
rie, a wealthy shipping magnate. Mid cruise, he decided on impulse to
accompany his fellow-passengers, including Tennyson, on a trip to
Scandinavia. This modest Norwegian cruise became, quite by chance, a
royal progress. The King of Denmark asked them to dinner to meet to
Tsar of Russia, the King and Queen of Greece, the Princess of Wales and
other royal relatives. The hospitality was returned on board the yacht,
where guns were fired, flags flew, the Poet Laureate recited and Gladstone made a speech. But Victoria was not amused. She was jealous. As
she had done years before with Palmerston, she complained that her
Prime Minister – 'especially one *not* gifted with prudence' – was not
entitled to go where he liked with impunity and that his actions could
be misconstrued. 'There are so many topics which cannot be discussed
with Foreign Sovereigns by the Prime Minister without ... the sanction
of the Sovereign.' She warned Gladstone: 'The Prime Minister of Great
Britain cannot move about ... as a private individual and any Trip like
the one he has just taken will lead ... to Political speculations which it
is better to avoid.'[40] Privately, Gladstone found her letter to him
'unmannerly'. However, ever the loyal subject of Her Imperial Majesty,
he wrote an ostensibly abject apology, blaming 'increasing weariness of
mind under public cares for which he feels himself less and less fitted'
for blunting his 'faculty of anticipation'.[41] Of anticipating what? The
Queen's ill humour?

In his final premiership, the relationship between them remained as bad
as ever – almost wilfully so on her part, one suspects. Shortly after taking

up office again, on 15 August 1892, Gladstone wrote to Catherine that he had had an audience with the Queen at Osborne, her home on the Isle of Wight.

> She enquired for you with evident sincerity, and perhaps a touch of warmth. In all other respects the interview was carefully polite and nothing else. There is a great change since 1886 [the end of his last premiership]; another lurch in the direction opposed to ours. I am to see the Prince of Wales tonight when, as I expect, the case will be different.[42]

Seven months later, after another audience with the Queen, he wrote to his wife from the House of Commons, referring to a letter of the previous day, since lost:

> In my note of yesterday, I described the formal and menacing character of my audience at Buckingham Palace: but I ought to have mentioned that she enquires somewhat kindly after your health. But a painful sense of unreality pervades these conversations; and the public announcement of an 'audience' hoodwinks the public.[43]

Victoria felt herself to be, and indeed was, Gladstone's intellectual inferior. He could, however, have tried harder to be more accessible – and less didactic. Melbourne, her early mentor, had advised that 'she wanted the whole truth – in one word'. That was never Gladstone's style. She felt he never listened. As the years went by, he reconciled himself to being forever excluded from intimacy with her: 'I am always outside an iron ring, and without any desire, had I the power, to break it through'.[44] The inability of Victoria and Gladstone to converse together seriously and naturally in their later years was a prominent aspect of their unhappy relationship. Curiously, both appeared to have longed to break the boring circle of small talk, and each accused the other in their diaries of obstinately clinging to trivialities.

There was a final element in the Queen's attitude to Gladstone, the significance of which should not be underestimated, particularly in the way it defined their relationship in later years. After Albert's death, Victoria was desperately lonely. She had always been jealous by temperament. She was also, understandably, powerfully attracted to father figures. Victoria, whose father Edward, Duke of Kent, had died when she was eight months old, found great comfort in her relationship with her uncle, King Leopold of the Belgians. This was also partly why, as a young Queen, she had found such comfort in Lord Melbourne.

Gladstone was comfortable with, and accomplished in, the role of father figure, which he practised with great success within his vast extended family. But Gladstone wasn't widowed. Gladstone wasn't fundamentally lonely. And Gladstone, unlike Disraeli, wasn't emotionally available. Victoria preferred men who were. In contrast with Gladstone, Melbourne – Victoria's first Prime Minister – was both widowed and had known great sadness. His late wife, better know as the novelist Lady Caroline Lamb, had conducted a scandalous affair with the Lord Byron, who was famously described by her as 'mad, bad and dangerous to know'. Melbourne's son, who suffered from epilepsy, died shortly before Victoria's accession. As for John Brown, Albert's former ghillie and the Highland servant – and possibly more – who caused such trouble in the royal household during Victoria's protracted bereavement, he, too, was single, although there were unsubstantiated rumours that he married a Highland girl in later years. Even Lord Rosebery, whom Victoria was delighted to accept as Liberal Prime Minister in 1894 after Gladstone retired for the last time, had been widowed four years earlier when his wife Hannah died at the age of thirty-nine. 'Personally I am very fond of Rosebery', she wrote, 'and prefer him (not his politics) to Lord Salisbury – he is so much attached to me personally.' In 1872, between Disraeli's first and second premierships, Lady Beaconsfield also died, leaving him free to give, or at least appear to give, his undivided attention to the Queen.

The Queen longed for a soul mate. She needed fellow feeling. It led her to seek out the company of fellow sufferers. In this respect, even Albert qualified: his own mother had left the family home when he was young, following a series of mutual and public infidelities by his parents, and had died soon afterwards. The widowed Disraeli declared himself 'fortunate in having a female sovereign. I owe everything to woman; and if in the sunset of life I still have a young heart it is due to that influence'. His was an arm for Victoria to lean on; and, as Disraeli cast his spell, the Queen leant. In the face of this competition, Gladstone was handicapped by enjoying a happy and enduring marriage. Devoted though he was to the monarchy, it precluded his being able to give the Queen the exclusive personal devotion for which she craved – or to receive her pity. And, as Disraeli said to Matthew Arnold: 'Everyone likes flattery; and when you come to Royalty, you should lay it on with a trowel'.[45]

The later relationship between the Queen and Gladstone ran entirely to form. Gladstone, four times her Prime Minister in a parliamentary career spanning more than six decades – he who had craved for years a period of peace between 'the theatre and the grave' – resigned for the last time in early 1894, ostensibly on grounds of poor health, although the vexed issue of increasing expenditure on the navy was a contributing factor. By now Gladstone was eighty-four. His hearing and eyesight were failing, and he felt increasingly irritable and isolated as a result. Characteristically, the manner of his resignation was a tortuous and protracted affair.

After driving out with his daughter Mary, followed by a family discussion on the situation, Gladstone wrote to the Queen on 27 February 1894 that his departure was imminent with the approaching end of the parliamentary session. The following afternoon he had a half-hour audience with the monarch, who, he observed, 'had much difficulty in finding topics for an adequate prolongation, but fog and rain and [her] coming journey to Italy helped ... I thought I never saw her looking better. She was at the highest point of cheerfulness'. Gladstone was mortified. At his last audience with the Queen, after a lifetime of public service, the monarch was cheerful. He guessed at the reason for her cheerfulness, and he was probably right. 'Any fear that the intelligence I had to give her would be a shock to her, has been entirely dispelled', he wrote in his diary on the night of 28 February. 'Certainly the impression on my mind is that she does not even consider it a trouble but regards it as the immediate precursor of an arrangement more agreeable.'[46]

The following day, 1 March, he chaired his 556th Cabinet session, where he formally broke the news to his tearful colleagues. John Morley, who would become his official biographer, noted in his diary that the atmosphere of 'simple and unaffected emotion was as manly as could be, and touched every one of us to the core ... a good many of us were ... near breaking down'. At the end of the meeting, Gladstone 'went slowly out of one door; while we with downcast looks and depressed hearts filed out by the other; much as men walk away from the graveside'.[47]

Gladstone then drove to the House of Commons for his final session of Prime Minister's questions. He never set foot in Parliament again. That same evening, Gladstone and his wife Catherine were invited to Windsor Castle to dine with the Queen and to stay the night. Victoria was courteous at dinner but keen to steer Gladstone into conversations with other guests, rather than engage with him herself. After breakfast the following morning, the Queen found Catherine Gladstone 'very much upset, poor thing' and anxious to stress that William had always been devoted to his sovereign.

> [She] begged me to allow her to tell him that I believed it which I did; for I am convinced it is the case, though at times his actions might have made it difficult to believe. She spoke of former days and how long he had known me and dear Albert. I kissed her when she left.[48]

But the retirement rigmarole wasn't over yet. Before lunch that day, 2 March, Gladstone carried in to the Queen a box containing his definitive resignation letter. Victoria, who must have known what was in it, 'asked whether she ought then to read it. I said there was nothing in the letter to require it'. Later, after reading the letter, the Queen dutifully wrote back, reiterating her concerns for his health and her recognition for his 'arduous labour & responsibility' on her behalf, and that he was 'right in wishing to be relieved at his age of these arduous duties'. She made no pretence, as protocol required, of seeking his advice as to his successor; but repeated the offer made at previous resignations: 'The Queen would gladly have conferred a peerage on Mr Gladstone, but she knows he would not accept it'.[49]

Gladstone was both hurt and offended. 'It seems that [the resignation] was in some way accepted *before* it was tendered', he wrote, ignoring the fact that the affair had already been dragging on for weeks. He deplored the curtness of the note. On 10 March, a week after his definitive resignation, he wrote: 'The same brevity perhaps prevails in settling a tradesman's bill, when it reaches over many years'.[50] Earlier that week, at a dinner given by the Duke of York, the new (but, as it turned out, short-lived) Prime Minister, Lord Rosebery, asked Mrs Gladstone whether her husband hated the Queen. Catherine defended William, 'but the proper defence', Gladstone wrote, 'would have been to say that any one giving countenance to this cruel imputation, ought at least to be supplied with the evidence'. And, deferential and devoted though Gladstone undoubtedly was to his sovereign, he could nevertheless not resist a parting shot in his diary entry for 10 March.

Let me now make in a few words a clean breast of it.

I am as I hope loyal to the Throne.

I admire in the Queen many fine qualities which she possesses.

I certainly used [to] admire still more: and frankly I do not see that the Queen has improved in the last twenty years. (Dean Wellesley spoke to me of a change in her before I perceived it myself.) But there is plenty of room remaining for the admiration of which I speak. Further I am grateful to the Queen as I have expressed it in my letter for many kindnesses received at various periods of my service under her.

Every one knows her attitude towards Liberalism. But taking relations to me since 1874, as a whole, there is in them something of a mystery, which I have not been able to fathom, and probably never shall.

I hope my duty to her and her family has never in fact, as it has never in intention, fallen short.

And I have a new cause of gratitude to H.M. in her having on this last occasion admitted my wife to a new footing of confidence and freedom. She had too long, I think, been suffering on my behalf. I am delighted that this chapter is well closed.

God save the Queen.[51]

The Queen had not always disliked Gladstone. Kind mentions are scattered throughout her earlier letters. But she knew instinctively that he disapproved in principle of the concept of Empire that was so dear to her. And she disapproved fundamentally of his desire for Irish Home Rule. So, when he resigned, she was too honest to feign regret. He had lost her love and therefore had to forego her gratitude. He felt it keenly, for none of her ministers had desired to serve the Queen more loyally. Yet, after nearly sixty-four years in politics and fifty-three in public office, this most loyal servant of the Queen felt she had dealt with him like the mule he had ridden many years before on holiday in Sicily. The comparison also admits a certain insight into his own stubborn streak.

The beast was wholly inaccessible to notes of kindness by voice or hand, and was disposed to lag. But we rode usually from 6 a.m. to 4 p.m., and its undemonstrative unsympathetic service was not inefficiently performed. In due time ... my mule and I of necessity parted company. I well remember having at the time a mental experience which was not unlike indigestion. I had been on the back of the beast for many scores of hours, it had done me no wrong; it had rendered me much valuable service; there was the fact staring me in the face. I could not get up the smallest shred of feeling for the brute. I could neither love it nor like it ... What the Sicilian mule was to me, I have been to the Queen.[52]

10

Final Years

Gladstone resigned from the premiership for the fourth and final time in March 1894. He was eighty-four years old. The whole of his long political career – sixty-three years – had been spent in the service of his country. Before he died, he was to enjoy just four years of the peace he had so long craved: the peace 'between the theatre and the grave'. It was a time, as he wrote in his last diary entry on his eighty-seventh birthday in 1896, 'appointed for the gradual loosening or successive snapping of the threads'.

The last letter that Gladstone wrote before he left 10 Downing Street for the final time was to his wife, Catherine. He was busy sorting out his papers to make way for the new Prime Minister, Lord Rosebery: 'I have been working hard all day and it will be difficult for me to manage by tomorrow the clearing out from these rooms'. But there was a more important matter than house removals to discuss. A suggestion had been made that Mrs Gladstone might like to receive a peerage in her own right. The idea did not appeal to either of them, and Gladstone had already turned down an honour for himself. Catherine, however, had some claim, via her Glynne ancestry, to the baronies of Percy and Poynings. These Gladstone would have liked to have seen restored to her.

> Marjoribanks [Lord Tweedmouth, the new Lord Privy Seal] has been here and enquired, on Rosebery's behalf, whether it would be agreeable to us that *you* should receive a peerage. I said that the subject must go to you for consideration, and that I would write it today. For my part, I look upon it with no favour but should not in any way press this. I should on all grounds very greatly prefer what would *cost* more, viz. the recovery of the old title to which you are supposed to have a good claim.[1]

The offer was duly declined. Lord Tweedmouth spoke for many when he wrote later that he was 'very glad that Mrs Gladstone is to keep her name unchanged, and to go down to posterity with the simple appellation we have been so familiar with, and which has been so dear to us all'.[2]

Of the girls and women with whose lives Gladstone had been closely involved, most had gone before. He had outlived both his sisters and one daughter. Anne Robertson, Helen Jane and Catherine Jessy Gladstone were now all interred together in the vault of the family chapel at Fasque, alongside his mother, Anne Mackenzie Gladstone. Suzie Opdebeck, the former Lady Lincoln, had died five years previously and was buried at Burgess Hill, near Brighton. As to Laura Thistlethwayte, the relationship that had begun just weeks into his first term as Prime Minister ended with her death just weeks after the end of his last term. Her estate amounted to just over £40,000. Lincoln's son, Edward, was the principal executor.[3] There were generous bequests from Laura to friends and family, but nothing to embarrass Gladstone. Whatever else, she had at least always been discreet and remained so to the end. Most of her money was intended to convert her last home, Woodbine Cottage in Hampstead, into a modest version of Gladstone's own St Deiniol's library at Hawarden, but this never materialised. Gladstone and his wife had visited Laura three weeks before her death. A cataract operation shortly afterwards, for which the treatment then was bandaged eyes and two weeks' bed-rest, meant he was unable to attend the funeral. It must have seemed to him like the end of an era.

After his retirement, Gladstone sometimes referred to his relationship with Queen Victoria as a reason for leaving office. Freedom from her constant nagging was certainly one of the bonuses. His relationship with the Prince of Wales and his elder son, the Duke of York, continued to be cordial. But he remained haunted by the memory of his personal failure with Victoria. They met from time to time at events, but he found her remote and restrained. She haunted his sleeping hours, too. Of the very few dreams that Gladstone recorded during his lifetime, only two involved people: Disraeli and Victoria. It was nearly two years after his final resignation that Gladstone dreamt of the Queen. The family were staying at Cannes to celebrate his eighty-sixth birthday when Gladstone wrote in his diary, on 2 January 1896, of his 'strong desire that after my decease my family shall be most careful to keep in the background all information respecting the personal relations of the

Queen and myself during these later years, down to 1894 when they died a kind of natural death'. This preoccupation was prompted by a dream he had the previous night, about which he wrote:

> We may sometimes, even if it be rarely, obtain a morsel of self-knowledge through the medium of a dream. Aware [of] the state of the Queen's feelings towards me, I have regretted to be in such ill odour with one in whom there is so much to admire and respect; but, as I seem to myself conscious without mistrust of having invariably rendered to her the best service that I could, I have striven to keep down that regret, and set it, as it were, behind me, and to attain, as nearly as I could to indifference in the matter. Since my retirement I have dreamt sometimes of Parliament and sometimes … of the Court, but without much meaning. Last night I dreamed that I was at Windsor. There had been a sort of breakfast, fugitive and early, at which several attended, and the Queen appeared, but without incident. However, it was conveyed to me through one of the 'pages' … that *I* of all people in the world was to breakfast alone with the Queen at ten o'clock … Well the time slid on, and the hour approached, and I was getting duly into what I may call a small perturbation as to the how and where of access. But the dream had lost its tail. The hour never came. And the sole force and effect of the incident is to show that the subject of my personal relation to the Queen, and all the unsatisfactory ending of my over half a century of service, had more hold upon me, down at the root, than I was aware.[4]

It is poignant that a statesman who had achieved so much should be haunted in his final years by this failure to inspire positive emotion in such a difficult woman. Gladstone's dream of having breakfast with Victoria may have had a sexual dimension, for he records having 'a small perturbation as to the how and where of access'. 'Reserved for access' was the phrase he had used in 1839 to describe his virginity on marriage.[5] But it seems more likely that it was in fact the absence of any sexual *frisson* between the Queen and Gladstone that was part of the problem. This meant their personal and political differences could not be negotiated a spirit of cooperation and accord. At the same time, the Queen – who was prone to jealousy – may have resented the fact that her Prime Minister, who flirted with so many society ladies, failed singularly to flirt with her as Disraeli had done. Gladstone was not immune to charm. Quite the contrary. He was as delighted to be charmed as he was to charm, when appropriate. But, despite Catherine's early exhortation to 'pet the Queen; and do believe you can', he failed. That he failed was probably due more to excess of regard than to lack of it.

The Queen seemed determined to outlive him.[6] And, even in retirement, she succeeded in causing offence. On 27 July 1896, Victoria's granddaughter Princess Maud, daughter of the Prince of Wales, married Prince Charles of Denmark. The Gladstones, now both in their mid eighties, made the arduous journey from North Wales to London to attend the marriage. Yet the Queen failed either to acknowledge their presence or to invite them to the wedding breakfast. Gladstone was hurt, particularly on Catherine's behalf.

> So, after nearly two and a half years we saw the Queen once more ... From want of information, we did not stay for the luncheon. The Prince of Wales as we heard expressed regret and we were invited to Marlborough House at 1.30 ... They were both extraordinarily kind. The Prince kissed Catherine's hand. I cannot avoid thinking that they do so much towards us from a sense of the Queen's deficiencies. For it was surely strange that H.M. should have taken *no* notice ... of a lady of eighty-four who had come near two hundred miles to attend the service.

Gladstone was no less frail than his frail lady wife of eighty-four. By now, for example, his failing sight meant he was unable to read as much as he would have aspired to do in retirement, but his life-long enthusiasm for books and learning continued unabated. For many years he had dreamed of creating a library and theological centre at Hawarden. The germ of the idea had been planted in 1882, when he attended the funeral of his fellow student and Oxford Movement leader, Edward Pusey, in whose memory just such an institution was later established on St Giles. By 1889, Gladstone had begun turning his own dream into the reality that would become St Deiniol's Library. Two large corrugated iron buildings had been erected to provide study bedrooms, plus a library which Gladstone had fitted with a shelving system, designed by himself, to house an initial donation of around 30,000 books. Many of these books he carted across himself from the Temple of Peace, his private study at Hawarden Castle. Gladstone pushing a wheelbarrow laden with books between the castle and the library was a regular sight locally. In 1895, he gave over £40,000 into a trust fund to support the future development of St Deiniol's.[7] In 1896, he appointed the library's first full-time warden.

It was about this time that Gladstone's daughter Helen was coming to the reluctant conclusion that her presence was needed back at Hawarden on a permanent basis. But, before she left Newnham, there were some issues she hoped to see through to a successful conclusion. Among them was the question of the admission of women to degrees at Cambridge. In January 1896, Helen wrote to her father, asking him to put his name to a petition.

> We are making a great effort to get the University to grant degrees to women in some form; a memorial is being signed by members of the Cambridge Senate, asking for the appointment of a Syndicate 'to consider on what conditions and with what restrictions if any' this might be done. This has been signed by near 2000 members of the Cambridge Senate, including the Archbishop of Canterbury, about eight bishops, Mr Balfour, Mr Childers, Sir George Trevelyan, Lord Crewe, Lord Justice Rigby, with headmasters, doctors, lawyers, and perfect swarms of clergymen. A general memorial from non-Cambridge people is also being signed in support ... if you could and would sign it, we should be enormously pleased. I have sent the form to Mary, also papers from which she can give you fuller information if you should want it. At present we may take the Honours examinations – and 659 women have done so with success – but we can get no degree. Signing does not involve approval of any particular form or extent of concession – only of a wish for the opening of university degrees to women in some form. I would not trouble you of I did not care much about this, and immensely about your opinion.[8]

Gladstone's reply is not recorded. But the fact that Helen felt confident enough to request his support implies that she knew that his mind was not totally set against the idea. In the event, it would be another half-century before women were admitted to degrees at Cambridge University. By November that year, Helen had finally made her decision to return full time to Hawarden.

> It seems as if the time has now come when I ought to take my share regularly of home duties, so I have now given notice to leave Newnham – at Christmas if they can arrange it with my successor, and if not, at Easter (with absence in the early part of next term). You will not think that I have done this lightly or easily – although I shall be so glad to do what I can at home. I can only thank you and others at home for making it possible that I should be here for nineteen and a half years. I should be grateful if you will keep this

entirely private, excepting with Mary ... I do not want Mama to know – I am
sure that at present it would only worry her.[9]

Gladstone replied that he was 'stunned by the disclosure' of the news
and overwhelmed by 'the unselfish and careful generosity with which
you have acted ... May God bless you. What you now meditate, come
what may, is so highminded and good, that good must come of it'.[10] To
the Newnham colleagues she was leaving, Helen wrote: 'There is so
much love and kindness mixed up with the pain; and the very pain of
leaving comes so much from the good things and happiness of the place,
that there is satisfaction even in it'.

There is some evidence that Gladstone may have been attempting to
set up an alternative support system that would liberate Helen, or perhaps at least provide additional back-up in coping with Catherine, who
was failing both physically and mentally. On 4 January 1897, he wrote to
the Bishop of St Asaph asking for the living at nearby Buckley to be given
to his son-in-law Harry Drew. Drew had resigned the Hawarden curacy
in 1893 with a view to acquiring a wider experience. In 1894, he completed a seven month 'term of duty' in South Africa. On his return he
helped set up St Deiniol's Library – Gladstone's gift to the nation – and
then spent a couple of months in the Holy Land, before returning to his
St Deiniol's duties. He was reluctant to take up the rectorship at Hawarden. But a post at Buckley was apparently about to become vacant. Mary
Drew was already oiling the wheels when she wrote to her brother Henry
about her husband Harry's future career on 10 December 1896.

> Something surely will soon turn up [you say]. I think we must face this fact:
> that only *two* 'somethings' can turn up that fulfil the two necessary condi-
> tions. 1. nearness of parents for M[ary] D[rew]; 2. Pastoral work for H[arry]
> D[rew]. You know that a place like Buckley appeals to Harry specially, as
> does any place that requires working up. Also that he has no taste any more
> than Stephy has, for a bigger position such as Hawarden affords, so that, if
> both Buckley and Hawarden were by nature vacant, and he was given his
> choice, he would leap at Buckley.[11]

It was just four weeks later that Gladstone wrote to the Bishop of
St Asaph.

> Mr Drew, my son-in-law, is just demitting important duties ... and
> we should be very sorry were he, with his excellent abilities, to remain

unemployed. [Also] it would be a matter of great importance to us, to my wife in particular, that such employment should be so near as not to remove our daughter, his wife, beyond the circle of constant domestic intercourse. At our time of life my wife would feel her removal very seriously.[12]

Harry Drew duly became Vicar of Buckley and Mary stayed close to her parents. It was the second time Gladstone had advanced the career of a son-in-law. His last act of ecclesiastical patronage before leaving office in 1894 had been to make Agnes's husband Edward Wickham the Dean of Lincoln.

Early in 1897, the Gladstones spent a couple of months in Cannes in the south of France, where there was something of a minor reconciliation with the Queen, who was staying nearby at Cimiez. Again the meeting was orchestrated by a member of the royal family – this time Victoria's daughter, Princess Louise – rather than being initiated by the Queen herself. This reinforced William's impression that the royal family may have felt embarrassed by their mother's coldness and apparent ingratitude, and were seeking to mitigate it. The meeting was not a success. Conversation dried up after ten minutes. But Gladstone noted that, for the first time that he could remember in over fifty years' acquaintance, the Queen shook his hand. It was the last time they met.

Gladstone's final winter was also spent back at Cannes, with Helen acting as her parents' companion. It was a difficult and depressing time for her. This time, the resort failed to work its magic. Her letters to Mary back in Buckley are dominated by the problem of her father's increasing remoteness, while her mother remained 'rather muddled' as the doctors strove to find a drug regime that would lift her ailing spirits. On their return from France the family stayed first in Bournemouth, then in London, before returning to Hawarden Castle, from where Helen wrote to her friend, Lady Aberdeen, outlining the current situation. Gladstone had been suffering facial neuralgia for some considerable time. Now terminal cancer of the mouth was diagnosed.

Suddenly on March 13th [the doctors in Bournemouth] discovered a swelling on the palate. They had always been aware of the possibility of this symptom, and had kept a look-out, but the long continued improvement in the state of the mouth had seemed a proof that there could be no deep-seated mischief ... From that day the doctors practically knew he could not recover, though it was decided to have the surgeon in consultation on the 18th.

He could only confirm the worst construction. It was a relief to Father to be told he could not recover. He has long, though with entire submission, desired the end; for him, I only fear the (probable) months of waiting may seem terribly long. But now the doctors can feel it right to do all they can to ease the pain, and so far with success: for the last week, I do not think that he has had any severe pain. May this only continue. My mother does not fully know yet: we dread the shock for her, and want her to understand gradually. I think she must be dimly aware that we never now speak of cure, but only of relief from pain. So if you should write to her, do not be too explicit; though we want her by degrees to think it more and more serious. You will understand the sadness and solemnity of this time – but there is so much that is holy and peaceful in it, too. It was most touching when we left Bournemouth, when he passed through the crowds, stirred by the audible blessings of men, he turned and spoke his farewell: 'God bless you all, and this place, and the land you love'. Was it not the spirit and seal of his whole political career?[13]

So Gladstone came home to Hawarden to die. No secret was made of his terminal condition. Indeed, a formal announcement was made to the press, and for eight weeks his family – and the nation – waited for him to die a very public death. His last public statement was a reply to a letter of 'sorrow and affection' from the University of Oxford with whose affairs he had been closely involved as an undergraduate, as one of its two MPs, and as a political reformer. He dictated this letter to his daughter, Helen:

There is no expression of Christian sympathy that I value more than that of the University of Oxford ... I served her perhaps mistakenly, but to the best of my ability. My most earnest prayers are hers to the uttermost and the last.[14]

Gladstone's world began to shrink around him. He gave up his ordinary habits, one by one. He ceased to go outdoors, ceased to come downstairs, and finally ceased to leave his bed except to kneel beside it to take Holy Communion. He joined visitors in reading hymns as best he could, and his family gathered closer. He began to drift in and out of consciousness, saying little but to thank those around for their 'kindness, kindness, kindness; nothing but kindness on every side'. Two days before he died, when his attendants asked if he were in pain, he answered: 'I am quite comfortable. I am only waiting, only waiting'. He had not long to wait.

As the end drew near, Hawarden gradually filled up with journalists – artists and photographers, as well as special correspondents. Two dozen extra postmen were drafted in to cope with the volume of mail and telegraphs. The press were given their own office in the smoking room at Hawarden Castle, just under Gladstone's bedroom. They suspected the struggle was over when, early on the morning of Sunday 19 May – Ascension Day – they heard the rector of Hawarden, Gladstone's son Stephen, begin to recite prayers for the dead. As the passing bell at Hawarden Church rang out the sad message to the local community, the journalists raced down the hill on their bikes to the telegraph office to relay the news to the world at large.

Dressed in the scarlet robes of a Doctor of Civil Law of the University of Oxford, Gladstone was laid out in his library, the Temple of Peace, where thousands of people came to pay their last respects. 'He lay on his bed like a king', his daughter Mary wrote, adding that he looked exactly as he had done the last time he wore the robes in 1892, to give the Romanes Lecture in Oxford's Sheldonian Theatre. A family friend, William Blake Richmond, drew a sketch of Gladstone dead, and wrote on it a dedication to Sister Kate Pitts, who, together with Sister Heslop, had cared for him during the final decline.

Four days later, Gladstone's plain oak coffin – crafted by the village carpenter – was taken the short distance from Hawarden Castle to Hawarden Church for a service of Communion.[15] From there the bier was drawn back through the castle grounds to the local railway station by four parties of bearers made up of colliers, estate workmen, tenants and neighbours. At each point where the cortège stopped to change bearers one of Gladstone's favourite hymns was sung. Along the way, inmates of the orphanage and the workhouse turned out to pay their respects. At the station, the coffin – accompanied by family members, attendants and journalists – was transferred to a private train and drawn through the night to London by a jet-black engine that, thirty-two years earlier, had been given the name *Gladstone*. At Willesden, the train was diverted to Earls Court, where the coffin was transferred to the District Line of the London Underground for the final stage of its journey to Westminster Hall. There was no procession through the capital, no parading of the coffin through the streets. There was no need to take the body to the people. The people came all by themselves to say goodbye to the 'People's William'. An estimated quarter of a million filed past his coffin during its two days of lying in state – or two hundred a minute, according to police reports. Gladstone had specified that there was to be no pomp, and the spectacle was magnificent in its simplicity. Just a black sable cloth on the platform that supported the coffin, a tall candle at each corner, and a plain brass cross at the head.

The state funeral took place on 28 May in Westminster Abbey. It was equally simple. The *Times* commented that the venue had witnessed 'more imposing, more magnificent rites ... but none more impressively austere'. The guests included leading figures of the day from many walks of life. The artistic community, for example, was represented, amongst others, by Edward Burne-Jones – a friend of Gladstone's daughter Mary – who sadly caught a cold on the day and died shortly afterwards as a result. Thomas Hardy was there, and described the scene to his sister as 'plain even to bareness'.[16] Clara Blake Richmond, wife of the artist responsible for Gladstone's death-bed portrait and afterwards for the design of his memorial at Hawarden, wrote:

> We were allowed to be in the Abbey for Mr Gladstone's funeral. It was beautiful, solemn and grand beyond words – the very air seemed to be full of affection and reverence for him. Dear old Mrs Gladstone was there, very brave and not so frail as one would have expected – but so lonely. *That* broke us down. Many others were in tears also.[17]

Eton schoolboys provided the guard of honour, and the principal two of the ten pall-bearers were future kings. Leading the cortège on the right was the Prince of Wales (Edward VII) and, on the left, his son the Duke of York (George V). The *Times* commented that they were there 'to represent for the Royal family their regard for one who was ever their loyal and chivalrous defender'. Mary Drew recorded that her mother went into the Abbey a widow, but came out a bride.

On hearing of Gladstone's death, Victoria had confided to a lady-in-waiting: 'I did not like the man. How can I say I am sorry when I am not?'[18] To Catherine, she wrote in guarded tones that she would 'always gratefully remember how anxious he always was to serve me and mine in all that concerned my personal comfort and welfare ... as well as that of my family'.[19] Gladstone may have served the royal family well; but in a letter to her eldest daughter, Vicky, the Empress Frederick of Germany,

Victoria singled out South Africa, Sudan and Ireland as areas in which her personal feeling was that Gladstone's policies had failed the country. It says more about Victoria Imperatrix than about him.

> I cannot say I think he was 'a great Englishman'. He was a clever man, full of talent, but he never tried to keep up the honour and prestige of Great Britain. He gave away the Transvaal and he abandoned Gordon, he destroyed the Irish Church and tried to separate England from Ireland and he set class against class. The harm he did cannot be easily undone ... But he was a good and very religious man.[20]

When she heard that her son and grandson were to carry Gladstone to his final resting-place, the Queen, in a final flash of hostility at the thought of his enjoying such a privilege in having them act in this capacity, took the Prince of Wales to task. She wrote to him, asking what the precedents were for royal mourners, and on whose advice they had acted. The Prince telegraphed back that there was no precedent and that he took no advice – nor would he ever forget what a friend Mr Gladstone had been to the royal family. And he doubly stressed the point on the day of the funeral. For as Catherine Gladstone stopped to thank the pall-bearers as she left the Abbey, the Prince of Wales bent to kiss her hand. The others followed suit. It was a gracious gesture interpreted by many as an apology for the final snub delivered by his mother: for, by what the Queen claimed was an oversight, Gladstone's death had not been mentioned in the Court circular. On the day of the funeral, the Queen confined herself to sending a polite telegram to Catherine. The monarch did not attend public funerals. She may, however, have enjoyed a taste of revenge in one final snub to the man who, seventeen years earlier, had declared himself too busy to attend the funeral of her beloved Disraeli.

In his will, Gladstone had stipulated that he would only be buried where Catherine could join him. And this she did, two years later, on 14 June 1900. It was a sweet but short ceremony. Their son Harry said it was more like a marriage than a funeral as she was laid to rest beside him in Westminster Abbey.

Victoria died six months later and was buried with her own beloved Albert in the mausoleum in the gardens of Frogmore House, Windsor. She and Gladstone had each served their country, in their different ways, for six and a half decades. In the end, what she perhaps found so hard to bear was that the 'People's William' was – and would remain – as much of a symbol of the Victorian age as was its eponymous Queen.

But more than that was involved. Gladstone's attitude to all women, not just his revered sovereign, encapsulated one of the nineteenth century's major anxieties. In an age of dramatic technological, social and economic change, many Victorians looked back with nostalgia to what they perceived, rightly or wrongly, to be the more straightforward values of the middle ages. This manifested itself in many ways: in Pre-Raphaelite art, in neo-Gothic architecture, in Anglo-Catholicism. For Gladstone, it manifested itself in a lifetime's campaign to celebrate the virtue of honourable women; or, where their virtue seemed threatened by prostitution, opium or simple feminine weakness, to do his best to save them. He understood from his own beloved and respected daughters and nieces that change was in the wind – that, sooner or later, there would be university degrees for women, votes for women, ultimately equal rights as well. If that was what they wanted, they should have it, eventually. That was only right and just. But he feared lest, in becoming strong, their uniquely feminine graces should be compromised as a result. And of that he wished to be no part.

Notes

Notes to Introduction

1. *Times*, 4 February 1927.
2. Herbert Gladstone, *After Thirty Years* (London, 1928), p. 435. Within five years, both brothers were dead.
3. *Manchester Guardian*, 4 February 1927.
4. Ibid.
5. Ibid.
6. *Daily Mail*, 4 February 1927.
7. Ibid.
8. TNA, CHAR 2/1 142/29.
9. Ibid.
10. At the time, she would have been under the patronage of the Prince of Wales, the future Edward VII.
11. Lillie Langtry, *The Days I Knew: An Autobiography* (Jersey, 1989), p. 103.
12. *Daily Telegraph*, 4 February 1927.
13. GG MSS 2773.
14. *Diaries*, xiii, p. 428.

Notes to Chapter 1: Early Years

1. The house survives, as number 62, and now comprises thirteen flats.
2. The 's' was dropped by John Gladstone. Even earlier, the family name was 'Gledstanes'.
3. Equivalent to about £30 million today. See: 'Inflation: The Value of the Pound 1750–1998', House of Commons Research Paper, 99/20, 23 February 1999.
4. In later life, genealogists sought to prove that Gladstone was a blood relation, through his maternal grandmother, and via the royal Stewarts, of Queen Victoria herself. See S. G. Checkland, *The Gladstones: A Family Biography, 1864–1851* (Cambridge, 1971), p. 38.

5. W. E. Gladstone, *Autobiographica*, ed. John Brooke and Mary Sorensen (London, 1971), 3 vols, i, p. 18.

6. H. C. G. Matthew, *Gladstone* (Oxford, 1997), p. 5.

7. Visiting spas without one's husband was recommended by some doctors of the time as a practical contraceptive device.

8. Gladstone, *Autobiographica*, i, p. 21.

9. Gladstone, *Autobiographica*, i , pp. 16, 149.

10. GG MSS 741.

11. Gladstone, *Autobiographica*, i, p. 16.

12. Gladstone, *Autobiographica*, i, p. 18.

13. Gladstone, *Autoniographica*, i, pp. 19–20.

14. John Gladstone named the house in honour of his wife, whose clan chief was the Earl of Seaforth.

15. BL, Add MS 44291, fol. 1, quoted in Richard Shannon, *Gladstone: Peel's Inheritor* (London, 1992), p. 21.

16. He did not subscribe to all her opinions. Anne, who believed one should go nowhere where God could not be present, disapproved strongly of the theatre – which became one of Gladstone's abiding pleasures.

17. Anne seems to have sensed that she would die almost from the beginning. In her day book she wrote, shortly after becoming ill, that God was 'chastening her with love/to fit her for the realms above'. Shortly before Christmas 1824 she wrote a 'prayer – when suffering': Lord! If it is thy will / That I should suffer still / I pray Thee, sanctify my pain, / And send Thy peace again.'; and, later: 'Come, Pain! Thou faithful monitor / Teach me that I may die ere long'. GG MSS 1741.

18. *Diaries*, i, 21 February 1829.

19. *Diaries*, i, 22 February 1829.

20. *Diaries*, i, 23 February 1829.

21. Anne had expressed the wish to be buried next to her parents when the time came. This happened in 1847, after her father built St Andrew's Chapel on the Fasque estate in Kincardineshire in Scotland where the family had its main home from 1833. Her body was brought from Liverpool, together with that of Sir John's mother-in-law and sister-in-law, and placed in the vault of St Andrew's with the body of his wife, which was brought home from the church in the nearby village of Fettercairn.

22. GG MSS 629, 29 February 1829.

23. GG MSS 629, 26 June 1829.

24. GG MSS 629, 22 May and 1 April 1829. Gladstone expressed annoyance with his brothers over this, insisting he did mention it to Tom and John

Neilson one evening, but they were tired and didn't listen. (GG MSS 751).
An endless capacity to listen may have been one of young Helen's
attractions for William.

25. As gynaecological complaints seem to have plagued Helen's ill health, this
comes as no surprise.

26. GG MSS 751, fos 41–42, 26 June 1829.

27. This 'covenant' was not Anne Mackenzie Gladstone's only legacy. Just
weeks before her death, she had been drawing up plans for an asylum for
female incurables. Within days of her funeral, John Gladstone had begun
discussions with other potential benefactors, originally with a view to
realising his daughter's plans by setting up an establishment in Liverpool
that would provide a compassionate alternative to the workhouse for a
dozen or so terminally ill and destitute persons. In the event it was ten
years – by which time the Gladstones has established themselves on their
Scottish estate at Fasque – before a trust was created to provide an asylum in the grounds of St Thomas's church and hospital in Leith, the
port district of Edinburgh. John Gladstone had the asylum built in his
daughter's memory entirely at his own expense with an annual budget
to fund ten patients, a matron and two servants. Together with their
responsibilities for ensuring good behaviour and sobriety, the staff were
specifically instructed to 'be kind to the inmates and attentive to their
comfort'. The asylum was closed, the remaining inmate being given a
pension, and the building sold in 1877. GG MSS 1232.

28. GG MSS 629, 2 July 1829.

29. GG MSS 751, fos 46, 11 October 1829.

30. GG MSS 751, fos 47–48, 11 October 1829.

31. GG MSS 751, fol. 49, 11 October 1829.

32. GG MSS 629, 18 October 1829.

33. GG MSS 604, 20 January 1830.

34. GG MSS 754, 18 June 1835.

Notes to Chapter 2: Eton and Christ Church

1. And some Dames were men.

2. W. E. Gladstone, *Autobiographica*, eds John Brooke and Mary Sorensen
(London, 1971), p. 20.

3. Quoted in S. G. Checkland, *The Gladstones: A Family Biography* (Cambridge, 1971), p. 138.

4. Gladstone, *Autobiographica*, i, p. 24.

5. Gladstone, *Autobiographica*, i, p. 24.

6. Gladstone, *Autobiographica*, i, pp. 24–5.

7. R. Jenkins, *Gladstone* (London, 1995), p. 16. Jenkins also calls Hallam a 'minx'.

8. On his death in Vienna in 1833, Francis Doyle described Hallam as 'the most ebullient and charming Etonian of his time. To all of us who knew, and I may say worshipped, him, his early death was a misfortune which we have never forgotten'. See Doyle's preface to James Milnes Gaskell, *Records of an Eton Schoolboy*, ed. Charles Milnes Gaskell (printed privately, 1833), p. ix.

9. John Morley, *Life of Gladstone* (London, 1908), 2 vols, i, p. 108.

10. Gladstone, *Autobiographica*, i, pp. 28–29.

11. *Diaries*, i, 24 September 1826.

12. Gladstone, *Autobiographica*, i, pp. 29–30.

13. *Diaries*, i, 14 September 1829.

14. John Morley, *Life of Gladstone*, (London, 1908), 2 vols, i, pp. 30–31.

15. Morley, *Gladstone*, p. 32.

16. Hallam and Gaskell also amicably shared a devotion to the young English beauty Anna Wintour, whom they met in Rome after university.

17. Gaskell, *Records of an Eton Schoolboy*, p. 85.

18. Ibid.

19. Gladstone, *Autobiographica*, i, p. 108.

20. *Diaries*, i, 2 December 1827.

21. Gladstone, *Autobiographica*, i, p. 189.

22. *Diaries*, i, 29 October 1828.

23. Gladstone, *Autobiographica*, i, p. 209.

24. Gaskell, *Records of an Eton Schoolboy*, p. 164.

25. Gaskell, *Records of an Eton Schoolboy*, p. 167.

26. Ibid.

27. Gladstone, *Autobiographica*, i, p. 217.

28. GG MSS 222.

29. *Diaries*, i, 15 July 1832.

30. Gladstone, *Autobiographica*, i, p. 53.

31. GG MSS 394, fol. 223.

32. GG MSS 394, fos 235–39.

33. *Diaries*, ii, 11 May 1835.

34. *Diaries*, ii, 8 July 1835.

35. GG MSS 1383–85, 'Reflections by WEG Concerning his Proposal of Marriage to Caroline Farquhar'.

36. GG MSS 705, 1 August 1835

37. GG MSS 707, 27 August 1835.

38. GG MSS 707, 31 August 1835.
39. GG MSS 707, 31 August 1835.
40. GG MSS 705, 3 September 1835.
41. GG MSS 705, 4 September 1835.
42. GG MSS 705, 15 July 1835.
43. GG MSS 705, 6 September 1835.
44. GG MSS 705, 13 February 1835.
45. GG MSS 705, 22 February 1835.
46. GG MSS 1385.
47. Widowed herself in 1861, Queen Victoria often used Court appointments as a means of providing financial security for the widows and daughters of former courtiers. For example, Grey's niece Theresa married Henry Ponsonby, who succeeded Grey as Private Secretary to Victoria. When Ponsonby died, Theresa became a Woman of the Bedchamber.
48. Edward Hamilton, *Gladstone: A Monograph* (London, 1899), p. 32.
49. *Diaries*, ii, 22 September 1835.
50. Gladstone, *Autobiographica*, i, p. 59.
51. Gladstone, *Autobiographica*, i, p. 61.
52. *Diaries*, ii, 25 September 1835: 'che si rincrescessero di aver finito le cose così subito: e questo mi piace muovendo ringraziamente all Sapienza di Dio senza troppo turbare il mio cuore fatto da mestizia più stabile e più chiaro.'
53. Later it would be transferred to the vault of the newly-built chapel of St Andrew's at Fasque.
54. *Diaries*, ii, 30 September 1835.
55. *Diaries*, ii, 20 November 1835: 'un'allegria che pessimamente s'accorda col spirito di dentro'.
56. *Diaries*, ii, 23 November 1835: 'pensieri sulle mie cose; fa d'uopo disimbrogliarle: e più mi sento come sono infelice per un sposo. E fra volieri e le pratiche, c'è tanta differenza: a delle due parti di mia natura, quale si mariterebbe?'
57. GG MSS 708, 15 November 1837.
58. GG MSS 708, 15 November 1837.
59. GG MSS 708.
60. *Diaries*, ii, 14 November 1837.
61. *Diaries*, ii, 17 November 1837.
62. *Diaries*, ii, 8 January 1838: 'Di quando in quando non mi potei sapere se la musica venisse dal cielo o fosse della terra, e volontieri avrei restato fisso al luogo. Udiva la dicendomi "la sposa ti sarà come una vigna in sulle pareti della tua casa. Tuoi figli come i rami dell'uliva, dintorno alla tua

tavola ... E vedrai gli figli de' tuo' figli e la pace in sull'Israele." Questa non mi fu veramente una Providenza? Ed affatto senza che io vo avessi parte. Ed anche un promesso: di nozze no, ma, siccome fissamente io credo, di quell'eterno amore che finora mi ha salvato'.

63. GG MSS 708, 13 January 1838.
64. *Diaries*, ii, 30 March 1838.
65. *Diaries*, ii, 28 April 1838: 'Quei pochi che mi guardano, parebbero facilmente ingannarsi circa i miei perigli, i quali vengono, mi pare, da dentro massimamente. Tutto il di fuori è in qualche maniera disarmato per ora, mediante la freddezza, come di gelo, del cuore ... Adesso cammino fra le pompe del mondo come morto, fra negozi come necribondo, portando il petto di pietra ... Questo viene da pochissime agrissime cose che mi sono andate a contrappelo. Può cambiarsi. E mentre dura, bisogna aver cura ... O vivere or morire: o gioire o aver pena: riuscire o forte o debole, o sprezzato o ben stimato: che sia sempre pronto, stando da giorno in giorno nella Divina voglia.'
66. *Diaries*, ii, 23 May 1838.
67. *Diaries*, ii, 4 June 1838.
68. *Diaries*, ii, 19 June 1838: 'Le nozze stan fisse; sian felici.'
69. GG MSS 697, n.d.

Notes to Chapter 3: Catherine

1. *Diaries*, i, 23 August 1826. Gladstone, aged sixteen, bought a copy of *Aristotle's Master Piece* [sic] which had been, for over a century, the principal popular handbook in English of sex physiology – 'and read part of it. It seems to me not bad; whether useful or not, I do not know'. The entry is written in Greek and scored through.
2. *Diaries*, iii, p. xliv.
3. *Diaries*, i, 12 January 1831.
4. Matthew suggests that one of the reasons Gladstone felt comfortable in the company of prostitutes was that he had spent much time with servants in his youth because of his mother's illness.
5. D. C. Lathbury, *Correspondence on Church and Religion of W. E. Gladstone* (London, 1910), pp. 437–43. The original 'Thirty-Nine Articles' were doctrinal statements of the Church of England which, at the time, all Anglican clergy – and Oxford students – were required formally to accept.
6. Harriet Brooke, quoted in Georgina Battiscombe, *Mrs Gladstone* (London, 1956), p. 20.

7. BL, Add MS 44727, fol. 175, September 1837, quoted in Richard Shannon, *Gladstone: Peel's Inheritor* (London, 1982), p. 63.
8. For a detailed account of Catherine Glynne's antecedents, see Mary Drew, *Catherine Gladstone* (London, 1919).
9. Drew, *Catherine Gladstone*, pp. 8–9.
10. Drew, *Catherine Gladstone*, p. 14ff.
11. Battiscombe, *Mrs Gladstone*, p. 23.
12. *Diaries*, ii, 6 February 1839.
13. *Diaries*, ii, 22 September 1838.
14. GG MSS 751, fol. 125, 22 September 1838.
15. *Diaries*, 29 September 1838.
16. *Diaries*, 8 October 1838.
17. *Diaries*, ii, 1 November 1838.
18. GG MSS 629, 6 December 1838.
19. *Diaries*, ii, 6 December 1838.
20. *Diaries*, ii, 17 December 1838.
21. GG MSS 751, fos 131–34, 17 December 1838.
22. *Diaries*, ii, 3 January 1838.
23. *Diaries*, ii, 6 February 1839. The church is identified as Santa Maria Maggiore in Battiscombe, *Mrs Gladstone*, p. 26.
24. Philip Magnus, *Gladstone* (London, 1954), pp. 38–39.
25. Magnus, *Gladstone*, pp. 39–40.
26. Battiscombe, *Mrs Gladstone*, p. 27.
27. In Glynnese, a sham appearance was 'a false flash'; an excessively well-behaved child was 'pintoed', while a querulous one was 'twarly'. A 'bathing-feel' was something one experienced before going to the dentist. By 1841, Gladstone was so au fait with Glynnese that, when asked how he felt on becoming Vice-President of the Board of Trade, he replied: 'bathing-feel'. See George William, Lord Lyttelton, *Contributions Towards a Glossary of the Glynne Language by a Student* (St Deiniol's, M 34.9 GL15). The work is prefaced with a quotation from the French diplomat Talleyrand: 'Language was given to man to conceal his tongues'.
28. *Diaries*, ii, 23 January 1839.
29. *Diaries*, ii, 6 February 1839.
30. *Diaries*, ii, 6 February 1839.
31. *Diaries*, ii, 27 May 1839.
32. The theme of the book was that membership of the Church of England ought to be a fundamental qualification for membership of the national community. This meant, amongst other things, the maintenance of the Anglican Church in predominantly Roman Catholic Ireland, and the

exclusion of Roman Catholics and Non-Conformists from public office. It was broadly accepted by the Church and universities, while most lay opinion was hostile.

33. *Diaries*, ii, 9 June 1839.
34. Colonel Francis Vernon Harcourt was the worst offender. Having plighted his troth to Catherine, he married the much richer Lady Catherine Julia Jenkinson, daughter of the Earl of Liverpool. Catherine was apparently very upset. Her friend Harriet Brooke, later Lady Brabazon, consoled her: 'Thank God our dearest Pussy [Catherine's family nickname] has been spared such a fate, reserved, we may dare to trust and believe, for one more worthy of appreciating the treasures of her heart'. Battiscombe, *Mrs Gladstone*, p. 19.
35. *Diaries*, ii, 17 June 1839.
36. *Diaries*, ii, 24 July 1839.
37. *Diaries*, ii, 25 July 1839.
38. The conspicuous absentee at the wedding was Lady Glynne (widowed in 1816), who was suffering from depression and felt unable to attend. Pondering this, Gladstone wrote that life was wonderful 'yet is has had its warning voice. Just before setting out, we saw Lady Glynne: birth, beauty, riches, energy, the respect of men, all were hers: and she has not passed middle age: but she remained in uneasy depression at the Castle, and did not venture to attend while she felt being absent. How strong are the contrasts of this mortal life – whereof today has been the flower – for that mingling of sanctity, joy and love, which sin hardly ever suffers to manifest itself on earth, and there but for a moment'. *Diaries*, ii, 25 June 1839.
39. *Diaries*, ii, 25 July 1839.
40. *Diaries*, ii, 26 July 1839.
41. *Diaries*, ii 29 July 1839.
42. *Diaries*, ii, 6 August 1839.
43. *Diaries*, ii, 20 August 1839.
44. *Diaries*, ii, 30 August 1839. It was money that he would spend, primarily, on his prostitute rescue work.
45. *Diaries*, ii, 20 September 1839.
46. On comparing notes after their honeymoons, Catherine and Mary found that both their husbands had the habit of pulling books out of their pockets and becoming engrossed in them, whenever there was a spare moment. See Magnus, *Gladstone*, p. 46.
47. *Diaries*, ii, 24 September 1839.
48. One wonders whether she was not in a very similar state of depression to

Lady Glynne, who was faced with not seeing her elder daughter for five months after her marriage.

49. *Diaries*, ii, 26 November 1839

50. *Diaries*, ii, 17 December 1839.

51. *Diaries*, ii, 29 December 1839.

52. Battiscombe, *Mrs Gladstone*, p. 37.

53. This incident is related in Battiscombe, *Mrs Gladstone*, p. 37.

54. Since her brother Sir Stephen Glynne never married, and her brother Henry's only son died shortly after birth, the Hawarden estate eventually passed to Catherine and William's son, by which time it had long since become the Gladstone family home as well as the Glynnes, and a second home for the Lytteltons and their many children.

Notes to Chapter 4: Helen

1. John Morley, *Life of Gladstone* (London, 1908), 2 vols, i, p. 171.

2. Henry also died prematurely, in Florence in 1850. Gladstone heard the news directly from his father, also Henry Hallam, whom he met by chance in Italy as Hallam was returning home after the sad event.

3. Morley, *Gladstone*, i, 168–69.

4. Quoted in Jack Beeching, *The Chinese Opium Wars* (San Diego and New York, 1975), p. 109.

5. It was a sentiment that would be echoed nearly forty years later in Gladstone's famous Midlothian speech on the plight of the Afghan peasant.

6. Sir James was Home Secretary in the next Tory administration, 1841–46.

7. In the event, it failed by only a handful of votes.

8. Aspirin was first introduced in 1899 by the German company Friedrich Bayer, which, like many chemical manufacturers at the time, had made the transition from dye production to pharmaceuticals in the late 1880s.

9. 'Addiction' originally meant the condition of a slave given over to a master.

10. GG MSS 751, fos 5 and 9.

11. GG MSS 751, fol. 15.

12. Presumably the 'circumstances' were her constant 'ill health'.

13. GG MSS 751, fos 146–59, 10 January 1841.

14. This is, in fact, quite possible. Helen left many of her letters unopened, to be read for the first time by John Morley. When pressurised by him, her response was often silence.

15. GG MSS 751, fos 150–59, 30 May 1842.

16. GG MSS 751, fos 160, 12 June 1842.

17. Throughout Europe, it was even deemed 'fashionable'.

18. GG MSS 751, fol. 160, 12 June 1842.

19. GG MSS 630, 2 July 1842.

20. *Record*, 18 July 1842.

21. S. G. Checkland, *The Gladstones: A Family Biography, 1764–1851* (Cambridge, 1971), p. 357.

22. Anthony Ashley Cooper (1801–1885) was later to become the seventh Earl of Shaftesbury. As Lord Ashley he had piloted the Lunacy Act of 1845, which achieved considerable reforms. He had chaired the previous Lunacy Commission since 1834.

23. Bagshawe's chambers were at 4 Lamb's Conduit Place; his home address was 35 Fitzroy Square.

24. This took the form of a note Helen left with William 'by way of a testament' when she left for the Continent in early 1845. She wrote a second will in 1855 at the Rome convent where she was again being treated for drug addiction. This was verified by the then mother superior. This second will was lost, which her executors regarded as a matter of extreme negligence on the part of the Gladstones. It seems likely that she may have left her estate to the Dominican Order. Her lawyers were Pears, Logan & Gibbons, Liverpool, who stated: 'There is great uncertainty as to the late Miss Gladstone's testamentary dispositions'. GG MSS 1750 and 1754, December, 1881.

25. The Gladstones successfully contested this bequest. H. R. Bagshawe had predeceased Helen.

26. Minutes of the Commissioners in Lunacy, TNA, MH 50/1, pp. 146–47.

27. GG MSS 531, 9 January 1846.

28. Ibid.

29. Checkland, *The Gladstones*, p. 353

30. *Diaries*, iii, p. 152.

31. Lunacy Commissioners, TNA, Kew, MH 50/1, p. 152.

32. Lunacy Commissioners, TNA, Kew, MH 50/1, p. 169.

33. Checkland, *The Gladstones*, p. 353.

34. GG MSS 633, undated.

35. Checkland, *The Gladstones*, p. 353. Checkland also registered Helen's defiance, noting that she was 'fierce against her brothers, crying that she would bring them to their knees'.

36. For example, in his letter to Helen on her conversion to Rome, GG MS 751, fol. 158, 30 May, 1842.

37. GG MSS 531, 11 December 1845.

38. GG MSS 630, 7 January 1846.

39. GG MSS 69, undated.
40. Helen's room, which was originally the house chapel before John Gladstone built a church on the estate, has since been returned to its original state and the secret door to the back stairs filled in again.
41. GG MSS 747, 18 March 1847.
42. GG MSS 747, 22 May, 1843.
43. *Diaries*, iii, p. 658.
44. Ibid.
45. *Diaries*, iii, p. 659. Interestingly, this entry implies that laudanum – opium in alcohol – was being used to control the greater habit.
46. GG MSS 365, 2 November 1847.
47. GG MSS 366, January 1848.
48. Ibid.
49. GG MSS 365, 23 October 1847.
50. GG MSS 366, January 1848.
51. Thomas Litchfield, 'On the Use and Abuse of the Speculum', *Lancet*, 1 (8 June, 1850), p. 705. See also Barbara Harrison, 'Women and Health', *Women's History: Britain, 1850–1945*, ed. June Purvis (1995), p. 167.
52. Robert Brudenell Carter, *On the Pathology and Treatment of Hysteria* (London, 1853), p. 69, quoted on the website of the University of Virginia, www.virginia.edu/~wwc2r/vicstudies/vicstudies.new.html.
53. GG MSS 366, January 1848.
54. Philip Magnus, *Gladstone* (London, 1963), p. 83, and GG MSS 360. Such symptoms can, however, be caused by calcium depletion following prolonged opium consumption; in which case, Wiseman's intervention would have been a genuine miracle.
55. Magnus, *Gladstone*, p. 84.
56. GG MSS 751, 24 November 1848.
57. Magnus, *Gladstone*, p. 84. Magnus comments that there was 'a piquant and symbolic quality about the disclosure of that last act of defiance when Miss Gladstone's physical and mental health were at last re-established'.
58. A private analysis of Helen's handwriting, by graphologist Ruth Rostron in June 2002, suggested that, as well as strong organisational abilities, Helen was highly intelligent, energetic and sexual, though suffering from low self-esteem.
59. In Helen's case, much of the published information about her is literally in footnotes, and adverse comments, by others. Yet there are about a thousand of her letters at St Deiniol's Library, with the same amount again either to her or about her. Most of the correspondence is with William. Helen's letters are usually undated and must therefore be dated by replies

from others. Most carry no address, and many are illegible. In moments of extreme stress, particularly in her relationship with William, probably the most stressful of her life, Helen's defence mechanism was not to write at all. Several of William's letters to her were opened only after they were both dead, by his first official biographer, John Morley.

60. Beeching, *The Chinese Opium Wars*, p. 110. Beeching, amongst others, maintains that his experience with Helen's addiction was what made William Gladstone so vehemently opposed to the opium trade with China: 'He spoke [in Parliament] as one who had mastered the subject, yet with an undertone of passion ... Indian opium casts a ... shadow over his as over many other Victorian homes'.

61. For a discussion of Gladstone and courtly love, see Anne Isba, 'Gladstone and Dante: The Place of Dante in the Life and Thought of a Victorian Statesman' (unpublished Ph.D. thesis, Keele University, 2001), pp. 78–81.

62. *Diaries*, iii, p. 662 (20 October 1847).

63. GG MS 630, 11 June 1842.

64. GG MSS 630, 11 June 1842.

65. GG MSS 366, January 1848.

66. GG MSS 354, 10 February 1829. While the age of consent at the time was twelve, the average age on marriage in the mid-nineteenth century was twenty-five for a woman and twenty-seven for a man.

67. GG MSS 354.12 February 1829.

68. GG MSS 354, n. d.

69. GG MSS 354, 8 December 1829.

Notes to Chapter 5: Lady Lincoln

1. Philip Magnus, *Gladstone* (London, 1954), p. 21.

2. The Duchess of Hamilton was wealthy in her own right. A daughter of the fabulously extravagant but decadent William Beckford, she grew up amid the Gothic splendour of Fonthill Abbey.

3. *Diaries*, ii (1833–39).

4. GG MSS 751, fol. 100, 15 April 1836.

5. *Diaries*, ii (1833–39).

6. From the Newcastle Papers in the University of Nottingham Library, quoted in Virginia Surtees, *A Beckford Inheritance: The Lady Lincoln Scandal* (Salisbury, 1977), p. 37. Ironically, the child weaned to facilitate the affair – Edward Pelham-Clinton – was the only one of the Lincolns' five children who turned out well.

7. *Diaries*, ii (1833–39).

8. The Duke claimed the French dukedom of Châtelherault, and the family communicated with each other in French.
9. Quoted in Surtees, *A Beckford Inheritance*, p. 48.
10. The solicitors were W. Pemberton and Sir William Follett, by then Solicitor-General, who, five years earlier, had appeared for George Norton in the action he brought against Lord Melbourne for alleged adultery with his wife Caroline.
11. Quoted in Surtees, *A Beckford Inheritance*, pp. 51–52.
12. Ibid., p. 52.
13. *Private Letters of Sir Robert Peel*, ed. George Peel (London, 1920), pp. 193, 195.
14. *Diaries*, iii (1840–47).
15. Newcastle Papers, quoted in Surtees, *A Beckford Inheritance*, p. 60.
16. GG MSS 788.
17. Surtees, *A Beckford Inheritance*, p. 70.
18. Ibid.
19. Horace Walpole was the eldest son of the third Earl of Orford.
20. *Diaries*, iv, 26 May 1843.
21. Ibid. It is interesting that Lincoln seems also to have been convinced that his wife, who planned to travel to Italy from Germany, would, like Helen Gladstone, convert to Roman Catholicism. Gladstone certainly saw opium abuse and Roman Catholicism as part of the same 'web of moral deceit'.
22. Quoted in Surtees, *A Beckford Inheritance*, p. 76.
23. 'I must not let myself be defeated – I have made the right decision for my happiness, if not for my position.'
24. GG MSS 788.
25. GG MSS 2944, undated but, from the content, between November 1848 and June 1849.
26. GG MSS 2945.
27. GG MSS 2947. John Nichol MP contacted Gladstone to provide the names of witnesses to the effect that the couple were living at Naples under an assumed identity, with permission for these to be made known to Lord Lincoln.
28. *Diaries*, iv (1848–54).
29. Ibid. 7 July, 1849.
30. Henry Manning, then Archdeacon of Chichester, had been seriously ill the previous year and was temperamentally unsuited to chasing across Europe to snatch an erring wife from the arms of her lover. He was also contemplating his conversion to Roman Catholicism, a move that was to alienate Gladstone from him for many years.

31. *Diaries*, iv (1848–54). The next day, 12 July 1849, Gladstone wrote: 'Late at night, I made copies of parts of the painful and shameful points of Lady W's case'. This presumable refers to the evidence that Lady Walpole, in a parallel operation, was gathering against her persistently philandering and violent husband.

32. Surtees, *A Beckford Inheritance*, p. 97.

33. GG MSS 2945, 12 July 1849.

34. *Diaries*, iv, 15 July 1849.

35. GG MSS 771.

36. GG MSS 2945, undated, but from the content likely to be 1 August 1849.

37. *Diaries*, iv, 31 July 1849.

38. *Diaries*, iv, 2 August 1849.

39. *Diaries*, iv, 5 August 1849.

40. Ibid., 9 August 1849.

41. Quoted in Surtees, *A Beckford Inheritance*, p. 110.

42. GG MSS 611.

43. *Diaries*, iv, 9 August 1849.

44. The codes of propriety that governed behaviour in nineteenth-century aristocratic circles required that there must be no doubt about the legitimacy of the first son and preferably the second, after which social discretion was required rather than strict fidelity. See K. D. Reynolds, *Aristocratic Women and Political Society in Victorian Britain* (Oxford, 1998), pp. 9–10.

45. Quoted in Surtees, *A Beckford Inheritance*, p. 120.

46. GG MSS 771.

47. GG MSS 2947.

48. Surtees, *A Beckford Inheritance*, pp. 129–30.

49. Ibid.

50. *Diaries*, iv (1848–54).

51. All references to the evidence given to the House of Lords are in GG MSS 2953: 'Petition, Minutes of Evidence and Act Concerning Divorce of Lord and Lady Lincoln'.

52. Presumably Gladstone would have recognised Lady Lincoln's handwriting.

53. GG MSS 2953.

54. GG MSS 2950.

55. His father's correct name, though he was generally known as 'Horace' was apparently also 'Horatio', according to the details contained in the divorce petition.

56. Surtees, *A Beckford Inheritance*, p. 135. Virginia Surtees also recalls being visited in the late seventies by a mother and daughter claiming to

be descendants of Horatio, but no further details are known (private information).

57. *Diaries*, iv (1848–54).

58. GG MSS 2952. 'A Memorandum as to Lord and Lady Lincoln's Settlement'.

59. They are now at St Deiniol's Library and can be accessed via the Flintshire Record Office.

60. GG MSS 2945.

61. His great-grandfather, William Beckford, was a known homosexual. Before she married the Duke of Hamilton, he had attempted to marry off Suzie's mother, when she was a young girl, to a homosexual friend.

62. It has not been possible to trace the child's birth through local records. The Prince of Wales allegedly kept Susan Vane's love letters to him for forty years after her death.

63. The same request was made to Gladstone by his old friend and reformed courtesan, Laura Thistlethwayte.

64. 'At the end her death was very gentle, today her face is very calm, smiling, she looks like a sleeping child.'

65. BL, Add. MS 44508, fol. 198, 29 November 1889, Lord Edward Pelham-Clinton to W. E. Gladstone.

66. Ibid., 12 December 1889, W. E. Gladstone to Laura Thistlethwayte.

Notes to Chapter 6: Fallen Women

1. Richard Deacon, *The Private Life of Mr Gladstone* (London, 1965), p. 13.

2. Only rarely did Catherine Gladstone question the wisdom of any of her husband's rescue work. When a court case threatened as a result in 1873, she merely commented: 'You are too credulous'. Gladstone admitted: 'She was wiser than I'. *Diaries*, 14 June 1873.

3. Quoted in H. C. G. Matthew, *Gladstone* (Oxford, 1997), p. 94.

4. Stephen Gladstone wrote to his brother Henry on 27 January 1908: '[Father] sometimes said things which unconsciously to himself raised suspicions outside his own circle – suspicions which could never be met'. GG MS 950. These suspicions were refuelled by the Wright case.

5. By comparison, a 2004 Home Office report gave a figure for sex workers in the twenty-first century in the entire United Kingdom as 80,000.

6. *Guardian*, 20 August 2004, p. 5. This is also about the same size as the entire current UK prison population.

7. Henry Mayhew, *London Labour and the London Poor* (London, 1985), p. 259.

8. See Michael Rose, ed., *The Poor and the City: The English Poor Law in its Urban Context, 1834–1914* (Leicester, 1985).

9. Quoted in Deacon, *The Private Life of Mr Gladstone*, p. 39.

10. James Greenwood, *The Seven Curses of London* (Oxford, 1981), p. 173. First published 1869. The other six 'curses' were neglected children, professional thieves, beggars and vagabonds, drunkenness, gambling and a waste of charity.

11. Though a friend of prostitutes, Gladstone voted with the government on the Contagious Diseases Acts. His public persona and private passions were always kept well apart, where possible. Josephine Butler campaigned simultaneously on two fronts: against the insidious Contagious Diseases Acts, which were repealed in the 1880s; and on behalf of the cause of female suffrage.

12. Every year thereafter, on the anniversary of his incarceration, Stead travelled up to London by train wearing his prison uniform. His distinguished career as a journalist and editor ended in 1912 when he went down with the *Titanic*.

13. Mayhew, *London Labour*, p. xxxvi.

14. Mayhew, *London Labour*, p. *xxxv*.

15. Ibid.

16. Ibid.

17. Now All Saints, Margaret Street.

18. The pornography he read consisted mainly of Restoration poems, lewd works by Classical authors, and bawdy French ballads.

19. *Diaries*, 19 July 1848.

20. Some dates for this were added to the document begun on 26 October 1845.

21. Followed by (R) for rescue case, added by Foot and Matthew.

22. *Diaries*, 1 August 1850.

23. *Diaries*, 2 October 1850.

24. *Diaries*, 5 October 1850.

25. *Diaries*, 28 March 1851.

26. *Diaries*, 30 March 1851.

27. *Diaries*, 9 May 1851.

28. *Diaries*, 16 July 1851.

29. *Diaries*, 13 October 1852.

30. Dyce Papers, quoted in Marcia Pointon, 'W. E. Gladstone as an Art Patron and Collector', *Victorian Studies*, 19 (1975), p. 92.

31. The portrait now hangs in the Aberdeen Art Gallery. Until the publication in 1978 of volume five of the Gladstone *Diaries* identified Summerhayes as

the subject the identity of the sitter was unknown, although it had been suspected that she may have been a rescue case.

32. Ibid.

33. Pre-Raphaelite painters were not, however, over-fastidious in their choice of models. Dante Gabriel Rossetti's painting *Dante's Dream* has, as the model for Beatrice, William Morris's wife Jane; at the time of painting, Jane Morris was Rossetti's mistress.

34. *Diaries*, 25 August 1859.

35. Hamilton to Gladstone, 6 February 1884, Lambeth Palace Library, MS 2760, fol. 188, quoted in Matthew, *Gladstone*, p. 542

36. Ibid.

37. Deacon, *Private Life*, p. 49.

38. Joyce Marlow, *Mr and Mrs Gladstone: An Intimate Biography* (London, 1977), pp. 110–11.

39. The wife of the Bishop of London took responsibility for the girls.

40. GG MS 1868.

41. Charles Dickens, *An Appeal to Fallen Women*, pamphlet (London, 1849), p. 1.

42. Matthew has described this attitude as 'a willingness to court evil while doing good ... [a] feeling that he must expose his soul and body to spiritual danger'.

43. *Diaries*, iv, p. 586.

44. *Diaries*, xii, p. 157n.

45. Memorandum by Charles Vickers, 4 February 1904, quoted in Deacon, *Private Life*, p. 168.

46. Deacon, *Private Life*, p. 149, quoting Hamilton's diaries.

47. Deacon, *Private Life*, p. 178.

48. Deacon, *Private* Life, p. 28.

Notes to Chapter 7: Daughters

1. *Diaries*, 4 June 1840.

2. *Diaries*, 17 October 1842.

3. *Diaries*, 7 January 1854. Lawley was Gladstone's secretary.

4. GG MSS 984, fol. 24. Gladstone to daughter Helen for her birthday, 27 August 1866.

5. GG MSS 628, Helen to her father, 28 December 1868.

6. Lucy Masterman, *Mary Gladstone: Her Letters and Diaries* (New York, 1930), p. 4.

7. The incident soon blew over. Also, it came at the end of a tense period

during which Agnes was very ill and her life hung in the balance. It should not, therefore, be taken as indicative. The fact that it warranted a diary entry says as much.

8. *Diaries*, 14 January 1864.

9. David Bebbington, *The Mind of Gladstone: Religion, Homer, and Politics* (Oxford, 2004), p. 270.

10. *Diaries*, 7 April 1850.

11. *Diaries*, 8 April 1850.

12. *Diaries*, 12 April 1850.

13. From a copy of the original made by Helen Gladstone between 29 March and 5 April 1888, GG MS 2096.

14. Lyttelton was a member of the Taunton Commission on Secondary Education which sat from 1864–68, and was the author of the section of its report that recommended secondary education for girls. See National Archive, ED 27.

15. Mary Wollstonecraft, *A Vindication of the Rights of Woman* (London, 1792), fly-leaf. Gladstone's own (1796) annotated copy is at St Deiniol's Library, U 44.21.25.

16. Wollstonecraft, *Rights of Woman*, p. 387.

17. *Times*, 18 July 1890, p. 10.

18. Philip Magnus, *Gladstone* (London, 1954), p. 383.

19. Georgina Battiscombe, *Mrs Gladstone* (London, 1836), p. 71.

20. When she was breast-feeding, he would massage her breasts to relieve engorgement; and he would help the nurse massage her abdomen when, post-partum, she was constipated.

21. *Diaries*, 20 September 1847.

22. *Diaries*, 28 September 1847.

23. The evidence for this is that Gladstone wrote on 25 August 1859: 'Catherine on her back with certain appearances, long disused'. And again, on 30 August: '[Returned to] Hawarden where found Catherine going on well: Saw [doctors] and learned from them that this indisposition only marks an effort of nature to regain equilibrium at a stage of transition'.

24. Catherine's distress may have been compounded by two factors. She was forty-six at the time and almost certainly menopausal. But, more importantly, Gladstone had paid only fleeting visits to the Lyttelton home at Hagley Hall, near Birmingham, during Mary's final illness; mainly he was in London to oppose and amend the government's Divorce Bill. It would be surprising if Catherine had not felt unsupported at this time.

25. GG MSS 603.

26. On New Year's Day 1867, while the Gladstone family were in Rome, Liszt came to visit 'for love of Catherine his old pupil, and played. It was marvellous', Gladstone wrote. Mary added: 'The execution was astonishing, immense form and feeling and more exciting than anything I ever heard. The awful part was that I had to play to him first, which brought on a slight attack of palsy'. Masterman, *Mary Gladstone*, p. 39.

27. Masterman, *Mary Gladstone*, p. 2. She added: 'It is a curious sidelight on those Victorian houses now held up for our admiration that Lady Lyttelton and Mrs Gladstone, both extremely affectionate mothers, seemed to have ... surrendered their daughters to governesses whose severities would now be called cruelty'.

28. Georgina Battiscombe, *Mrs Gladstone* (London, 1956), p. 144.

29. Masterman, *Mary Gladstone*, p. 7.

30. Masterman, *Mary Gladstone*, p. 195.

31. It was May, his third daughter, who had been the great love of future Prime Minister Arthur Balfour. Balfour placed inside May's coffin an emerald ring of his mother's which he had intended as an engagement ring.

32. Quoted in Sheila Fletcher, *Victorian Girls: Lord Lyttelton's Daughters* (London, 1997), p. 215.

33. Masterman, *Mary Gladstone*, p. 199.

34. Masterman, *Mary Gladstone*, p. 202.

35. Quoted in Patricia Jalland, 'Mr Gladstone's Daughters: The Domestic Price of Victorian Politics', in *The Gladstonian Turn of Mind: Essays Presented to J. B. Conacher*, ed. Bruce L. Kinzer (Toronto, 1985), p. 97.

36. The Drews had a daughter, Dorothy ('Dossie') in 1890, when Mary was forty-three.

37. And it was one that her spinster niece would replicate at Hawarden in the mid-1890s.

38. GG MSS 1898, *Newnham College Letter* (January 1926), containing (pp. 68–86) memoirs of Helen Gladstone, p. 80.

39. *Diaries*, 12 May 1874.

40. Fellow student Constance Ashford, quoted in *Newnham College Letter*, January 1926, p. 68.

41. Mary to her brother Henry in May 1878, quoted in Jalland, 'Mr Gladstone's Daughters', p. 115.

42. *Newnham College Letter*, p. 68.

43. Ibid.

44. *Diaries*, 5 January 1877.

45. 'We are very sad over the theft of our treasured little tree – a mean trick,

though probably meant as a practical joke'. Helen Gladstone to William Gladstone, 13 February 1887, GG MS 628.

46. On Helen's death, Newnham sent a wreath that included leaves from Mr Gladstone's oak tree.

47. Mary to her brother Henry in May 1878, quoted in Jalland, 'Mr Gladstone's Daughters', p. 115.

48. GG MS 984, fos 69–70. Gladstone himself used his earned income for charitable purposes, while the family lived off the income from family interests, and these, in turn, were passed on to the next generation.

49. GG MSS 628.

50. *Newnham College Letter*, January 1926, 'Helen Gladstone: In Memoriam', quoted in Jalland, 'Mr Gladstone's Daughters', p. 114.

51. *Newnham College Letter*, p. 70.

52. *Newnham College Letter*, p. 72.

53. GG MSS 628, 7 December 1886.

54. GG MSS 1888.

55. GG MSS 1888.

56. GG MSS 984, fol. 78.

57. GG MSS 984, fos 79–80.

58. GG MSS 638, 20 June 1886.

59. GG MSS 1888.

60. Helen and her mother did not always get on particularly well. In an undated note to Helen, apparently written after some falling-out, Catherine wrote: 'It will help you and it will help me if you will bear in mind I never intend to hurt you, and as my ways have had that *effect*, I *must* have been to blame. Forgive me ... I in all sincerity admire the work you have done. Thank you so much. I do know you do wish to help old Mother. The chief of what I wish to say is let us each bear with one another's faults'. GG MS 985.

61. GG MSS 1888.

62. GG MSS 984, fol. 85.

63. Helen had a second chance. In 1901, after her mother's death, she became Warden of the Women's University Settlement at Southwark.

64. *Diaries*, 26 June 1882, quoting note to the Dean of Windsor, BL, Add MS 44545, fol. 157.

65. *Diaries*, 15 July, 1885.

66. *Diaries*, 31 July 1885, quoting BL, Add. MS 44548, fol. 41.

67. Dilke strenuously denied the allegation, and Gladstone may have suspected an intrigue to undermine the Liberal Party by discrediting his colleague.

68. John Morley, *Life of Gladstone* (London, 1908), ii, p. 213–15. There was also

the case of the prominent politician, and Gladstone's associate, the Marquess of Hartington ('Harty Tarty'), brother-in-law of Gladstone's Lyttelton niece, Lucy Cavendish, who lived with the Duchess of Manchester until she was widowed and free to marry him.

69. W. E. Gladstone, 'Divorce', *Quarterly Review*, July 1857, p. 51.

70. W. E. Gladstone, 'Divorce: A Novel', *Nineteenth Century*, 25, February 1889, pp. 213–15.

71. Ibid.

72. W. E. Gladstone, *New American Review*, November 1889, quoted in *Dairies*, 28 October 1889.

73. *Diaries*, xii, p. 157n.

74. GG MSS 603.

75. *Diaries*, xii, p. 157n.

76. It was 1928 before women were given the right to vote under the same conditions as men.

77. H. C. G. Matthew, *Gladstone* (Oxford, 1997), p. 428.

78. *Diaries*, quoting BL, Add. MS 43875, fol. 165.

79. *Diaries*, quoting BL, Add. MS 44486, fol. 238.

80. Matthew, *Gladstone*, p. 615.

81. The affair seems to have dragged on. On 1 May 1892, Gladstone wrote in his diary that he had been discussing 'this unending resignation business' with his wife.

82. GG MSS 1798, not dated.

83. Adèle Crepaz, *Die Gefahren der Frauen-Emancipation* (Leipzig, 1892), pp. 2–6.

84. *Diaries*, xiii, p. 99, quoting BL, Add. MS 44549, fol. 17.

85. Samuel Smith, *My Life-Work* (London 1902), appendix xi, quoted in *Diaries*, xiii, p. 19.

86. *Nineteenth Century*, 25, August 1889, pp. 355–84. This was the anti-suffrage statement to which Mrs Gladstone had refused to put her name, as she had equally declined to endorse the votes for women movement either.

87. Smith, *My Life-Work*, appendix xi.

88. St Augustine, *Confessions*, vii, c. 7: 'Da mihi castitatem et continentiam – sed noli modo'. Augustine was one of Gladstone's four acknowledged 'doctors' or teachers. The others were Dante, Aristotle and the eighteenth-century theologian Bishop Butler. See Morley, *Life of Gladstone*, i, p. 115.

Notes to Chapter 8: Harriet, Laura and Olga

1. He was once, however, caught at a party stealing a kiss from pretty Mrs Cornwallis West.
2. K. D. Reynolds, 'Gower, Harriet Elizabeth Georgiana Leveson, Duchess of Sutherland (1806–1868)', *Oxford Dictionary of National Biography*, Oxford 2004.
3. *Diaries*, iv, 14 September 1853.
4. *Diaries*, iv, 3–27 September 1853.
5. *Diaries*, viii, p. 570, W. E. Gladstone to Laura Thistlethwayte, 25 October 1869.
6. *Diaries*, xi, 28 October 1886.
7. *Diaries*, xi, 3 November 1886.
8. Mitigated to some extent in 1880, when Gladstone's eldest son Willy eventually got married, at the age of forty, to Harriet's grand-daughter, Gertrude Stuart.
9. For a full account of Laura Thistlethwayte's life, see Jean Gilliland, *Dear Spirit* (Oxford, 1994).
10. According to the 1881 English census.
11. Gilliland, *Dear Spirit*, p. 8, quoting Gladstone family archivist, A. Tilney Bassett. Laura also began to sculpt a bust of Gladstone, but no trace of it remains. *Diaries*, 9 January 1875.
12. *Diaries*, vi, 30 April 1865.
13. They also had a mutual friend in Arthur Kinnaird, who had accompanied Gladstone on the European tour of 1838–39, when he fell in love with Catherine Glynne.
14. *Diaries*, vi, 5 February 1865.
15. W. E. Gladstone to Laura Thistlethwayte, 19 October 1869. A collection of his letters to her, returned by the Thistlethwayte family after her death, is included as an appendix to the *Diaries*, viii, pp. 557–87. The few letters from her to him that survive (Gladstone having burned those that he held in 1893) are at Lambeth Palace. See Jean Gilliland, *Dear Spirit* (Oxford, 1994), passim.
16. Gilliland, *Dear Spirit*, p. 13.
17. *Diaries*, vii, 2 July 1869.
18. *Diaries*, viii, p. 557, W. E. Gladstone to Laura Thistethwayte.
19. Ibid.
20. Ibid.
21. *Diaries*, vii, p. 563.
22. *Diaries*, vii, p. 564.

23. *Diaries*, vii, p. 560.
24. *Diaries*, vii, p. 563.
25. Ibid.
26. This was a quality shared by his daughter, Helen. Her fellow-students at Newnham College said that Helen was 'almost comically penitent if she thought anyone's feelings had been hurt'.
27. His old friends Hope and Manning were about to convert to Roman Catholicism.
28. Mary was also suffering from the old family complaint, erysipelas. In her case, it was affecting her eyes.
29. *Diaries*, vii, pp. 572–73, 27 October 1869. In the event, Gladstone accepted Laura's counter-suggestion that her name should simply be rendered as 'L'.
30. It was, however, for the Thistlethwayte correspondence that Gladstone's system of double-envelopes was introduced. Under this system, the inner envelope was marked with a code indicating that it was only to be opened personally by the addressee. It was a system that Olga Novikoff tried to emulate, but without success.
31. *Diaries*, vii, pp 576–77.
32. Ibid.
33. H. C. G Matthew, *Gladstone*, (Oxford, 1997), p. 242, quoting J. Vincent, ed., *Disraeli, Derby and the Conservative Party* (Hassocks, 1978), p. 346.
34. *Diaries*, vii, p. 579–80.
35. *Diaries*, vii, p. 580.
36. Ibid.
37. *Diaries*, vii, p. 582.
38. *Diaries*, vii, p. 583.
39. Ibid.
40. *Diaries*, vii, p. 587, 22 April 1870.
41. Quoted in Gilliland, *Dear Spirit*, p. 17.
42. 26 March 1871, quote in Gilliland, *Dear Spirit*, p. 17.
43. *Diaries*, vii, 29 April 1871.
44. Quoted in Gilliland, *Dear Spirit*, p. 19.
45. Ibid.
46. Ibid.
47. Madame Novikov was unlike the other women mentioned in the Wright case. Katherine O'Shea had simply been substituted for her husband when his ability as a go-between between Charles Parnell and Gladstone was questioned. Lillie Langtry, in common with other actresses, had never been more than an object of 'artistic' admiration.
48. BL, Add. MS 44542, fol. 92, quoted in *Diaries*, viii, p. 291n.

49. GG MSS 1974.
50. Ibid.
51. While Viscount Gladstone's gratuitous assessment, given at the time of the Wright trial, may have been intended to counter suggestions that his father was sexually attracted to Madame Novikov, it is less kind than the picture of her, by an anonymous photographer, that appears in W. T. Stead, ed, *Olga Novikoff: The MP for Russia* (London, 1909), facing frontispiece.
52. Stead, *Novikoff*, pp. x–xi.
53. W. E. Gladstone, *The Bulgarian Horrors and the Question of the East'* (1876).
54. Stead, *Olga Novikoff,*, p. 243.
55. Quoted in Stead, *Olga Novikoff*, p. 243.
56. Stead, *Olga Novikoff*, p. 244.
57. Stead, *Olga Novikoff*, p. 441.
58. Stead, *Olga Novikoff*, pp. 356–57.
59. Stead, *Olga Novikoff*, p. 381.
60. Stead, *Olga Novikoff*, p. 463.
61. Stead, *Olga Novikoff*, p. 441.
62. *Nineteenth Century*, 7, March 1880, p. 538.
63. Stead, *Olga Novikoff*, p. 185.
64. Quoted in Matthew, *Gladstone* p. 322.
65. Gilliand, *Dear Spirit*, p. 24.
66. Ibid.
67. Gilliland, *Dear Spirit*, p. 28.
68. Gilliland, *Dear Spirit*, p. 27.

Notes to Chapter 9: Victoria

1. Frederick Ponsonby, *Sidelights on Queen Victoria* (London, 1930), p. 282.
2. Mary Drew, *Catherine Gladstone* (London, 1928), p. 17.
3. *Diaries*, ii, 28 May 1834.
4. Ibid.
5. Philip Guedalla, *The Queen and Mr Gladstone*, 2 vols (London, 1933), i, p. 28. Individual letters from this selected correspondence are referred to by number as well as page.
6. Drew, *Catherine Gladstone*, pp. 91–92.
7. Guedalla, *The Queen and Mr Gladstone*, i, no. 55, p. 123.
8. 'The queen bee was taken away, but the hive went on.' Walter Bagehot, *The English Constitution* (London, 1878), p. 51.

9. Ibid., i, no. 273, p. 253.

10. Ibid.

11. 'Fritz' was already terminally ill when he became Emperor of Germany on 9 March 1888. He lived for just ninety-nine days, during which time both Victorias – mother and daughter – were Queen Empresses.

12. Guedalla, *The Queen and Mr Gladstone*, i, no. 273, p. 253.

13. Ibid., i, no, 372, pp. 298–300.

14. Ibid., i, no. 376, p. 302.

15. Ibid., i, no. 379, pp. 303–4.

16. Ibid., i, no. 132, p. 180.

17. Ibid., i, no. 135, pp 183–84.

18. Ibid., i, no. 388, pp 308–9.

19. Ibid., i, no. 413, pp. 326–27.

20. Bagehot, *The English Constitution*, p. 51.

21. Memorandum quoted in Bagehot, *The English Constitution*, p. 74.

22. Guedalla, *The Queen and Mr Gladstone*, i, no. 573, p. 426.

23. Ibid., i, no. 574, pp. 426–27.

24. Ibid., i, no. 575, p. 427.

25. Ibid., i, p. 433.

26. Ibid., i, no. 608, p. 447.

27. Ponsonby, *Sidelights on Queen Victoria*, p. 282.

28. Gladstone memorandum, 30 January, 1886, quoted in H. C. G. Matthew, *Gladstone* (Oxford, 1997), p. 491.

29. Guedalla, *The Queen and Mr Gladstone*, ii, no. 1334, pp. 422–23.

30. Gladstone to Ripon, 4 November 1881, quoted in Matthew, *Gladstone* (Oxford, 1997), p. 378.

31. Ibid.

32. Guedalla, *The Queen and Mr Gladstone*, i, no. 489.

33. Ibid., i, no. 490, p. 380.

34. 'The full impact of the blow fell on Mr Gladstone. For the Queen, from whose service he had retired in 1884, had completely vanished, That sovereign had lived on terms of friendship with him, fussed about his health, shared some of his ideals, and shared small, improving presents. Six years had passed over them; and he returned to find a changed woman, who surveyed him with a stony stare and conveyed a silent hope that he would act as much as possible as dear Lord Beaconsfield.' Ibid., i , pp. 15–16.

35. Ibid., ii, p. 21.

36. Marquess of Crewe, *Lord Rosebery* (1931), i, p. 165; quoted in Guedalla, *The Queen and Mr Gladstone*, p. 80.

37. Ibid., ii, no. 1334, pp. 422–23.

38. Guedalla, *The Queen and Mr Gladstone*, ii, no. 1162.
39. Guedalla, *The Queen and Mr Gladstone*, ii, no. 1163.
40. Ibid., ii, no. 989, p. 343.
41. Ibid., ii, no. 992, pp. 246–47.
42. GG MSS 780, 15 August 1892.
43. GG MSS 780, 11 March 1893.
44. *Diaries*, x, 30 November 1881.
45. Benjamin Disraeli, *To Matthew Arnold*, ch. 23.
46. *Diaries*, xiii, 28 Feruary 1894.
47. John Morley's diaries, quoted in appendix to *Diaries*, xiii, p. 439.
48. Queen Victoria's Journal, 3 March 1894; quoted in Elizabeth Longford, *Victoria R. I. (London, 1964), p. 525.*
49. Guedalla, *The Queen and Mr Gladstone*, ii, no. 1467, p. 493.
50. *Diaries*, xiii, 10 March 1894.
51. Ibid.
52. Guedalla, *The Queen and Mr Gladstone*, ii, pp. 75–76.

Notes to Chapter 10: Final Years

1. GG MSS 780, fol. 240, 21 March 1894.
2. A. Tilney Bassett, ed., *Gladstone to his Wife* (London, 1936), p. 259.
3. Edward was only four years younger than Laura. His wife had died childless in 1892, the year that Laura wrote her will, naming him as executor. Had Laura hoped for a closer connection? See Jean Gilliland, *Dear Spirit* (Oxford 1994), p. 29.
4. *Diaries*, xiii, 2 January 1896.
5. H. C. G. Matthew, *Gladstone* (Oxford, 1997), p. 610n.
6. Certainly, in the case of her son, Victoria is rumoured to have said she tried to live as long as she could to delay his coming to the throne. In the event, Bertie was fifty-nine when he became Edward VII and reigned only for ten years.
7. After Gladstone's death, his wife's last public act, in September 1899, was to cut the first sod prior to the building of the library as we know it today. The number of books has since risen to a quarter of a million.
8. GG MSS 628, 26 January 1896.
9. GG MSS 628, 2 November 1896.
10. GG MSS 984, fos 106–7, 9 November 1896.
11. GG MS 849, 10 December 1896.
12. G. M. Russell, *Harry Drew: A Memorial Sketch* (Oxford, 1911), p. 70.
13. GG MSS 985.

14. Matthew, *Gladstone*, p. 633.

15. W. T. Bailey was the carpenter.

16. Matthew, *Gladstone*, p. 637.

17. Quoted in Simon Reynolds, *William Blake Richmond: An Artist's Life, 1842–1921* (Norwich, 1995), p. 271.

18. Elizabeth Longford, *Victoria R.I.* (London, 1964), p. 550.

19. Ibid.

20. Ibid., p. 551.

Bibliography

ARCHIVE SOURCES

GG MSS: Glynne-Gladstone manuscripts, St Deiniol's Library, Hawarden (accessed via Flintshire Record Office, Hawarden).
National Archive, Kew, London.

PRIMARY SOURCES

Acton, William, *Prostitution* (London, 1857).

Bagehot, Walter, *The English Constitution* (London, 1878).

Crepaz, Adèle, *The Emancipation of Women* (London, 1893).

Drew, Mary, *Catherine Gladstone* (London, 1928).

Gaskell, James Milnes, *Records of an Eton Schoolboy* (privately printed, 1883), ed. Charles Milnes Gaskell, with preface by Francis Doyle.

Gladstone, Herbert, *After Thirty Years* (London, 1928).

Gladstone, W. E., *Diaries*, ed. M. R. D. Foot and H. C. G. Matthew (Oxford, 1968–94), 14 vols.

Gladstone, W. E., *Autobiographica*. ed. John Brooke and Mary Sorensen (London, 1971), 3 vols.

Langtry, Lillie, *The Days I Knew* (Jersey, 1989). First published in 1925.

Masterman, Lucy, *Mary Gladstone: Her Diaries and Letters* (New York, 1930).

Mayhew, Henry, *The Morning Chronicle Survey of London Labour and the London Poor* (Firle, 1980), 4 vols.

Morley, John, *Life of Gladstone* (London, 1908), 2 vols.

Newnham College Letter (January 1926), containing memoirs of Helen Gladstone junior, pp. 68–88.

Ponsonby, Frederick, *Sidelights on Queen Victoria* (London, 1930).

Schlüter, Auguste, *A Lady's Maid in Downing Street* (London, 1922).

O'Shea, Katherine, *Charles Stewart Parnell* (London, 1921).

Stead, W. T., *Olga Novikoff: The MP for Russia* (London, 1909), 2 vols.

Victoria, Queen, *Dearest Child: Letters between Queen Victoria and the Princess Royal*, ed. Roger Fulford (London, 1964).

Victoria, Queen, *Leaves from a Journal* (London, 1977).

Victoria, Queen, *More Leaves from the Journal of a Life in the Highlands* (London, 1884).

Woolstonecraft, Mary, *A Vindication of the Rights of Woman* (3rd edn, London, 1798).

SECONDARY SOURCES

Aronson, Theo, *The King in Love: King Edward VII's Mistresses* (New York, 1988).

Aronson, Theo, *Victoria and Disraeli* (London, 1977).

Askwith, Betty, *The Lytteltons: A Family Chronicle of the Nineteenth Century* (London, 1875).

Battiscombe, Georgina, *Mrs Gladstone* (London, 1956).

Bebbington, David, *The Mind of Gladstone: Religion, Homer and Politics* (Oxford, 2004).

Blake, Robert, *Disraeli and Gladstone* (London, 1969).

Cecil, Algernon, *Queen Victoria and her Prime Ministers* (London, 1953).

Checkland, S. G., *The Gladstones: A Family Biography, 1764–1851* (Cambridge, 1971).

Deacon, Richard, *The Private Life of Mr Gladstone* (London, 1965)

Eldridge, C. C., 'The Lincoln Divorce Case: A Study in Victorian Morality', typescript, St Deiniol's Library, M34.9G/191.

Emden, Paul, *Behind the Throne* (London, 1934).

Fairbairn, W. R. D., *Psychoanalytical Studies of the Personality* (London, 1999).

Finnegan, Frances, *Poverty and Prostitution* (Cambridge, 1979).

Fletcher, Sheila, *Victorian Girls: Lord Lyttelton's Daughters* (London, 1997).

Fulford, Roger, ed., *Dearest Child: Letters between Queen Victoria and the Princess Royal* (London, 1964).

Gilliland, Jean, *Gladstone's 'Dear Spirit': Laura Thistlethwayte* (Oxford, 1994).

Guedalla, Philip, *Idylls of the Queen* (London, 1937).

Guedalla, Philip, *The Queen and Mr Gladstone* (London, 1933), 2 vols.

Harris, Susan K., *The Cultural Work of the Late Nineteenth-Century Hostesses* (New York, 2002).

Hibbert, Christopher, *Queen Victoria in her Letters and Journals* (Stroud, 2003).

Jenkins, Roy, *Gladstone* (London, 1995).

Magnus, Philip, *Gladstone: A Biography* (London, 1954).

Marlow, Joyce, *Mr and Mrs Gladstone: An Intimate Biography* (London, 1977).

Matthew, H. C. G., *Gladstone* (Oxford, 1997).

McHugh, Paul, *Prostitution and Victorian Social Reform* (London, 1980).

Munsell, F. Darrell, *The Unfortunate Duke: Henry Pelham, Fifth Duke of Newcastle, 1811–1864* (Columbia, 1985).

Nevill, Barry St John, *Life at the Court of Queen Victoria* (Stroud, 1997).

Pearsall, Ronald, *The Worm in the Bud: The World of Victorian Sexuality* (London, 1969).

Pearson, Michael, *The Age of Consent: Victorian Prostitution and its Enemies* (Newton Abbot, 1972).

Pugh, Martin, *The March of the Women* (Oxford, 2000).

Quennel, Peter, ed., *London's Underworld* (London, 1950).

Reynolds, K. D., *Aristocratic Women and Political Society in Victorian Britain* (London, 1998).

Shannon, Richard, *Gladstone and the Bulgarian Agitation* (London, 1963).

Shannon, Richard, *Gladstone: Peel's Inheritor, 1809–1865* (London, 1988).

Shannon, Richard, *Gladstone: Heroic Minister, 1865–1898* (London, 1999).

St-John Neville, Barry, *Life at the Court of Queen Victoria* (Stroud, 1997).

Stone, Lawrence, *Broken Lives: Separation and Divorce in England, 1660–1857* (Oxford, 1993).

Surtees, Virginia, *A Beckford Inheritance* (Salisbury, 1977).

Index

Acton, William 102
age of consent 119, 143, 224 n. 66
Albert, Prince Consort
    death of 180, 181–83, 195
    and Gladstone 179
American Civil War 181
'American sin, the', *see* birth control
Anglo-Russian entente 173
'Appeal against Female Suffrage, An'
    151
Appeal to Fallen Women, An
    (Dickens) 118
aristocracy 72, 90–91, 226 n. 44
Aristotle's Master Piece 218 n. 1
Ashley, Lord 57, 58–59
Asman, Joseph 88, 90
Aspirin 221 n. 8
Augusta, Princess 78
Augustine, St 15
autoeroticism 106, 107, 109
Avery, Mr Justice xiii
Ayscough, Rebecca 116

Bad Ems 33, 79
Bagshawe, Frederick Gladstone 57
Bagshawe, Henry 57, 59
Balfour, Arthur 131
Balzari, Dr 85
Bathe, Lady de, *see* Langtry, Lillie
Beatrice (Dyce) 113
Bell, Captain Robert Henry 156
Birmingham Advertizer 55
birth control 145–46
Blake Richmond, Clara 210
Booth, Bramwell xii

Braybrooke, Lord 33
Brown, John 183, 196
Buckley, Wales 206–7
Burdett Coutts, Angela 118
Burlington Hall
    Gladstone's address at (1890) 128
Burnes-Jones, Sir Edward 131, 210
Butler, Josephine 104, 142, 228 n. 11
Byron, George Gordon, Lord 196

Cambridge University 128, 205
Carnarvon, Lord Henry Howard
    Molyneux Herbert 157–58
Cavendish, Lady Lucy 132, 151
Cavendish, Lord Frederick 132–33
Charlemagne 33
China 49–50
chivalry 67, 71, 121, 172, 212
cholera epidemics 116–17
Church Congress 146
Church of England 105, 218 n. 5, 219
    n. 32
Church of England Purity Society
    146
Churchill, Winston xiv
Clewer House of Mercy 107, 110, 116
Clifton, Emma 107–9
Clinton, Lord William 74–75
Coliseum, Rome 37
Collins, Elizabeth 110–11, 112
Commissioners in Lunacy 56, 57–59
Coningsby (Disraeli) 156
Contagious Diseases Acts 104, 142–43,
    152, 228 n. 11
Cooper, Anthony Ashley 222 n. 22

Coutts, Angela Burdett, *see* Burdett
   Coutts, Angela
Crepaz, Adèle 149–50
Criminal Law Amendment Act 143
Cuddesdon 18, 19

Daily Mail xiii, xiv
Daily Telegraph xiv
Dale, Mrs *see* Summerhays, Marian
Dangers of Female Emancipation, The
   (Crepaz) 149–50
Dante, *Divine Comedy* 41, 113
   Gladstone's reading of 27
   Paradiso 41
'Declaration, The' xv
Dickens, Charles 103, 118
Dilke, Charles 143, 147, 184
Dingwall, Ross-shire 2
Disraeli, Benjamin xii, 186
   and Gladstone 177, 237 n. 34
   as Prime Minister 187, 193
   and Victoria 177, 191–92, 196–97,
      237 n. 34
Divine Comedy, see Dante
divorce
   American situation 144
   Gladstone's attitude towards
      143–45
Divorce Act 89, 144, 152
Divorce (Lee) 144
Douglas, Lady Frances, *see* Milton,
   Lady Frances
Douglas, Lady Susan, *see* Lincoln,
   Lady Susan
Doyle, Francis 216 n. 8
Drew, Harry
   career 206–7
   marries Mary Gladstone 134
drug abuse 76–77, 79
Dyce, William 112–13

Eastern Question 171–72
Ecclesiastical Titles Bill 110

education of females 127, 205, 230
   n. 14
   Wollstonecraft on 127–28
Edward, Prince of Wales
   duties 185
   at Gladstone's funeral 110
   illness 184
Elementary Education Act (1870)
   127
Elliot, Mrs 62, 63, 64
Emancipation of Women and its
   Probable Consequences, The 150
Empire 190
'Engagement, The' 105
Essay Club 19
Eton College 13–18, 49

Faithful or Unfaithful (Lee) 144
Farquhar, Caroline 21–24
Farquhar, Lady 23–24, 26
Farr, William 15, 18
Fasque, Scotland 21, 44–45, 61–62,
   64–65, 214 n. 21
Fellowes, Laura 21
female suffrage
   Catherine Gladstone's attitude
      towards 148–49, 233 n. 86
   Gladstone's attitude towards 142,
      146–51
   see also Women's Suffrage Bill
Finlay, Thomas Kirkman 68–69
Franchise Bill (1884) 147–48
Franco-Prussian War 181

Garibaldi, Giuseppe 154
Gaskell, James Milnes 17, 19
Gefahren der Frauen-Emancipation,
   Die (Crepaz) 149–50
George, Duke of York 210
Gladstone, Agnes (daughter)
   birth 124
   childhood 128
   courted by Arthur Gordon 129

illness 129
marries Edward Wickham 130, 187
Gladstone, Anne Mackenzie (sister)
    birth 2
    burial 214 n. 21
    establishes asylum 215 n. 27
    and Gladstone 5, 32, 214 n. 16
    illness and death 5–6, 202, 214 n. 17
    management of Gladstone family
        4–7
Gladstone, Anne Robertson (mother)
    1, 11
    death 25–26, 129, 202
    illness 3–4
    on romance 24
Gladstone, Catherine, née Glynne
    (wife)
    character 32, 41, 46, 47
    charity work 116–17
    courted by Gladstone 38–41
    death 211
    education 33–34
    at Fasque 44–45
    and female suffrage 148–49, 233 n.
        86
    and Hawarden 107
    health 129, 206, 230 nn. 23, 24
    and Helen (daughter) 232 n. 60
    influence over Gladstone 43–44
    and Lady Lincoln 78, 80, 83, 88,
        95–96
    and Lady Milton 46
    and Laura Thistlethwayte 167, 175
    marries Gladstone 42
    offered peerage 201–2
    and Olga Novikov 172
    personal life 107
    physical appearance 43
    and political secrets 47
    popularity 148
    pregnancies 45, 49
    and prostitutes 99, 100, 103, 108,
        116, 218 n. 4
    romances 41–42
    and Victoria 178, 198
    and Women's Liberal Federation
        148–49
Gladstone, Catherine Jessy
    (daughter)
    death 89, 125–26, 202
Gladstone family 56
    erysipelas 129
    and women 66–67
Gladstone, Helen (daughter) 124, 128,
    133
    academic career 136–37, 138–41, 205
    character 135, 235 n. 26
    childhood 135–41
    at Hawarden 205–6
    relations with Gladstone 137
    relations with mother 232 n. 60
Gladstone, Helen Jane (sister)
    and Aunt Johanna 61, 62, 64, 66,
        67
    birth 2
    and Catherine Gladstone 45
    confined by family 56–60
    death 66, 202
    and the Dominicans 66
    engagement 36–37, 40
    at Fasque 61–62, 64–65, 135
    friendships with women 67
    illness 56–60, 62–64
    at Leamington 62–64
    opium addiction 45–46, 50–51, 62,
        66, 222 n. 24
    place in family 65–66
    reaction to mother's death 25–26
    relations with father 61–62, 64–65,
        135
    relations with Gladstone 7–11, 30,
        34, 35, 51–68
    relations with sister 66, 67
    Roman Catholicism 52–56, 60, 225
        n. 21
    at spa towns 32–33, 35, 56

Gladstone, Henry (son)
  sues Peter Wright xi–xv
Gladstone, Herbert (son)
  birth 124
  on Olga Novikov 171, 236 n. 51
  sues Peter Wright xi–xv
Gladstone, John (father)
  attends Gladstone's wedding 43
  daughter Helen's illness 59–60,
    63–64
  and Lady Farquhar 24
  relations with daughter Helen
    61–62, 64–65, 68–69
  wealth and business activities 1–3,
    45, 100
Gladstone, John Neilson (brother)
  birth 2
Gladstone, Mary (daughter)
  on birth control 145–46
  as Gladstone's private secretary
    132, 133–34
  intellectual life 134
  marries Harry Drew 134
  youth 130–32
Gladstone, Robertson (brother)
  birth 2
  at Eton 14
Gladstone, Stephen (son) xv, 130
Gladstone, Thomas (brother)
  birth 2
  education 14, 18
  marriage 21
  and sister Helen 58–59
Gladstone, Thomas (grandfather) 1
Gladstone, William (son)
  birth 123–24
  and death of sister Catherine Jessy
    126
Gladstone, William Ewart
  academic career 14, 13–18, 18–20
  Agnes (daughter), birth 124
  and Albert, Prince Consort 179
  and aristocracy 72, 90–91, 153

autoeroticism 106, 107, 109
'Baden Rules' 106
'besetting sin' 106
birth 1
on birth control 145–46
at Boveridge 164–65
Burlington Hall address (1890)
  128
and Catherine (wife) 38–41, 42,
  43–44, 84, 95–96, 119, 220 n. 48
childhood 4–5
chivalry 67, 71, 121, 172, 212
at Cuddesdon 18, 19
death and funeral 209–11
devotion to duty 183
diary 5
and Disraeli 177, 237 n. 34
on divorce 143–45
and the Eastern Question 171–72
education of daughters 126–28
education of women 205
as father 124–25, 196
on female suffrage 142, 146–51
Grand Tour 20, 34–39
health 29, 30, 154, 197, 207–9
and Helen (sister) 7–11, 30, 34, 35,
  51–69
Herbert (son), birth 124
honeymoon 44–45
illness, attitude towards 3–4
inherits Demerara 45
in Italy 35–39
Jessy (daughter), death 89, 125–24
Lady Lincoln, attempts to 'rescue'
  79–89, 91–94, 97–98
Lord High Commissioner
  Extraordinary of Ionia 129
Lord Lincoln, death 95–96
on marriage and religion 21–24, 41
on mules 35
Norwegian cruise 194
'People's William' 194
personal values 81–82

physical appearance 43
political career 20–21, 47, 71, 177, 180–81
pornography 103, 106, 228 n. 18
prostitutes, rescue work among 103–21; *see also* prostitutes; prostitution
and religion 7, 22–24, 41, 220 nn. 32, 30
reputation 162, 167, 169, 172, 175, 235 n. 30
retirement 197–98, 202
romances 21–24, 27, 32
self-flagellation 99–100, 106, 110
sexuality 44, 118–19, 203–4
on slavery 21
translates Farini 109
and Victoria 48, 177–200, 202–4, 207, 213 n. 4
William (son), birth 123–24
at Wilmslow 18
and women 31–32, 67, 81, 90–91, 212
Glynne, Catherine, *see* Gladstone, Catherine
Glynne family
background 33
European travels 33–39
and Gladstone 34, 35–36, 38, 39, 40–41
private vocabulary 39, 219 n. 27
Glynne, Lady Mary *née* Neville (mother-in-law) 33, 51, 220 nn. 38, 48
Glynne, Lavinia 108
Glynne, Mary *see* Lyttelton, Lady Mary
Glynne, Sir Stephen (father-in-law) 33
Glynne, Stephen (brother-in-law) 25
Gordon, Arthur 129
Gordon, General Charles 193
Graham, Sir James 50

Gower, *see* Sutherland
Greenwood, James 103–4
Grenville, Richard de 33
Grey, Charles 2nd Earl 25

Hall, Jane 1–2
Hallam, Arthur 15–17, 216 n. 8
death 25
Hallam, Henry 49
Hamilton, Eddie 115
Hamilton, Lady Susan, *see* Lincoln, Lady Susan
Harcourt, Colonel Francis Vernon 220 n. 34
Hardy, Thomas 210
Hawarden Castle 24–25, 124, 178
estate 33, 42, 48, 107, 108, 117, 204, 205–6, 221 n. 54
Hawtrey, Edward Craven 14–15, 49
Hertford, Marquis of 155–56
High Church Anglicanism 55
Hohenlohe-Langenburg, Princess 184–85
Home Rule for Ireland 137–38, 189–90
Hope, James 109
House of Saint Barnabas 105, 116
Houses of Mercy, *see* Clewer House of Mercy; House of Saint Barnabas; Magdalen Hospital
Hughes, Marian 103

In Memoriam (Tennyson) 16
India 190–91
Ireland Bill 189–90
Irish Nationalists 188
Irish University Bill 186
Italian language 27, 110

Jane Eyre (Brontë) 59, 66
Jenner, Sir William 183
Jephson, Dr 62, 63
Jones, Ellen 90

Jung Bahadur, Maharaja 156

Keate, John 'Flogger' 14
Kent, Duchess of 178
Kingsley, Charles 184
Kinnaird, Arthur 34, 234 n. 13
Kiréev, Aleksander 171
Kiréev, Nicholas 171, 172
Kirkman, Finlay Thomas, see Finlay,
    Thomas Kirkman

Labouchère, Henry 115
Lady with a Coronet of Jasmine
    (Dyce) 113
Lamb, Lady Caroline 196
Landseer, Edwin 156
Langtry, Lillie xiv, 235 n. 47
Lansdowne, Lord, Viceroy of India
    188
Leamington
    Helen Gladstone (sister) at 62–64
Lee, Margaret 144
Leighton, Frederic 131
Leveson-Gower, see Sutherland
Lightfoot, P. 109–10, 111, 112
Lincoln, Henry Clinton, Earl of see
    Newcastle, Henry Clinton 5th
    Duke of
Lincoln, Lady Susan, née Hamilton
    71, 72–73
    and Catherine Gladstone 78, 80,
        83, 88, 95–96
    character 73–74, 75
    children 96
        see also Pelham-Clinton, Edward
    death 97, 202
    divorce 82, 87–94
    drug abuse 76–77, 79
    Gladstone's attempts to 'rescue'
        79–89, 91–94, 97–98
    and Laura Thistlethwayte 174
    and Lord Walpole 78–79, 84–85, 94
    marital infidelity 74–75, 76–78

at spa towns 77
    treated for hysteria 75
    see also Opdebeck, Lady Susan
Lincoln, Lord Henry Clinton 71, 143,
    156, 157
    academic career 72
    children 96
        see also Pelham-Clinton, Edward
    death 95–96
    inspiration for 'Plantagenet
        Palliser' 71
    love for wife 75
Liszt, Franz 34, 131, 231 n. 26
Loader, A. 111
London
    prostitution in 100–2, 103–4
London Committee for the
    Suppression of Traffic in English
    Girls for the Purposes of
    Continental Prostitution 120
London Labour and the London Poor
    (Mayhew) 100
London Society for the Protection of
    Young Females and Prevention of
    Juvenile Prostitution 108
Lyttelton, Mary, Lady, née Glynne
    (sister-in-law)
    death 129
    marriage to Lord Lyttelton 42–44,
        178.220 n. 48
Lyttelton, George, Lord 49
    and education of females 127
    marriage to Mary Glynne 42–44,
        178, 220 n. 48

Magdalen Hospital 104
Magnus, Philip 64, 223 n. 57
Manchester Guardian xii
Manning, Henry 83, 109, 225 n. 30
marriage and religion 21–24, 41
Married Women's Property Acts
    151
Mayhew, Henry 100, 104–5

Melbourne, William Lamb, Viscount
  195, 196
Mill, J. S. 150
Millais, John 131
Miller, Professor 64
Milton, Lady Francis, *née* Douglas
  27–28, 46
Milton, Lord 29–30
Morley, John xv, 16, 143, 197
Morris, Jane 229 n. 33
Morton, Lady 28
Morton, Lord 27, 29, 46

Napoleon, Louis 156
Neville, Mary, *see* Glynne, Lady Mary
New American Review 144–45
Newark, parliamentary seat 20–21
Newcastle, Henry Clinton 5th Duke
  of (formerly Earl of Lincoln), 20,
  49, 71, 72, 77, 78
Newcastle Scholarship 49
Newport Market Refuge 117
Nichol, John MP 225 n. 27
Nineteenth Century 144, 151, 173
Non-Conformists 220 n. 32
Norwich Cathedral 28
Novikov, Olga 171
  death xiv
  and Laura Thistlethwayte 173–75

Opdebeck, Jean Alexis 95
Opdebeck, Lady Susan, *see* Lincoln,
  Lady Susan
opium 50–51, 223 n. 54, 224 n. 60, 225
  n. 21
Opium War 49–50
O'Shea, Katherine xiv, 143, 235 n. 47
Outdoor Relief 102
Oxford Union 19
Oxford Movement 19, 105
Oxford University 128, 208
  Christ Church 18–20
  Oriel 19

Padwick, Henry 174
Page Saunders, Augustus, *see*
  Saunders, Augustus Page
Pall Mall Gazette 143
Palmerston, Henry John Temple,
  Lord 144, 186
Paovick, Noel 90
Parnell, Charles Stewart xiv, 143
Peel, Sir Robert 21, 49, 77, 82, 102
Pelham-Clinton, Edward 96–97
Percy, William de 33
photography 113
Poor Law Amendment Act 102
Portraits and Criticisms (Wright) xi
Potter, Beatrice 151
Pre-Raphaelite Movement 131, 229 n.
  33
Princess (Tennyson) 113
prostitutes
  ages of 115–16
    see also age of consent
  Catherine Gladstone and 99, 103,
    108, 116, 218 n. 4
  class divisions 105, 115, 116
  Gladstone's 'rescue' of 103–21
  Gladstone's sexual response to
    118–19
  and Poor Law Amendment Act
    102
  refuges for 104, 105, 107, 110, 116
  rescue work among 103
  see also Ayscough, Rebecca;
    Clifton, Emma; Collins,
    Elizabeth; Lightfoot, P.; Loader,
    A.; Summerhays, Marian;
    Thistlethwayte, Laura
prostitution
  causes of 121
  defined 101
  employment among 101
  topography 100–2, 103–4
  and urban deprivation 102
Pusey, Edward 204

'Question of Divorce, The' 144

Ramsay, Edward 27–28
Ramsay, Isabella 28, 32
Raphael, Lewis 88, 90
Rawson, Elizabeth 62–64, 67–68
Rawson, William 3, 13, 14, 62
Record 55
Reform Bill 150
religion
    in marriage 21–24, 41
    and the rescue of prostitutes 120
republicanism 183, 184
revolution 183
Richmond, Clara Blake, *see* Blake
    Richmond, Clara
Ripon, George Robinson, Marquess
    of, Viceroy of India 190
Robertson, Eliza 29
Robertson, Johanna (Gladstone's
    aunt) 61, 62, 64, 66, 67
Roman Catholicism 109, 220 n. 32,
    225 n. 30
Rosebery, Lord 114, 196, 198, 201
Rossetti, Dante Gabriel 229 n. 33
Rostron, Ruth 223 n. 58
Russell, Lord John 186
Russia
    entente with England 173
    Gladstone's interest in 171–72
Russia and England from 1876 to 1880
    (Novikov) 173
Russian Society of Friends of
    Religious Enlightenment 171
Russian-Turkish War 171

Santo Spirito 35
Saunders, Augustus Page 18
Scottish Presbyterianism 1
Seaforth House 2–3
self-flagellation 99–100, 106, 110
Seven Curses of London, The
    (Greenwood) 103–4

Sherry, Rebecca 14
Sidgwick, Nora 136, 139, 140
Smith, Samuel 150–51
Sollohub, Léon, Count 36, 40
spa towns 1–2, 32–33, 35, 56, 77
    see also Bad Ems
St Deiniol's Library 204, 223 n. 59,
    238 n. 7
*State and its Relations with the
    Church, The* (Gladstone) 31, 41
Stead, W. T. 104, 119, 143, 173
Sudan 193
Summerhayes, Marian 112–14
    sits for William Dyce 112–13
Sutherland, Harriet Leveson-Gower,
    Duchess of 178
    and Gladstone 153–55
Sutherland, George Granville
    Leveson-Gower, Duke of
    Sutherland 114, 153

Talbot, James Beard 108
Talbot, Lavinia 151
Talleyrand-Périgord, Charles
    Maurice 219 n. 27
Taunton Commission on Secondary
    Education 230 n. 14
Temple of Peace 204
Tennant, Mrs 107, 108
Tennyson, Alfred, Lord 16
Tennyson, Emily 16
Tennyson, Hallam 125, 134
Thirty-Nine Articles 217 n. 5
Thistlethwayte, Arthur 156–57
Thistlethwayte, Captain Frederick
    157, 168, 175
Thistlethwayte, Laura 97, 112
    autobiography 158, 159, 160, 162,
        165–66, 167, 168, 175
    and Catherine Gladstone 167, 175
    death xiv, 202
    early life 155–56
    evangelism 157

and Gladstone 158–71, 173, 174, 235
  n. 30
jealously over Olga Novikov
  173–75
and Lady Lincoln 174
letters destroyed by Gladstone 162,
  175, 234 n. 15
marriage 157, 170
Times xii
Tractarianism 55, 119
Turner, Rev. John 18
Tweedmouth, Lord 201–2

United States of America
  divorce in 144

Vanity Fair (Thackeray) 156
Vernon Harcourt, Colonel Francis
  220 n. 34
Vickers, Charles 119–20
Victoria, Queen
  Albert, death of 180, 181–83, 195
  and Catherine Gladstone 178, 198
  conservatism 180
  death 211
  and Disraeli 177, 180, 191–92,
    196–97, 237 n. 34
  family 185
  and Gladstone 48, 177–200, 202–4,
    207, 210–11
  health 183–84
  loneliness 195–97

and royal prerogative 185–86
widowhood 217 n. 47
Vindication of the Rights of Woman,
  A (Wollstonecraft) 127

Walpole, Lady 226 n. 31
Walpole, Lord Horatio 78, 95
  and Lady Lincoln 78–79, 84–85, 94
Walpole, Orazio 94–95
Watkins, Ann 64
Wickham, Edward 130, 207
Wilde, William 156
Wilmslow 18
Wiseman, Cardinal Nicholas Patrick
  Stephen 56, 64
Wollstonecraft, Mary
  on education of females 127–28
women
  Gladstone and 31–32, 67, 81, 90–91,
    212
  Gladstone family and 66–67
Women's Liberal Federation 148–49
women's suffrage
  Catherine Gladstone's attitude
    towards 148–49, 233 n. 86
  Gladstone's attitude towards 142,
    146–51
Women's Suffrage Bill 151
Woodall, William 147–48
Wright, Captain Peter xi–xv
Wright, Ellis 150
Wright v. Gladstone xi–xiv, 227 n. 4